Black Cosmopolitanism
and Anticolonialism

This book examines the cosmopolitanism and anticolonialism that black intellectuals, such as the African American W.E.B. Du Bois, the Caribbeans Marcus Garvey and George Padmore, and the Francophone West Africans (Kojo Touvalou-Houénou, Lamine Senghor, and Léopold Sédar Senghor) developed during the two world wars by fighting for freedom, equality, and justice for Senegalese and other West African colonial soldiers (known as *tirailleurs*) who made enormous sacrifices to liberate France from German oppression.

Focusing on the solidarity between this special group of African American, Caribbean, and Francophone West African intellectuals against French colonialism, this book uncovers pivotal moments of black Anglophone and Francophone cosmopolitanism and traces them to published and archived writings produced between 1914 and the middle of the twentieth century.

Babacar M'Baye is Associate Professor in the Department of English and the Department of Pan-African Studies at Kent State University, USA.

Routledge Studies in Modern History

4 Charity and Mutual Aid in Europe and North America since 1800
Edited by Paul Bridgen and Bernard Harris

5 Churchill, Roosevelt and India
Propaganda during World War II
Auriol Weigold

6 Genocide and Fascism
The eliminationist drive in Fascist Europe
Aristotle Kallis

7 Scientific Research in World War II
What scientists did in the War
Edited by Ad Maas and Hans Hooijmaijers

8 Restoration and History
The search for a useable environmental past
Edited by Marcus Hall

9 Foundations of Modernity
Human agency and the imperial state
By Isa Blumi

10 Transpacific Revolutionaries
The Chinese Revolution in Latin America
By Matthew D. Rothwell

11 First World War Nursing
New perspectives
Edited by Alison S. Fell and Christine E. Hallett

12 The Ideological Cold War
The politics of neutrality in Austria and Finland
Johanna Rainio-Niemi

13 War and Displacement in the Twentieth Century
Global conflicts
Edited by Sandra Barkhof and Angela K. Smith

14 Longue Durée of the Far-Right
An international historical sociology
Edited by Richard Saul, Alexander Anievas, Neil Davidson and Adam Fabry

15 Transnational Perspectives on Modern Irish History
Edited by Niall Whelehan

16 Ireland in the World
Comparative, Transnational, and Personal Perspectives
Edited by Angela McCarthy

17 The Global History of the Balfour Declaration
Declared Nation
Maryanne A. Rhett

18 Colonial Soldiers in Europe, 1914–1945
"Aliens in Uniform" in Wartime Societies
Edited by Eric Storm and Ali Al Tuma

19 Immigration Policy from 1970 to the Present
Rachel Stevens

20 Public Goods versus Economic Interests
Global Perspectives on the History of Squatting
Edited by Freia Anders and Alexander Sedlmaier

21 Histories of Productivity
Genealogical Perspectives on the Body and Modern Economy
Edited by Peter-Paul Bänziger and Mischa Suter

22 Landscapes and Voices of the Great War
Edited by Angela K. Smith and Krista Cowman

23 War, Peace and International Order?
The Legacies of The Hague Conferences of 1899 and 1907
Edited by Maartje Abbenhuis, Christopher Ernest Barber and Annalise R. Higgins

24 Black Cosmopolitanism and Anticolonialism
Pivotal Moments
Babacar M'Baye

Black Cosmopolitanism and Anticolonialism
Pivotal Moments

Babacar M'Baye

LONDON AND NEW YORK

First published 2017
by Routledge
2 Park Square, Milton Park, Abingdon, Oxon OX14 4RN

and by Routledge
711 Third Avenue, New York, NY 10017

Routledge is an imprint of the Taylor & Francis Group, an informa business

© 2017 Babacar M'Baye

The right of Babacar M'Baye to be identified as author of this work has been asserted by him in accordance with sections 77 and 78 of the Copyright, Designs and Patents Act 1988.

All rights reserved. No part of this book may be reprinted or reproduced or utilised in any form or by any electronic, mechanical, or other means, now known or hereafter invented, including photocopying and recording, or in any information storage or retrieval system, without permission in writing from the publishers.

Trademark notice: Product or corporate names may be trademarks or registered trademarks, and are used only for identification and explanation without intent to infringe.

British Library Cataloguing-in-Publication Data
A catalogue record for this book is available from the British Library

Library of Congress Cataloging-in-Publication Data
Names: M'Baye, Babacar, 1967– author.
Title: Black cosmopolitanism and anticolonialism : pivotal moments / Babacar M'Baye.
Other titles: Routledge studies in modern history.
Description: New York : Routledge, 2017. | Series: Routledge studies in modern history | Includes index.
Identifiers: LCCN 2016044660 | ISBN 9781138281011 (hardback : alk. paper) | ISBN 9781315271408 (ebook)
Subjects: LCSH: Cosmopolitanism. | Imperialism. | Transnationalism. | France. Armâee. Troupes coloniales—History—20th century. | France. Armâee. Tirailleurs sâenâegalais—History—20th century. | France— Colonies—History—20th century. | Africa, French-speaking West—Race relations. | Africa, French-speaking West—History, Military. | Africa, French-speaking West—Relations—France. | France—Relations—Africa, French-speaking.
Classification: LCC DT532.5.M38 2017 | DDC 966.0097541—dc23
LC record available at https://lccn.loc.gov/2016044660

ISBN: 978-1-138-28101-1 (hbk)
ISBN: 978-1-315-27140-8 (ebk)

Typeset in Sabon
by Florence Production Ltd, Stoodleigh, Devon

In memory of all *tirailleurs*, including my grandfather
Mamadou Wade.

Also in memory of my father, Moussa M'Baye,
our grandmother Yoshiko Noda, and our beloved
cat Nuke.

Contents

	List of figures	ix
	Acknowledgements	xi
	Introduction: Writing Africa into black Atlantic studies	1
1	Blaise Diagne's cosmopolitanism and views on French colonialism	31
2	W. E. B. Du Bois's cosmopolitanism, anticolonialism, and relations with Blaise Diagne	59
3	Marcus Garvey's cosmopolitanism, anticolonialism, and responses to Blaise Diagne	87
4	Kojo Touvalou-Houénou's cosmopolitanism, anticolonialism, and relations with Marcus Garvey	114
5	Lamine Senghor's cosmopolitanism, anticolonialism, and similarities with Marcus Garvey	137
6	George Padmore's cosmopolitanism and views on French colonialism	168
7	Léopold Sédar Senghor's cosmopolitanism and responses to French colonialism	191
	Conclusion: Roadblocks to black cosmopolitanism and France's integration of its minorities	218
	Notes	224
	Index	233

List of figures

0.1 "Débarquement aux Dardanelles" [Disembarking in Dardanelles], 1915. Collections Eric Deroo.   26

1.1 "Tournée de recrutement au Soudan" [Recruitment tour in Soudan], 1918. Collections Eric Deroo.   48

1.2 "Mitrailleurs sénégalais à l'exercice, camp du Sud-Est. Carte photos, 1914" [Senegalese gunners in exercise, Southeast camp, Photo card, 1914]. Collections Eric Deroo.   53

2.1 "Soldat africain originaire de l'une des Quatre communes et une amie, Paris, vers 1930" [African soldier from one of the four communes and a friend. Paris, circa 1930]. Collections Eric Deroo.   66

2.2 Clipping from *The Crisis*, March 1919. *W. E. B. Du Bois Papers* (MS 312). Special Collections and University Archives, University of Massachusetts Amherst Libraries.   70

3.1 "Corps de tirailleurs sénégalais. Carte photo de source allemande, 1916" [Bodies of Senegalese tirailleurs. German source Photo Card, 1916]. Collections Eric Deroo.   104

5.1 "Carte postale, fin 1914. Vendangeuse offrant du raisin à un blessé Sénégalais" [Postcard, end of 1914. Vintager offering grape to a wounded Senegalese]. Collections Eric Deroo.   156

5.2 "Respectueux hommages" [Respectful homages]. Musere Goré, 1914. Collections Eric Deroo.   157

5.3 "Banania y'a bon" [Banania is good] / [Affiche non identifié] [Unknown image source], Bibliothèque nationale de France [National Library of France] / gallica.bnf.fr /   159

5.4 "Prisonniers sénégalais blessés. Carte photo de source allemande, janvier 1918." [Senegalese wounded prisoners. German photo card source, January 1918]. Collections Eric Deroo.   162

6.1 "Tirailleurs du 12e RTS sortant du métro porte de Clignancourt pour rejoindre leur casernement lors du défilé du 14 juillet 1939. Paris. Photographie." [Tirailleurs of the 12th RTS leaving Clignancourt's metro entrance to

x *List of figures*

return to their barracks during the July 14, 1939, parade. Paris. Photography]. Collections Eric Deroo.   173

7.1 "Corps de tirailleurs sénégalais dont la disposition et l'absence de blessures peuvent indiquer une exécution collective. Front nord-est, juin 1940. Photographie de source allemande" [Bodies of Senegalese tirailleurs whose position and lack of injuries may indicate a collective execution. Northeast Front, June 1940. German source photograph]. Collections Eric Deroo.   210

Acknowledgements

First and foremost, I thank my editors, Robert Langham and Michael Bourne, for having provided me with much professional guidance and support that have made the publication of this book possible. I am also grateful to the entire staff of Kent State University's main library, especially to Diane May, who diligently helped my research throughout these past years. Diane gave me numerous extensions that allowed me to consult rare books by Senegalese or French scholars such as Lamine Gueye, Iba Der Thiam, Amady Aly Dieng, Marc Michel, Pascal Blanchard, Nicolas Bancel, Eric Deroo, and many others, who enabled me to understand the historical contexts of the relations between France and colonial Senegal. I am equally indebted to Ibra Sene, a notable African historian at Wooster College, whose seminal study of prisons in colonial Senegal also helped me to comprehend the interactions between the métropole and its overseas territories during the first half of the twentieth century. I am also thankful to other titanic intellectuals, such as Tyler Stovall, Dominic Thomas, Brent Hayes Edwards, Patrick Manning, Robin D.G. Kelley, Gary Wilder, and David Murphy, to name a few, who have given me a more solid foundation in the field of black transnational studies to which I am deeply devoted. But I owe most thanks to Paul Gilroy whose pioneer book, *The Black Atlantic: Modernity and Double Consciousness*, opened my eyes during the start of my doctoral education in American Studies at Bowling Green State University. Through the years, my admiration for Gilroy has grown as I have become increasingly aware of the full potential of his theories and have learned to assess them critically based on groundbreaking research provided by Simon Gikandi, Laura Chrisman, Tunde Adeleke, and other major scholars that I also admire greatly. Thanks to all these scholars for having laid the foundations on which I tread.

I also thank my friends and colleagues Fallou Ngom, Djiby Diagne, Babacar Dieng, Ahmed Iyane Faye, and Samuel Sene, and all my mentors from Gaston Berger University. I especially thank Baydallaye Kane, who recommended that I include Lamine Senghor in my project, and his wonderful spouse Raki, whose support has also been tremendous. In the same vein, I thank my American mother, Frances Novack, who brought me

xii *Acknowledgements*

to the United States many years ago as a French Teaching Assistant at Ursinus College. I remember how generous everyone was at this school where I could dress like a superstar, recklessly lose my Senegalese hats and find them on my door knob the next morning. Thanks to all those wonderful classmates that I had at Ursinus and the coworkers with whom I flipped hamburgers and shared leftover cheese late in the evenings.

I am also very grateful to Simon Bronner, whose generosity and dedication to scholarship and diversity made it possible for me to be awarded a fellowship in the American Studies Program at Penn State Harrisburg where I earned a Master's degree in 1998. I am equally indebted to all my mentors at Bowling Green State University, who opened my mind about the complex, rich, and meaningful history and literature of the United States. Lillian Ashcraft-Eason and her wonderful and late husband Baba Djisovi Eason, my other mentors, Apollos O. Nwauwa, Donald McQuarie, Donald Nieman, Michael E. Staub, Philip G. Terrie, William E. Grant, Cecilia A. Green, Scott C. Martin, Michael T. Martin, and many other scholars at Bowling Green State University strengthened my love for interdisciplinary studies that my previous mentors at Penn State University, such as Theodora Rapp Graham, John Patterson, Eaton Churchill, Timothy Evans, and Michael Barton, had instilled in me. Most of what I teach in my courses was inspired by these mentors and my earlier professors at Ursinus, such as Patricia Schroeder, Tony Castell, and the late Douglas M. Cameron, Juan Espaldas, and Shirley Eaton, whose humane qualities fostered the cosmopolitanism that I cherish dearly.

I also thank all my colleagues of the Department of English and the Department of Pan-African Studies at Kent State University as well as those from the other units of our dear institution, who have also dearly encouraged me over these years. Special thanks to James Gleeson and his spouse Rachel whose kindness is enthralling. Special thanks also to my two Chairs, Robert Trogdon and Amoaba Gooden, whose support has been very motivating. In a related vein, I extend my gratitude to Zachery Williams, Seneca Vaught, Robert Smith, Timothy Lake, Camille Rodger, and Tara Jabbaar-Gyambrah, who have also been very supportive since we were graduate students at BGSU.

Last but not least, I thank my dear wife Eriko Tanaka and my daughters Fatou M'Baye and Amina M'Baye, whose love and support have been tremendously helpful to me. My thanks also go to my in-laws and all of my wife's relatives in Japan who have been so generous to my family and have entertained them during summer vacations when I was deeply involved in research. I also thank our family in Senegal who have been very understanding and patient over these years. Above all, I thank all my high school, middle school, and elementary school teachers who first taught me to read, write, and think.

Introduction: Writing Africa into black Atlantic studies

The rhetoric that absolves France of the suffering of colonization and presents the métropole as the purveyor of cosmopolitanism is traceable to the discourse that generations of French imperialists used to subdue West African colonial soldiers known as *tirailleurs Sénégalais*. This cosmopolitan discourse was entrenched in French political culture since Blaise Diagne, the first Senegalese deputy of France, and his white parliamentarian colleagues employed it during and after World War I to convince Africans of the rightfulness of the sacrifices that they made by providing colonial soldiers and hard labor which enabled the empire to resist foreign competition and oppression during World War I. Early signs of this cosmopolitan discourse are found in the rhetoric that Diagne developed to convince colonial African soldiers to fight for an empire that actually gave little importance to their lives.

Between the two world wars, a number of black Anglophone and Francophone intellectuals challenged Diagne's cosmopolitan discourses about France's treatment of its colonial soldiers and other Africans. The black transnational detractors of Diagne's discourses included the African American W. E. B. Du Bois, the Caribbeans Marcus Garvey and George Padmore, and Francophone West Africans (such as the Senegalese Lamine Senghor and Léopold S. Senghor and the Beninese Kojo Touvalou-Houénou). To varying degrees, these black intellectuals condemned French imperial policies toward Senegal and their effects on *tirailleurs* and other Africans of the colonies during the two world wars. They challenged French cosmopolitan discourses by exposing the colonialist, racist, and fascist doctrines that shaped them. Moreover, the black intellectuals resisted the dehumanization, prejudices, and alienation of French cosmopolitan rhetoric by replacing this ideology with one in which black radicalism is consistent with the republican idea of liberty, equality, and justice for all. As they individually and collectively assessed the impact of French colonialism and racism on *tirailleurs* and other Africans, the black intellectuals created alternative cosmopolitan philosophies which reflected their genuine, legitimate, and resilient aims to improve the plight of people of African descent worldwide.

2 Writing Africa into black Atlantic studies

The figures on whom this book focuses were special because they were outspoken critics of French colonialism and cosmopolitanism in West Africa. These personalities dismantled the myth of France's extension of democracy and human rights to Africans, which permeated the cosmopolitan discourses of Diagne and other French imperial leaders during the first part of the twentieth century. Rather than being cosmopolitan, the policies that France developed toward Africans during this period were exclusionary and manipulative because they subjugated the peasants and *tirailleurs* and confined them in low and degrading positions in which racism, violence, and prejudice maintained the authority of an imperial system that defined rights as the privileges of the upper-class whites of the métropole (known here as metropolitan France) to the detriment of blacks and other colored people who lived in the overseas territories including those in Africa. French cosmopolitan theories were contradicted by racist and draconian colonial ideologies and practices that aimed to transform *tirailleurs* and other West Africans into a totally subjugated population rather than increasingly emancipated people. Studying the ways in which the black intellectuals denounced such policies and discourses at pivotal moments such as World War I, the 1919 and 1921 Pan-African congresses, the interwar period, and World War II enables us to uncover a neglected history of black cosmopolitanisms buried in black transnational writings, colonial papers, and other sources. Juxtaposing these black cosmopolitan responses to French colonialism will help us to correct the limited space that has been given to Francophone African intellectuals in black Atlantic studies.

Therefore, this current book has a double aim, because it traces the roots of twentieth-century black Anglophone and Francophone solidarity to the anticolonialism and cosmopolitanism that the selected black intellectuals reveal in their published and (or) archived writings which were produced between 1914 and the middle of the twentieth century. The published texts include a large sample of Du Bois's commentaries about Africa (especially those from *The Crisis*), Garvey's *The Philosophy and Opinions of Marcus Garvey* (1923), Lamine Senghor's *La violation d'un pays* [the abuse of a country] (1927), Touvalou's "The Problem of Negroes in French Colonial Africa" (1924) and other essays, Padmore's *The Life and Struggles of Negro Toilers* (1931), and Léopold Sédar Senghor's *Collected Poetry* (1991), as well as other writings. The archived texts include letters, notes, and news clippings of (or about) the above black intellectuals gathered from the W. E. B. Du Bois Collection of the University of Massachusetts in Amherst, the Gallica database of the National Library of France, and the main library of the University of Cheikh Anta Diop. Yet many of the archival materials come from numerous issues of French imperial newspapers such as *Les Annales Coloniales* and *La Dépêche Coloniale et Maritime*. Similar documents include speeches, essays, and testimonies of Houénou and Garvey found in Robert Hill's edited multi-volume collection entitled *The Marcus Garvey and Universal Negro Improvement Association Papers*. Analyzing the archived

Writing Africa into black Atlantic studies 3

sources in conjunction with the published writings, I show how the black thinkers from the two sides of the Atlantic Ocean responded to one another's ideas about the impact of French colonialism and racism on blacks of Africa and the diaspora. Exploring the anticolonialism and cosmopolitanism that permeate these intellectuals' political writings will enable us to uncover the neglected history of *tirailleurs* and the pivotal moments of black Francophone and Anglophone solidarity which occurred between the two world wars.

Through their assessments of France's treatment of *tirailleurs* and other Africans, Diagne, Du Bois, Garvey, Touvalou, Padmore, and the two Senghors represented similar and different forms of black cosmopolitanism, anticolonialism, and views of France. While they shared a radical respite of a French republic that epitomized brutal exploitations of Africans under the false civilizationist rhetoric of cosmopolitanism, the seven black intellectuals differed in the ways in which they each critiqued the métropole's failure to live up to its ideals of liberty, equality, and justice. Working against the dominant imperial status quo that Diagne embodied, Du Bois, Garvey, Touvalou, Padmore, and the two Senghors criticized French cosmopolitanism and republicanism based on the horrible, subordinate, and exploitative status of *tirailleurs* in both the colonies and the métropole. These intellectuals, who were aware of the French colonials' use of Diagne as a tool for marketing their brand of cosmopolitanism in Africa and ushering imperial soldiers to Europe's trenches, condemned the parliamentarian's ideologies and expectations about these combatants as deceptive and fascist. Countering the cosmopolitan frameworks through which Diagne and his white colleagues praised France as a nation that loved Africans, Du Bois and the other black thinkers developed their own types of cosmopolitanism (that I call "black cosmopolitanisms") which radically condemned the hypocritical ways in which the métropole ostracized *tirailleurs* and other Africans while claiming to fight for their advancement.

Yet Du Bois, Garvey, and Touvalou were not completely different from Diagne since they also had special attachments with French cosmopolitanism and republicanism. However, these three black intellectuals were in stark contrast to Diagne to the extent that they were primarily loyal to Africa rather than to France. Also, being aware of the social and economic privileges that Diagne had due to his intimacy with France, Du Bois, Garvey, and Touvalou devised forms of cosmopolitanism and radicalism that were intended to be distinct from the deputy's. Nevertheless, these other intellectuals were not fundamentally dissimilar from Diagne since their cosmopolitanisms also sought to appropriate French republicanism for the benefit of anticolonial and antiracist struggles. Focusing on the seven black intellectuals' creations of distinct forms of cosmopolitanism that shared certain common fascinations with France and radical desires to protect *tirailleurs* and other blacks from racism and colonialism, I attempt to study the political discourses of Diagne, Du Bois, Garvey, Touvalou, Padmore,

4 Writing Africa into black Atlantic studies

and Lamine and Léopold Senghor beyond the traditional categorizations of these intellectuals as either apologists or opponents of the colonial system. Another goal of this book is to blur the categorization of these intellectuals as either proponents or detractors of a radical black nationalist agenda. The black intellectuals reflect all of these patterns at different times and in discrete contexts.

My conception of black cosmopolitanism is indebted to Ifeoma Kiddoe Nwankwo's argument, in *Black Cosmopolitanism: Racial Consciousness and Transnational Identity in the Nineteenth-Century Americas*, that "imperialism and colonialism themselves are forms of cosmopolitanism" and that "responses and resistance to these forms, then, are often also cosmopolitanism" (2005, 162). Nwankwo also writes:

> In using this term [black cosmopolitanism] to describe a nineteenth-century person of African descent, I aim to suggest that this, along with the other manifestations of cosmopolitanism during the period (and slavery, of course), helped to shape the terms of people of African descents' public articulations of self and representations of each other.
> (2005, 162)

Like Nwankwo, I use the term "black cosmopolitanism" as a concept that describes how African-descended peoples have attempted to counter Western hegemonies by acknowledging the linkages between their local and transnational histories.

Yet cosmopolitanism is not a call for essentialism since it allows blacks to invent a transnational consciousness without neglecting their disrupted individual and national aspirations and identities. As Nwankwo suggests, when "national identity may be desired but [is] inaccessible," cosmopolitanism serves, for blacks, "as a means to the end of gaining access to national identity . . . and/or as the basis of a substitute national identity" (2005, 12). In this sense, black cosmopolitanism is a resistive tool that enables various blacks, whose lives are intertwined with the West, to embrace their hybrid and diverse selves and mitigate the anguish of their fragmented and marginalized identities while preserving a sense of a shared history of struggle. Black cosmopolitanism, then, emphasizes race not as an essentialist idea, but as a notion signifying black alliances for social, political, and economic transformations in Africa and the black diaspora. This conception of cosmopolitanism as a broad form of black unity that refuses dogmatism is appropriate for studying the transnational solidarity that Diagne, Du Bois, Garvey, Touvalou, Padmore, and both Lamine and Léopold Senghor expressed toward the plight of *tirailleurs* in spite of their differing relationships with France and its republican ideals.

Moreover, black cosmopolitanism stands in opposition to a Western totalizing view of civilization as an idea that assumes the existence of undeniable values, principles, and cultures (such as the benefits of education, science, and other knowledge) to which all the citizens of the world should aspire. This essentialist Western concept of civilization is apparent in the ways in which the late eighteenth-century German writer Christoph Martin Wieland defined the qualities of "ideal cosmopolitans" in universalistic terms. As Kwame A. Appiah argues, in *Cosmopolitanism: Ethics in a World of Strangers*, Martin defined "ideal cosmopolitans" as individuals who

> regard all the people of the earth as so many branches of a single family, and the universe as a state, of which they, with innumerable other rational beings, are citizens, promoting together under the general laws of nature the perfection of the whole, while each in his own fashion is busy about his own well-being.
>
> (2006, xv)

Although it provides opportunities for nations to be both similar to and different from one another, Western cosmopolitanism is usually universalistic and absolutist, because it claims ownership and knowledge of the "general laws of nature" and "perfection" and presents them as ideal models of development for the rest of the world.

The study of *tirailleurs* in French history is not new and can be traced to the archival materials in which such combatants are often idealized as heroic "noble savages." These archetypes are found in classic French books such as Charles Mangin's *La Force Noire* (1910) and Lucie Couturier's *Des inconnus chez moi* (1920) which blend primitivizing and romanticization of *tirailleurs* while praising the Africans' devotions to the métropole.[1] In an attempt to dismantle such stereotypes, scholars such as Marc Michel, Pascal Blanchard, Nicolas Bancel, Eric Deroo, and many others have explored the contributions of West African colonial soldiers in French history. They have provided us with key statistics, photographs, and testimonies about the enormous sacrifices *tirailleurs* made for France during the two world wars. Furthermore, in preparation of the centennial commemoration of World War I, numerous papers, exhibits, public lectures, conferences, and films about *tirailleurs* had been produced by the French research collective called Achac.[2]

Michel's work is uniquely important since it recognizes the difficult historical context in which *tirailleurs*' fights for France in World War I must be understood. Describing the attitude of the *indigènes* toward the French administration during World War I, Michel writes:

> À l'époque, les autorités y voient la manifestation d'un loyalisme sincère, en tout cas elles la présentèrent comme telle. Elle a peut-être été tout cela à la fois, mais a traduit aussi de véritables stratégies politiques d'accommodation qui prouvent l'existence d'espaces de négociation.
>
> [At the time, the authorities saw it as a manifestation of sincere loyalty, at least they presented it as such. This attitude may have been all this

6 Writing Africa into black Atlantic studies

at once, but also reflects genuine political strategies of accommodation that prove the existence of negotiation spaces.]

(2003, 32)

Michel's perception of *indigènes'* relationships with France as associations that potentially led to "accommodation" and "negotiation spaces" enables us to understand how Diagne and the other black intellectuals viewed *tirailleurs'* participation in the war as a tool for gaining a degree of admissibility and rights for Africans.

In a similar vein, Blanchard, Deroo, and Gilles Manceron have recognized *tirailleurs'* contributions to France's history. In their book, *Le Paris Noir*, the three French scholars pay homage to the 34,000 fallen African *tirailleurs* who had severely suffered from the cold in France and had been punctually deployed in 1918 from "la bataille de la Marne aux combats de Champagne" [the battle of the Marne to the combats of Champagne] (2001, 46). Drawing on similar testimonies, I attempt to show that not all *tirailleurs* who were stationed in France between the start of World War I and the late 1920s were ill-treated. Despite the racism that was directed toward them, a few *tirailleurs* crossed the color line and, as indicated in *Le Paris Noir*, had romantic relationships with young French women with whom they exchanged letters during and after the first war (2001, 58). Such cosmopolitan moments symbolize special instances of natural coexistence between blacks and whites of the French empire that the Senegalese historian Iba Der Thiam praises in his essay "Réflexions sur les Forces noires" (2009). Thiam's essay was part of the proceedings of a conference held in Metz, France, on January 24th and 25th, 2008, on the history of European war recruitment of Africans. In the essay, Thiam describes the geopolitical importance that French administrators, who later supported Diagne's political ascendance in Senegal, gave to their overseas territories in 1909-1910 when they knew that

> les colonies pouvaient apporter une contribution économique importante qui est le pendant de la force démographique qu'elles apportent avec la Force noire ... Dès ce moment-là se pose la nécessité d'une alliance fondée sur l'intérêt mutuel entre les colonies et la métropole.

> [the settlements could make an important economic contribution which is the counterpart of the demographic strength they bring with the black Force ... From that point, there arises the need of an alliance based on mutual interest between the colonies and the metropole.]

(2009, 223)

Therefore, like Michel, Blanchard, and many other scholars, Thiam interprets the relations between France and *tirailleurs* as those of mutual reliance. Conversely, I assess these relations differently by seeing them as also founded on social, political, and economic inequalities and subjugations reinforced by racism and fascism.

In spite of the sporadic attention given to *tirailleurs*, the painful history of these combatants' relations with France and their conditions in the métropole and Senegal between the wars are underexplored. Realizing this problem, Thiam launched in March 2014 a project aimed to write a general history of Senegal "des origines à nos jours" [from the beginning to the present] because "les Sénégalais ne connaissent pas leur histoire" [the Senegalese do not know their history].[3] Lamenting the limited knowledge about *tirailleurs* who demanded the right to do military service in the early twentieth century, Thiam urges African scholars to study a history that began before World War II and served the role "de moteur et de détonateur à la prise de conscience politique" [of motor force and catalyst of political consciousness] in Africa (1992, 50). Giving Africans the opportunity to participate in this academic endeavor will help to correct the limited presence of *tirailleurs* in mainstream (and especially Western) scholarship and media which continue to represent heroes of the two world wars as white and European men, ignoring the sacrifices of black African and other colonial and ethnic soldiers in these conflicts. In their book, *Empires at War: 1911–1923 (Greater War)*, Robert Gerwarth and Erez Manela address this situation when they assert:

> Neither the First World War nor its effects on Europe's political landscape are neglected subjects of historical research. Yet—understandably perhaps, given the imprint of the fighting on Western Europe—most of the literature produced since 1918 has focused on the events on the Western Front and their impact on metropolitan Britain, France, and Germany.
>
> (2014, 2)

The main focus on Europe in world-war studies has led to the neglect of the effects of these conflicts on colonial Senegal and other non-Western nations.

Also, the scholarship on *tirailleurs* remains limited. With the exception of books such as Gregory Mann's *Native Sons: West African Veterans and France in the Twentieth Century* (2006), Joe Lunn's *Memoirs of the Maelstrom: A Senegalese Oral History of the First World War* (1999), and Myron Echenberg's *Colonial Conscripts: The Tirailleurs Senegalais in French West Africa, 1857–1960* (1991), the history of these combatants between the two world wars is insufficiently studied. Besides, the perspectives of Senegalese intellectuals are underrepresented in a research which is dominated by the few Western scholars who may lack the personal and emotional attachments and connections to the experiences of these soldiers, though they usually have strong interests, expertise, and investments in this history. It is this personal commitment to this history that I hope to display

8 *Writing Africa into black Atlantic studies*

while letting the archives talk and provide us with fresh perspectives on France's troubling relations with colonial Senegal.

Fortunately, there is a growing call for scholars to examine the importance of the two world wars in Pan-African history. Michelle M. Wright explains:

> [A]s more scholars—from undergraduates to full professors—seek to integrate their own interests, projects, departments, or disciplines with African diaspora studies, World War II as a shaping trope offers a far broader and more immediate set of connections than the Middle Passage and allows us to explore a variety of Black identities that intersect as they differ.
>
> (2009, 272)

Answering Wright's call, I use the *tirailleur* as the pivotal agent whose dire circumstances during the two great wars ruptured the mirage of French cosmopolitanism that frequently bedazzled Touvalou (who was also called Tovalou or Tovalou-Quénum) and the two Senghors, whose portrayals of the plight of the colonial soldiers resonated with those of Du Bois and Garvey. Using the *tirailleur* as the uniting element and the central historical trope that activated black Anglophone and Francophone critiques of French imperialism during the first half of the twentieth century, I organize this book around the seminal influence that the exchanges between Diagne and Du Bois on France's treatment of the soldiers and other West Africans had on the ensuing discourses about cosmopolitanism and colonialism. The first two chapters focus on the disagreements and dialogues between Diagne and Du Bois on blacks' relationships with France and the role of *tirailleurs* in the empire, allowing the next five chapters to show how the problems grew and were understood over time through a series of conversations between other black intellectuals.

The scholars' neglect of *tirailleurs* has contributed to the lack of knowledge about the cosmopolitanism to which blacks of Africa and the diaspora contributed during the two world wars. Both *tirailleurs* and black intellectuals demonstrated their cosmopolitanisms during pivotal struggles that exposed the fascism, imperialism, colonialism, and racism which betrayed France's cosmopolitan claims to spread liberty, fraternity, and equality throughout the world. Achille Mbembe alludes to France's ambiguous cosmopolitanism as the nation's glorification of "son modèle civique républicain" [its civic republican model] and "son modèle quasi censitaire de représentation démocratique" [its quasi census model of democratic representation] (2010, 212). France's self-representation as the emblem of republicanism and democracy glamorizes it as a symbol of "cosmopolitisme" [cosmopolitanism]. This philosophy was more fictive than real since *tirailleurs* and black Francophone and Anglophone intellectuals hardly experienced it and were forced to invoke the republican principles to invent and articulate their own individual and collective

Writing Africa into black Atlantic studies 9

cosmopolitanisms. Using alternative forms of cosmopolitanism, these black intellectuals became the weapon and voice of the silenced and ostracized black masses of the French empire.

Presenting *tirailleurs* and black intellectuals as cosmopolitans with conflicting relations to and understandings of the ideals of the French republic pushes further Paul Gilroy's black Atlantic theory. The theorizing and imagining of Africa in the works of black intellectuals of the diaspora is part of the growing field of interdisciplinary transatlantic studies that explores the interactions and negotiations between authors and political figures from both sides of the Atlantic Ocean. Transatlantic research calls into question established disciplinary boundaries that segregate between various national and cultural literatures, challenging the traditional academic emphasis upon periodization and canonization. By examining numerous topics such as travel and exploration, migration and diaspora, slavery, colonialism, and anti-colonial resistances, this scholarship offers new insights into the hybrid and intercultural basis of transatlantic identity, politics, and aesthetics. Focusing on the contributions of black people to the history of the transatlantic scholarship, Gilroy coined the term "black Atlantic," in his book *The Black Atlantic: Modernity and Double Consciousness*, in order to refer to a set of political and philosophical ideas about vernacular culture and identities which reveal how, throughout history, black nationalists have expressed their relationships with Africa in antithetical ways that often contradict the transnational nature of black culture (1993, 4).

Following Gilroy's definition, one must recognize the diverse nature of black cultures and question any essential unity among them. Rather than being monolithic, black cultures have multiple "stereophonic, bilingual, or bifocal cultural forms originated by, but no longer the exclusive property of, blacks dispersed within the structures of feeling, producing, communicating, and remembering" (1993, 3). Yet such hybridism should not lead one to assume that Africa has not played a major and continuous role in modern or world history and cultures. By conceptualizing hybridism as a fluidity of ideas and identities occurring mainly in the West, Gilroy somewhat ignores Africa's contributions to black cosmopolitan and anticolonial resistances against tyranny between the two world wars. Gilroy could have avoided this dismissal of Africa by including the continent in his theorizing of black transnational spaces. As Charles Piot contends, Gilroy's theory could be more instrumental in black Atlantic studies "by including rather than excluding Africa and exploring the complex traffic in meanings that has long circulated throughout this Atlantic world and produced cross-hatched histories of the black modern" (2001, 168).

Yet, Gilroy's black Atlantic theory should not be dismissed since it can serve as a starting point for exploring the areas of both tension and interconnectedness that characterize black cosmopolitanisms. Gilroy's hypothesis allows us to view black cultures as complex and dynamic. Recognizing this potential, Annalisa Oboe and Anna Scacchi praise Gilroy's

10   *Writing Africa into black Atlantic studies*

theory for focusing on the "black Atlantic" as a "contact zone" and a "system of cultural exchanges" which is "defined by flows and contingent exchanges—rather than by national constituencies and racial authenticity—both central and marginal to the contemporary hegemonic discourses of modernity" (2008, 3). The two critics also laud Gilroy's thesis for having provided

> the concept of the Black Atlantic as a unifying site of hybridization, linking together Africa, Europe, and the Americas, and joining in critical dialogue with the West both the Africans transported in the slave ships to the plantations of the New World and their nationally diverse descendants, bound by their common history of enslavement, racial oppression, and double consciousness.
>
> (2008, 3)

However, as Oboe and Scacchi indicate, Gilroy's black Atlantic theory has pitfalls which are visible in its "Americocentrism and the paradox of an effort to debunk African American parochialism that ends up taking the African American experience as paradigmatic of the black diaspora" (2008, 4). These limitations partly stem from Gilroy's minimization of the historical exchanges between Africa and the black diaspora.

Relatedly, my book expands the study of the global movement that Edwards theorizes, in *The Practice of Diaspora: Literature, Translation, and the Rise of Black Internationalism*, as the influence of Paris in black novelistic production during the 1920s and 30s and the creation of "a special space for black transnational interaction, exchange, and dialogue" (2003, 5). While I also focus on black associations and activisms in France, I study the crucial role that a group of black intellectuals from both Africa and the diaspora played in the resistances of subjugated West Africans against colonialism and racism between the two world wars. Moreover, offsetting the preponderance of the United States in black Atlantic studies, my book uncovers a neglected history of black transnationalism by discussing the conversations that the black Francophone and Anglophone intellectuals had about colonialism and *tirailleurs* during the two world wars. Consequently, my study widens the geographical spaces in which African and diasporic transnational exchanges can be theorized. Such other points of black transnational exchanges of ideas have been neglected in the Atlantic-studies scholarship that tends to focus predominantly on African Americans, at the exclusion of Africans and Caribbeans. One example of such a scholarship is that on "black Paris" which presents key research issues that Aedín Ní Loingsigh synopsizes in his book, *Postcolonial Eyes: Intercontinental Travel in Francophone African Literature*, as follows:

> Indeed, impressive as the growing body of scholarship on "black Paris" is, converging on the French capital in order to explore the complex

Writing Africa into black Atlantic studies   11

transnational network of black relations arguably threatens to reinforce at some level a colonial geography of political and cultural domination. Of course, operating exclusively within this framework also risks the creation of a reductive topography that excludes other networks of exchange that either bypass or extend beyond the European center.

(2009, 100)

My book attempts to overcome these theoretical and methodological hurdles by looking at Paris not as the main site of black transnational contact, but as one of the key locations where the relationships between French West Africa and its métropole were discussed through the prisms of parliamentarian debates and colonial newspapers in which segregating and capitalist power relationships between European colonials and African laborers were noticeable. My study also seeks to surmount the challenges by juxtaposing the cosmopolitan ideas of selected diasporan and African leaders and putting them in conversation with one another, breaking the overemphasis on Paris and other metropolises in black diaspora studies. Reading archival or published writings, such as *The Marcus Garvey and Universal Negro Improvement Association Papers*, *The Crisis*, W. E. B. Du Bois Papers, Diagne's colonial speeches, and Léopold Senghor's poems, as cosmopolitan texts that put French colonialism and racism on trial, this book revives a significant body of political narratives that has been either ignored or insufficiently examined in black Atlantic and black diaspora studies. By analyzing the representations of cosmopolitanism, the two great wars, anticolonialism, and racism in such texts, I want to disrupt the colonial topography of the "black Paris" scholarship through a juxtaposition of African American, Caribbean, and Francophone West African political and literary voices on the plight of the *tirailleurs* and other disadvantaged blacks during the first half of the twentieth century. Moreover, by including and interpreting such marginalized transnational voices, I want to enlarge the scopes through which blackness can be understood in terms of both solidarity and disunity.

Another scholarship to which my book contributes is the one about Pan-Africanism. Even if it is massive, this research is hampered by an overemphasis on Anglophone relations and a frequent neglect of the connections between English-speaking diasporan black intellectuals and their French-speaking West African counterparts. Works that stand out in this scholarship include Jabez Ayodele Langley's *Pan-Africanism and Nationalism in West Africa, 1900–1945* (1973), Wilson Jeremiah Moses's *The Golden Age of Black Nationalism, 1850–1925* (1978), Robert Hill's *Pan-African Biography* (1987), Hakim Adi and Marika Sherwood's *Pan-African History: Political figures from Africa and the Diaspora since 1787* (2003), and James Campbell's *Middle Passages: African American Journeys to Africa, 1787–2005* (2006). While these books explore the main trajectories, biographies, and tenets of Pan-Africanism, they tend to be

12 *Writing Africa into black Atlantic studies*

primarily Anglophone and generally exclude Francophone Africans' contributions to the movement and their relationships with diasporan blacks. Moreover, these works limit their study of Africa's role in Pan-Africanism to analyses of Ralph Bunche and Thurgood Marshall's influence on anti-Apartheid resistances in South Africa or Du Bois's impact on nationalism in Ghana, Nigeria, or Kenya. The impact of African American and Caribbean intellectuals on the anticolonial resistances of Francophone West Africans is often ignored in this scholarship. For instance, Adi and Sherwood's *Pan-African History* makes no mention of the role of Du Bois and Garvey in Senegal's anticolonialism. Moreover, this book ignores Diagne, Touvalou, and Alioune Diop even if it counts Léopold Senghor, Sékou Touré, and Cheikh Anta Diop among the notable Pan-African leaders of the twentieth century.

Other studies which have neglected the relations between black Anglophone and Francophone intellectuals are those which have paid no attention to the influence of Diagne, Touvalou, and Lamine Senghor on Pan-Africanism. Such works include Tony Martin's *Race First: The Ideological and Organizational Struggles of Marcus Garvey and the Universal Negro Improvement Association* (1976), Ronald W. Walters's *Pan-Africanism in the African Diaspora* (1993), and Campbell's *Middle Passages*. These books represent Pan-Africanism as Garvey's vision of an African nation, Bunch's and Marshall's anti-Apartheid struggles, and Wright's support of Kwame Nkrumah's anticolonialism respectively. Yet they do not locate or inscribe Pan-Africanism in the relations between Garvey and Houénou or those between Du Bois and Diagne. In addition, although they refer to Diagne's discords with Garvey and Du Bois on the issue of black participation in World War I, Martin, Walters, and Campbell do not provide a deeper analysis of these disagreements and, subsequently, ignore the three intellectuals' analogous and dissimilar concepts of black freedom. While Du Bois and Garvey represented freedom as unmitigated equality under the law, Diagne theorized it as incremental autonomy. Yet Diagne was quite similar to Du Bois and Garvey with whom he shared a sporadic rivalry and naive fascination with French cosmopolitanism that somewhat marred and contradicted their Pan-Africanist convictions.

However, there are a few exceptions to the neglect of African Francophone intellectuals in Pan-African studies. Works such as Lilyan Kesteloot's *Black Writers in French* (1974) and Michel Fabre's *From Harlem to Paris: Black American Writers in France, 1840–1980* (1993) have shown that Paris was a major point of contact for African American, Caribbean, and African writers in the 1940s. As Kesteloot argues, during that decade, Diop, Wright, Césaire, and Léopold Senghor founded the journal *Présence Africaine* as "the principal voice of the black world in France" (1974, 280–281). In a similar vein, numerous essays of V. Y. Mudimbe's *The Surreptitious Speech: Présence Africaine and the Politics of Otherness 1947–1987* have examined the seminal journal's role as a mouthpiece whose "loyalty to the ideals of

Writing Africa into black Atlantic studies 13

Pan-Africanism" turned away "from the temptations to become an interpreter of the micronationalisms" in post-independence Africa (1992, xix). A major contribution to this book is Bennetta Jules-Rosette's essay which, as Mudimbe argues, shows how a young generation of black intellectuals became critical of *Presence Africaine*'s "political prudence" and its romanticization of Africa as idyllic and pure (1992, xix) just as was common in Negritude literature. My study attempts to reduce the idealization and essentialization of Africa by representing black cosmopolitanism as a set of Francophone and Anglophone ideological and political discourses which, albeit radical in their collective denunciations of France's mistreatment of West Africans, did not succumb to racial or cultural purism.

Though it was pioneering when it was first published in the early 1960s, Kesteloot's book has been dramatically updated in such landmark contributions as Christopher Miller's *Nationalists and Nomads: Essays on Francophone African Literature and Culture* (1998), F. Abiola Irele's *The Negritude Moment* (2011), T. Denean Sharpley-Whiting's *Beyond Negritude: Essays from Woman in the City* (2009) and *Bricktop's Paris: African American Women in Paris Between the Two World Wars* (2015), and Dominic Thomas's *Black France: Colonialism, Immigration, and Transnationalism* (2007). These works have paved the way for a deeper analysis of the relations between France and its colonial populations and cultures beyond the prism of Negritude which had traditionally occupied scholars.[4] They provide a revisionist approach to black Francophone literature that places the ideology and colonial culture which preceded Negritude at the center of academic inquiry. Miller's *Nationalists and Nomads* is particularly groundbreaking in this scholarship since it charts the history of black Francophone radicalism beyond the eras of Negritude by focusing on the neglected interwar period (1918–1939). Miller writes:

> [T]he literary historiography of francophone Africa has been incomplete and distorted. The Negritude movement that emerged in the late 1930s is too often seen as the first organized intellectual response by blacks to French colonialism ... Negritude was in fact preceded by a generation of far more radical thinkers and activists.
>
> (1998, 2)

Among these pioneers of black radicalism associated with Negritude Miller counts Touvalou and Lamine Senghor who, he asserts, "should be much more well-known to us" since "before the generation of Léopold Sédar Senghor and Aimé Césaire, these and other activists had begun the process of resisting and rethinking French colonialism" (1998, 2). Miller's acknowledgement of Touvalou's activism is principally crucial, because it suggests the primary importance of this African intellectual whose relationships with Garvey, Diagne, and the French administration were complex since they oscillated between black cosmopolitanism and radicalism.

14   *Writing Africa into black Atlantic studies*

Another innovative scholarship on Negritude is Irele's which perceives African Americans as sources of inspiration for the pioneers of the movement. For instance, in *The Negritude Moment*, Irele interprets Du Bois's view of African American culture and identity as an early expression of Negritude. He writes:

> Du Bois gives voice here to certain sentiments which his Negro compatriots were the first to echo, although we have come to associate them with Léopold Sédar Senghor. The cultivation of a Negro identity, culturally as well as socially and politically, and the expression of a total racial solidarity based not only on a common social experience but also on a common spiritual feeling, came to dominate the literature of the American Negro.
>
> (2011, 15)

Irele's view of Du Bois as a seminal expression of racial solidarity and militancy that was later identified with Senghor gives us an opportunity to compare the radicalisms of black Anglophone and Francophone intellectuals during the two world wars. Yet making such a comparison requires us to explore the meaning of black Francophone radicalism both within and outside of Negritude's confines. Sharpley-Whiting makes a strong case for this endeavor in her book, *Bricktop's Paris*, where she explores the contributions of African American women artists, writers, and entrepreneurs such as Ada "Bricktop" Smith, Jessie Fauset, and Josephine Baker to the formation of a transnational and racially conscious black expatriate community for which "France became a place where" they "could realize personal freedom and creativity, in narrative or in performance" during the 1920s and 30s (2015, 5). In a similar streak, Sharpley-Whiting has shown in another book, entitled *Negritude Women*, how France was, during the interwar years, a country where globally and racially aware black Francophone Caribbean women found a home. Among such women, she argues, were the Nardal Sisters who were "black internationalists," since

> They saw a world that linked a people by historical processes and conditions such as violent dispersal, a racialized identity (imposed from without), and a commitment to an originary homeland of Africa. They also saw this black diaspora as being part and parcel of world history and modernity.
>
> (2002, 2)

My book contributes to the seminal scholarship mentioned above by focusing on the other formative experiences of black radicalism and internationalism that preceded and influenced Negritude. Such pivotal moments include the 1919 and 1921 Pan-African congresses, the two world wars, and the interwar period which prompted blacks of both sides of the

Writing Africa into black Atlantic studies 15

Atlantic Ocean to forge collective battles against colonialism and racism. By exploring early formations of solidarity and frictions among these blacks and their responses to French cosmopolitanism, colonialism, and racism, my book provides a deeper analysis of black and Anglophone-Francophone connections that are traceable both beyond the moment of Negritude and prior to it. Therefore, my study hopes to give early historical contexts for future studies of black transatlantic ties such as those of the 1956 Congress in Paris and the 1966 World Festival of Negro Art in Dakar.

Other scholarly works linking French-speaking Africa with the black diaspora to which this study is indebted include Edwards's *The Practice of Diaspora* (2003) and Jonathan Derrick's *Africa's 'Agitators': Militant Anti-Colonialism in Africa and the West, 1918–1939* (2008). These two books exemplify the importance of including French-speaking Africans in the study of Pan-Africanism. Edwards's *The Practice of Diaspora* focuses on Paris as a locus for the development of black modernism and internationalism during the interwar years. Edwards also makes unique contributions to black diaspora studies by calling for the crossing of linguistic boundaries in the field through a valuation of writings in idioms other than English. He states:

> [T]he cultures of black internationalism can be seen only *in translation.* It is not possible to take up the question of "diaspora" without taking account of the fact that the great majority of peoples of African descent do not speak or write in English.
>
> (2003, 7)

Like Edwards, I seek to revive the French linguistic heritage which has been written out of black diaspora studies by translating passages from speeches, newspaper articles, letters, and other writings of African Francophone intellectuals whose ideas about France between the two world wars enable us to uncover a neglected history of Anglophone and Francophone internationalism. In an attempt to express the authentic voices of Francophone intellectuals such as Diagne and white French administrators, who expressed controversial ideas about *tirailleurs* and other blacks in both parliamentary debates and imperial papers, such as *Les Annales Coloniales* and *La Dépêche Coloniale et Maritime*, I have consistently cited these officials' original words and have translated them into English within the discussions.

Like Edwards's *The Practice of Diaspora*, Derrick's *Africa's 'Agitators'* expands current studies of the relations between Africa and the black diaspora. The book includes various contexts in which blacks in France, South Africa, and the United States rose up against European imperialism during the interwar years. Like Edwards, Derrick pays special attention to the associations of Lamine Senghor and Touvalou with French communists against colonialism during the mid-1920s, which is a history that my book also explores to a reasonable extent. However, unlike Edwards and Derrick,

16   *Writing Africa into black Atlantic studies*

I analyze not just the anticolonialisms of the two black intellectuals but also their cosmopolitanisms. Moreover, rather than assessing Lamine Senghor's and Touvalou's activisms in isolation, I juxtapose them with Garvey's in order to display the Jamaican's strong influence on the two Francophone leaders and their critical views on Diagne's cultural assimilationism. Furthermore, unlike Edwards and Derrick, I deconstruct the anticolonialisms of the black Francophone thinkers through not just the historical contexts that produced them, but also the archival sources that reflected them.

Another groundbreaking scholarship to which I owe a favor is the one dealing with France's colonial relationships with Senegal. A key contribution in this scholarship is Wilder's *The French Imperial Nation-State: Negritude and Colonial Humanism Between the Two World Wars* (2005). Wilder decodes the notion of republicanism, or France's moral duty to bring liberty and civilization to Africa and the rest of the world, that I consider as the source of the métropole's cosmopolitanism. Specifically, Wilder explains how, after World War I, the country's "republicans promoted the general but imprecise idea that the colonies were somehow integral parts of *la plus grande France*, an expanded French nation" (2005, 29). In order to understand this republicanism, I focus on its idea of the "rights of man" which was also the core element of French cosmopolitanism that all the black intellectuals discussed in this book, with the exception of Diagne, shattered by vehemently denouncing the imperial oppressions in the colonies that contradicted it. Discussing the paradoxes of French republicanism, Wilder states: "Colonial humanism was simultaneously universalizing and particularizing; the imperial nation-state was at once republican and illiberal" (2005, 8). While I study how the métropole's cosmopolitanism vacillated between universalism, racism, and fascism, I also examine the ways in which the transnational black intellectuals attempted to salvage the universalism that inspired the French Revolution by devising alternative forms of cosmopolitanism which opposed colonialism. In spite of their ambivalent attitudes toward French cosmopolitanism, the black intellectuals, who admired its revolutionary origins, substituted the discourse's colonialist and racist elements with a spirit of international collaborations between races and working classes that could topple imperial tyranny. Although they hoped that such cosmopolitanism would lead to freedom, equality, and citizenship for France's African populations, the black intellectuals were ultimately dismayed that it did not do so during the interwar period.

Alice Conklin's *A Mission to Civilize: The Republican Idea of Empire in France and West Africa, 1895–1930* (1997) is another innovative work that inspired my study. Explaining the ideological convictions that inspired both the republican credo "Becoming French!" and the métropole's colonial discourse about West Africa, Conklin writes: "Abolishing slavery, like eradicating indigenous languages and customs, pestilence, poverty, and ignorance, was central to the French understanding of their mandate in West Africa"

Writing Africa into black Atlantic studies   17

(1997, 102). Yet Conklin discusses another crucial aspect of the French *mission civilisatrice* [civilizing mission] when she asserts:

> This was the extent to which the French believed that their republican heritage imposed upon them not only a special obligation to uplift the oppressed of the earth materially, in whatever way they could, but also a specific duty to defend the individual rights of man wherever they were threatened.
>
> (1997, 102)

Drawing on Conklin's theorizing of French republicanism and "civilizing mission," I demonstrate how these ideologies were compromised by the métropole's maltreatment of blacks in colonial Senegal.

Situating my study within the above scholarship, I attempt to bring twentieth-century Africa firmly into the discussion of diaspora and criss-cross linguistic worlds to show the complexity of Anglophone US and Caribbean intellectuals' engagements with the black francophone world. Moreover, I explore black-diasporan and Francophone West African cosmopolitan resistances against colonialism and racism while analyzing the transnational contexts of global struggles against oppression from which they also evolved. Drawing from the fields of history, literature, political science, philosophy, and critical theory, I put the black diasporan scholars' views about French cosmopolitanism in conversation with those of their counterparts from Africa. By juxtaposing these views, I reveal the scholars' different depictions of the effects of colonialism, racism, and fascism in Senegal between the two world wars. This method reveals both the similarities and differences among black intellectuals of Africa, the United States, and the Caribbean who struggled for political freedom, equality, and sovereignty during the first half of the twentieth century. While I reveal the comparable cosmopolitanisms and radicalisms that the black intellectuals shared in their disparagements of France and praises of the *tirailleurs*' valor in battles, I show the thinkers' discrete acclaims of French republican ideals and vilifications of Garvey's Pan-Africanism. Therefore, while studying the connections between the black intellectuals, I also unveil the disconnections among them and the different views about France that complicated their ties. This approach reveals the contributions of the cosmopolitan black intellectuals to transnational literary and political sites of resistances outside of the United States, such as France and Senegal, where they developed close relations with one another while sometimes disagreeing on the meaning of black identity, crossracial alliances, and anticolonial struggles. Studying these connections and disconnections helps us to acknowledge the significant and complex roles of diasporan black intellectuals in the independence struggles of Francophone West Africans.

However, this book's methodology is primarily transnational since I interpret the cosmopolitan works and ideologies of key black intellectuals

18 *Writing Africa into black Atlantic studies*

in their local spheres of black-diasporan or Francophone West African resistances against colonialism, racism, and socio-economic alienation while showing the global contexts from which such rebellions also evolved. Using a transnational approach, I analyze the writings of Francophone West Africans in the intercontinental context of resistance against racism and socio-economic alienation in which blacks of the diaspora made great contributions. This methodology provides a counterpoint to the "mystification of transatlanticism" that Laura Chrisman decries, in one of her fascinating appraisals of Gilroy's theory, as a situation that "threatens to foreclose rather than expand critical studies of black diasporic cultures, African cultures and their relationship" (2001, 12). Questioning Gilroy's "transatlanticism," which regards African nationalism and black Atlanticism as mutually exclusive, Chrisman calls for a new theory that considers the two traditions as reciprocally supportive (2001, 17). In a similar vein, Chrisman urges a new black Atlantic studies methodology that reveals both similarities and differences between black cultures. As Thomas Jeffery argues,

> Her [Chrisman's] primary concern is the need for the development of approaches to black Atlanticism which can take into account the various (national) points of view in which it consists, without lumping them together in such a fashion as to mask their distinct characteristics and concerns.
>
> (2004, 155)

Like Chrisman, I reposition Africa in novel constructions of blackness, within the wide transnational contexts from which it has been usually excluded, in an attempt to induce new critical inquiries about the complex relations among various blacks.

Furthermore, this book's methodology is both diachronistic and synchronistic since I explore the development of conversations about colonialism and cosmopolitanism among selected black intellectuals between 1914 and 1945 while showing these thinkers' contributions to the study of the two world wars. While I place the intellectuals' writings and ideas in their historical contexts, I also analyze their depictions of the effects of these battles, colonialism, and racism on Africans. My approach is consistent with the two research strategies that Lois Tyson defines as synchronic and diachronic methods. Tyson explains:

> To analyze the semiotics of food as it is expressed in restaurant menus, for example, one would not examine menus from a single restaurant as they have changed over time (diachronically). Instead, one would examine a large number of menus produced by different restaurants at the same point in time (synchronically) in order to discover their *semiotic*

codes, the underlying structural components that carry a nonverbal cultural message of some sort.

(2006, 218–219)

My book disrupts the binary between the diachronic and synchronic research methods because it considers both the history of individual black Francophone and Anglophone ideas about cosmopolitanism, colonialism, and Pan-Africanism over time (diachrony) and the development of particular relationships among proponents or detractors of such ideas at specific points in time (synchrony). I use the diachronic approach since I focus on the development of conversations about cosmopolitanism across time and how this philosophy was either celebrated or criticized by black thinkers who invoked black solidarity as a means to resist French colonialism, racism, and fascism. Yet, I also employ the synchronic approach by relating the contributions of black diasporans and Africans at specific moments and conjunctures, establishing connections across black transnational groups and spaces whose cosmopolitan and anticolonial ideas reveal lingering inconsistencies not only in the relations between the black intellectuals and the West but also in the ties among the intellectuals themselves.

Having explained this book's major research contributions, it is now befitting to define its main concepts. As Aubrey W. Bonnett and G. Llewellyn Watson suggest, the term "diaspora" comes from the Greek word "*Diaspeirein*" (to spread about) (1990, 2). Originally referring to the dispersion of Jews outside Israel in the twentieth century, the concept of "diaspora" has been enlarged to include the dispersal of Africans in New-World societies by historical forces such as slavery, colonization, wars, and migrations (Bonnett & Watson, 1990, 2). Discussing the resulting notions of "African diaspora" or "black diaspora," Paul Lovejoy defines them as the various locations where people originating from Africa (their homeland) live.[5] Thus, the black diaspora is wider than one could cover in a single book, since it includes black communities living in all the regions outside of continental Africa. Accordingly, I use the concept of the "black diaspora" to refer to the United States, the Caribbean, and England only, and not to all the other regions where African-descended people live.

On the other hand, "Pan-Africanism" is a political ideology that resists Western global oppression against blacks. Summarizing Maulena Karenga's explanation of this concept, Walters states:

Speaking practically, continental Pan Africanism is the *principal task* of Africans on the continent and the Black solidarity expressed in the thrust of global Pan Africanism must ultimately and essentially be translated into the struggle we as Black people wage to free ourselves right here.

(1997, 83)

20 *Writing Africa into black Atlantic studies*

In a similar logic, Jerry Gafio Watts writes:

> Political Pan-Africanism views Africans and the diaspora as constituting a shared political struggle against a common enemy (i.e., European colonialism or white racism). Less emphasis is placed on international black cultural similarities than on the various struggles against European racist colonization and white racist practices throughout Africa and the African diaspora.
>
> (2001, 378)

Instead of theorizing Pan-Africanism as a fixed and homogeneous resistance against domination, I conceptualize it as a fluid and multilayered subversive movement and intellectual tradition that is shaped by varying cosmopolitan responses to colonialism and racism. Thus, while it is distinct from both cosmopolitanism and anticolonialism, Pan-Africanism is slightly similar to the two movements because it is viscerally antithetical to imperialism, fascism, and racism. My conception of Pan-Africanism derives from Iris Schmeisser's interpretation of the adjective "Pan-African" as a word that "signifies a specific construction of black otherness" and

> how ideas about black otherness functioned within the actual cultural, historical and political contexts of their times, as they [Africans] were embedded in the specific dialogues and significations of the contemporaneous discursive order that characterized the cultural landscape of Paris in the interwar years.
>
> (2004, 117)

Schmeisser's definition of Pan-Africanism enables us to stress both continuities and transformations in the development of the ideology as well as the specific contexts out of which it evolved.

Like the term "Pan-Africanism," the concepts of "colonialism" and "imperialism" mean different things depending on the historical contexts, regions, and theories in consideration. As Robert J. C. Young argues, colonialism functioned as an activity on the periphery and was economically driven "from the home government's perspective," while imperialism operated from the center as a policy of state and was driven by the grandiose projects of power (2001, 17). Moreover, Young states: "[W]hile imperialism is susceptible to analysis as a concept ... colonialism needs to be analyzed primarily as a practice" (2001, 17). Another contrast between colonialism and imperialism is that they developed in various parts of the world (2001, 17). However, although it is different from imperialism, colonialism shares with the other system degrading characteristics such as cultural primitivizing and social and economic exploitation. In *Discourse on Colonialism*, Césaire captures the nature of such subjugating processes when he says that the decisive actors in colonization are "neither

Writing Africa into black Atlantic studies 21

evangelization, nor a philanthropic enterprise, nor a desire to push back the frontiers of ignorance, disease, and tyranny, nor a project undertaken for the greater glory of God, nor an attempt to extend the rule of law," but

> the adventurer and the pirate, the wholesale grocer and the ship owner, the gold digger and the merchant, appetite and force, and behind them, the baleful projected shadow of a form of civilization which, at a certain point in its history, finds itself obliged, for internal reasons, to extend to a world scale the competition of its antagonistic economies.
>
> (2000, 32–33)

Césaire's rationale shows that colonialism is a form of transnational exploitative capitalism because it thrives on the conquest of new territories and on the expropriation of foreign goods.

One more recurrent concept in this book is "black transnationalism," which refers to the liberation ideologies of blacks from various nations against colonialism and racism. This term has materialist and subversive connotations since it also refers to these blacks' continuous efforts to free their people from capitalist exploitation and white racial supremacy. Michelle Stephens explains:

> Black transnationalism is not a universalist doctrine, but a vision of the liberation of a very particular, historical racial and class community. This vision seeks to overcome racial division by overthrowing systems of unequal power relations between races and peoples. This vision never assumes that cultural intermingling across lines of difference will occur until peoples can interact with each other on a level social, political and economic playing field.
>
> (2005, 267)

Theorizing black transnationalism in such a flexible way, my book explores both known and little-known Pan-African encounters, writings, speeches, and events when a special group of black intellectuals became adamant defenders of Africa against French colonialism.

Another frequent term in this book is *"indigène."* The French used this expression to demarcate Africans socially, economically, politically, and culturally as "others" in relation to the "colonial masters and mistresses." Mamadou Diouf represents this unequal class system as "a dualistic political and administrative division of colonial Senegalese society between French *sujets* [subjects], who followed the *code de l'indigénat* [the *indigénat* code], and French *citoyens* [citizens]—the *originaires* from the Four Communes of Saint-Louis, Gorée, Rufisque and Dakar," who abided by the laws of the Republic (2001, 197). In order to convey such demarcations, I employ the word *"indigène"* as it appears in imperial texts.

22 Writing Africa into black Atlantic studies

An additional recurrent concept in this study is "fascism." My definition of this word hails from Robin D.G. Kelley's description of the term "anti-fascism," in *Freedom Dreams: The Black Radical Imagination*, as a resistance against slavery, colonialism, and racism (2002, 56–57). Locating the movement in a long and radical tradition involving many black intellectuals, such as Padmore and Césaire, Kelley asserts: "They viewed fascism as a blood relative of slavery and imperialism, global systems rooted not only in capitalist political economy but in racist ideologies that were already in place at the dawn of modernity" (2002, 56). Using a similar framework, I define fascism as a coherent and systemic Western oppression that expressed itself in the form of colonialism, racism, or slavery. Fascism also signifies the racist and violent manners in which France confined Africans to subhuman conditions during the first half of the twentieth century.

Last but not least, the term *"tirailleur"* (which is often referred to in English as "sharpshooters" or "riflemen") is used in this study to describe black colonial soldiers who served France in either Senegal or other West African parts of its empire between the two world wars. French administrators employed this word as a concept which was also applicable to colonial soldiers from Soudan [Mali], Guinée-Conakry, Ivory Coast, Upper Volta [Burkina Faso], Gabon, Dahomey [Benin], Niger, Congo-Brazzaville, Algeria, Tunisia, Madagascar, and other overseas territories. By contrast, the word *"tirailleurs Sénégalais"* [Senegalese *tirailleurs*], which is the focus of this book, has a specific definition that is drawn from the colonial archival materials themselves where various meanings of the concept emerge. For instance, Colonel Debon states:

> Nous appelons Sénégalais tous les indigènes de l'Afrique noire, dont les siècles d'atavisme militaire et d'entraînement ont fait des merveilleux guerriers de race ... C'est en 1857 que le général Faidherbe, alors commandant et gouverneur du Sénégal créa le 1er bataillon sénégalais, et pendant la guerre nous avons eu jusqu'à 100 bataillons de Sénégalais sur le front français, ou ils se sont toujours admirablement conduits, dans les batailles les plus rudes.[6]

> [We call Senegalese all the natives of black Africa whose centuries of atavism and military training turned into wonderful race warriors .... It was in 1857 that General Faidherbe, then commander and governor of Senegal, created the first Senegalese battalion, and during the war we had up to 100 battalions of Senegalese on the French front in which they have always admirably conducted themselves in the toughest battles.]

In a similar vein, Aminata Diakhaté suggests that it was under the order, dated July 21, 1857, of Napoleon III (the Emperor of the Second French Empire), that the battalion of *tirailleurs* was founded, replacing the 1820s'

Writing Africa into black Atlantic studies   23

corps of African soldiers of the Gorée island formerly known as the "*laptots*" (2008, 16). Thus, the expression "*tirailleurs Sénégalais*" has a dual meaning. According to Charles Cros, Diagne considered this denomination as a tribute to the inhabitants of the four communes of Senegal who had shed their blood for France throughout Africa (1972, 81-82). Yet the term "*tirailleurs Sénégalais*" generally refers to various African soldiers who served France during colonization.

The exact number of *tirailleurs* from French West Africa who served in World War I remains unknown since scholars estimate it differently. While Colonel Debon evaluates the number to be 164,351, Moulaye Aïdara and Pap Ndiaye estimate it to be 161,250 and 189,000 respectively.[7] The last number is 9000 higher than the 180,000 that Blanchard, Deroo, and Manceron give as the total size of the African forces from Senegal, Soudan, Niger, Guinée, Upper Volta, Ivory Coast, Dahomey, Somali, and Madagascar, who were mobilized during World War I.[8] According to the three scholars, 134,000 of these soldiers, who were all called *tirailleurs sénégalais*, reached Europe and were joined by tens of thousands of combatants from the old colonies such as Guyana [17,000], Réunion [10,000], and the four communes of Senegal [5,400] (2001, 46).

The discrepancy about the number of *tirailleurs* who fought in World War I partly derives from the fact that estimates do not generally include the colonial soldiers who actually landed in France as opposed to those who were only stationed in Africa. Thus, according to Ndiaye, 134,000 *tirailleurs* disembarked in France and 31,000 died in the first war (2008, 154). Though his final statistics corroborate those of Ndiaye, Lunn observes:

> The total African casualties during the war, based on the most consistent and generally accepted official estimates, can be reckoned at approximately 31,000 soldiers . . . Although almost certainly an underestimate because incidental deaths—including those from disease—were probably not included.
>
> (1999, 142)

These statistics differ largely from those that one finds in other historical studies. For instance, as Manning Marable argues in *Black Leadership*, upon Clemenceau's call for soldiers from French West Africa, "within twelve months, under Diagne's direction, 680,000 soldiers and 238,000 laborers from French West Africa were in France" (1998, 82–83). These estimates are in contrast with those of Aïdara, Ndiaye, and Lunn, suggesting the need for more scholarship on the exact number of *tirailleurs* who fought in World War I. In spite of this discrepancy, it is undeniable that *tirailleurs* distinguished themselves through their bravery at home and abroad and their enormous sacrifices that need to be remembered.

Drawing from numerous issues of *Les Annales Coloniales*, *La Dépêche Coloniale et Maritime,* and other archival sources, the first chapter discusses

24 *Writing Africa into black Atlantic studies*

Diagne's upbringing, his early contacts with the métropole, and his rise as an elite member of the French National Assembly. The chapter then explores Diagne's cosmopolitanism and his role in recruiting colonial soldiers for France during World War I. The rest of the chapter deals with the numerous contradictions that emerged in Diagne's cosmopolitanism as his discourse about an idyllic France that was a protector of blacks collided with the racist and colonialist manners in which the empire mistreated *tirailleurs* and other West Africans. Diagne himself suffered from this paradox as he faced racism from some of his parliamentarian colleagues who disdained his support for Africans in spite of his staunch loyalty to France.

Focusing on numerous articles, essays, editorials, and other commentaries from *The Crisis* magazine, the W. E. B. Du Bois Papers of the University of Massachusetts in Amherst, and the edited *Marcus Garvey and Universal Negro Improvement Association Papers*, the second chapter explores Du Bois's cosmopolitanism and Pan-Africanism in relation to those of Diagne. Major contradictions surfaced as Du Bois, who was fascinated by a few aspects of French cosmopolitanism, opposed the imperialism against Africans that Diagne and other colonial administrators legitimized. In addition, dissensions between Du Bois and Diagne emerged as the African American criticized the Senegalese's support of black participation in World War I even if he previously lauded this involvement as a commendable black contribution to French cosmopolitanism. However, Du Bois shared a few parallels with Diagne since the Senegalese deputy was also a Pan-Africanist like him, despite his allegiance to French colonization. Discussing the relationships between Du Bois and Diagne at the two Pan-African congresses, this chapter also examines pivotal moments during which the two leaders shared common racial solidarity despite their differing attitudes toward French cosmopolitanism.

Drawing from speeches, articles, and convention proceedings from *The Philosophy and Opinions of Marcus Garvey* and *The Marcus Garvey and Universal Negro Improvement Association Papers*, the third chapter analyzes the Jamaican's views on Diagne and colonial Senegal. These documents suggest Garvey's strong understanding of the real issues facing West Africans during and after World War I. Garvey played major roles in global struggles for freedom and equality when he worked on the key issues of black participation in World War I and the racism against Senegalese soldiers and other blacks of Africa which contradicted French cosmopolitanism. Moreover, Garvey was aware of and involved in the plight of blacks of Senegal even if the French strived to keep both the Universal Negro Improvement Association (UNIA) and him out of Africa. These atrocities transformed Garvey into a declared enemy of Diagne whom he perceived as a traitor who had sacrificed racial unity to placate his unwavering loyalty to a France that was oppressing black Africans. Another irony was that Garvey was fascinated with the republican ideals of French cosmopolitanism

Writing Africa into black Atlantic studies   25

in spite of the hostility that the métropole developed toward the UNIA in Senegal in the 1920s.

Referring to similar archival materials from the UNIA Papers and Touvalou's post-World War I speeches, the fourth chapter discusses the convergences and divergences between Garvey and the French Dahomean intellectual. Even if they had different backgrounds, these two leaders shared a fascination with the core ideals of universal freedom and equality of the 1789 Revolution which gave birth to French cosmopolitanism. Yet, both black leaders ended up developing an aversion to this cosmopolitanism as they decried France's unwillingness to liberate West Africans from colonialism and racism. Another focus of this chapter is on the schism that occurred between Garvey and Touvalou as the Jamaican became dismayed by his contemporary's unwarranted fascination with France in spite of the demeaning ways in which the empire treated Africans.

Reviving neglected sources such as Lamine Senghor's *La violation d'un pays* and a few of his articles which were published in David Murphy's 2012 collection of the Senegalese activist's writings, the fifth chapter explores the major roles Senghor played in France in the 1920s as a strong voice of African liberation from colonialism. Exhibiting a Pan-Africanism that was similar to Garvey's, Senghor expressed toward French cosmopolitanism deep aversions that were apparent in his sturdy communist-inspired denunciations of the impact of colonialism on *tirailleurs* and other Africans. Furthermore, like Garvey, Senghor hated Diagne's elitism and French cultural assimilationism which he viewed as debilitating. Yet, unlike Garvey, Senghor effectively transcended race and developed a cosmopolitanism that was very successful in its calls for collaborations between blacks and whites who could topple colonialism, racism, and fascism.

Discussing Padmore's *The Life and Struggles of Negro Toilers*, the sixth chapter assesses the Trinidadian scholar's disparagements of the effects of colonialism and fascism on *tirailleurs* and other West Africans. Padmore, who was born in 1903 as Malcolm Ivan Meredith Nurse, played a pivotal role in the history of black anticolonialism and cosmopolitanism during the interwar period, since he consistently denounced the exploitation that England, France, and the United States perpetrated against blacks between 1919 and 1939. Moreover, Padmore was able to witness the tense relationships that France had with Germany, Russia, and Britain, allowing us to map out the complex geopolitical contexts out of which the métropole's difficult ties with other powers compelled it to draw on Senegal and *tirailleurs* as a means of saving the declining empire. In addition, Padmore vehemently condemned French fascism in colonial Senegal. He was another Caribbean intellectual who understood the fascist nature of France's stronghold in Senegal, namely, the métropole's use of this colony and its populations as mere laborers of a subtly ruthless empire.

Drawing from selected poems of Léopold Sédar Senghor written during the first half of the twentieth century and translated from French to English

Figure 0.1 "Débarquement aux Dardanelles" [Disembarking in Dardanelles], 1915.
Source: Collections Eric Deroo.

Writing Africa into black Atlantic studies 27

by Melvin Dixon, the seventh chapter explores the Senegalese intellectual's representations of the impact of World War II on *tirailleurs* who fought on the side of France against Nazi Germans. Using Negritude and surrealism as weapons of resistance and liberation, this Senghor (who must not be confused with Lamine Senghor) aptly depicts the cosmopolitanism that *tirailleurs* expressed toward French people who reciprocated their humanism with racism, colonialism, violence, and fascism. Senghor was able to soothe the pain of black participation in World War II by emphasizing the respect for life and world freedom that *tirailleurs* showed to France.

Bibliography

Adi, Hakim and Marika Sherwood, eds. *Pan-African History: Political figures from Africa and the Diaspora since 1787*. New York: Routledge, 2003.

Aïdara, Moulaye. *L'Histoire Oubliée des Tirailleurs Sénégalais de la Seconde Guerre Mondiale*. Paris: Le Manuscrit, 2005.

Appiah, Kwame A. *Cosmopolitanism: Ethics in a World of Strangers*. New York: Norton, 2006.

Blanchard, Pascal, Eric Deroo, and Gilles Manceron. *Le Paris Noir*. Paris: Hazan, 2001.

Bonnett, Aubrey W. and G. Llewellyn Watson. *Emerging Perspectives on the Black Diaspora*. Lanham, MD: University Press of America, 1990.

Campbell, James. *Middle Passages: African American Journeys to Africa, 1787–2005*. New York: Penguin, 2006.

Césaire, Aimé. *Discourse on Colonialism*. Translated by Joan Pinkham. New York: Monthly Review Press, 2000.

Chrisman, Laura. "Rethinking Black Atlanticism." *The Black Scholar* 30, no. 3–4 (2001): 12–17.

Colonel Debon. "Les Troupes coloniales: importance du recrutement indigène colonial." *La Dépêche Coloniale et Maritime*, April 1, 1920.

Conklin, Alice L. *A Mission to Civilize: The Republican Idea of Empire in France and West Africa. 1895–1930*. Stanford, CA: Stanford University Press, 1997.

Couturier, Lucie. *Des inconnus chez moi*. Paris: Éditions de la Sirène, 1920.

Cros, Charles. *La Parole est à M. Blaise Diagne, premier homme d'Etat africain*. Dakar: Edition Maison du Livre, 1972.

Derrick, Jonathan. *Africa's 'Agitators': Militant Anti-Colonialism in Africa and the West, 1918–1939*. New York: Columbia University Press, 2008.

Diakhaté, Aminata. *Les Motivations de l'engagement volontaire des jeunes au Centre d'Instruction de Dakar-Bango*. B.A. thesis, Université Cheikh Anta Diop, 2008.

Diouf, Mamadou. *Histoire du Sénégal: le modèle islamo-wolof et ses périphéries*. Paris: Maisonneuve & Larose, 2001.

Echenberg, Myron. *Colonial Conscripts: The Tirailleurs Senegalais in French West Africa, 1857-1960*. Portsmouth, NH: Heinemann, 1991.

Edwards, Brent Hayes. "The 'Autonomy' of Black Radicalism." *Social Text* 19, no. 2 (Summer 2001): 1–13.

——, *The Practice of Diaspora: Literature, Translation, and the Rise of Black Internationalism*. Cambridge, MA: Harvard University Press, 2003.

28 *Writing Africa into black Atlantic studies*

Fabre, Michel. *From Harlem to Paris: Black American Writers in France, 1840–1980*. Urbana: University of Illinois Press, 1993.

Gerwarth, Robert and Erez Manela. "Introduction." In *Empires at War: 1911–1923 (Greater War)*, edited by Robert Gerwarth and Erez Manela, 1–17. New York: Oxford University Press, 2014.

Gikandi, Simon. "Afterword: Outside the Black Atlantic." *Research in African Literatures* 45, no. 3 (Fall 2014): 241–244.

Gilroy, Paul. *The Black Atlantic: Modernity and Double Consciousness*. Cambridge, MA: Harvard University Press, 1993.

Hill, Robert, ed. *Pan-African Biography*. Los Angeles, CA: African Studies Center, University of California Los Angeles, 1987.

Irele, F. Abiola. *The Negritude Moment: Explorations in Francophone African and Caribbean Literature and Thought*. Trenton: Africa World Press, 2011.

Jeffery, Thomas. Review of *Postcolonial Contraventions: Cultural Readings of Race, Imperialism and Transnationalism*, by Laura Chrisman. *English in Africa* 31, no. 1 (May 2004): 153–156.

Kelley, Robin D. G. *Freedom Dreams: The Black Radical Imagination*. Boston, MA: Beacon Press, 2002.

Kesteloot, Lillian. *Black Writers in French: A Literary History of Negritude*. Philadelphia, PA: Temple University Press, 1974.

Langley, Jabez Ayodele. *Pan-Africanism and Nationalism in West Africa, 1900–1945: A Study in Ideology and Social Classes*. Oxford: Clarendon Press, 1973.

"Le Groupe de recherche Achac." Accessed October 4, 2015. http://www.achac.com/.

"Le projet d'écriture d'une histoire générale 'vient combler un vide' (Iba Der Thiam)." Accessed March 27, 2014. http://www.seneweb.com/news/Societe/le-projet-d-ecriture-d-une-histoire-generale-vient-combler-un-vide-iba-der-thiam_n_122098.html.

Loingsigh, Aedín Ní. *Postcolonial Eyes: Intercontinental Travel in Francophone African Literature*. Liverpool, UK: Liverpool University Press, 2009.

Lovejoy, Paul. "The African Diaspora: Revisionist Interpretations of Ethnicity, Culture and Religion under Slavery." *Studies in the World History of Slavery, Abolition and Emancipation* 2, no. 1 (1997). Accessed January 1, 2014. http://www.yorku.ca/nhp/publications/Lovejoy_Studies%20in%20the%20World%20History%20of%20Slavery.pdf.

Lunn, Joe. *Memoirs of the Maelstrom: A Senegalese Oral History of the First World War*. Portsmouth, NH: Heinemann, 1999.

Mangin, Général [Charles]. *La Force Noire*. Paris: Librairie Hachette, 1910.

——, *Regards sur la France d'Afrique avec quatre cartes*. Paris: Librairie Plon, 1924.

Mann, Gregory. *Native Sons: West African Veterans and France in the Twentieth Century*. Durham, NC: Duke University Press, 2006.

Marable, Manning. *Black Leadership*. New York: Columbia University Press, 1998.

Martin, Tony. *Race First: The Ideological and Organizational Struggles of Marcus Garvey and the Universal Negro Improvement Association*. Dover, MA : The Majority Press, 1986.

Mbembe, Achille. "La République et l'impensé de la 'race.'" In *Ruptures post-coloniales: Les nouveaux visages de la société française*, edited by Nicolas Bancel, Florence Bernault, Pascal Blanchard, and Valérie Amiraux, 205–216. Paris: La Découverte, 2010.

Writing Africa into black Atlantic studies   29

Michel, Marc. *Les Africains et la grande guerre: l'appel à l'Afrique, 1914–1918*. Paris: Éditions Karthala, 2003.

Miller, Christopher L. *Nationalists and Nomads: Essays on Francophone African Literature and Culture*. Chicago: University of Chicago Press, 1998.

Moses, Wilson Jeremiah. *The Golden Age of Black Nationalism*. Hamden, CT: Archon Books, 1978.

Mudimbe, V. Y. "Introduction." In *The Surreptitious Speech: Présence Africaine and the Politics of Otherness, 1947–1987*, edited by V.Y. Mudimbe, xvii–xxvi. Chicago: The University of Chicago Press, 1992.

Mudimbe-Boyi, Elisabeth. "Harlem Renaissance and Africa: An Ambiguous Adventure." In *The Surreptitious Speech: Présence Africaine and the Politics of Otherness, 1947–1987*, edited by V.Y. Mudimbe, 174–184. Chicago: The University of Chicago Press, 1992.

Ndiaye, Pap. *La condition noire: Essai sur une minorité française*. Paris: Calmann-Lévy, 2008.

Nwankwo, Ifeoma Kiddoe. *Black Cosmopolitanism: Racial Consciousness and Transnational Identity in the Nineteenth-Century Americas*. Philadelphia: University of Pennsylvania Press, 2005.

Oboe, Annalisa and Anna Scacchi. "Introduction." In *Recharting the Black Atlantic: Modern Cultures, Local Communities, Global Connections*, edited by Annalisa Oboe and Anna Scacchi, 2–8. New York: Routledge, 2008.

Padmore, George. *The Life and Struggles of Negro Toilers*. 1931. Hollywood: Sun Dance Press, 1971.

Piot, Charles. "Atlantic Aporias: Africa and Gilroy's Black Atlantic." *The South Atlantic Quarterly* 100, no. 1 (Winter 2001): 155–170.

Robinson, Cedric J. *Black Marxism: The Making of the Black Radical Tradition*. 1983. Chapel Hill: The University of North Carolina Press, 2000.

Rodney, Walter. "Upper Guinea and the Significance of the Origins of Africans Enslaved in the New World." *Journal of Negro History* 54, no. 4 (October 1969): 327–345.

Sarkozy, Nicolas. "Allocution de M. Nicolas Sarkozy, Président de la République, prononcée à l'Université de Dakar." In *L'Afrique de Sarkozy: un deni d'histoire*, edited by Jean-Pierre Chrétien, 191–202. Paris: Karthala, 2008.

Schmeisser, Iris. "'Vive l'union de tous les noirs, et vive l'Afrique': Paris and the Black Diaspora in the Interwar Years." *Sources: Revue d'Études Anglophones* 17 (Automne 2004): 114–143.

Senghor, Lamine. "La Violation d'un Pays." In *La Violation d'un Pays et autres écrits anticolonialistes*, edited by David Murphy, 1–30. Paris: L'Harmattan, 2012.

Senghor, Léopold Sédar. *Léopold Sédar Senghor: The Collected Poetry*, edited and translated by Melvin Dixon, 12–13. Charlottesville: University of Virginia Press, 1991.

Sharpley-Whiting, T. Denean. *Beyond Negritude: Essays from Woman in the City*. Albany: State University of New York Press, 2009.

——, *Bricktop's Paris: African American Women in Paris between the Two World Wars*. New York: State University of New York Press, 2015.

——, *Negritude Women*. Minneapolis: University of Minnesota Press, 2002.

Stephens, Michelle Ann. *Black Empire: The Masculine Global Imaginary of Caribbean Intellectuals in the United States, 1914–1962*. Durham, NC: Duke University Press, 2005.

30 *Writing Africa into black Atlantic studies*

The Philosophy and Opinions of Marcus Garvey, or Africa for Africans. 1923. Edited by Amy Jacques-Garvey and Tony Martin. 2 vols. Dover, MA: The Majority Press, 1986.

Thiam, Iba Der. "Réflexions sur les Forces noires." In *Forces Noires des puissances coloniales Européennes*, edited by Antoine Champeaux, Éric Deroo, and János Riesz, 229–236. Panazol: Lavauzelle, 2009.

——, *Le Sénégal dans la Guerre 14–18, ou, Le prix du combat pour l'égalité.* Sénégal: Nouvelles Editions africaines du Sénégal, 1992.

Thomas, Dominic. "Immigration and National Identity in France." In *Black France/France Noire: The History and Politics of Blackness*, edited by Trica Danielle Keaton, T. Denean Sharpley-Whiting, and Tyler Stovall, 110–122. Durham: Duke University Press, 2012.

——, *Black France: Colonialism, Immigration, and Transnationalism.* Bloomington: Indiana University Press, 2007.

Tovalou-Houénou, Prince Kojo. "The Problem of Negroes in French Colonial Africa." *Opportunity* 2 (July 1924): 203–207.

Tyson, Lois. *Critical Theory Today: A User-Friendly Guide.* New York: Routledge, 2006.

Walters, Ronald W. *Pan Africanism in the African Diaspora: An Analysis of Modern Afrocentric Political Movements.* 1993. Detroit, MI: Wayne State University Press, 1997 edition.

Watts, Jerry Gafio. *The Politics and Arts of a Black Intellectual.* New York: New York University Press, 2001.

Wilder, Gary. *Freedom Time: Negritude, Decolonization, and the Future of the World.* Durham, NC: Duke University Press, 2015.

——, *The French Imperial Nation-State: Negritude and Colonial Humanism Between the Two World Wars.* Chicago: University of Chicago Press, 2005.

Wright, Michelle M. "Pale by Comparison: Black Liberal Humanism and the Postwar Era in the African Diaspora." In *Black Europe and the African Diaspora*, edited by Darlene Clark Hine, Trica Danielle Keaton, and Stephen Small, 260–276. Urbana: University of Illinois Press, 2009.

Young, Robert J. C. *Postcolonialism: An Historical Introduction.* Malden, MA: Blackwell Publishing, 2001.

1 Blaise Diagne's cosmopolitanism and views on French colonialism

In her essay, "Who Speaks for Africa?", Conklin argues that both the Guyanese intellectual René Maran and Diagne

> moved in multiple worlds, with considerably more complex identities than simply black or white, French or *noir* that the sharp dichotomies of Pan-Africanism might suggest—complexities that echoed the permeable and unstable boundaries of the French color line overseas and at home.
>
> (2003, 303–304)

Conklin introduces a concept that is desperately needed in the study of African political and intellectual figures—this is the notion that a continental African can be both black and French in the same way an American or Caribbean can be black, white, Anglophone, Francophone and more at the same time. Therefore, blacks of both Africa and the diaspora can have multiple consciousnesses and identities. Emphasizing this diversity is vital since, unlike blacks of the diaspora, those of Africa are not usually perceived as having complex and "fragmented" selves. One of these complex black Africans was the Senegalese leader Blaise Diagne, who used his privileged space within the métropole's administration to be a voice of both French and black cosmopolitanisms. Drawing on French republicanism, he developed a cosmopolitan discourse that firmly believed in the métropole's will to uplift the conditions of its colonial populations. In defense of this cosmopolitanism, Diagne developed a fervor and loyalty to the French empire and a civilizing mission that often led him to minimize the colonial populations' agony. Nonetheless, in spite of his unbending assimilationism and allegiance to the French empire, Diagne ultimately was a black cosmopolitan and radical leader. His fascination with French cosmopolitanism did not prevent him from developing a black African equivalent of this discourse that sometimes prioritized the needs of the colonial populations over the empire's exigencies.

Indeed, Diagne was a black cosmopolitan since he often denounced *indigènes'* unfair status and limited rights and the inequalities between

32 Blaise Diagne's cosmopolitanism

tirailleurs and their white French counterparts. Yet, he often contradicted his black cosmopolitanism by frequently ignoring these inequities and supporting the use of forced labor in Senegal. Therefore, Diagne was an enigmatic and conflicted leader whose ambivalent ideas about *indigènes*, servitude, and *tirailleurs* must be understood in the troubling World War I context when his role of spokesperson for French colonialism in Africa prevented him from publicly disparaging this system. Re-inscribing Diagne into the anticolonialism to which he contributed despite his frequent support of colonization and obligatory labor, this chapter examines the ways in which he contradicted his self-defeatist, elitist, and condescending views about *indigènes* by sometimes defending the rights of *tirailleurs* in unflinching ways. Referring to speeches that he gave at *la Chambre des députés* [the French Chamber of Deputies hereafter referred to as the Chamber] and comments that he made in *La Dépêche Coloniale et Maritime* and *Les Annales Coloniales*, this chapter shows how Diagne was a paradoxical black intellectual who was so obsessed with his cosmopolitan loyalties to France that he was willing to tolerate the suffering of members of his own race and birth-country for the benefit of an empire that was bitterly struggling to control its West African dominions.

A major problem in African studies is the critics' neglect of Diagne's role in black anticolonialism even if this leader did not resist French imperialism in the same ways in which Du Bois, Garvey, Touvalou, Padmore, and the two Senghors did. The critics' denial of Diagne's contributions to this history stems from their reluctance to acknowledge this leader's deserved place in black radical traditions. In "Politics and Nationalism in West Africa, 1919–1935," A. Adu Boahen argues that many "radical intellectuals" later "came to regard the Blaise Diagne of the 1920s and 30s as conservative and even anti-African" (1985, 646). Similarly, in reference to the Maran-Diagne litigation of November 1924, Hillary Jones states:

> Diagne won the case. The trial, which captured the attention of the mainstream press in Paris, however, symbolized the shifting politics of black identity and politics in the post-World War I period. Blaise Diagne's position appeared more conservative vis à vis this increasingly radical and anticolonial movement.
>
> (2010, 100)

One of the reasons why Diagne is taken out of black radicalism is the historical association of early twentieth-century Pan-Africanism with elitism. In *Framing a Radical African Atlantic: African American Agency, West African Intellectuals and the International Trade Union Committee of Negro Workers*, Holger Weiss explains the roots of this concordance when he observes:

> Political Pan-Africanism, it seemed in the eyes of the radical African American intelligentsia, by the 1920s, was a bourgeoisie intellectual

movement, which had little interest towards the masses and their plight in the African Atlantic. In their view, a totally different approach had to be taken if one wanted to challenge to [sic] [the] racial and the colonial system, namely one that would engage the masses of downtrodden toilers and agricultural workers.

(2014, 53–54)

Diagne must not be written out of Pan-Africanism and anticolonialism because he stressed the importance of black solidarity numerous times even if he envisioned this unity to be balanced and constructive rather than just reactionary. His ideologies reveal divergences in his association with Du Bois and the Pan-African movement. Yet they should not exclude him from black radicalism, anticolonialism, and other liberation movements that must be conceived in terms of variations, disagreements, and contradictions as well as similarities, consensus, and accords. Dismissing Diagne from such struggles flattens black history by representing it as a linear trajectory in which intellectuals fight oppression only in similar ways. This methodology is problematic because it neglects the different ways in which black intellectuals resist domination through different means that may include Pan-Africanism, cosmopolitanism, and (or) radicalism, among other ideologies. Addressing these issues requires a reconceptualization of black radicalism as liberation strategies with cosmopolitan representations of the world that may sometimes involve negotiations with the status quo or hegemony. The need to re-theorize black radicalism is apparent in the 2009 essay "The African Diaspora Today: Flows and Motions," in which Anthony Bogues argues that the "ideas of black liberation, pan-Africanism, and forms of black internationalism," that evolved in London, Paris, New York, Cape Town, São Paulo, and Moscow during the early twentieth century emerged "sometimes independently, at other times in collaboration and then in competition" and developed "a set of political ideas about what would constitute black freedom" (2009, 2).

Bogues's flexible conception of black radicalism as a pliable, rather than rigid, set of ideas allows us to understand how Diagne could have both defended and disparaged the French colonial establishment while working within the métropole to reduce and, later, end the empire's injustices toward Africans. Although he defended colonialism, Diagne was often anticolonial because his support of French cosmopolitanism enabled him to take a radical stance against a colonial administration that ignored its ill-treatment of World War I *tirailleurs*. Denouncing these injustices, Diagne appealed to a fair cosmopolitanism founded on loyalty to a transnational French empire in which he saw the métropole and Senegal as making equal contributions. His cosmopolitanism accepted French colonialism while rejecting undemocratic, racist, and prejudiced European attitudes toward *tirailleurs* that he viewed as counterproductive for the empire's reputation and prosperity. Examining Diagne's views on colonialism within the theoretical framework

34 *Blaise Diagne's cosmopolitanism*

of his cosmopolitanism helps us to uncover his pivotal role in the development of a subtly radical intellectual and political tradition about the relations between the métropole (France) and Senegal. My definition of "métropole" is informed by the materialistic praxis which theorizes this term as a central locus of the empire where directives about vital colonies are made. The métropole and the colonies are socially, economically, politically, and, above all, financially, dependent on each other. Discussing the interactions between the two regions, Carla Freeman alludes to "the structural relationship of dependency between 'the hinterland' (the supplier of raw material) and the '*métropole*' (the center for decision making)" (2000, 82).

Another issue in the scholarship about Diagne is how critics mainly represent him as an assimilationist or hypocritical leader who either betrayed his people or failed to defend them against European oppression. In *Nationalists and Nomads*, Miller describes Diagne "as the walking embodiment of assimilation" who "succeeded in recruiting 60,000 soldiers with 'virtually no armed resistance'" (1998, 17). Likewise, Martin Thomas represents Diagne, in *The French Empire Between The Wars: Imperialism, Politics And Society*, as a proponent of assimilationism from whom Senghor, Césaire, and other black students in 1930s Paris wanted to distinguish themselves (2005, 256). In a similar vein, Michael Crowder depicts Diagne as a "prime example of the French pursuing a policy of assimilation when it suited them, and abandoning it when it did not" (1962, 30). First, the three scholars ignore that assimilationism was a strategy Diagne frequently used to defend the Senegalese in the French empire. Second, Diagne did not remain assimilationist since he often supported in his speeches the idea of an autonomous Senegalese society that could become independent from the métropole in the future. Although it was a part of his rhetoric, assimilationism was not the major trait of Diagne's philosophy. Instead, cosmopolitanism was the dominant attribute in Diagne's discourse since he always attempted to find a balance between a France that theoretically accepted Senegalese as equals while practically oppressing these populations and denying their humanity.

Diagne's story is that of a tragic hero who rose from humble beginnings to become the highest administrative public officer from colonies known as A.O.F. (Afrique Occidentale Française [French West Africa]). Most records show that Diagne was born on October 13, 1872, on Gorée Island, in Senegal, although Jean-Francois Maurel dates the figure's birth to October 14, 1872.[1] Diagne's birth on Gorée is symbolically important since this island was one of the major slave houses in West Africa during the Atlantic human trade. Moreover, as Amady Aly Dieng argues, Diagne's nativity is historically significant because it occurred two years after the fall of the Second French Empire and the beginning of the Second French Republic (1990, 19).

Diagne's mother was a millet pounder while his father was a cook on Gorée (Gerbi, 2006, 75). Diagne was a product of local ethnic and cultural mixing that reflected the hybridity of colonial Senegalese society. A 1934

Blaise Diagne's cosmopolitanism 35

posthumous homage indicates that "M. Blaise Diagne devait avoir des ascendances confuses que l'histoire même de l'île justifiait" [Mr. Blaise Diagne must have confused ancestries that stemmed from the history of the island]."[2] Discussing his ethnic origins, Jones writes:

> She [Diagne's mother Gnagna Preira] traced her maternal line to the Lebou ethnic group of Rufisque and her paternal line to the Afro-Portuguese population of today's Guinea-Bissau. Diagne's father, Niokhar Diagne, came from the Serer ethnic group and grew up in the town of Joal.
>
> (2010, 93)

While his ethnic origins remain unclear, it is established that Diagne was an intellectually precocious child who had already mastered the French language at a very young age. His gifted intelligence soon caught the attention of his uncle Adolphe Crespin, who allowed the child to finish elementary education in Senegal and be sent to France. Diagne graduated from the École Laïque de Saint-Louis in August 1884 with a *palmarès* prize shortly before a letter from the Governor of Senegal, dated August 24, 1884, awarded him a scholarship to the École Professionnelle Fabre, in Aix-en-Provence, France.[3] Suffering from loneliness and maladjustment, Diagne failed in his studies in the métropole and was sent back to Senegal in 1890. There, as G. Wesley Johnson states, "he [Diagne] redeemed himself in Saint-Louis by graduating at the head of his class in secondary school. Then Diagne passed a rigorous competition for entering the French colonial customs service, which was still open to qualified African applicants" (1966, 237).[4] Diagne completed his administrative education in a timely manner in 1892 (the same year he was admitted to the colonial customs officers' administration school and was, thereafter, sent to numerous parts of the French empire. The areas where he served included: Dahomey (1892), Congo (July 1897–October 1898), Réunion (1898–1902), Madagascar (1902–1909), and Cayenne (1910–1913). In 1913, following a six-month leave of convalescence in France, Diagne returned to Senegal to be involved in politics.

Though it is uncertain whether Diagne became a human rights defender at this point, it is quite sure that the paradox of French cosmopolitanism became stark to him. For instance, as Bakari Kamian writes:

> Il se rendit compte à Cayenne que la France de la Révolution qui renversa la monarchie absolue n'était plus la République des idées généreuses de liberté, d'égalité et de fraternité. Il perdit ses dernières illusions face aux réalités de la vie quotidienne dans la cité du bagne.
>
> [He [Diagne] realized in Cayenne that the France of the Revolution era that toppled the monarchy was no longer the Republic of liberal ideas of liberty, equality, and fraternity. Faced with the daily life

36 *Blaise Diagne's cosmopolitanism*

realities of the city which was a penal colony, he lost all his remaining illusions.]

(2001, 131)

Diagne's disillusionment about France partially came from his dejection with the ways in which race, not character, was the criterion upon which a person's worth was determined in the colonies where he served. His disenchantment about this racism is apparent in an August 8, 1900, letter to the *Vénerable* head of the Masonic order of Saint-Denis-de-la-Réunion, in which he asked to be reassigned to a colony that had a similar lodge. His main reason for preferring such a relocation was, he said, that "j'ai appris à mes dépens à redouter certains milieux coloniaux fort puissants dans les colonies nouvelles surtout, qui mettent en pratique le principe barbare de l'inégalité des races, basée sur la couleur de l'épiderme" [I learned at my own expense to fear a few powerful colonial circles, especially those in the new settlements, which put into practice the belief in the inequality of races based on the color of one's skin].[5] Diagne's frustration about the racism in French colonies led him to develop a cosmopolitanism that was based on his deep conviction in the core sameness of all human beings. According to Diagne, ignorance, not racial difference, is the only criterion that distinguishes people. He says: "Tout membre de la société humaine y a sa place marquée, s'il en est digne . . . Telles sont les raisons pour lesquelles je souhaiterai une résidence ayant une loge maçonnique" [Every human being has a place in this world of intelligence as long as they deserve to be admitted into it . . . These are the reasons why I prefer to reside in a colony that has a masonic order].[6]

Diagne's cosmopolitanism is also apparent in his view of merit and dignity as the main factors that define individual worth and character. In this cosmopolitan philosophy, race is sterile since it confines human value in bodily features, leading Diagne to say that "L'intelligence humaine me semble bien petite si elle s'arrête à un état physique qui ne peut constituer scientifiquement une dégénérescence."[7] [Human intelligence will be so meaningless if it is reduced to a physical nature which cannot scientifically be considered as evidence of degeneracy.] Diagne's refusal to associate skin color with inferiority reveals his cosmopolitan view of humanity as an indiscriminately shared quality and his staunch opposition against racial hierarchy. In this sense, Diagne was a radical and cosmopolitan intellectual since he believed that all races deserve to be treated equally because they have the same worth. He also believed that history eventually leads to the victory of justice over tyranny. Acknowledging this quality of Diagne, the eminent Senegalese intellectual Doudou Gueye writes:

Pour Blaise Diagne, dans la longue histoire de l'humanité, la philosophie de la liberté, de l'égalité des hommes, de la fraternité, de la justice sociale s'exprimait, de la manière la mieux achevée, à travers les diverses Institutions enfantées par la Révolution française, singulièrement la

Blaise Diagne's cosmopolitanism 37

République et, à travers elles, par des actes concrets : la suppression de l'esclavage, la destruction de la féodalité et des privilèges injustes qui se rattachaient à elle, etc.

[For Blaise Diagne, in the history of mankind, the ideas of liberty, equality of races, fraternity, and social justice have been fully expressed in the diverse Institutions, notably the concept of the Republic, that resulted from the French Revolution and led to concrete actions such as: the abolition of slavery, the destruction of feudalism and other privileges that came with it, etc.]

(1974, 75)

Nevertheless, Diagne was radical in spite of his cosmopolitanism. Diagne's radicalism is noticeable in the fact that he despised the racism that Cayenne's black populations faced even if he espoused French republican ideals, leading many of his white superiors to perceive him as a despondent and rebellious person. In a 1911 correspondence, the Governor of Cayenne said that Diagne "souffre d'une indigestion d'assimilation" [suffers from indigested assimilation].[8] The Governor's negative view of Diagne stemmed from the latter's refusal to succumb to the racial prejudice and civilizing mission of his white administrative supervisors. Gueye explains:

Au cours de toute sa carrière de fonctionnaire colonial, Blaise Diagne resta fidèle à lui-même, opposé à la discrimination sous toutes ses formes et à l'injustice. Ses supérieurs hiérarchiques le notèrent comme un fonctionnaire indiscipliné, ambitieux, revendiquant sans cesse une impossible assimilation.

[Throughout his colonial administrative career, Blaise Diagne stuck to his core principles. He opposed injustice and all forms of discrimination. His official superiors categorized him as an undisciplined and immodest civil servant who incessantly demanded an impossible assimilation.]

(1974, 69)

The assertion reflects the systemic racism that Diagne faced in Réunion and French Guyana due to his blackness and *indigène* descendance.

Yet racism was not always tolerated in French colonies. In the following quotation, Johnson describes a case in which racial prejudice against Diagne that occurred in the French Caribbean was reprimanded. Johnson writes: "Called derogatory names by three drunken sailors, he [Diagne] demanded and ultimately got severe punishment for them, but antagonized his own colleagues by his obstinacy and insistence" (1966, 238). The sailors' punishment suggests that Diagne's status as a black man from Rufisque gave him the same right to equal protection that his white French colleagues had.

38   Blaise Diagne's cosmopolitanism

This right was more tangible in Réunion where blacks had more privileges, such as universal suffrage and closer relations with whites, than their counterparts in Senegal and other French colonies.[9] Unlike blacks of Réunion, those of colonial Senegal had few rights. First, by the 1910s, French administrators in Senegal, who believed more in "association" than in "assimilation," wanted to take away the citizenship and voting rights of the colony's Africans who were not regarded as "*assimilés*" [assimilated]. In this vein, as Johnson argues in *The Emergence of Black Politics in Senegal*, in 1905, M. Verrier, a French inspector-general, "recommended reducing the numbers of voters in Senegal from 9,441 to 898, leaving only white Frenchmen and 'those who were assimilated' on the lists" (1971, 81). But, as Johnson indicates, those who were regarded as "assimilated" included the biracial population (*métis*) and the black Africans (*originaires*) whose political rights were also being threatened by both M. Verrier's proposal and the racist French administrative climate that supported it (1971, 81). The harsh words that Diagne's superiors expressed toward him must be placed in this racial context that exposes the blatant unwillingness of French officials to integrate blacks from the colonies in the affairs and management of the overseas territories. This racism prompted Diagne to return to Senegal to fight for the political freedom that would guarantee citizenship and voting rights for blacks of the four communes.

When he returned to Senegal, Diagne pioneered local protests against a French administration that denied the human rights of *indigènes*. Even if they were better regarded by the French, the colonial blacks who were perceived as assimilated were not considered very differently from *indigènes* since their race and class rendered them customary victims of French prejudices which considered all blacks as savages even if the latter theoretically were citizens according to an 1848 French law. In spite of this legislation, privileged blacks of colonial Senegal did not gain citizenship until France approved the *Loi Blaise Diagne* in 1916. Such a legal victory was not widespread because the majority of blacks in Senegal and other parts of French West Africa were considered as *indigènes* and thus inferior to both whites and *originaires*. Such inequities are apparent in a passage in which Baba Diarra, a Malian *tirailleur* of the 1910s, says: "Martinaique, Gadouloup, Larégnon, Guyane avec Dakarou n Dara, Rofis avec Gorée. Ca y a citouin français, ca y a comme boulan" [Martinique, Guadaloupe, La Réunion, Guyana, Dakar, N Dara (Saint-Louis of Senegal), Rofis (Rufisque), and Gorée. There you find French citizens, here people are like whites] (2012, 104). Diarra's account suggests the discriminatory ways in which blacks from outside Senegal's communes and the few Caribbean dominions that the French culturally and administratively attached to the métropole were mostly disenfranchised and legally ostracized due to their *indigène* status.

Diagne's method for fighting against racial bigotry drew on a cosmopolitanism that was founded on his allegiance to France over all loyalties. With

Blaise Diagne's cosmopolitanism 39

a fanatic vigor, Diagne wanted the colonies to subsume all their devotions under France's priorities. On January 30, 1930, he had a heated parliamentarian debate with the deputy M. Alexandre Varenne, who initially believed that *indigènes* of Indochina must be allowed to have their own version of a French-influenced nation. Diagne disagreed by saying that all *indigènes* must regard France as their mother country.[10] According to Diagne, this allegiance must go to "La plus grande France! Partout où la France se trouve!" [To the greatest France! Wherever France is!].[11] This statement suggests Diagne's conception of France as a transnational meta-identity that brings all the colonies of the empire together while being superior to all its constitutive parts. His conception of this meta-identity is strategic since it guarantees equal rights and protection to all the members of the empire whether they are colonials or *indigènes*.

Diagne's cosmopolitanism also stemmed from freemasonry's influence on his intellectual outlook. During the late 1890s and early twentieth century, when he served as a colonial officer in French overseas territories and in the métropole, Diagne succumbed to the cosmopolitan appeal of a masonic brotherhood that theoretically privileged individual or collective will to do good for humanity over racial membership. This cosmopolitanism was "theoretical" because the Europeans' freemason lodges in Senegal and in the colonies were not devoid of racism. Revealing this bigotry, Dieng argues that Diagne was refused admittance to the masonic lodge in Saint-Louis, Senegal, in 1897, even if he was able to join a similar group in la Réunion in 1899 (1990, 59–60). Yet, in spite of its intrinsic racism, French colonial freemasonry allowed Diagne to relate to different people on the basis of intelligence, reason, and rationality and a refutation of dogmas. This freemasonry gave Diagne a greater appeal to cosmopolitan idealism, specifically to what Dieng calls "idéaux d'amitié, de fraternité et de protection qui constituaient les piliers de la confrérie maçonnique" [ideals of friendship, fraternity and protection which constituted the pillars of the masonic brotherhood] (1990, 59). However, while it taught him these cosmopolitan ideals of a republicanism in which people are supposed to embrace one another as humans, French colonial freemasonry solidified Diagne's elitism by transforming him into a person who was socially, intellectually, and spiritually remote from ordinary blacks.

Diagne's cosmopolitanism also stems from a discourse in which France becomes the métropole that has the moral obligation to extend the benefits of civilization and education to its overseas territories and, in return, use the resources drawn from such lands for the betterment of itself and the rest of the world. In this imperial cosmopolitanism, France and its colonies are perceived as inseparable entities bound by reciprocal, moral, and social loyalties and responsibilities. In this sense, the French colonial project is transnational since it reflects the global dimension of cosmopolitanism. Defining "cosmopolitanism," Garrett Wallace Brown and David Held write:

40 *Blaise Diagne's cosmopolitanism*

[A]s the etymology of the word suggests, cosmopolitanism is universal in its scope, maintaining that all humans are equal in their moral standing and that this moral standing applies to everyone everywhere, *as if we are* all citizens of the world.

(2010, 2)

Working within this framework, Diagne's cosmopolitanism transcended the mere idea of assimilating or adapting the colonies' customs to those of the métropole, because it also stressed the mutual interdependence between the two civilizations. In a June 1924 article of *La Dépêche Coloniale et Maritime*, Diagne said that "l'avenir de la France est lié au développement général de son domaine colonial" [France's future is tied to the general development of its colonial dominion] and that the colonial policies of France "doivent être liées à la politique nationale tant à l'intérieur qu'à l'extérieur" [must be tied to the national policy both internally and externally].[12] Diagne's cosmopolitanism was then a conception of French nationality as a global political identity and unity that allowed France and its colonies to rely on one another.

Moreover, Diagne's cosmopolitanism evolved from relationships that were historically romanticized as unbreakable cultural and economic bonds between the métropole and its colonies when, in fact, the rapports between these entities were based on France's exploitation of Africans. This romanticized cosmopolitanism prevailed not only in the civilizing mission which, as Guy Martin suggests, attempted "to associate or assimilate Africans into the ideals of French civilization by imparting to them the essentials of that language and culture" (2002, 56), but also in the French imperial policy that viewed "Africa as provider of raw materials, and Europe as supplier of finished goods" (2002, 56). Despite this inegalitarian history, France has, since the late nineteenth century, idealized its cosmopolitan links with Africa as indestructible political, cultural, and linguistic ties. To this effect, Martin has shown how the twentieth-century concepts of *"France-Afrique"* and *"EurAfrique"* have "symbolized the intensity with which many French people came to believe that links with Africa were indissoluble" (2002, 56). Such a glorification of the relations between France and Africa is cosmopolitan because it depicts the métropole as an entity that shares with its overseas territories culture, knowledge, and other elements of progress under a common ideology of reciprocity and mutuality. This cosmopolitan discourse resurfaced during the middle of the twentieth century in the philosophy of *Francité*, or what Manthia Diawara calls "thinking through French grammar and logic" (1998, 288). In a similar fashion, Murphy describes *Francité* as "a manner of expression shared by all French-speakers" and "a profound Franco-African hybridity, in which the values of French and African 'civilization' could coexist" (2008, 185). The metropolitan romanticization of cohabitation between French and African customs registers the idea of cultural juxtaposition that also permeated Diagne's cosmopolitanism.

Yet, another origin of Diagne's cosmopolitanism is the legislation that guaranteed citizenship to all the French empire's inhabitants. The roots of this citizenship are found in many French legal documents, notably the 1848 law of The Second Republic that abolished slavery in France and its colonies and transformed the male inhabitants of the possessions into citizens.[13] Diagne used this law as an opportunity to demand the extension of military service to Senegalese. In one 1915 speech at the Chamber, Diagne said:

> J'estime qu'on nous doit cette satisfaction du service militaire, surtout après tant d'années consacrées à l'enseignement donné avec un esprit empreint de tant de libéralisme, surtout après les manifestations qui se sont fait jour depuis 1848, grâce auxquelles les droits de citoyens nous étaient rendus. Qu'on ne vienne donc plus nous les discuter par des subtilités du genre de celle qui consiste à dire que nous avons les droits de citoyens, mais que nous ne sommes pas des citoyens français!

> [We deserve to have military service obligation extended to us, especially after so many years that have been spent on education that has been delivered with so much spirit of liberalism, and, above all, after the changes that have taken place since 1848 and have allowed us to gain citizenship rights. Let us, therefore, not allow anyone to oppose these developments with ambiguous claims which consist of saying that we are not French citizens even if we have citizenship rights!][14]

The excerpt reflects the dilemma Diagne had throughout his political life—which was to diplomatically defend the rights of populations in the colonies without offending his French parliamentarian colleagues who abhorred racial particularity and viewed the empire as stable and just. In order to avoid appearing as a radical leader, Diagne walked a fine line between demanding rights and being cautious at the Chamber of Representatives. Thus, as Nancy J. Jacobs explains, Diagne's "language" in the above speech "is indirect and complicated, perhaps because of the challenge of expressing loyalty and demanding rights at the same time" (2014, 174).

Yet, because he was steeped in French cosmopolitan discourse, Diagne somewhat transcended his dilemma by appealing to the right of all inhabitants of the French empire to protect the motherland (the métropole). Diagne's strategy was effective since his invocation of the 1848 law culminated in legislation that granted citizenship to Senegalese. In his book, *De la Situation Politique des Sénégalais Originaires des Communes*, the pioneer Senegalese political leader Lamine Gueye describes a French decree stating that:

> [Le] territoire de la colonie est considéré, dans l'application du Code civil, comme partie intégrante de la Métropole, et que tout individu né libre et habitant le Sénégal ou ses dépendances jouira, dans la colonie, des droits accordés par le Code civil aux citoyens français.

42 *Blaise Diagne's cosmopolitanism*

[[The] territory of the colony is considered in the application of the Civil Code, as part of the métropole, and that everyone born free and living in Senegal and its dependencies will enjoy, in the colony, the same rights granted to French citizens by the Civil Code.]

(1922, 11)

This law was not entirely put into practice since, as discussed earlier, all the inhabitants of the four communes were not actual citizens. Also, few Senegalese fully benefited from the ruling because of racism. Yet the legislation provided many Senegalese with a legal opportunity to be recognized as French citizens.

Consequently, French cosmopolitanism, or the colonial ideal that promised Senegalese people political assimilation, did not partially materialize until Diagne's election to the French National Assembly in 1914 occurred. This was a pivotal moment since it allowed Diagne to use French cosmopolitan discourse to partially defeat the racism and bigotry that jeopardized the Senegalese *originaires*' acquisition of citizenship. Even if nationality was given only to *originaires*, Diagne waged a struggle that later allowed *indigènes* to gain it as well in a Senegal that became independent thirty-five years after his death. Senegal's struggle for independence from France was the long-term result of Diagne's cosmopolitan wars. As Boahen argues in his essay, "Politics and Nationalism in West Africa," "his [Diagne's] political awakening of Senegal did lay the foundation for the Senegalese politicians and nationalists of the 1940s and 50s" (1985, 646). Therefore, Diagne must not be neglected in black nationalism since he was the first major twentieth-century architect of Senegalese struggle for independence.

On the other hand, Diagne's cosmopolitanism is visible in his opposition against the French's general view of the colonies as the inferior entities that needed metropolitan support. On April 18 1921, Albert de Pouvourville, a former French military and colonial officer, wrote an article which reflects this conception of unequal dependence between France and its colonies as a one-way stream. In the article, Pouvourville writes: "La politique française aux colonies doit comprendre la politique *indigène*. Mais la politique *indigène* doit dépendre de la politique française" [French policy in the colonies must include the policy of the indigenous populations. But the policy of the indigenous populations must depend on French policy] (1921, 1). Opposing this conception of dependence as a need that was stronger in the colonies than in the métropole, Diagne developed a philosophy of cosmopolitanism in which the two entities equally relied on each other. His firm belief in this ideology led him to write to Mr. Marcel Ruedel, the director of the *Annales Coloniales*, on April 8, 1926, a letter summarizing his views on colonialism.[15] In the letter, Diagne displays a fervent loyalty to France's mission that he theorizes as a cosmopolitanism that allows the empire to draw vitality and succor from colonies that can never become autonomous from the métropole. Diagne's use of the collective pronoun "our" to describe the "overseas possessions" as territories that must remain dependent on the métropole for their own "interest" emanates from his view of France and its colonies as inseparable units working for a "common profit."[16]

As I demonstrate later in this book, Diagne's cosmopolitan philosophy ignored the cruelty and deprivation that France created in its colonies. Nevertheless, in spite of his failure to address this oppression in the letter to Ruedel, Diagne's theorizing of the métropole and the colonies as two parts of a same umbilical cord is a subtle attempt to humanize French colonialism by giving it a cosmopolitan appeal. By attempting to permanently attach France to its overseas territories, Diagne conveys the idea of "association" that is central to cosmopolitanism. According to Appiah, "it [cosmopolitanism] begins with the simple idea that in the human community, as in national communities, we need to develop habits of coexistence: conversation in its older meaning, of living together, association" (xviii–xix). This cosmopolitanism is consistent with Diagne's representation of the relations between France and its colonies as bonds founded on association and unity as opposed to disassociation and fragmentation.

Diagne's argument that French policy encouraged association and unity between the métropole and the colonies was in line with the cosmopolitan discourse of the French administration of his generation. This cosmopolitanism is apparent in numerous articles of *Les Annales Coloniales* and *La Dépêche Coloniale et Maritime* in which many French leaders and intellectuals depicted the two concepts as pillars of French diplomacy.[17] For instance, Albert Sarraut placed the cosmopolitan search for unity and association between the métropole and the overseas dominions at the core of his political philosophy. Sarraut—France's minister for the colonies (from 1920 to 1924 and 1932 to 1933) and a member of the Chamber of Deputies (between 1902 and 1924)—wrote an important treatise on colonialism entitled *Grandeur et Servitude Coloniales* (1931). While he recognized that colonization had historically been a personal, unilateral, and selfish enterprise accomplished by the strong over the weak (1931, 108), Sarraut proposed an alternative policy of imperialism that was grounded on cosmopolitanism. He writes:

> Supérieur à tous les droits, se dresse le droit total de l'espèce humaine à vivre sur la planète une vie meilleure, par l'usage plus abondant des biens matériels et des richesses spirituelles susceptibles d'être fournis à l'ensemble des vivants. Cette double abondance ne peut résulter que d'une collaboration solidaire des races, échangeant amplement leurs ressources naturelles et les facultés propres à leur génie créateur.
>
> [Above all rights, there is the inalienable right of the human species to have a better life on this planet, through a more abundant use of the

44 Blaise Diagne's cosmopolitanism

material goods and the spiritual wealth that could benefit all human beings. This double abundance can only come from a united collaboration among races who all share their natural resources and skills that are proper to their creative genius.]

(Sarraut, 1931, 108–109)

Sarraut's conception of the world's wealth as resources that must benefit everyone signifies a cosmopolitan ideology that he used to justify French colonialism. If one puts aside the fact that French colonization was as personal, unilateral, selfish, and hegemonic as its historical precedents, one realizes that Sarraut humanizes this colonialism by giving it a cosmopolitan appeal. This idealized cosmopolitanism is apparent in Sarraut's representation of colonization as an endeavor that seeks solidarity and sharing of resources between races and peoples.

Sarraut's cosmopolitan ideology is also perceptible in an October 12, 1921, article of *Les Annales Coloniales* that includes a summary of a speech that he gave in France shortly after his October 7, 1921, trip to Dakar. In the speech, Sarraut conveys his view of civilization as a common culture involving the contribution of many races and peoples. As a colonial news report suggests,

Il [Sarraut] s'éleva énergiquement contre la thèse divisant l'humanité en races supérieures et races irréductiblement inférieures et montra la solidarité de la Grande Famille humaine dont les nations évoluées doivent se porter au secours des frères attardés sur le chemin de la civilisation pour les aider à regagner le retard et franchir les étapes accomplies par les autres races.

[He [Sarraut] vigorously spoke against the thesis that strictly divides humanity between superior and irreducibly inferior races and showed the solidarity within the Great human Family out of which the advanced nations must be ready to rescue their primitive brothers on the road of civilization in order to help them make up for their delay and go through the same stages that other races have experienced.][18]

Sarraut's cosmopolitanism was, therefore, founded on prejudice since it was based on a primitivistic view of France's colonized populations. Calling the colonization of Senegal a rescue from backwardness is a racist theory that stemmed from France's civilizing mission and use of cosmopolitanism as a means of masking and justifying brutal appropriation and domination of the overseas territories. Contrary to popular beliefs, French colonization of Senegal was not benign, compassionate, and slow. It was brutal, cruel, and swift. Ignoring the consequences of French colonization on Senegal, Sarraut's cosmopolitanism veils itself with a philanthropic discourse that attempts to humanize Africans through imperial force.

Blaise Diagne's cosmopolitanism   45

Yet, even if it is a racist philosophy that depicts Africans and other colonized populations as people that the métropole must help to civilize, Sarraut's ideology is partly cosmopolitan since it represents the world as a fraternal space in which individuals from various locations could create a universal civilization which is built on solidarity. In this sense, although it is logically flawed and prejudiced, Sarraut's depiction of the relations between France and the colonies in terms of harmony is relevant since it fits with the cosmopolitan intellectual tradition that also influenced Diagne.

Like Sarraut's, Diagne's cosmopolitanism is founded on a perception of France and the colonies as parts of the same nation, body, soul, and destiny. Diagne believed in this union so ardently that he snapped at any attempt to sever the métropole from the *outre-mer*, as was apparent in a heated exchange that he had at the Chamber with M. Varenne. Diagne challenged his deputy colleague for having proposed that France let Indochina develop a sort of autonomy in its education system.[19] Diagne attacked Varenne's theory by invoking his cosmopolitan conception of France and its colonies as parts of one indivisible empire. He said :

> A-t-on honte de la France? Ne plus enseigner l'histoire de la France, et sa géographie, aux indigènes, c'est à la fois témoigner de mépris pour nous-mêmes, et constituer un certain danger.

> Il ne faut pas décider que désormais les indigènes devront être éduqués sur place, sans venir demander à nos Facultés, à nos Universités, à notre contact même, la signification même de leur existence. Désire-t-on atténuer le sentiment qu'ils nous portent, supprimer la liaison qui existe entre eux et nous? Il faut agir de telle sorte que les indigènes doivent, au contraire, avoir le désir de venir s'accoler à nous.[20]

> [Are we ashamed of France? Not teaching the history and geography of France to the *indigènes* is both evidence of contempt for ourselves and a danger.

> We should not decide now that the natives should be educated where they are, without coming to ask our professors, universities, and contact for the meaning of their existence. Do we want to weaken the sentiment they have for us and end the bonds that exist between us and them? We must act so that the *indigènes* have the desire to be adjoined to us.]
> ("A La Chambre", 1930, 2)

This declaration shows that the foundation of Diagne's cosmopolitanism is his conception of an extension of France's intellectual and cultural knowledge into the colonies as a partnership that solidifies and guarantees the métropole's intimacies with its overseas territories. When M. Varenne attempted to clarify his argument by saying, "J'ai dit que la séparation était

46 Blaise Diagne's cosmopolitanism

impossible" [I have said that separation is impossible], Diagne retorted, "Justement! Il n'y a pas deux patries!" [This is my point! We are not talking about two nations!"].[21] Thus, Diagne considers any philosophy that threatens to split France from its colonies as jeopardizing the empire's cosmopolitan ties with its conjoined parts.

Moreover, Diagne's exchange with Mr. Varenne attests to the vital role that he gave to education in the promotion of cosmopolitan bonds. Instead of perceiving France's involvement in Senegal's education system as a form of indoctrination and conquest, Diagne viewed it as an imperial duty that could enhance the conditions of people in both the colony and the métropole. A December 1924 article of *Les Annales Coloniales* mentions a meeting of "la Commission des colonies à la Chambre," presided by M. Diagne, at which many documents, including the Senegalese deputy's resolution for the establishment of a medical school in Lyon, were discussed.[22] The editorial claims that a medical school would help to increase the number of doctors for the colonial troops.[23] This attempt to palliate the lack of French doctors in the colonial army fits into Diagne's cosmopolitan goal of encouraging the métropole to support Africans. Representing this support as a cosmopolitan duty of both Europeans and Africans, Diagne jovially spoke to a group of French students who were getting ready to travel to Senegal under a program funded by the *Journal Officiel*, which was the main organ of the colonial administration. Encouraging these French students to regard Senegal as an important part of their own world, Diagne told them: "Quand vous serez à Saint-Louis, fondée en 1658, . . . souvenez-vous que le Sénégal est la pierre angulaire de notre domaine ouest africain" [When you are in Saint-Louis, which was founded in 1658, . . . remember that Senegal is the angular stone of our West African dominion].[24] Urging the students not to waste time, Diagne told them to use their journey as an opportunity to understand and resolve the predicaments of the colony. He said: "N'allez point satisfaire une curiosité et n'allez pas là-bas en dilettantes; la connaissance approfondie des mœurs, des habitudes, des choses coloniales doit être la moralité de ce voyage, car vous êtes l'avenir!" [Do not go there in order to just satisfy a curiosity or wander; the journey must be morally motivated by a thorough knowledge of values, customs, and other colonial elements, because you are the future!"][25] Diagne's statements show his conception of cosmopolitanism as France's responsibility to use its brightest individuals in order to assure the economic and social development of both its colonies and empire. Therefore, Diagne's cosmopolitanism was not devoid of imperialist and paternalistic ambitions since it was partially imbibed with the nationalistic view of colonization as French citizens' noble task of preserving their imperial garden and children.

A similar nationalistic and paternalistic perception of the colonies as France's natural treasure and family is apparent in the rhetoric of other colonial leaders. This representation is perceptible in a 1926 speech in which Pierre de Taittinger, a colonial fascist leader, said: "It was just as important ... for Frenchmen to be taught how to colonize as how to read."[26] Taittinger's and Diagne's views of the colonies are analogous in their representations of imperial conquest as an ennobling, virtuous, and civic enterprise rather than a despicable, immoral, and unpatriotic project. Nevertheless, Diagne's cosmopolitanism was distinct from those of his fascist French colleagues because its ultimate goal was the liberation of the colonial subject.

Moreover, in spite of its support of French imperialism, Diagne's cosmopolitanism was somewhat redemptive because it was also based on the belief that France and its colonies were parts of one nation with inhabitants of various races whose common fates were conjoined by the blood that the colonial soldiers spilt for the métropole's freedom during World War I. For Diagne, the sacrifice that Africans made on behalf of France's freedom ushered in a new era in which all the benefits of civilization, that were previously considered as the sole privileges of the métropole, must be shared with the colonized Africans whose loyalties equaled and complimented those of the Europeans. In this vein, Diagne told Mr. Varenne:

> Les temps ont changé. L'éducation s'est faite. Il y a eu quatre années de guerre. Durant ces quatre années, nous avons mené à nos côtés, aux combats, des hommes de couleur auxquels nous avons demandé le même sacrifice que celui que nous consentions nous-mêmes.

> [Times have changed. Education has been achieved. There were four years of war during which we have fought side by side with colored men from whom we have asked the same sacrifice that we have agreed to make ourselves.][27]

The passage reveals Diagne's representation of French soldiers and *tirailleurs* as brave people who demonstrated strong cosmopolitan loyalties to the empire they defended in World War I. For Diagne, this cosmopolitanism needed to be recompensed with the full admissibility, accommodation, and equality of colonial soldiers who proved their faith in France and the rest of humanity.

Diagne's conception of patriotism as a conjoined sacrifice of both Senegalese and European soldiers stemmed from a French cosmopolitanism that viewed the colonial combatants' participation in World War I as a demonstration of the loyalty to empire that they learned from their colonizers. An example of this sacrifice is apparent in the book *Faith in Empire: Religion, Politics, and Colonial Rule in French Senegal*, in which Elizabeth Foster discusses a moment in 1919 when a group of French Catholics called the "Spiritans" prepared a memorial that would recognize the joint sacrifices of Senegalese and French troops during the war. Foster writes:

48 *Blaise Diagne's cosmopolitanism*

West African troops had played an important role in the defense of metropolitan France, and many people began to look to the empire as a crucial reserve of military and economic strength. The Spiritans adapted to this new context by expanding the memorial meaning of the cathedral to commemorate the French colonialists and the Africans who had died in the conflict and by emphasizing the link between the sacrifices of prewar colonizers and those of African troops in the war.

(2013, 127)

Diagne's theorizing of the sacrifices of the African soldiers as a joint loyalty fits into this French cosmopolitanism that viewed the bravery of the Senegalese troops as a devotion to empire that the Europeans had taught *tirailleurs*. Yet, unlike the Europeans who somewhat represented the "courage" of Africans as unexceptional (since they viewed it as a valor that was preceded and made possible by the heroism of the colonizers), Diagne's interpretation of the war stemmed less from nostalgia or cult of paternalism and imperialism than cosmopolitanism.

In addition, Diagne sometimes gave tremendous support to *tirailleurs*. He often fought hard to integrate them into the French army and, thus, ideologically disrupt the racial barriers in the empire's military. His support

Figure 1.1 "Tournée de recrutement au Soudan" [Recruitment tour in French Sudan], 1918.
Source: Collections Eric Deroo.

Blaise Diagne's cosmopolitanism   49

for *tirailleurs* is noticeable in the numerous bills that he submitted and defended at the Chamber in 1916.[28] The first proposal sought to authorize *indigènes* and *sujets français* [créoles] of the colonies to be voluntarily recruited into the French metropolitan, colonial, or marine army corps, while the second one, according to Doudou Gueye, attempted to "create the employment of *indigène* adjutant in the units of *tirailleurs* and spahis of North Africa" (1974, 85). Even though they were all successful, Diagne's bills faced the strong biases of many French colonials even after they were passed. These prejudices are apparent in an anonymous September 1918 correspondence which laments "La loi du 19 Octobre 1915 [qui] assimile les ressortissants des Quatre communes du Sénégal, sur le plan militaire, aux citoyens français, compliquant encore la cohabitation des 'tirailleurs sénégalais' avec ces hommes" [The law of October 19, 1915 [which] treats the *originaires* of the Four communes of Senegal, in military terms, like French citizens, further complicating the cohabitation of "Senegalese *tirailleurs*" with these men].[29] This concern about the cohabitation of *indigène*, créole, and European soldiers in the French army is further noticeable in a letter dated September 25, 1918, in which Aubé, the Major Director of the French Colonial Armies, writes:

> Les créoles et originaires, étant citoyens français, sont entièrement soumis au régime européen (soldes, alimentation, permission après dix-huit mois, etc.); les tirailleurs sénégalais ne comprendraient pas la différence de traitement d'hommes de même couleur, placés dans les mêmes unités qu'eux. Jusqu'ici la 8ᵉ direction a toujours évité le contact entre ces deux catégories de militaires. Cette mesure doit continuer à être appliquée, dans le but d'éviter tout germe de discorde et d'indiscipline.
>
> [As French citizens, the creoles and originaires are fully under the same European regime (salaries, nutrition, permits after eighteen months, etc.); if they were put in the units of these soldiers, the Senegalese *tirailleurs* would not understand the differential treatment of men of the same color. Up to now, the eighth direction has always avoided contact between the two military categories. This method must continue to be practiced so as to avoid all risks of discord and indiscipline.][30]

This excerpt reflects the acerbic racism that Diagne continued to face from the French military and other colonial officials who were deeply disturbed by his effort to extend rights to *tirailleurs*. Mr. Aubé's refusal to let *tirailleurs* join the units of *originaires* and créoles segregates against Senegalese who shared a similar racial background and cosmopolitan patriotism independently of the colorism that colonists used to differentiate them.

Though it did exist, the conflict between *originaires* and *créoles* to which Aubé alludes should not be overemphasized since it hinders the real motive

50 *Blaise Diagne's cosmopolitanism*

of the white colonial officer, which was to deflect attention from the French racism that confronted both black and biracial soldiers from Senegal. Such racism created a horrid atmosphere in which both *originaires* and *tirailleurs* were alienated in a separate-and-unequal system (resembling Apartheid). *Tirailleurs* were directly affected by this discriminatory system because they mostly came from the social class of the *sujets*, who worked as peasants, servants, domestics, and other laborers. The *sujets* were placed below both whites and *originaires*. Diouf explains:

> Contrary to the *originaires* who benefitted from political privileges from political assimilation, the sujets—the population living in spaces that were circumscribed earlier [the Four Communes], were subjected to the *indigénat* code—they had no right. The *commandant de Cercle* (a European) and the *chef de canton* (an African) could imprison them without trial or send them to do *corvées* (forced labor to build infrastructure, etc.).
>
> (199)

While they were initially protected by the above measures, *originaires* soon realized that this advantage was mostly abstract since they were physically and customarily classified as *sujets*.

An example of the segregation toward *sujets* is perceptible in the book *Itinéraire Africain*, in which Lamine Gueye, a former protégé of Diagne who studied in France and later returned to become a major leader of Senegal, decries how the infirmary of Dakar (later known as Hôpital Indigène) was for *indigènes* while the one called *Hôpital Militaire* (now Hôpital Principal de Dakar) was for Europeans (1966, 7–8). In addition, having French citizenship did not always give *originaires* more power than *sujets* had. Discussing this paradox, Johnson observes in his essay "The Senegalese Urban Elite, 1900–1945:"

> Some *originaires* were poverty-stricken urban dwellers, working as messengers or clerks, while some *sujets* were wealthy traders, with connections throughout the interior. But compared with most peasants of the interior, older inhabitants of the communes, such as the *originaires*, had a higher standard of living.
>
> (1972, 145)

Therefore the *sujets'* privilege lay in their informal wealth while the *originaires'* depended on their purchasing power and networking skills. Otherwise, the two groups had the same value in the eyes of Europeans.

However, racism and segregation did not lead Diagne to completely ignore the plight of *tirailleurs*, since he sometimes took advantage of his parliamentarian status to denounce the predicament of these combatants and call for a cosmopolitanism that could remedy it. For instance, on November

27, 1916, Diagne complained at the Chamber about the excruciating conditions in which many *tirailleurs* lived in French war fronts. Although he was satisfied when the minister of war, Alexandre Millerand, consented to his demand that *tirailleurs* in France and the East be relieved during the winter, Diagne was despondent toward Mr. Pascal Ceccaldi, the Budget Reporter of the colonial troops, who opposed his request.[31] After chiding him for not recognizing how impossible it was for the *tirailleurs* to live in freezing Adrian barracks during severe winters, Diagne read this fitting passage from an official report (dated April 24, 1916) that illustrated these soldiers' suffering:

> La pluie tomba toute la nuit: les hommes enfoncés dans la boue jusqu'aux genoux souffrirent beaucoup du froid, sous un bombardement constant d'une exceptionnelle intensité. La plupart des tirailleurs, ayant les pieds et les mains atteints [sic] de gelures, sont restés néanmoins vigilants à leur poste. Comme ils n'avaient plus la possibilité de nettoyer leurs armes enduites d'une épaisse couche de boue, ce furent les Européens qui s'y employèrent.

> [It rained all night: the men, whose legs were deeply buried into mud up to the knee as they were constantly bombarded with an exceptional intensity, suffered from cold. Although they had frostbitten feet and hands, most tirailleurs alertly remained at their post. Since they were unable to clean their weapons which were covered with thick mud, the Europeans did this for them.][32]

This quotation suggests not only the dilemma of *tirailleurs* who were stationed at the fronts, but also the rare moments of cosmopolitan solidarity that white soldiers sometimes extended to their black counterparts. By cleaning the weapons of *tirailleurs*, the white French soldiers demonstrated their perception of the African combatants as "brothers-in-arms" who had the same dignity, respect, humanity, and patriotism. The example shows the equalizing role that war trenches had on the black and white soldiers by providing them with a brief opportunity for cosmopolitan equality and unity that replaced racism with mutual valuation of human worth. Understanding this cosmopolitanism and solidarity, Diagne asked his colleagues:

> Ce geste de solidarité fraternelle, au milieu du danger, ne vous fait-il pas comprendre l'hérésie qui consiste à envoyer à la mort, dans l'incapacité de se défendre, des hommes dont la vaillance au contraire devrait être tant profitable à ce pays?

> [Doesn't this gesture of fraternal solidarity, which is expressed in the midst of danger, make you understand the heresy that consists of sending to death men whose valor should instead be more profitable for this country?].[33]

52 Blaise Diagne's cosmopolitanism

This quotation reflects Diagne's criticism of a French colonial policy which deployed *tirailleurs* to the trenches in droves without realizing the labor force and stability these men could provide the empire if they remained in the colonies. Such an irrational deployment of *tirailleurs* stemmed from the French colonials' romantic view of Senegal as an inexhaustible reservoir of valiant African warriors who were willing to die for the métropole. In the January 1, 1916, issue of *Les Annales Coloniales*, Ruedel cites a passage from *Le Journal des Débats* boasting about the métropole's limitless military reserves:

> On puisera en Afrique, on puisera en Asie, on puisera même au besoin en Océanie, d'innombrables régiments de toutes races et de toutes couleurs; on leur mettra sur le dos des uniformes, on leur donnera des canons, des fusils, des mitrailleuses, tout ce qu'il faut pour se battre. Et alors . . . . Alors les Allemands n'auront qu'à se bien tenir.
>
> [We will draw from Africa, Asia and, if necessary, Oceania, countless regiments of all races and all colors; we will give them uniforms, cannons, rifles, machine guns, all they need to fight. And then . . . . Then the Germans will know how to behave.][34]

This perception of the overseas territories as boundless depositories of combatants that can be deployed to intimidate the métropole's enemies also derives from a long history of French army officers' portrayal of the colonies' populations as extensions of the empire's power. Conveying a similar ideology, Mangin writes in the conclusion of *La Force Noire*:

> La création de l'armée noire démontrera l'unité du domaine national; tous les Français comprendront que la France ne s'arrête ni à la Méditerranée, ni au Sahara; qu'elle s'étend jusqu'au Congo; qu'elle constitue un empire plus vaste que l'Europe et qui, dans un demi-siècle, aura 100 millions d'habitants, et que les peuples valent par le nombre et par l'élite, beaucoup plus que par la moyenne.
>
> [The creation of the black army will demonstrate the unity of the national domain; all French people will understand that France does not stop either at the Mediterranean or the Sahara—it extends to the Congo, it constitutes a vast empire larger than Europe and, in half a century, will have 100 million people. They will know that the worth of nations is determined by their number and elite, much more than by their average size.]

(1910, 355)

Yet Mangin did not really value the men who constituted the black army since he, like most French colonials, viewed these soldiers as disposable cannon fodder. In this vein, Kamian describes colonials who spread the rumors of African human availability as "les racoleurs de 'l'Armée noire', de la 'Force noire', chère au général Mangin, et envoyé à l'abattoir sur les champs de bataille d'Europe et du Moyen-Orient" (2001, 128) [the raiders of the "black army," of the "Black Force," who are dear to General Mangin and are sent to be slaughtered on the battlefields of Europe and the Middle East"].

Even if he was the major recruiter of World War I *tirailleurs*, Diagne was against the reckless deployment of these men overseas. Calling Mangin's theory an "illusion," he required that the war efforts not lead the colonial administration to botch the cosmopolitan reciprocity between France and African troops. On November 27, 1916, Diagne told his parliamentarian colleagues: "Eh bien! Moi, j'ai une autre confiance en moi-même et en vous: notre effort de guerre est légitime, nous devions le fournir, mais nous attendons que vous l'imposiez dans des conditions meilleures, pour l'intérêt même du pays" [Well! I have another faith in myself and you: our war effort is legitimate and we should make it; but we hope that you will impose it in better conditions for the interest of the country].[35] Diagne's statement reflects his conception of cosmopolitanism as France's moral and political obligation to equally treat all the members of its empire. For Diagne, this equality would enable France to practice its cosmopolitanism and increase its imperial power. In this sense, giving equality to Africans was a diplomatic

Figure 1.2 "Mitrailleurs sénégalais à l'exercice, camp du Sud-Est. Carte photos, 1914" [Senegalese gunners in exercise, Southeast camp, Photo card, 1914].

Source: Collections Eric Deroo.

54 Blaise Diagne's cosmopolitanism

and economic necessity that would help France to use the support and patriotism of its colonial populations to become an indestructible global empire. Diagne's cosmopolitanism is consistent with the ethical and institutional forms of human solidarity that Thomas Pogge describes as "moral cosmopolitanism." For Pogge, this kind of cosmopolitanism

> holds that all persons stand in certain moral relations to one another: we are required to respect one another's status as ultimate units of moral concern—a requirement that imposes limits on our conduct and, in particular, on our efforts to construct institutional schemes.
>
> (2010, 114)

Drawing on this type of cosmopolitanism, Diagne refuted, on March 16, 1917, Mangin's thesis on the inexhaustible availability of African men. Countering Mangin's theory, Diagne complained about European soldiers stationed in Senegal who were happy to see *tirailleurs* go fight in their place.[36] He also said:

> Ajoutez à cela, messieurs, le recrutement de nos admirables tirailleurs et retenez cette infamie publiée dans un journal du 15 janvier: "Plutôt que de faire partir 300 ou 400 Européens, il vaut mieux recruter 1,000 ou 10,000 indigènes." Pendant cette guerre, où l'égalité du sang s'impose, de telles théories sont odieuses.

> [Let's add, gentlemen, the recruitment of our admirable *tirailleurs* and recall the indignity that was expressed in a January 15 journal article which stated: "Instead of sending 300 or 400 Europeans, it is better to recruit 1,000 or 10,000 *indigènes*." Such theories are repulsive during this war in which equality of blood is much needed].[37]

Therefore, Diagne believed that true cosmopolitanism is one in which both *tirailleurs* and France demonstrate parity and patriotism through an even blood sacrifice. By asking the French to go to the front as much as *tirailleurs* did, Diagne found in equivalent loyalty to the empire the cosmopolitan tool through which citizenship and humanity could be measured, weakening the power of race and other superficial categories. Substituting color with character traits, Diagne once told an audience of French freemasons (in 1900) that "Logiquement, je me suis permis de n'admettre de comparaisons entre les êtres humains qu'au seul critère de l'intelligence" [Reason leads me to view intelligence as the only criterion upon which human beings can be compared].[38] By replacing race with reason, mental power, and morality, Diagne developed a cosmopolitanism that was part of the French republican nationalism that Niall Ferguson summarizes as follows:

> It was an ingenious appeal to the tradition of the French Revolution, with its ideal of the nation in arms—everyone a citizen with the right

Blaise Diagne's cosmopolitanism 55

to liberty, equality and fraternity, but also with the solemn duty to bear arms for the defence of the nation.

(2011, 184)

Moreover, Diagne invoked cosmopolitan philosophy by stressing the egalitarian right of Senegalese to be treated as French and integrated into the metropolitan army. On April 1, 1915, he defended an amendment in which he declared the readiness of *originaires* to be stationed in different parts of French West Africa. When this amendment, which stated that selected units would undergo "service militaire obligatoire" [obligatory military service], was dismissed by the Minister of War (who deemed it as more appropriate for a different agenda than the one under discussion), Diagne withdrew the bill saying:

Cet élément, qui m'a envoyé à la Chambre, a le droit de considérer que le mandat qu'on me donne ne peut être complet qu'à la condition que vous le placiez dans la même situation que l'élément de population qui vous envoie au parlement.

[The entity, which brought me to the Chamber, has the right to know that the mandate it gave to me can be complete only if you put me in the same situation in which the population that brought you to the parliament lives].[39]

This passage shows Diagne's deft attempt to negotiate the incremental freedom of Senegalese from France by deploying cosmopolitanism from within the empire. Such cosmopolitanism wanted the Senegalese soldiers to have the same right to die as combatants of the French Republic that their white counterparts had.

Further displaying his cosmopolitanism, Diagne said: "La question est celle-ci: si nous pouvons être ici pour légiférer, c'est que nous sommes citoyens français; et, si nous le sommes, nous réclamons le droit de servir au même titre que tous les citoyens français" [The real question is: We are able to make laws here because we are French citizens; if we [the population of Senegal] are French citizens, we, therefore, claim the right to serve in the military with the same title accorded to all French citizens].[40] This passage shows that Diagne considered the integration of Senegalese into the French armies as an opportunity for *tirailleurs* to prove their cosmopolitan loyalty to a France they considered as theirs. Diagne viewed this cosmopolitanism as a Senegalese debt toward the mother country. Diagne's parliamentarian speech was successful since, as Tyler Stovall and Ferguson have argued, it allowed him to have "the promise of French citizenship" from the French President George Clemenceau.[41] Yet this citizenship was mostly nominal since, as I will show in subsequent chapters, during both the interwar years and the World War II period, France denied many *tirailleurs* and other Senegalese equal rights and justice.

56 *Blaise Diagne's cosmopolitanism*

By painting an image of a fair and just France that was historically bound to its Senegalese colony, Diagne sought and gained remarkable legal victories guaranteeing important rights and privileges to Senegalese people. Yet such rights, such as military obligation and nationality, did not amount to full cosmopolitanism since most Senegalese, including those living out of the four communes, did not enjoy these benefits. Moreover, Diagne himself contradicted his rhetoric of a cosmopolitan France by suggesting in his speeches this nation's partial unwillingness to integrate the Senegalese into its midst and allow them to equally rule the colonies. Yet these contradictions did not weaken the deputy's cosmopolitanism since he maintained a firm loyalty to and faith in France's moral and legal responsibilities to extend to Senegalese soldiers the same equality and freedom accorded to other members of its empire. In spite of these limitations, Diagne's views on France deserve to be studied because they are part of a neglected West African history about the empire's complex relations with Senegal during the early twentieth century.

Bibliography

"A la chambre: le Budget des colonies: Deuxième séance du 30 Janvier: M. Varenne." *Les Annales Coloniales*, January 31, 1930: 2.

"A la commission de l'Algérie, des colonies, et des protectorats." *Les Annales Coloniales*, December 1, 1924: 1.

Appiah, Kwame A. *Cosmopolitanism: Ethics in a World of Strangers*. New York: Norton, 2006.

Balesi, Charles John. *From Adversaries to Comrades-in-arms: West Africans and the French Military, 1885–1918*. Waltham, MA: Crossroads Press, 1979.

"Blaise Diagne est mort hier à Cambo." *Les Annales Coloniales*, May 12, 1934: 1.

Boahen, A. Adu. "Politics and Nationalism in West Africa, 1919–1935." In *Africa under Colonial Domination 1880–1935*, edited by A. Adu Boahen, 624–647. Berkeley: University of California Press, 1985.

Bogues, Anthony. "The African Diaspora Today: Flows and Motions." *Radical History Review* 103 (Winter 2009): 215–219.

Brown, Garrett Wallace and David Held. "Introduction." In *The Cosmopolitanism Reader*, edited by Garrett Wallace Brown and David Held Cambridge, 1–15. Cambridge, UK: Polity, 2010.

Conklin, Alice L. "Who Speaks for Africa? The René Maran-Blaise Diagne Trial in 1920s Paris." In *The Color of Liberty: Histories of Race in France*, edited by Sue Peabody and Tyler Stovall, 302–337. Durham, NC: Duke University Press, 2003.

——, Sarah Fishman, and Robert Zaretsky. *France and its Empire Since 1870*. New York: Oxford University Press, 2011.

"Courrier de l'Afrique Occidentale: Gouvernement General." *Les Annales Coloniales*, October 12, 1921: 1.

Cros, Charles. *La Parole est à M. Blaise Diagne, premier homme d'Etat africain*. Dakar: Edition Maison du Livre, 1972.

——. "La première intervention à la Chambre, son premier succès." In *La Parole est à M. Blaise Diagne, premier homme d'Etat africain*, 76–78. Dakar: Edition Maison du Livre, 1972.

———. "Son premier discours à la tribune, sa première bataille, sa première victoire." In *La Parole est à M. Blaise Diagne, premier homme d'Etat africain*, 79–84. Dakar: Edition Maison du Livre, 1972.

Crowder, Michael. *Senegal: A Study of French Assimilation Policy*. London: Methuen, 1962.

Delafosse, Maurice. "Colonisateurs et colonisés: Juxtaposition, assimilation, association." *La Dépêche Coloniale et Maritime* June 21, 1924: 1

Devaux, Eugène. "Cinéma et causerie sur l'A.O.F." *Les Annales Coloniales*, June 10, 1934: 1.

Diagne, Blaise. "Le Gouvernement de demain et les colonies." *La Dépêche Coloniale et Maritime*, June 10–11, 1924: 1.

———. "Lettre de Diagne au maître de la loge maçonnique de Saint-Denis-de-la-Réunion. 8 aout, 1900." In *Blaise Diagne: Sa vie, son œuvre*, edited by Obèye Diop, 24–25. Dakar: Nouvelles Editions Africaines, 1974.

———. "Mon cher directeur." *Les Annales Coloniales*, April 8, 1926: 1.

Diarra, Baba. "Réponse d'un ancien tirailleur sénégalais à M. Paul Boncour." In *Lamine Senghor: La Violation d'un Pays et autres écrits anticolonialistes*, edited by David Murphy, 104–105. Paris: L'Harmattan, 2012.

Diawara, Manthia. "Afro-Kitsch." In *Black Popular Culture*, edited by Gina Dent, 285–291. New York: The New Press, 1998.

Dieng, Amady Aly. *Blaise Diagne, premier député africain*. Vol. 7 of *Afrique Contemporaine*, edited by Ibrahima Baba Kaké. Paris: Editions Chaka, 1990.

Diouf, Mamadou. *Histoire du Sénégal: le modèle islamo-wolof et ses périphéries*. Paris: Maisonneuve & Larose, 2001.

"Discours de Monsieur Fred Zeller." In *Blaise Diagne: Sa vie, son œuvre*, edited by Obèye Diop, 23–29. Dakar: Nouvelles Editions Africaines, 1974.

Douaire, Anne. *"Traces et absence de la Grande Guerre aux Antilles."* In *Mémoires et antimémoires littéraires au XXe siècle: la Première Guerre mondiale: colloque de Cerisy-la-Salle, 2005*, edited by Annamaria Laserra, Nicole Leclercq, and Marc Quaghebeur, 129–145. Bruxelles: P. I. E. Peter Lang, 2008.

Ferguson, Niall. *Civilization: The West and the Rest*. New York: Penguin, 2011.

Foster, Elizabeth. *Faith in Empire: Religion, Politics, and Colonial Rule in French Senegal, 1880–1940*. Stanford, CA: Stanford University Press, 2013.

Freeman, Carla. *High Tech and High Heels in the Global Economy: Women, Work, and Pink-collar identities in the Caribbean*. Durham, NC: Duke University Press, 2000.

Gerbi, Alexandre. *Histoire occultée de la décolonisation franco-africaine: Imposture, refoulements et névroses*. Paris: L'Harmattan, 2006.

Gueye, Doudou. "Allocution du Docteur Doudou Gueye." In *Blaise Diagne: Sa vie, son œuvre*, edited by Obèye Diop, 65–108. Dakar: Nouvelles Editions Africaines, 1974.

Gueye, Lamine. *De la situation politique des Sénégalais originaires des communes de plein exercice telle qu'elle résulte des Lois des 19 Octobre 1915, 29 Septembre 1916 et de la jurisprudence antérieure, conséquences au point de vue du conflit des lois françaises et musulmanes en matière civile*. Paris: Editions de La vie Universitaire, 1922.

———. *Itinéraire Africain*. Paris: Présence Africaine, 1966.

Jacobs, Nancy J. *Colonial Contexts and Everyday Experiences c. 1850–1946*. Vol. 1 of *African History through Sources*. Cambridge, UK: Cambridge University Press, 2014.

58 Blaise Diagne's cosmopolitanism

Johnson, G. Wesley, Jr. "The Ascendancy of Blaise Diagne and the Beginning of African Politics in Senegal." *Journal of the International African Institute* 36, no. 3 (July 1966): 235–253.

——. *The Emergence of Black Politics in Senegal: The Struggle for Power in the Four Communes, 1900–1920*. Stanford, CA: Stanford University Press, 1971.

——. "The Senegalese Urban Elite, 1900–1945." In *Africa & the West: Intellectual Responses to European Culture*, edited by Philip D. Curtin, 139–188. Madison: University of Wisconsin Press, 1972.

Jones, Hilary. "Blaise Diagne (1872–1934): Senegal's Deputy to the French National Assembly." In *The Human Tradition in the Black Atlantic: 1500–2000*, edited by Beatriz G. Mamigonian and Karen Racine, 89–102. New York: Rowman and Littlefield, 2010.

Kamian, Bakari. *Des tranchées de Verdun à l'église Saint-Bernard: 80000 combattants maliens au secours de la France: (1914–18 et 1939–45)*. Paris: Karthala, 2001.

"Les obligations militaires des Sénégalais." *Les Annales Coloniales*, June 10, 1916: 2.

Mangin, Général [Charles]. *La Force Noire*. Paris: Librairie Hachette, 1910.

Martin, Guy. *Africa in World Politics: A Pan-African Perspective*. Trenton: Africa World Press, 2002.

Maurel, Jean-François. *Blaise Diagne et son temps: catalogue de l'exposition d'Archive*. Dakar: Archives du Sénégal, 1972.

Michel, Marc. *L'appel à l'Afrique: Contributions et réactions à l'effort de guerre en A.O.F. (1914–1919)*. Paris: Cujas, 1982.

Miller, Christopher L. *Nationalists and Nomads: Essays on Francophone African Literature and Culture*. Chicago: University of Chicago Press, 1998.

Murphy, David. "Sub-Saharan Africa." In *A Historical Companion to Postcolonial Literatures: Continental Europe and its Empires*, edited by Prem Poddar, Rajeev S. Patke, Lars Jensen, and John Beverley, 184–188. Edinburgh: Edinburgh University Press, 2008.

Pogge, Thomas. "Cosmopolitanism and Sovereignty." In *The Cosmopolitan Reader*, edited by Garrett Wallace Brown and David Held, 114–133. Malden, MA: Polity, 2010.

Pouvourville, Albert de. "France d'abord." *La Dépêche Coloniale et Maritime*, April 18, 1921: 1.

Ruedel, Marcel. "Renforts Coloniaux." *Les Annales Coloniales*, January 1, 1916: 1.

Sarraut, Albert. *Grandeur et Servitude Coloniales*. Paris: Editions du Sagittaire, 1931.

Soucy, Robert. *French Fascism: The First Wave, 1924–1933*. New Haven, CT: Yale University Press, 1986.

Stovall, Tyler. "Black Modernism and the Making of the Twentieth Century: Paris, 1919." In *Afromodernisms: Paris, Harlem, Haiti and the Avant-garde*, edited by Fionnghuala Sweeney, 19–42. New York: Columbia University Press, 2013.

Thomas, Martin. *The French Empire between the Wars: Imperialism, Politics and Society*. Manchester, UK: Manchester University Press, 2005.

Valran, Gaston. "Education du sens social chez les Indigènes: Encourageons le génie de l'association." *La Dépêche Coloniale et Maritime*, August 25, 1922: 1.

Weiss, Holger. *Framing a Radical African Atlantic: African American Agency, West African Intellectuals and the International Trade Union Committee of Negro Workers*. Leiden, NL: Brill, 2014.

2 W. E. B. Du Bois's cosmopolitanism, anticolonialism, and relations with Blaise Diagne

For the most part, W. E. B. Du Bois was a doppelganger of Diagne since he often praised *tirailleurs*, as the Senegalese deputy also did, as symbols of a humane and egalitarian French cosmopolitanism. Du Bois was very fascinated with this French cosmopolitanism that he frequently lauded for allowing black Africans to fight alongside whites. For him, the admissibility of Francophone blacks in World War I trenches showed that whites outside of the United States were not always racist since they sometimes were not afraid to integrate blacks into their societies.

However, there were many levels on which Du Bois was critical toward French cosmopolitanism, especially the one that Diagne embodied during the two Pan-African congresses that he co-organized with him. In addition, Du Bois's cosmopolitanism was usually antithetical to those of both France and Diagne, which were based on a sustained romanticization of the métropole as a flawless global power that extended selfless fraternity to blacks. Unlike those of the métropole and Diagne, Du Bois's cosmopolitanism was founded on frequent criticisms against the métropole's colonial impositions on Africans. In this sense, Du Bois's cosmopolitanism was more radical than Diagne's since it always ended with a disparagement of a French colonialism that the Senegalese leader was reluctant to denounce.

Focusing on Du Bois's collaborations with Diagne to coordinate the 1919 and 1921 Pan-African congresses, this chapter examines the extents to which Du Bois's anticolonialist views often changed his attitudes toward both French cosmopolitanism and Diagne. The chapter will also show how Du Bois's relationships with Diagne became soured by the ruthless French colonialism that the Senegalese deputy approved despite his support of the Pan-Africanist movement. Such a paradox ultimately severed the relations between Du Bois and Diagne as the latter's reluctance to criticize France's colonial supremacy in Africa led him to be dismissive toward African American participants of the 1921 congress that he perceived as radicals.

While there are many works on Du Bois's relations with Pan-Africanism, they rarely include the scholar's connections with or disconnections from Diagne. With the exception of Eric J. Sundquist's *To Wake the Nations: Race in the Making of American Literature* (1993), David Levering Lewis's

60 W. E. B. Du Bois's cosmopolitanism

W. E. B. Du Bois: The Fight for Equality and the American Century, 1919–1963 (2000) and Edwards's *The Practice of Diaspora*, most critical works overlook the relations between Du Bois and Francophone West Africans. Moreover, although there is a massive scholarship on Du Bois's attitudes toward Africa, this research mainly focuses on his relationships with Anglophone African countries such as Ghana, Liberia, and South Africa, ignoring his associations with French West Africa. Walters's *Pan Africanism in the African Diaspora* is crucial in the extant scholarship since it discusses Du Bois's emigration to Ghana in 1966, following many years of harassment from the Central Intelligence Agency (CIA) which had "handcuffed" both Paul Robeson and him numerous times and revoked their passports during "a highly volatile competition between the United States and the Soviet Union in a Cold War Context" (113). Walters's book is also indispensable since it shows the close connections that Du Bois established with Kwame Nkrumah and Ghana after his emigration to the country (119–123). However, the book ignores similar relations that Du Bois established with Diagne and Senegal in the early twentieth century, decades before he moved to Ghana.

In a similar vein, Sundquist's *To Wake the Nations* examines Du Bois's relations with Africa. Sundquist identifies parallels between Du Bois's "liberating leadership in America and messianic independence movements in Africa," linking his ethiopianism and the Congolese spiritualism of the early post World War I era, known as "Kimbanguism," where he finds "the same ideology of protest" (1993, 553) and "the figure of the Black Christ" (1993, 600–609) which also permeate African American liberation traditions. Yet Sundquist does not include any West African Francophone leader in his important study of Du Bois's connections with Africa.

Another neglect of Africa's significance in Du Bois's work is apparent in *Reconsidering The Souls of Black Folk* (2002) in which Stanley Crouch ignores Africa's influence on an African American cosmopolitanism that he theorizes as a gift from Europe and North America only. Even if he does not use the term "cosmopolitanism," Crouch alludes to it in his depiction of Du Bois as an intellectual who countered Teutonic "barbarism" not with "warrior culture" but with "the input of the 'submissive man'" and the Judeo-Christian philosophical construct of humanity that is the product of the "I and Thou" principle (2002, 62). Therefore, Crouch perceives Du Bois as the inheritor of a Judeo-Christian cosmopolitanism that enabled him to rise above primitivism and embrace Western civilization. Crouch's statements reveal his representation of Du Bois's cosmopolitanism as being mainly the outcome of the intellectual's personal encounters with the West. He writes:

> DuBois, so confident and so given to study, walked through Europe with his head held high and his intentions limited by nothing he knew, taking in the art and culture of people who had built nothing for him but whose

W. E. B. Du Bois's cosmopolitanism   61

humanity spoke to a man unimpressed by those who thought that his
heritage was anything less than whatever in the world inspired him,
regardless of its source, regardless of the color of its makers.

(Crouch, 2002, 85)

Crouch's declarations are problematic since they perceive Africans as
absent in the Western world that influenced Du Bois. As a result, Crouch
ignores Diagne, who, like Du Bois, also treaded the streets of France and
the rest of Europe in the 1920s and was heavily engaged with the main issues
facing Africa and the world at large during and after World War I.

Unlike Crouch, Chrisman favors a black Atlantic theory that connects Du
Bois with Africa and recognizes the continent's pivotal role in the widening
of black international circuits. In her book, *Postcolonial Contraventions:
Cultural Readings of Race, Imperialism and Transnationalism*, Chrisman
explores the relations between the nationalism of Du Bois and that of the
South African leader Sol Plaatje, among many other themes. Yet, unlike
Crouch and Gilroy, Chrisman calls for a black Atlantic studies scholarship
which recognizes "that cultural study of black transnationalism could benefit
from greater attention to the circuits of capital within and against which
Africans and diasporic black peoples operated" and "could give greater
attention to alliances that were primarily political rather than racial" (2003,
9). Motivated by a similar urgency, I will examine in this chapter Du Bois's
cosmopolitanism and anticolonialism through the prism of his familiarity
with colonial Senegal.

Like Diagne's, Du Bois's cosmopolitanism was founded on racial equality
and a view of human worth as a quality that is determined by character,
not skin color. Developing this cosmopolitan view of human beings, Du Bois
said in a November 16, 1927, letter to Miss Bernice E. Brand: "I believe
that all men, white and black, should be accepted and rated according to
their individual accomplishment."[1] Therefore, like Diagne's, Du Bois's
cosmopolitanism was based on the conception of personal virtues, not racial
traits, as the measures of humanity. Du Bois's cosmopolitanism was
influenced by his own relationships with France, a country he visited numerous times during the first half of the twentieth century. Du Bois's trips to
France produced the two major patterns of his cosmopolitanism in which
he attempted to balance his romanticization of the métropole as a symbol
of freedom with his de-idealization of this nation as an emblem of colonial
subjugation. Within both discourses, Du Bois maintained a cosmopolitan
faith in the power of world nations and leaders to stop oppressing individuals
by prioritizing ethical reasons over economic interests. The dualism in Du
Bois's cosmopolitan philosophy and attitudes toward France is apparent at
the beginning of his essay, "Sketches from Abroad: le grand voyage,"
published in *The Crisis* in March 1924. In the report, one notes Du Bois's
love and hate relationships with France. This ambivalence is visible when
he says that France, England, and other parts of the West that he had visited

62 W. E. B. Du Bois's cosmopolitanism

were "white, kindly on the whole—intensely interesting, but painfully white" (1924, 203). Du Bois's representation of whiteness in this passage stemmed from the limited number and dismal conditions of blacks living in France and the rest of Europe during the 1920s.

However, when he talks about France, Du Bois is usually reluctant to criticize the nation's racism and colonialism, preferring to depict the country as an idyllic paradise. Describing Marseilles and Carcassonne, where he visited historical ruins in 1924, Du Bois represents the first French city as the land "beneath the moon" that "shone like a jewel in a jewelled sea" before comparing the second region with "a tale that is told above the earth" (1924, 204). These quotations reveal a strong romantic love for the métropole, corroborating Fabre's argument that "it would be difficult to find a more discerning American admirer of French culture than Du Bois" (1993, 47). Second, Du Bois's statements convey his attraction to a charming France which he regards as stretching beyond the nation's relics, landscape, geography, and material culture. The assertions show that Du Bois also romanticizes France as an idyllic land of cosmopolitan possibilities. For him, France's beauty extends to a captivating transnational openness to diversity that he finds lacking in the United States. Describing his visit to St. Etienne, France, Du Bois shares a pleasing discovery when he says:

> [T]he most popular man in town—the head of the French and Foreign Club, the chief sportsman, the guest of a hundred hosts, and the welcomed of all business men—is one of us—Hunt, the only American Consul of Negro descent in Europe.
>
> (1924, 203)

Hunt's minoritarian status corroborates Du Bois's lamentation of the lack of "darkness" in Europe in the early part of his essay. Yet this lack of diversity is undercut by Europe's increasing admissibility of blacks that Du Bois celebrates as a cosmopolitanism that was missing in the United States. For instance, at the Lisbon Coliseum, where he went during a trip to Spain and Portugal, Du Bois found a French-speaking man who treated him as a human being. He writes:

> My neighbor explained matters in polite French. He accepted a cigarette and commended its flavor. At the end he raised his hat and bowed and bade me a very good night. Imagine him in the Hippodrome, New York! He would have shouldered me warily and explained on the other side of the ubiquity of "damn niggers"!
>
> (Du Bois, 1924, 205)

The quotation registers Du Bois's view of Europe as a continent where blacks were perceived, in cosmopolitan terms, as human beings equal to everyone else, during the 1920s. This cosmopolitan acceptance of humanity that transcended race was the reason why Du Bois was so enamored with France. Lewis explains:

> Whenever he traveled outside the United States, Du Bois was invariably seized by an almost giddy feeling of liberation, an exhilaration that often billowed into magniloquent opinionatedness and archly inflected prose. To be free of America's enveloping racism and New Negro sniping was intoxicating. On this trip [to Europe], he spoke and wrote, as he had on past reprieves from his condition, in the manner of a man whose cosmopolitan, upper-class Edwardian birthright had been certified for the duration of his visa.
>
> (2000, 115)

France was then appropriate for Du Bois since it reflected a valuation of the individual over race and caste that he found as a mesmerizing cosmopolitanism. In "Sketches from Abroad," Du Bois further embraces this cosmopolitanism when he writes:

> Always and everywhere there is going on a subtle change. My brown face attracts no attention. I am darker than my neighbors but they are dark. I become, quite to my own surprise, simply a man. I cease to be specially selected for attention either elaborately pleasant or ostentatiously contemptible. Forgetting myself I study others. I feel relieved.
>
> (1924, 205)

Moreover, Du Bois was fascinated by the idea of universal equality and rights to freedom that lies at the center of French cosmopolitanism. This progressive philosophy is evident in Nicolas Di Méo's definition of French cosmopolitanism as "une idéologie ayant pour finalité la coïncidence de la nation et du monde" [an ideology aiming to establish coincidence between the nation and the world] that one can trace from the "Lumières" [Century of Light] to the nineteenth and twentieth centuries during which it served to foster revolutionary and patriotic purposes (2009, 116). Yet, as Di Méo suggests, at the end of the nineteenth century and the beginning of the twentieth century, French cosmopolitanism had a slightly particular goal, which was "d'offrir la France en exemple au reste du monde et d'inciter les autres pays à adopter ou à imiter les valeurs françaises" [to provide the example of France to the rest of the world and encourage other countries to adopt or imitate French values] (2009, 116). Du Bois espoused this French cosmopolitanism as long as it could bring universal acquisition of equality and rights. His fascination with the universal dimension of French cosmopolitanism is perceptible in his editorial of the September 1917 issue of *The Crisis* in which he describes Bastille as "a carven oriflamme of that liberty, fraternity and equality which is in verity the pride of France."[2] For Du Bois, this cosmopolitanism was tangible in the equality between blacks

64   W. E. B. Du Bois's cosmopolitanism

and whites in which many French people believed during the World War I period.

Du Bois's positive view of France's cosmopolitanism was not a fantasy since he saw its proof in the 1914 election of Diagne to the nation's parliament. Du Bois was so enthused by this appointment that he told his *Crisis* readers: "M. Diagne, formerly Collector of Customs, is a deputy from Senegal, West Africa. Imagine a black member of the English Parliament from South Africa, or a black Congressman from Mississippi! They do things better in France."[3] The quotation suggests the important symbolic meaning that Du Bois gave to Diagne's election as an example of the success that blacks could achieve in the modern world if they were freed from tyranny. Later, a brief note from the December 1914 issue of *The Crisis* reads:

> "A full-blooded Jollof of Senegambia has just been elected as a French Senator," is the message which reaches me from West Africa this week, and this fact is declared to be one of the most momentous in African history. It is, beyond question, the biggest native landmark in the evolution of Africa since the Basuto King, Moshesh, hurled back the republican armies of South Africa.[4]

This statement reveals *The Crisis*'s elation about Diagne's election and Du Bois's perception of this pivotal moment as France's acceptance of the intellectual capacity, leadership, and humanity of a black person, which was a cosmopolitanism he hoped to see in the United States. Du Bois's attraction to this cosmopolitanism is also apparent in a passage of his editorial of the March 1919 issue of *The Crisis* in which he praises the French for recognizing the contributions of Diagne and the colonial troops to their victory during World War I. Du Bois says:

> Seven black deputies represent black Frenchmen in the French Parliament. Deputy Diagne, of Senegal, was the first man introduced today by the Minister of Colonies and he sat in the place of honor in the President's box.
>
> The exploits of the black and yellow troops were acclaimed by actors from the Théâtre Française, singers from the opera and orators from the government with play and music, cheers and the great strains of the Marseillaise. France, "le jour de gloire est arrivé," and the honor is yours, Men of Africa! How fine a thing to be a black Frenchman in 1919—imagine such a celebration in America![5]

In a similar tone, Du Bois conveyed his respect for France by further perceiving it as a nation that supports the enfranchisement and integration of its colonial populations. This freedom is the cosmopolitanism that an anonymous author registers in a March 1917 article of *The Crisis* where he quotes Diagne's following words:

> We cannot be sufficiently grateful for the immense benefit we have received from the Convention which enables us to sit here with you on the footing of perfect equality. That is why, in 1914, when France was attacked, all Frenchmen of the colonies, without distinction of race or color, united in close solidarity to come forward to defend it.[6]

Such instances of France's accommodations of its colonial populations represented a cosmopolitanism that dazzled Du Bois. The scholar's admiration for this cosmopolitanism is also visible in a section of the April 1917 issue of *The Crisis* which represents the bravery of *tirailleurs* as sacrifices that were made possible by France's acceptance of the military men. This cosmopolitanism appears in these bold statements from the *Cleveland Plain Dealer* that were inserted into the April 1917 issue of *The Crisis*:

> The Senegalese (jet-black Negroes) have fought for France in the great war as heroically as they could have fought for any ancestral chieftain; for they have been fighting for their friend rather than for their master and despot . . .

> Judged solely by results, rather than by the meticulous criticism of professional fault-finders, France stands at the head of the empire builders of today. For France alone has put into practice her own irrefutable republican doctrine of fraternity. England and the rest scorn the brown or black man. France acknowledges him a human being, and measures him by his merit and not by his shade of complexion.[7]

By expressing a lavish admiration for France's cosmopolitanism toward colonial populations, Du Bois wanted to reveal the lack of such humanism in the United States toward blacks. In this vein, Lewis represents Du Bois's cosmopolitan view of France as stemming from a mystique of "the Third Republic" in which blacks had better conditions than their counterparts in the United States (2000, 45). Lewis explains:

> Africans sat in legislative assemblies in Paris and Lisbon; they held teaching posts at universities; they advanced in the army and civil service; intermarriage of Africans and Europeans occasioned little if any public controversy . . . Paris had been synonymous with sanctuary to a generation or more of American Negro expatriates.
>
> (2000, 45)

Du Bois was mesmerized by this cosmopolitanism and praised it as a model that Americans could use to better treat blacks. In his mind, France

Figure 2.1 "Soldat africain originaire de l'une des Quatre communes et une amie, Paris, vers 1930" [African soldier from one of the four communes and a friend. Paris, circa 1930].

Collections Eric Deroo.

was ahead of the United States in the promotion of impartiality because it agreed to increasingly integrate blacks. This progressive assimilationism is the idea that the preceding picture of a World War I Senegalese *originaire* soldier and a Parisian woman exemplifies.

Additionally, for Du Bois, black Francophone and African soldiers represented a cosmopolitanism that African Americans had sought by fighting for humanity in World War I. Like their African cousins, African Americans did not go to the trenches to oppress the weak or colonize people. They went there to liberate France from Germany and wish that such genuine love and respect for human lives would be reciprocated to them in America. Yet these soldiers' hopes did not come true since they faced racism, decrepit accommodation, and other delousing treatments in the United States after World War I.[8] This enduring racism suggests the drastic manner in which white Americans did not reciprocate the cosmopolitanism of their black soldiers, despite the invaluable sacrifices the combatants made in a struggle for global justice and citizenship. Denouncing America's disheartening attitudes toward blacks, the "Looking Glass" section of the December 1919 issue of *The Crisis* had a brief essay entitled "Benefits Forgot" in which an anonymous author asks:

Must the Negro race be ignored after the record made in this world war? Their country called for men, and they responded. The color of their skin was not questioned when they were asked to give their lives for the United States. Is it impossible to grant them a place in this country where loyal service as citizens is needed from all our resident races?[9]

This quotation expresses the contradiction of an American society that used blacks to fulfill its cosmopolitan support of France without giving them loyalty and freedom at home.

Correcting this unrequited cosmopolitanism, Du Bois praised the bravery that African American soldiers showed in the war by fighting valiantly, just as their African counterparts also did. A passage entitled "War," from the May 1917 issue of *The Crisis*, reads: "Francis Cain, an American Negro, has been recently decorated for bravery by the French. He has been wounded five times and has three colonial medals for distinguished conduct."[10] This quotation suggests that *The Crisis* acknowledged the valor that both *tirailleurs* and African American soldiers showed during World War I. Recognizing this common heroism, Du Bois revealed his unbound respect for both *tirailleurs* and black French officers who distinguished themselves in World War I with dignity like their African American brothers did. A cover page of *The Crisis* had the memorable image of Bak[h]ane Diop, a Chief of the Senegalese soldiers, who received from the French General Archinard the French Cross of Chevalier of the Legion of Honor, at the end of the war, in recognition of his distinctive action at the front.[11] Praising a

68 W. E. B. Du Bois's cosmopolitanism

similar appreciation of black men's valor that the French displayed by also decorating African American soldiers, Du Bois observes: "The colored Lieutenant-Colonel of the 370th, a colored Major, eight colored Captains, seventeen colored Lieutenants, eight colored under-officers and twenty-six colored privates received the *Croix de Guerre* in November."[12] By listing these awards, Du Bois registered not just France's cosmopolitan and egalitarian recognition of the humanity of African American veterans, but also the paradox of loyalty these soldiers faced in the United States where they lacked the democracy and equality for which they bled and died in Europe.

The first encounter between Du Bois and Diagne was the result of negotiations that George H. Jackson made in 1918 to facilitate contact between the two leaders. Jackson was an African American official from Connecticut (yet born in Massachusetts), who was the United States Consul to the French cities of Cognac and, then, La Rochelle, in France.[13] On December 27, 1918, Jackson wrote a letter to Du Bois saying, "I have seen Sénateur Diagne and had a very pleasant interview with him; he would like to have us call at his office 19 Rue de Bourgogne tomorrow morning at 10 o'clock."[14] This meeting inspired Du Bois and Diagne to connect with each other. Thanks to the established contact, on January 5, 1919, Diagne cordially wrote to Du Bois and invited him to a casual conversation at his office. In the letter, Diagne said:

> Cher Monsieur Du Bois,
> Je serais très heureux de pouvoir causer avec vous si demain, dans l'après-midi, vers 3h, vous vouliez bien venir jusqu'à mon cabinet.
> Cordialement vôtre
> [signature de Diagne].
> 19 Rue de Bourgogne
>
> [Dear Mr. Du Bois,
> I would be very pleased to talk with you tomorrow, in the afternoon, about 3 o'clock, if you would like to come to my office.
> Cordially yours,
> [signature of Diagne]
> 19 Rue de Bourgogne].[15]

This letter reveals Diagne's respect and friendliness toward Du Bois whom he perceived as a leader that should be consulted on important matters regarding blacks. Diagne saw Du Bois as a vetted representative of blacks who, like him, had full knowledge of the conditions of the race. Du Bois transformed this mutual deference, trust, and friendship into diplomacy by considering Diagne as a prime contact for African American leaders who traveled to France. One of these leaders was Lester B. Granger, a World War I veteran and future member of the National Urban League.[16] An

W. E. B. Du Bois's cosmopolitanism   69

anonymous correspondent, who could be Du Bois himself, wrote a letter to Diagne on October 18, 1919, saying:

> This will introduce to you Lester B. Granger, formerly Second Lieutenant in the 349th Field Artillery, A.S.F., and a graduate of Dartmouth College.
> Any courtesies that you can show him will be deeply appreciated.
> Very sincerely yours,[17]

This missive shows that Du Bois saw Diagne as an important partner who could facilitate the lives of African American soldiers who were deployed to France in World War I. As one of these soldiers, Granger was a future champion of the struggle for the integration of African Americans into the United States military service during World War II. By introducing Granger to Diagne, Du Bois recognized the Senegalese deputy's ability to inspire in young and talented African Americans a sense of leadership and awareness of the black world outside of the United States that they could later bring back to their country to fight for equality and justice. By supporting African Americans abroad, Du Bois developed a form of cosmopolitanism based on solidarity—one in which blacks support one another for the benefit of the world. This reliance on unity, commonality, and team spirit resonates with Robert Spencer's definition of cosmopolitanism as a "social solidarity [that] can result not just from our inherited identities and interests but also, more auspiciously, from our shared participation in the public spheres" (2011, 3–4). Considering cosmopolitanism as a mutual public work involving different parties allows us to regard solidarity between blacks as an expression of unity and camaraderie that can enhance the lives of these and other populations.

Du Bois's cosmopolitan relationships with Diagne are also visible in the mutual friendliness that the two leaders developed toward each other in 1919 when they were preparing for the First Pan-African Congress. On a personal photo that he dedicated to Du Bois on January 6, 1919, Diagne wrote the following autograph: "Hommage d'affectueuse amitié au Docteur Du Bois" [A token of affectionate tribute and friendship to Dr. Du Bois] (221).[18] Elated by this very kind gesture, Du Bois published the photograph in *The Crisis* issue of March 1919 perhaps as another testimony to his strong admiration for Diagne.[19]

Du Bois's respect for Diagne was further noticeable in a letter dated January 1, 1919, in which he invited the Senegalese and the rest of the seven black members of the French Parliament to the Pan-African convention which was scheduled to take place in Paris in February 1919.[20] The congress was convened at the Grand Hotel of Paris, from February 19 through 21, 1919, and, by Du Bois's own account, "was held with fifty-six delegates representing sixteen different groups of Negroes throughout the world."[21] Discussing the organization of the 1919 congress, Campbell writes: "Its

Figure 2.2 Clipping from *The Crisis*, March 1919. *W. E. B. Du Bois Papers* (MS 312).
Special Collections and University Archives, University of Massachusetts Amherst Libraries.

W. E. B. Du Bois's cosmopolitanism   71

nominal head was Blaise Diagne of Senegal . . . but it was Du Bois who called the congress, organized the sessions, and wrote the resolutions" (2006, 230–231). By enthusiastically supporting Du Bois, Diagne was perhaps being diplomatic while competing for international attention with a partially-selfish desire to be seen as the most important black leader in the world. Being one of two major official organizers of the 1919 congress gave Diagne this opportunity to represent the black race from the halls of the French métropole. Through the 1919 congress, Diagne attempted to be the spokesperson of African people in front of superpowers while publicly strengthening among blacks worldwide his recent popularity in French West Africa.

By seeking to be the representative of modern blacks in the European colonial world, Diagne selfishly appropriated luster and visibility that he should have equally shared with Du Bois and other black leaders, showing that black cosmopolitanism and unity are not easy to achieve since individual and national ambitions, proclivities, and obligations can hinder them. While seeking to be the voice of blacks in the transnational world, Diagne privately attempted to prevent Du Bois from outshining him at the congress. Also, by competing with Du Bois for world attention, Diagne prioritized his Francophone background and leadership over the black cosmopolitanism that he shared with the African American. Therefore, black cosmopolitanism has roadblocks which stem from personal interests' capacities to spoil it. In this sense, as David Hollinger argues,

> the problem of solidarity is inevitably located within one or another set of historical constraints, including the way in which power is distributed in any particular social setting. Some people have much more authority over their own affiliations than others do . . . Contingency does not imply easy rearrangement.
>
> (2006, xv)

Yet the obstacles against the black cosmopolitanism that Du Bois and Diagne wanted to create at the 1919 congress also came from racism. Even with Diagne's assistance, Du Bois's co-organization of the 1919 convention was difficult since it faced the lack of support of the United States Government. For instance, a major roadblock to the Paris conference was the State Department's denial of passports to many black participants because of the fear that "Negroes would tell Paris of lynching here [in the United States]."[22] This legal decision disillusioned Du Bois since it reflected, once again, America's lack of cosmopolitan sensitivity toward African Americans who needed to collaborate with other blacks to know what was happening in the rest of the world. In addition, as the film documentary *W. E. B. Du Bois: A Biography in Four Voices* suggests, another problem that Du Bois faced in the 1919 congress was to have a sponsor that could fund his own trip for the summit. Du Bois would have been unable to travel to

72 W. E. B. Du Bois's cosmopolitanism

Paris if he had not obtained the status of special envoy of the United States shortly before the voyage.[23] Du Bois viewed these challenges as further evidence of America's contrast from a cosmopolitan France where the world congress of black leaders was welcomed. In the métropole, Du Bois saw a government leader, the French Prime Minister Georges Clemenceau, publicly endorse the convention and attest to his nation's partial willingness to let blacks talk about their grievances about the white world in a free forum. Knowing that Diagne was Clemenceau's protégé, Du Bois relied on the Senegalese's power to influence French support of the congress. In a letter he sent to Jean de la Roche, the Chief of the French Press and Information Service in New York City, on April 11, 1945, Du Bois said:

> The first congress was convened in Paris directly after the armistice following the first World War early in 1919. The French Government was officially represented. Blaise Diagne and M. Candace presided at various meetings and we met by special permission of Premier Clemenceau.[24]

Therefore, the 1919 congress was a pivotal moment when a unique form of solidarity among twentieth-century Francophone West African and African American intellectuals was born. Du Bois understood this pivotal moment that prompted him to proudly declare in a May 1919 article of *The Crisis*: "The world-fight for black rights is on!"[25] However, for Du Bois, the congress transcended race since it allowed blacks from different nations and territories to gather their thoughts about a modern and cosmopolitan world that was bound to change the course of history. When Du Bois said, "We got, in fact, the ear of the civilized world,"[26] he signified his view of the 1919 congress as a pivotal cosmopolitan moment that enabled modern blacks to escape the narrow confines of dogmas, bitterness, and cynicism in which the local racial struggles confined them. In this logic, Anglophone and Francophone blacks who participated in the congress liberated themselves from psychic limitations while getting the attention of European officials who cared to listen to them even if they did not necessarily embrace their cause.

Incidentally, by attending the 1919 congress, African Americans established transnational contacts with Diagne and contributed to the development of a black cosmopolitanism that was rooted in the core spirit of the Talented Tenth. Bernard Bell, Emily R. Grosholz, and James B. Stewart allude to such a cosmopolitanism when they describe the Talented Tenth's foundation on Du Bois's "democratic and cosmopolitan view that the process of discovering the best way to live relied on the input of all cultural groups" (1996, 4). Du Bois conceptualized such groups in transnational terms since he viewed Diagne as another Pan-African leader with whom he could establish ties for the betterment of the lives of blacks worldwide despite the geographic and linguistic barriers that separated them. In 1919, Du Bois regarded Diagne as a Pan-Africanist who then believed in the principle of black solidarity which made the first major summit possible. Du Bois acknowledged this fact when he said, in his report on the summit, that Diagne "opened the Congress with words of praise for French colonial rule. He expressed the hope that the ideal of racial unity would inspire all of African descent throughout the entire world."[27] The quotation reveals a blend of pluralism and authenticity in Diagne's cosmopolitanism. Such a dualism is evident in Diagne's use of the 1919 congress as an opportunity for praising France's openness to egalitarian principles while calling for cohesion among blacks. Diagne could not easily fulfill the two priorities since he was unable to equally share loyalty and solidarity with both France and the colonial world which resisted her supremacy. Describing Diagne's dilemma, Debré asserts: "Il est difficile d'apparaître à la fois comme l'interprète des aspirations d'émancipation des Noirs, par ailleurs, de servir l'État 'colonial' et d'être lié aux intérêts économiques de grands groupes économiques européens" [It is difficult to appear at the same time as the interpreter of Black people's aspirations for emancipation and be, otherwise, a servant of the "colonial" State and remain tied to the economic interests of major European economic groups] (2008, 122).

Yet, in 1919, Du Bois did not disparage Diagne's divided loyalty toward France and colonized blacks as a contradiction because he experienced a similar ambivalence toward the métropole. Besides, for the Du Bois of 1919, Diagne's loyalty to France was not always detrimental since it gave the deputy the vetted status of France's diplomatic spokesperson of blacks on a global stage. Du Bois also saw in Diagne's elite position a chance for African Americans to show how remote the United States was from French colonies where lawmakers treated black leaders with respect. Du Bois's view of France as a cosmopolitan nation probably influenced his collaborative attitudes toward Diagne up through the 1921 congress. Until then, he had no major quibble with the deputy even if he was not fond of his assimilationism. Du Bois's lack of prior antagonism with Diagne also stemmed from their similar adoration of French cosmopolitanism and belief in their role as leaders who should secure support of liberal and progressive-minded whites for the improvement of the conditions of blacks worldwide. Like Diagne, Du Bois was kind to France because he espoused its cosmopolitan ideals of liberty, fraternity, and equality which they both wanted to see extended to blacks and other colonized peoples. This shared faith in French cosmopolitanism reinforces another similarity between the two leaders that Jean-Hervé Jézéquel describes as follows:

> "L'anticolonialisme modéré de Du Bois ne pose pas trop de problèmes à l'assimilationniste Diagne, car le leader américain est aussi un fervent admirateur de la France de 1789." Avant la tenue du congrès [Pan-Africain de 1919], il se serait d'ailleurs engagé à ne pas critiquer la colonisation française.

74 W. E. B. Du Bois's cosmopolitanism

> ['The assimilationist Diagne did not have many issues with the moderate anticolonialism of Du Bois, because the American leader was, like him, a fervent admirer of the France of 1789.' Before the [1919 Pan-African] congress, Du Bois had even agreed not to criticize French colonization]
>
> (1993, 84)

The two leaders' compromise enabled them to each create a cosmopolitan vision of the 1919 congress which did not visibly threaten France's imperial authority.

Du Bois's cosmopolitan view of the 1919 congress is apparent in a document entitled, "Memorandum to Mr. Diagne and Others on a Pan-African Congress to Be Held in Paris, in February 1919." In this January 1, 1919, memorandum, Du Bois argued that "the obtaining of authoritative statements of policy toward the Negro race from the Great Powers" was part of the chief "work" of the congress.[28] In the same text, Du Bois hoped that the summit would lead to "the cordial and sympathetic cooperation of the black, yellow and white races on terms of mutual respect and equality in the future development of the world."[29] The two quotations exemplify a version of Du Bois's cosmopolitanism which is based on a dismantlement of ethnic barriers and a development of racial collaboration for humanity's progress. Ethnic and cultural particularisms are non-existent in this ideology in which Du Bois envisioned a transnational and crossracial unity in which Western powers and formerly colonized people would work in harmony toward the betterment of the world. Such a cosmopolitanism is consistent with the Kantian definition of "a universal *cosmopolitan existence*" that Pheng Cheah describes as a concept which refers to "the regulative idea of 'a perfect civil union of mankind'" and a "constitutional global federation of all existing states 'based on cosmopolitan right' (*ius cosmopoliticum*)" and "articulated around the idea that 'individuals and states, co-existing in an external relationship of mutual influences, may be regarded as citizens of a universal state of mankind'" (1998, 23). Du Bois would have agreed with this Kantian view of cosmopolitanism since he dreamed of a pluralistic world in which the global North and the global South would work together to repair and prevent imperial injustices. In this sense, as Monica L. Miller explains, Du Bois is an "'antiracist' (vs. anti-race) Race Man" because he holds "an idea of culture that continually strives toward the goal of attaining cultural equality, or status as part of a universal, in tension with the particular historical circumstances that add their own demands to what constitutes that universal" (2009, 169).

Yet, Du Bois could not completely take race out of cosmopolitanism. He continued to value race in cosmopolitanism, as is visible in his January 1, 1919, memorandum in which he made numerous racial demands that reinscribed both autonomy and authenticity into his pluralism. Du Bois pointed out that the uncompromising platform of the congress included:

W. E. B. Du Bois's cosmopolitanism   75

[The] Development of autonomous government along lines of native custom, with the object of inaugurating gradually an Africa for the Africans.

[The] Full recognition of the independent governments of Abyssinia, Liberia, and Hayti, with their full natural boundaries, and the development of the former German colonies under the guarantee and oversight of the League of Nations.

The Cordial and sympathetic cooperation of the black, yellow and white races on terms of mutual respect and equality in the future development of the world.[30]

The last demand resonated with Diagne's cosmopolitanism which also sought mutual respect and equality between races. But this equality was for Diagne a natural and inherent human fact that racism threatened, while for Du Bois it was a set of rights, such as employment, equal treatment before the law, and other civil liberties, that blacks could gain only through ongoing struggle. The 1919 congress echoed Du Bois's radical legal philosophy by giving blacks an international platform where they demanded freedom globally. In their deliberations, the leaders from 57 countries of Africa and the black diaspora who attended the summit vowed to: protect the 200,000,000 blacks of the world; allow Africans and their descendants to take effective ownership of their land and natural resources; regulate the investment of capital to prevent the exploitation of the "natives;" abolish slavery and capital punishment and substitute them with free labor; make education, health care, cultural celebration, and religious worship be human rights; demand citizenship for Africans on account of their being "civilized and able to meet the tests of surrounding culture;" and use the power of the League of Nations to secure the life, property, and labor of Africans against any oppressive state.[31] The black congressioners' demand of "citizenship" and other rights on account of their humanity and ability to be "civilized" and pass "the tests of surrounding culture" reflects their embrace of European cosmopolitanism as long as it also leads to justice and equality for blacks.

Nevertheless, the other delegates had no strong faith in Europe's willingness to free the colonized and, as a result, agreed on a manisfesto that the Senegalese deputy would have perceived as radical toward France. While Diagne would have concurred with Du Bois's call for "the development of the former German colonies under the guarantee and oversight of the League of Nations," he would have required that France be given a preponderant role in the re-establishment of order in these colonies. Moreover, while cosmopolitanism inspired him to support, in his 1919 congress speech, the struggle of former African colonial populations of Germany for "[le] droit à la vie qui appartient à tout homme" [[the] right to life which belongs

76 W. E. B. Du Bois's cosmopolitanism

to every human being],[32] Diagne would not want these populations, such as those of the former German *Kamerun* (now Cameroun) and Togo, to be totally free from France's influence. Furthermore, unlike Du Bois who wanted such colonies and others, including Kionga Triangle (Portuguese Mozambique), Tanganyika (Tanzania), Ruanda-Urundi (Rwanda and Burundi), Wituland (Kenya), and *Deutsch-Südwestafrika* (Namibia and Botswana), to be liberated from imperialism, Diagne wanted France to have a stake and influence in these dominions after this freedom. Referring to the Paris Peace Conference, which took place on January 18, 1919, Diagne welcomed its decision to end Germany's rule on its African colonies.[33] But, as a loyal colonist, he preferred to see Germany's former settlements (Togo and Cameroun) go to France rather than to Britain, Italy, or the United States.

Although he did not criticize it at the 1919 congress, Du Bois felt uneasy about Diagne's colonialist attitudes since he later assessed the convention, in a correspondence with the deputy, in a disappointed tone. In a missive to Diagne, written sometime during the last half of August 1921, Du Bois writes:

> When I was here last matters were so unsettled that all I had to do was to have some sort of meeting. This second meeting is however much more significant and it is necessary for us who are seeking to lead the movement to have clear understanding and to work together for certain great principles.[34]

Du Bois's remarks sound like implicit criticisms against the lack of consensus between Diagne and him in their visions of the goals of the 1919 convention. Such a divergence, which Du Bois did not voice during the 1919 congress, became full-blown at the 1921 summit. By then, the two leaders had different conceptions of the 1921 congress's objectives and the cosmopolitan role that the West should play in the resolution of the challenges facing blacks in the early twentieth century.

Once again, it was thanks to the networking skills of Diagne that Clemenceau authorized the 1921 Pan-African Congress at the Grand Hotel in Paris.[35] The number of delegates at this summit almost doubled that of the 1919 meeting. While it estimates the number to be 110, a December 1921 article of *The Crisis* suggests that "Other persons were present from Swaziland, Jamaica, Martinique, French Congo, Trinidad, the Philippines and Liberia; and in addition to these there were at least 1,000 visitors."[36] According to Kenneth Robert Janken, "twenty-four participants were Africans or African Americans living in Europe, while forty-one people came from the United States and Seven from the British West Indies" (1993, 54). African American delegates included Rayford Logan, Walter White, Edward Franklin Frazier, the Minister and Dr. George Jackson, and Jessie Fauset, while the African and Caribbean delegates comprised the Congolese Paul

W. E. B. Du Bois's cosmopolitanism   77

Panda, the Guadeloupian Candace, and the Jamaican Nathan S. Russell, among others.[37]

Diagne's support for Du Bois was also consultative. In a letter which he wrote in the last half of August 1921, Du Bois sought Diagne's advice on a draft proposal that he had prepared for the 1921 congress. Du Bois told Diagne: "This [memorandum] is not for finalization but for information and comment and revision according to your ideas. Later I shall send you a draft of proposed resolutions for the matter."[38] Du Bois later described the meeting as an opportunity to discuss the future of the former German colonies and "to focus the attention of the peace delegates and the civilized world on the just claims of the Negro everywhere" (1921, 124–125). Therefore, Du Bois envisioned the 1921 congress as a transnational and cosmopolitan forum that could discuss the issues facing blacks. Yet, as is apparent in the following passage of *The Crisis* issue of January 1921, Du Bois focused the second summit on Africa:

> The Second Pan-African Conference under the Presidency of Blaise Diagne, Deputy from Senegal to the Parliament of France and Commissioner of African French Troops in the late war, has been called by the executive committee through its secretary, W. E. B. DuBois, to meet in Paris, in the early fall of 1921. All Negro governments and groups and all Negro organizations interested in the peoples of African descent will be invited to participate. Governments with colonies in Africa will be invited to send official spokesmen.[39]

Reciprocating Du Bois's plan to focus the congress on Africa, Diagne intimated, in a letter to Du Bois, written on November 15, 1920, his desire to center the summit on the conditions of African Americans. However, Diagne gave Du Bois a warning that suggested his fear of the potential radicalism of African American delegates at the meeting. He anxiously told Du Bois:

> Mais pour cela, il faut que la représentation américaine au Congrès ne nous arrive pas composée d'éléments divisés et manquant de solidarité aux yeux même de leurs congénères des autres pays. Vous nous permettrez ainsi à tous de faire un travail utile qui impressionnera assez les Gouvernements pour que notre race en tire un réel profit.
>
> [But, the American delegation for the Congress must not come to us with elements who will appear as divided and lacking solidarity in the eyes of their counterparts from other countries. By preventing this situation, you will allow all of us to do a useful work that will impress all the Governments so that our race can really profit from the event].[40]

Diagne's statements show that he was afraid of Du Bois's propensity to become radical at the congress. Diagne did not initially have this

78   *W. E. B. Du Bois's cosmopolitanism*

apprehension when he was co-planning the event with Du Bois since the latter had published an article in the *New York Tribune* issue of September 6, 1921, stating his disinterest in the hot subject of colonialism. In this article, Du Bois declared: "The colored American cannot withstand the African climate. We cannot oust the Europeans, and do not desire to do so."[41] Diagne might have relished these words which somewhat assured French colonials of the diasporan blacks' disinterest in agitating Africa and moving there to create free nations. Yet Diagne was probably not very consoled by the declaration since he was aware of Du Bois's propensity to condemn global problems affecting blacks. Diagne also feared that other African American delegates, such as James Weldon Johnson and Logan, would make irreverent remarks about France.

Diagne's trepidations made him so nervous at the 1921 congress that he ended up being stern and controlling at the September 2 meeting in Brussels. At that gathering, Diagne attempted to please the white observers, who were also present and busy spreading news about the events to different parts of the globe, by rushing the adoption of a motion that Paul Otlet, a utopian Belgian lawyer and political activist, brought to the floor. Florence Hackett summarizes Otlet's motion as follows:

> Mr. Otlet's proposition declared Negroes "susceptible" of advancement from their present backward condition and that their development would rid humanity of a weight of 200 millions of ignorant incompetents, and that collaboration between races on a basis of equality was an urgent duty today. He proposed, therefore, a federation of all uplift agencies of Negroes and their friends centering in the Palais Mondial, Belgium.
>
> (40)[42]

This motion that Otlet also proposed to avoid a clash between Diagne and the African American delegates produced damage rather than peace. By rushing Otlet's submission, Diagne had ignored a motion that Du Bois had proposed at a previous session of the congress which took place in London. Dismissing this early motion which called for democracy, independence, and education in Africa, Diagne supported Otlet's proposition which urged more Western tutelage and intervention in the continent.[43]

Yet the major factor that mostly aggravated Du Bois at the 1921 congress was Diagne's portrayal of African Americans as Anglophone blacks who were interfering into the "methods" of French Africans. A report of the congress reads:

> Et M. Diagne donne à entendre très nettement que les noirs qui vivent sous le drapeau français n'ont point à se plaindre de leur situation et que s'ils viennent au secours de leurs frères de race, c'est par bonté et affection fraternelles et non par égoïsme. Si on veut les entrainer trop loin, ils laisseront les autres se débrouiller tout seuls. . . .

W. E. B. Du Bois's cosmopolitanism 79

Quand on nous dit qu'avec nos méthodes de conciliation, ajoute t'il, nous n'arriverons à rien, nous verrons bien. Si nous n'arrivons à rien, il sera temps alors d'employer la violence; pour le moment, laissez-nous agir et ne venez pas compromettre notre effort dans je ne sais quel but et quel intérêt égoïste.

[Diagne made it clear that blacks who live under the French flag have nothing to complain about their situation and that, if they come to the aid of their kinsmen, it will be from kindness and brotherly affection and not selfishness. If they keep being pressured so much, they will have to let the others help themselves . . . .

Those who say that our methods of conciliation will achieve nothing should wait and see. If we achieve nothing, it will then be the time to use violence; for now, let us act freely and not compromise our effort for whatever purpose and selfish interest].[44]

Diagne's assertion reflects his perception of Du Bois as an outsider with minimal knowledge of Africa and his view of the African American delegates as black diasporan elite who were imposing an Anglophone form of cosmopolitanism on Francophone West Africans. Claiming an alternative cosmopolitanism, Diagne seemed to see West Africans as people who were able to determine their destiny and relations with the West without the tutelage and radicalism of their diasporan brothers. Consequently, Diagne's words displayed his elitist attempt to silence the African American delegates with black Francophone snobbery. His remarks deeply hurt Du Bois and the other African American delegates who felt belittled by the black French deputies at the summit. One of these deputies was Gratien Candace, whom Du Bois perceived, like Diagne, as another assimilated and a "virulently French" black man who "has no conception of Negro uplift, as apart from French development."[45]

Du Bois's troubling impressions about Diagne and Candace led him to retrospectively assess the 1921 congress in somewhat negative terms. For instance, listening to Diagne's words above, Du Bois felt betrayed by a man that he used to idealize as a savior of the black race. And here was Du Bois's romanticized, cultured, and modern African brother (Diagne) spitting in the faces of his black transatlantic siblings by speaking to them in patronizing and condescending ways in front of white patrons of the Belgian session. These white participants included the Belgians Otlet and Mr. and Mrs. LaFontaine as well as the French deputy of Pas-de-Calais George Barthelemy, who all admired Diagne's assimilationist and Eurocentric postures. The affront was too much for Du Bois and other African American delegates to bear, leading to this inevitable withdrawal that an anonymous reporter noted: "La salle devient un peu houleuse. M. Burghardt du Bois quitte le fauteuil qu'il occupait prés de M. Diagne et va dans un coin de la salle où plusieurs Américains viennent le rejoindre" [The room got a little hot.

80 *W. E. B. Du Bois's cosmopolitanism*

Mr. Burghardt du Bois left the chair where he was sitting near Diagne and went to a corner of the room where more Americans joined him].[46]

From that moment, Du Bois's relationships with Diagne were never the same. The former knight in shining armor became a betrayer of his people—one who was eager to sell his own soul for a colonial power that was as guilty of atrocities as its American counterpart was. Diagne's snap at his other black Atlantic siblings truly shocked and dejected Du Bois who still wanted to understand the real causes of the deputy's dismissive behavior. Du Bois registers his disappointment when he later says:

> We came to Paris with a sense of strain and apprehension, only partially allayed by a long, frank conference with Diagne who acknowledged that his methods in Brussels were high-handed but contended that he had only thought to prevent the "assassination of a race!"[47]

Du Bois's allusion to the selfless and cautionary motivations that might have led Diagne to be defensive toward diasporan blacks at the second congress suggests the Anglophone and Francophone leaders' capacity to somewhat put their shared struggle before their geographic, cultural, and political differences. In this vein, Clarence G. Contee writes: "In order to heal the division between the French-speaking and French civilization loving Negroes and the English-speaking Negroes and at the same get adopted the London resolutions adroit diplomacy was necessary" (1969, 297).

Yet the tension between Du Bois and Diagne was difficult to completely appease since it wounded the African American so deeply that he immediately wrote about it upon his return to the United States. Du Bois's reactions to the disconcerting incident appear in an essay entitled "A Second Journey to Pan-Africa" that he published in *The New Republic* on December 7, 1921, three months after the gathering. Reminiscing the conflict, Du Bois described Diagne as a person who "was beside himself with excitement after the resolutions were read," perhaps "as a successful investor in French colonial enterprise" who "was undoubtedly in a difficult position" (1995, 664). Du Bois continues:

> He [Diagne] felt that the cause of the black man in Belgium and France had been compromised by black American radicals; he especially denounced our demand for "the restoration of the ancient common ownership of the land in Africa" as rank communism.
>
> (1995, 664)

Diagne's perception of African American delegates' desire to protect African land from European expropriation as "rank communism" conveys his perception of the Anglophone blacks as radicals. Diagne's comments suggest a discord between Du Bois and him that is also apparent in a report that Fauset wrote in the November 1921 issue of *The Crisis*. Fauset's

W. E. B. Du Bois's cosmopolitanism 81

account reveals a blend of American elitism and exceptionalism that she expresses by representing the African American delegates as more disciplined and pragmatic than their black Francophone counterparts. For instance, Fauset contends that Du Bois's speech at the 1921 congress "gave facts and food for thoughts" while those of "Messieurs Diagne and Candace gave us fine oratory, magnificent gestures—but platitudes" (1921, 16). Yet Fauset's strongest reproaches appear later in the report when she indirectly accuses Diagne and Candace of having been silent about the brutality of colonialism. While she recognizes that the congress was a "finer example of unity and trust on the part of Negroes toward a Negro leader," which presumably refers to Diagne, Fauset disparages the latter personality for having "'jam[med] through' his resolutions and adjourn[ed] the session" (1921, 15). Discussing Fauset's participation in the 1921 congress, Edwards rightly argues that she "introduces gender issues" without "sustain[ing]" what he calls "an articulation of diaspora that would combine anti-imperialism with a feminist critique" (2003, 137–138).

One instance in which Fauset combines the elements that Edwards mentions is in her disparagement of Diagne, which hints at both the leader's masochism and support of colonialism. By lamenting how Diagne rushed resolutions, Fauset perceives him as a male "bully" who lacked the Anglophone blacks' finesse and patience and who would have spoiled the congress if Du Bois had not intervened. Revisiting this controversial moment, Contee writes:

> Miss Fauset maintained that it was at this point that the American delegation under the leadership of DuBois proved to be master of the situation and prevented the complete disruption of the sessions, which had not as yet been to Paris.
>
> (1969, 294)

Fauset's criticism against Diagne resonates with her vituperation of the Senegalese deputy's collaboration with colonialism in her report where she later asserts:

> And yet the shadow of Colonial dominion governed . . . For three days we listened to pleasant generalities without a word of criticism of Colonial Governments, without a murmur of complaint of Black Africa, without a suggestion that this was an international Congress called to define and make intelligible the greatest set of wrongs against human beings that the modern world has known.
>
> (1921, 14)

Fauset's observations condemn the elitist and imperialistic posture that Diagne assumed by not attacking imperialism as Anglophone blacks did. Such an expectation is somewhat unreasonable since Diagne was a declared advocate of colonialism.

82   *W. E. B. Du Bois's cosmopolitanism*

Moreover, Fauset's remonstrances posit that Anglophone blacks were swift and matter-of-fact in their attitudes toward Africa while their Francophone counterparts were tardy and elusive. This dichotomy is elitist and exceptionalist since it assumes that Du Bois had particular Western experiences and backgrounds that gave him more insights than Diagne, who was born and reared in Senegal, about Africa. Representing the African American delegates as more equipped than Diagne to liberate Africa is counterproductive since it dismisses the solidarity among the different blacks of the summit. Moreover, being Francophone and a part of the colonial administration did not prevent Diagne from sometimes developing a black cosmopolitan search for justice and equality that he shared with Du Bois. Even if he was patronizing toward African Americans, Diagne embraced Pan-Africanism. Diagne dovetailed this Pan-Africanism and his cosmopolitan message into Du Bois's anticolonial and nationalist concerns by agreeing with the congress's final resolutions that were adopted in Paris. When Diagne spoke to the French media about the Pan-African conference, he did it with a spirit of solidarity and communalism with the Anglophone blacks. According to an article entitled, "Le Congrès Pan-Noir," written on September 9, 1921, Diagne praised the event by saying:

> Nous avons dit les imperfections des systèmes coloniaux qui pèsent sur la race noire: nous avons indiqué les solutions qui apparaissent les mieux appropriées au développement rationnel de la masse noire; nous avons enfin proclamé notre vif désir que notre évolution se fasse dans la plus franche et étroite collaboration des races.

> [We talked about the imperfections of colonial systems that affect the black race. We have indicated the solutions that appear most appropriate to the rational development of the black masses; we finally proclaimed our strong desire that our development is done with the most open and close collaboration of races].[48]

The statement suggests that Diagne was finally accommodating toward the African American delegates, which is probably the reason why Fauset says that "the situation in Paris was less tense" than that in Brussels (1921, 16). This quotation shows that Diagne was also a Pan-Africanist since he ultimately subsumed all the differences he had with Du Bois under the collective needs and interests of transnational and cosmopolitan leaders who were fighting to uplift the conditions of all blacks.

In light of the interactions and communications they had during the 1919 congress, Du Bois and Diagne were on excellent terms during the first part of the twentieth century. Both leaders were fervent admirers of French cosmopolitanism and used it to establish Pan-African connections with each other and bring global awareness about Africa's plight during the early twentieth century. Furthermore, Du Bois was comparable to Diagne because

W. E. B. Du Bois's cosmopolitanism   83

he, too, experienced the dilemma of appreciating the cosmopolitanism of a French society that refused to acknowledge the damage of its imperial policies on *tirailleurs* and other Africans.

Yet the two leaders became ideological foes during the 1921 congress when their relations turned bitter although they remained fervent devotees of French cosmopolitanism. The two leaders' paradoxical relationships show the complexity of a black cosmopolitan tradition which was not stable because it was fraught with disagreements amidst ephemeral celebrations of Pan-Africanism. These fissures show that Du Bois and Diagne had a rivalry that ultimately undermined their cosmopolitanisms, Pan-Africanisms, and mutual affections. Yet Diagne might have been touched by Du Bois's celebrations of his accomplishments since he was very eager to have relationships with the African American although his attitudes toward him often stemmed from selfish and colonialist motives.

Bibliography

"110 Delegates to the Pan-African Congress by Countries." *The Crisis* 23, no. 2 (December 1921): 68–69.

"Article in *La Dépêche Coloniale et Maritime* [Brussel 2, 1921]." In *The Marcus Garvey and Universal Negro Improvement Association Papers*, Vol. 4, edited by Robert Hill, 165–166. Los Angeles: University of California Press, 1995.

"Au Congrès Pan-Noir: Une Séance de clôture Mouvementée." *La Dépêche Coloniale et Maritime*, September 4–5, 1921: 1.

Barbeau, Arthur E. and Florette Henri. *The Unknown Soldiers: African American Troops in World War I*. Philadelphia, PA: Temple University Press, 1974.

Bell, Bernard W., Emily R. Grosholz, and James B. Stewart. "Editors Introduction." In *W. E. B Du Bois on Race and Culture*, edited by Bernard W. Bell, Emily R. Grosholz, and James B. Stewart, 1–14. New York: Routledge, 1996.

"Benefits Forgot." *The Crisis* 19, no. 2 (December 1919): 76–77.

"Black Soldiers." *The Crisis* 15, no. 1 (November 1917): 33–35.

Campbell, James. *Middle Passages: African American Journeys to Africa, 1787–2005*. New York: Penguin, 2006.

Cheah, Pheng. "The Cosmopolitical – Today." In *Cosmopolitics: Thinking and Feeling beyond the Nation*, edited by Pheng Cheah and Bruce Robbins, 20–41. Minneapolis: University of Minnesota Press, 1998.

Chrisman, Laura. *Postcolonial Contraventions: Cultural Readings of Race, Imperialism and Transnationalism*. Manchester: Manchester University Press, 2003.

"Clippings." *The Evening Independent*, May 2, 1955: 18

Contee, Clarence Garner. *W. E. B Du Bois and African Nationalism: 1914–1945*. Washington, DC: The American University, 1969.

"Crisis (Firm)." Clipping from *The Crisis*, March 1919. W. E. B. Du Bois Papers (MS 312). Special Collections and University Archives, University of Massachusetts Amherst Libraries.

Crouch, Stanley. "A Reply from Stanley Crouch: A Two-Part Invention on the Black Willie Blues I: Blues To Be There." In *Reconsidering the Souls of Black Folk*, edited

84   W. E. B. Du Bois's cosmopolitanism

by Stanley Crouch and Playthell Benjamin, 69–79. Philadelphia, PA: Running Press, 2002.

Debré, Jean-Louis. *Les oubliés de la République*. Paris: Fayard, 2008.

Diagne, Blaise. "Letter to W. E. B. Du Bois." January 5 1919, W. E. B. Du Bois Papers (MS 312). Special Collections and University Archives, University of Massachusetts Amherst Libraries.

Diagne, Blaise. "Letter to Du Bois." *The Crisis* 17, no. 5 (March 1919): 221.

Diagne, Blaise. "Letter to W. E. B. Du Bois." November 15, 1920. W. E. B. Du Bois Papers (MS 312). Special Collections and University Archives. University of Massachusetts Amherst Libraries.

"Discours inaugural de M. Diagne au Congrès Pan-Africain des 19-20-21 février 1919," ca. February 1919. W. E. B. Du Bois Papers (MS 312), Special Collections and University Archives, University of Massachusetts Amherst Libraries, 1–5.

Di Méo, Nicolas. *Le Cosmopolitisme dans la littérature française de Paul Bourget à Marguerite Yourcenar*. Genève: Librairie Droz S. A., 2009.

Du Bois, W. E. B. "A Second Journey to Pan-Africa." *W. E. B. Du Bois: A Reader*, edited by David Levering Lewis, 662–67. New York: Henry Holt, 1995.

——. "An Essay Toward a History of the Black Man in the Great War." *The Crisis* 18, no. 2 (June 1919): 63–87.

——. "Du Bois, "Editorial." *The Crisis* 17, no. 5 (March 1919): 215–217.

——. "Editorial." *The Crisis* 14, no. 5 (September 1917): 215–218.

——. "Letter to A. Vinck." July 15, 1921. W. E. B. Du Bois Papers (MS 312). Special Collections and University Archives. University of Massachusetts Amherst Libraries.

——. "Letter to Blaise Diagne." October 18, 1919, W. E. B. Du Bois Papers (MS 312). Special Collections and University Archives, University of Massachusetts Amherst Libraries.

——. "Letter to Diagne." ca. August 1921. W. E. B. Du Bois Papers (MS 312). Special Collections and University Archives. University of Massachusetts Amherst Libraries.

——. "Letter to Jean de La Roche." *The Correspondence of W. E. B. Du Bois. Vol 3. Selections*, edited by Herbert Aptheker, 59. Amherst: University of Massachusetts Press, 1978.

——. "Letter to [Miss] Bernice E. Brand." November 16, 1927. W. E. B. Du Bois Papers (MS 312). Special Collections and University Archives. University of Massachusetts Amherst Libraries.

——. "Memorandum from W. E. B Du Bois to M. Diagne and Others on a Pan-African Congress to be Held in Paris in February 1919." January 1, 1919. W. E. B. Du Bois Papers (MS 312), Special Collections and University Archives, University of Massachusetts Amherst Libraries.

——. "Memorandum to Messrs. Diagne, Candace and their friends on the future of the PA Congress, 1921." W. E. B. Du Bois Papers (MS 312). Special Collections and University Archives, University of Massachusetts Amherst Libraries.

——. "Opinion of W.E.B. Du Bois." *The Crisis* 18, no. 1 (May 1919): 7–9.

——. "Opinion of W.E.B. Du Bois." *The Crisis* 21, no. 3 (January 1921): 101-104.

——. "Sketches from Abroad: le grand voyage." *The Crisis* 27, no. 5 (March 1924): 203–205.

——. "The Black Man in the Revolution of 1914–1918." *The Crisis* 17, no. 5 (March 1919): 218–223.

W. E. B. Du Bois's cosmopolitanism 85

——. "The Pan-African Congress." *The Crisis* 17, no. 6 (April 1919): 271–273.

——. "The Pan-African Movement." In *History of the Pan-African Congress*, edited by George Padmore, 13–26. London: The Hammersmith Bookshop, 1947.

——. "Worlds of Color." *The Crisis* 3, no. 3 (April 1925): 423–444.

Edwards, Brent Hayes. *The Practice of Diaspora: Literature, Translation, and the Rise of Black Internationalism.* Cambridge, MA: Harvard University Press, 2003.

"Enclosure: Resolutions Passed at the 1919 Pan-African Congress." In *The Marcus Garvey and Universal Negro Improvement Association Papers*, Vol. 4, edited by Robert Hill, 4–7. Los Angeles: University of California Press, 1995.

Fabre, Michel. *From Harlem to Paris: Black American Writers in France, 1840–1980.* Urbana: University of Illinois Press, 1993.

Fauset, Jessie. "Impressions of the Second Pan-African Congress." *The Crisis* 23, no. 1 (November 1921): 12–18.

"Foreign." *The Crisis* 13, no. 5 (March 1917): 245–246.

"From N. Y. Tribune." In *The Marcus Garvey and Universal Negro Improvement Association Papers*, Vol. 4, edited by Robert Hill, 186–187. Los Angeles: University of California Press, 1995.

Grayzel, Susan R. "Women and Men." In *A Companion to World War I*, edited by John Horne, 263–278. Malden, MA: Wiley-Blackwell, 2010.

Harlan, Louis R and Raymond W. Smock, eds. *The Booker T. Washington Papers: 1906–8.* Urbana: University of Illinois Press, 1972.

Hollinger, David A. *Cosmopolitanism and Solidarity: Studies in Ethnoracial, Religious, and Professional Affiliation in the United States.* Madison: University of Wisconsin Press, 2006.

Jackson, George H, "Letter to Blaise Diagne." December 27, 1918. W. E. B. Du Bois Papers (MS 312). Special Collections and University Archives. University of Massachusetts Amherst Libraries.

Janken, Kenneth Robert. *Rayford W. Logan and the Dilemma of the African American Intellectual.* Amherst: University of Massachusetts Press, 1993.

Jézéquel, Jean-Hervé. *L'action politique de Blaise Diagne, 1914–1934: des rapports entre les milieux coloniaux français et l'élite noire assimilée à travers l'exemple du premier élu noir africain à la Chambre des Députés.* Thesis: Institut d'Etudes Politiques de Paris, 1993.

Justesen, Benjamin R. "African-American Consuls Abroad, 1897–1909." *Foreign Service Journal* (September 2004): 72–76

"Le Congrès Pan-Noir: Ce Qu'il a Obtenu." *La Dépêche Coloniale et Maritime*, September 9, 1921: 1.

Lewis, David Levering. *W. E. B. Du Bois: The Fight for Equality and the American Century, 1919–1963.* New York: Henry Holt, 2000.

Miller, Monica L. *Slaves to Fashion: Black Dandyism and the Styling of Black Diasporic Identity.* Durham, NC: Duke University Press, 2009.

"Miscellaneous." *The Crisis* 13, no. 6 (April 1917): 303.

"Pan-African Delegates." *The Crisis* 23, no. 2 (December 1921): 68–69.

Roberts, Frank E. *The American Foreign Legion: Black Soldiers of the 93rd in World War I.* Annapolis, MD: Naval Institute Press, 2004.

Spencer, Robert. *Cosmopolitan Criticism and Postcolonial Literature.* Hampshire, UK: Palgrave Macmillan, 2011.

Sundquist, Eric J. *To Wake the Nations: Race in the Making of American Literature.* Cambridge, MA: Harvard University Press. 1993.

86 W. E. B. Du Bois's cosmopolitanism

"The Denial of Passports." *The Crisis* 17, no. 5 (March 1919): 237–238.

"The War." *The Crisis* 15, no. 4 (February 1918): 191–192.

"The War." *The Crisis* 16, no. 1 (May 1918): 21–24.

"The War." *The Crisis* 16, no. 3 (July 1918): 134.

"The World War: Causes and Effects." *The Crisis* 9, no. 2 (December 1914): 69–70.

"Three Members of Parliament." *The Crisis* 8, no. 4 (August 1914): 170.

Walters, Ronald W. *Pan Africanism in the African Diaspora: An Analysis of Modern Afrocentric Political Movements*. 1993. Detroit: Wayne State University Press, 1997.

"War." *The Crisis* 14, no.1 (May 1917): 37–38.

Williams, Chad L. *Torchbearers of Democracy: African American Soldiers in the World War I Era*. Chapel Hill: University of North Carolina Press, 2013.

W. E. B. Du Bois: A Biography in Four Voices. Directed by Louis Massiah. San Francisco: California Newsreel, 1995. Videocassette (VHS).

Wolters, Raymond. *Du Bois and His Rivals*. Columbia: University of Missouri Press, 2002.

3 Marcus Garvey's cosmopolitanism, anticolonialism, and responses to Blaise Diagne

Marcus Garvey influenced black transnational resistances against Western imperialism in fundamental ways that deserve more scholarly recognition. For instance, Garvey's liberation struggle had a strong impact on the fight for self-determination, equal rights, and justice for blacks of Senegal, particularly for *tirailleurs* combating for France's liberation from Germany during World War I. Garvey's global influence is also apparent in his sustained ideological battles against Diagne, whose cosmopolitanism was quite antithetical to his. Unlike Diagne's cosmopolitanism, which was often founded on Africans' subjection to French colonialism, Garvey's was based on these people's continuous resistance against this domination. Diagne's cosmopolitanism originated from a resolve to maintain French colonial hegemony and cultural assimilationism rather than the desire to fully liberate Senegalese from it. By contrast, Garvey's cosmopolitanism stemmed from a determination to free Senegalese and other Africans from French colonialism. Focusing on Garvey's and Diagne's different views about the treatment of African colonial soldiers during World War I and France's relationships with Senegal during this period, this chapter aims to reveal the two leaders' dissimilar forms of cosmopolitanism. The chapter hopes to also show the rare contexts in which Garvey and Diagne shared a few affinities in their Pan-Africanist approaches to French colonialism.

Although it is substantial, the scholarship on Garvey tends to be American-centric, focusing mainly on the significance of his nationalism in the United States, neglecting its importance in Africa. A major contribution to this scholarship is Judith Stein's *The World of Marcus Garvey: Race and Class in Modern Society* (1986), which tracks Garvey's journey from Europe to the United States in the mid-1910s. Stein provides key insights on the main individuals, such as the Guianese T. Ras Makonnen and the Sudanese-Egyptian Mohamed Ali, who exposed Garvey to nationalism. As Stein argues, these men taught Garvey the importance of wealth and knowledge for global African development (1986, 29). Moreover, Stein reveals the racism, violence, and disenfranchisement against blacks during the 1910s and 20s which prompted Garvey to adopt a radical approach to the inequalities in the United States (1986, 41–42). These historical episodes are

88 Marcus Garvey's cosmopolitanism

important since they later influenced Garvey to also fight for Africa's liberation from colonialism.

In a similar vein, Colin Grant's *Negro With a Hat: The Rise and Fall of Marcus Garvey* (2008) provides a thorough study of the impact of Garvey's nationalism in the United States. Discussing Garvey's influence in 1920s Harlem, Grant writes:

> Over the coming months, Garvey electrified audiences with speeches in which he exhorted his docile fellow blacks to stand up and fight back. He tapped into a deepening ground swell of fear and resentment. And if Garvey was sounding the alarm bells, as he surely was, then Americans (black and white) would soon be shaken by a frightening reveille on the streets of Houston.
>
> (2008, 102)

Grant's assertion portrays Garvey as an opportunist and a fearmonger whose American fame was accidental. Instead of representing Garvey as a newcomer who took advantage of African Americans' anxieties, I see him as a leader who provided these blacks with the confidence and defiance they needed to fight against racism, dehumanization, and economic alienation. Garvey appealed to oppressed African Americans because he calibrated their frustration toward a black radical and transnational liberation movement that ultimately placed Africa's anticolonial liberation at its central agenda.

In addition, most of the scholarship on Garvey focuses on English-speaking Africa, ignoring the relationships between the Jamaican leader and Francophone West Africa. Subsequently, Garvey's impact on black activism in Senegal is little known although there has been sporadic attention given to his influence in this country as well as in Nigeria, Liberia, and South Africa. In "Marcus Garvey and Nigeria," Adebowale Adefuye describes Garvey's strong resolve "to get Africa involved in his movement" when "in August 1920 at his convention in New York City, plans were worked out for the establishment of a negro state in Africa" (1991, 191). According to Adefuye, Garvey's impact on Africa was also noticeable in the establishment of UNIA branches in 1920s Nigeria where "events connected with the UNIA were closely followed, and the ideas preached by Garvey were being circulated to the Africans" (1991, 191).

In a similar vein, Elliot P. Skinner has explored Garvey's impact on South Africa. Skinner argues that, during his travels to South Africa in 1937–1938, the African American diplomat Ralph Bunch noticed the strong imprint of Garvey and the UNIA on the segregated blacks of the country (2010, 61). Skinner writes:

> He [Bunch] was especially intrigued by a black man, an apparent "Garveyite" who harangued crowds of colored and blacks during a parade. This man wore a UNIA (United Negro Improvement

Marcus Garvey's cosmopolitanism 89

Association) button on his lapel, carried copies of the *Pittsburgh Courier*, *The Bantu World*, and *The Black Man*, and spoke fairly good English. The political scientist in Bunch could not help noting the manner in which this Garveyite exemplified how the various "worlds of race" were coming together.

(2010, 61)

Skinner's declaration suggests Bunch's awareness of Garvey's stronghold on disenfranchised black South Africans and his realization of the Jamaican leader's power to dismantle colonialism and inequality through both international and local racial solidarity.

Yet, although Garvey's influence in English-speaking Africa is relatively known, his impact on French-speaking Africa remains underexplored. For instance, the only known study of Garvey's influence in Senegal is Aly Dramé's 1988 bachelor's thesis entitled "L'Impact du Mouvement Garveyiste et la Réaction de l'Administration Coloniale au Sénégal" [The Impact of Garveyism and the Reaction of the French Colonial Administration in Senegal]. Confirming the existence of UNIA branches in Senegal in the 1920s, Dramé writes:

La plus importante était la section rufisquoise, dirigée par le vétéran Selim Mustapha Gueye. Ensuite, venaient celles de Dakar et de Thiès, respectivement présidées par Duck Thomas et Amadou Jawarrah. Ces sections avaient de petites ramifications dans certaines localités comme Tivaouane, Diourbel, M'Backé.

[The most important branch was the rufisquoise section, which was led by veteran Selim Mustapha Gueye. Then came those of Dakar and Thiés, which were chaired by Duck Thomas and Amadou Jawarrah respectively. These sections had small branches in territories such as Tivaouane, Diourbel, and M'Backé.]

(1988, 53)

Building on Dramé's remarkable exploration of the UNIA's presence in Senegal, I examine the deeper influence that this organization had in this country through its leader's unyielding condemnations of French imperialism during the 1920s.

Fortunately, a few other major works have given some attention to Garvey's relations with French West Africa. These works, which include Walters's *Pan-Africanism in the African Diaspora* and Tony Martin's *Race First*, hint at Garvey's influence in a few connections between diasporan blacks and Francophone Africans during the 1920s. Walters argues that the word "Negritude" is "a term describing Negro-Africans both physically and psychologically, at home, but especially in the Diaspora" (359). In a related vein, Martin contends that, during his 1928 trip to France, Garvey claimed

90 Marcus Garvey's cosmopolitanism

to have "cemented a working plan with the French Negro" and "to have established a 'sub-European headquarters' in France" and "joined the Comité de Défense de la Race Nègre, a Paris-based Pan-African organization associated with the French Communist Party and the Comintern" (1976, 115–116). By drawing on Garvey's speeches and writings about *tirailleurs* and French colonialism, this chapter provides a deeper study of such connections between the Jamaican leader and Francophone Africa while focusing initially on his cosmopolitanism.

Garvey's cosmopolitanism is discernible in his perception of blacks as citizens of a world in which every race and culture contributes to the building of human civilization. He develops this cosmopolitanism in *The Philosophy* by representing Africa as the first continent whose future will determine the lives of all blacks. Unfortunately, black intellectuals tend to deny Garvey's cosmopolitanism. For instance, as Tania Friedel argues in her book, *Racial Discourse and Cosmopolitanism in Twentieth-Century African American Writing* (2008), Richard Wright

> urge[d] Negro writers to distance themselves from the "specious and blatant nationalism" of the 1920s, manifest in the Harlem Renaissance art and black nationalist movements, like Marcus Garvey's, based on essentialist notions of black identity, and to accept, instead, "the nationalist implications of Negro life."
>
> (2008, 105)

This thesis writes Garvey's radical nationalism out of cosmopolitanism by promoting an elitist minimization of his internationalist movement that must not be conceived as completely essentialist in spite of the power of authenticity and race that prevail in its conceptions of blackness in the modern world.

Challenging the elitist approach to cultural studies, Cheah argues that "nationalism is not antithetical to cosmopolitanism" (1998, 25) and "that nationalist politics is not necessarily a form of identity politics" (1998, 26). Garvey allows us to disrupt the distance between cosmopolitanism and nationalism because he persistently struggled for a liberated and autonomous black international community without denying this society's need to learn from other civilizations. Moreover, Garvey was not anticosmopolitan since he envisioned the UNIA as an organization that would lead to the recognition of the humanity of all races. Arguing that members of the UNIA "have been very misunderstood and very much misrepresented by men from within our own race, as well as others from without," Garvey writes:

> Any reform movement that seeks to bring about changes for the benefit of humanity is bound to be misrepresented by those who have always taken it upon themselves to administer to, and lead the unfortunate, and to direct those who may be placed under temporary disadvantages.
>
> ("The Principles", 94)

Marcus Garvey's cosmopolitanism 91

Therefore, Garvey conceptualized cosmopolitanism as a process through which societies that are more economically and technologically developed support those which are less fortunate so that there can be a prosperous world. Garvey's conception of "the benefit of humanity" as the central goal of his endeavors shows that he theorized cosmopolitanism as the synonym of universal freedom and human rights, just as Du Bois and Diagne also did. Discussing connections between Garvey and Du Bois, Contee states: "Both men maintained that it was extremely desirable and worthwhile to use their institutions, their Pan-African organizations, in order to consolidate the strengths of Negroes everywhere for racial uplift and for attaining for them dignity, respect, liberty and democracy" (1969, 202).

Furthermore, Garvey was inspired by the same ideas of human egalitarianism in Western revolutions that had influenced both Du Bois and Diagne. Garvey's belief in these principles is visible in a speech that he delivered at Liberty Hall, New York City, on November 25, 1922. In the address, Garvey said:

> It was not unreasonable for George Washington, the great hero and father of the country, to have fought for the freedom of America giving to us this great republic and this great democracy; it was not unreasonable for the Liberals of France to have fought against the Monarchy to give to the world French Democracy and French Republicanism; it was no unrighteous cause that led Tolstoi to sound the call of liberty in Russia, which has ended in giving to the world the social democracy of Russia, an experiment that will probably prove to be a boon and a blessing to mankind. If it was not an unrighteous cause that led Washington to fight for the independence of this country, and led the Liberals of France to establish the Republic, it is therefore not an unrighteous cause for the U.N.I.A. to lead 400,000,000 Negroes all over the world to fight for the liberation of our country.
>
> ("The Principles", 94)

This quotation reflects Garvey's cosmopolitan conception of the UNIA as an organization that thrived to participate in the long resistance tradition against tyranny in which French, American, and Russian republicanisms achieved democracy and human rights for downtrodden masses. By repeating the words "unreasonable" and "unrighteous cause," Garvey theorizes the UNIA's liberation struggle as a justified cosmopolitan resistance for freedom and equality. He tried to enlighten his critics on the point that the UNIA was also part of the transnational tradition of rebellions against injustice that inspired socialist movements across the world during the early twentieth century. It is from this patriotic and utopian logic that Garvey invoked the power of British resistance against tyranny as a cosmopolitanism that the English empire gave to the world. At a March 13, 1920, meeting with the UNIA members, Garvey told the audience:

92 Marcus Garvey's cosmopolitanism

> If you will read English history you will read what daring achievements the Englishman and the ancient Briton and the other white races that came from the other parts of Europe did to help them in their civilization and in the development of their government.
>
> ("Liberty Hall, New York Crowded to Doors", 256)

Garvey's statement suggests that he was a cosmopolitan leader since he believed in the universal rights of all human beings.

Yet Garvey's cosmopolitanism was also tactical since its main goal was black people's acquisition of inalienable rights in the West. Thus, as Yogita Goyal argues in *Romance, Diaspora, and Black Atlantic Literature*, Garvey's militancy "derived from his ability to tap into deep-seated feelings of disaffection from the failed promise of American democracy and in his promise of a black nation that could embody the desire for autonomy and freedom" (2010, 2). However, Garvey's liberation struggle transcended the West since it aimed to also bring cosmopolitan rights to blacks of Africa. His cosmopolitanism was transnational since it intended to give a sense of nation, pride, and dignity to many subjugated global black communities.

Garvey was therefore not the anticosmopolitan, essentialist, fanatic, irrational, and fascist intellectual that many critics see as a foil of Du Bois whom they perceive as an open-minded, flexible, logical and egalitarian intellectual who effectively reached out to whites to advance black liberation struggle in the United States. While Jacqueline M. Moore sees Garvey as a Jamaican whose approach Du Bois saw as "too emotional" and devoid of "real leadership" for the "working class" (116), Debra J. Dickerson dismisses the Jamaican leader from a cosmopolitanism that she fully credits to the African American philosopher who once said:

> I sit with Shakespeare and he winces not. Across the color line I move arm in arm with Balzac and Dumas, where smiling men and welcoming women glide in gilded halls . . . I summon Aristotle and Aurelius and what soul I will, and they come all graciously with no scorn nor condescension.
>
> (2004, 152)

According to Dickerson, Du Bois exemplifies how "knowledge and art don't discriminate, they give themselves to the world, just as the medicines derived from African knowledge work as effectively on a Montanan as on a Mauritanian" (2004, 152). Dickerson's assertions write Garvey out of cosmopolitanism by representing him as a leader who lacked Du Bois's widely learned qualities and ability to embrace and appreciate all knowledge and cultures. Garvey was as cosmopolitan as Du Bois was because he too validated the contributions of other races and cultures to world civilization. Garvey's cosmopolitanism is apparent in his representation of the UNIA as an organization that "believes in the rights of not only the black race, but the white race, the yellow race and the brown race" ("The Principles," 95).

Yet Garvey's cosmopolitanism was not a chimerical form of multiculturalism but an embrace of diversity founded on reciprocal recognition, respect, and justice between races. He writes:

> In view of the fact that the black man of Africa has contributed as much to the world as the white man of Europe, and the brown man and yellow man of Asia, we of the Universal Negro Improvement Association demand that the white, yellow and brown races give to the black man his place in the civilization of the world.
>
> ("The Principles", 95)

Garvey's statement reflects his cosmopolitan vision of the world as a universe in which members of every race and society should have equal rights, powers, and be considered as making contributions to human civilization. By depicting the "black man" as a person that the "white, yellow and brown races" must allow to take "his place in the civilization of the world," Garvey was also a participant in a black cosmopolitan tradition which stretched back to Phillis Wheatley, Toussaint Louverture, and early black intellectuals. This cosmopolitanism was founded on the right of blacks to be equal members of a global human civilization that has historically denied them admissibility and acceptance. Nwankwo explains:

> Faced with dehumanization and the Atlantic power structures' obsession with preventing the blossoming of their cosmopolitanism, people of African descent decided to stake their claim to personhood by defining themselves in relation to the new notions of "Black community" and ubiquitous manifestations of cosmopolitanism that the [Haitian] Revolution produced.
>
> (2005, 10–11)

Garvey was a champion of this transnationalist cosmopolitan tradition since he conceived blacks of Africa and the diaspora as people who deserve the same equality and rights that members of other races had. By steadfastly demanding equality for 400,000,000 blacks of the world without any desires "to destroy or disrupt the society or the government of other races," Garvey developed a radical, united, peaceful, and cosmopolitan understanding of right as a negotiated and reciprocated justice obtainable through both dialogue and civil resistance. "Cosmopolitan right," according to Jeremy Waldron, is "one's willingness to do what is required by the general principle of sharing this limited world with others" (2010, 173). Drawing on Kantian philosophy, Waldron also defines "cosmopolitan right" as "the department of jurisprudence concerned with people and peoples' sharing the world with

94 *Marcus Garvey's cosmopolitanism*

others, given the circumstance that this sharing is more or less inevitable, and likely to go drastically wrong, if not governed by juridical principles" (2010, 165). Garvey fought in resolute ways for blacks' acquisition of cosmopolitan right. For instance, he urged blacks in the United States to exercise their right to stand against racial violence and have pride, self-consciousness, and knowledge about Africa. In *Race Against Empire: Black Americans and Anticolonialism, 1937–1957*, Penny M. Von Eschen explains:

> It was Marcus Garvey and his Universal Negro Improvement Association that brought the notion of the links between the black world and Africa to a mass audience, creating a new working-class diaspora consciousness. By linking the entire black world to Africa and its members to one another, Garvey made the American Negro conscious of his African origins and created for the first time a feeling of international solidarity between Africans and peoples of African descent.
>
> (1997, 10)

Garvey also theorized this black cosmopolitanism in *The Philosophy* by representing Africa as the continent that will determine the future and development of the global black community. In his speech at the Second International Convention of Negroes, held in August 1921 in Liberty Hall, New York City, he exhorted blacks to assert that "we desire a freedom that will lift us to the common standard of all men" and that "we shall stop at nothing until there is a free and redeemed Africa" ("Speech Delivered at Liberty Hall," 95). Referring to one of the UNIA's slogans, he also declared: "We have pledged ourselves even unto the last drop of our sacred blood that Africa must be free" ("Speech Delivered at Liberty Hall, 95). These words suggest Garvey's use of Pan-Africanism as a black cosmopolitanism which resiliently struggles for Africa's liberation from colonialism. Yet a core aspect of Garvey's black cosmopolitanism is its denunciation of the colonial oppression that Diagne brought to Senegal during the 1920s.

In order to understand Garvey's conflictive relationships with Diagne, it is necessary to study their roots in the propaganda that the French mounted against the Jamaican to stanch his popularity in colonial Senegal. Garvey's influence in colonial Senegal is noticeable in the presence of Sierra Leonean Garveyites who profited from their passages in or immigration to the territory to promote the UNIA. According to Dramé, these Sierra Leonean migrants and UNIA activists in 1920s Senegal included John-Henri Farmer, Duck Thomas, Selim Mustapha Gueye, Alpha Renner, Ahmadou Jawarrah, Isaac Doherty, Clarence Randall, Winston Williams, and Venn Herni Adolph (1988, 49–50). Working under John Kamara's leadership, these migrants, who included shopkeepers, tailors, cola merchants, typists, and trading house employees, transmitted the UNIA's activities across West Africa (Dramé, 1988, 48–49). Through the help of individuals working on the British ship called Elder Dempster, Kamara spread Garveyite ideology

Marcus Garvey's cosmopolitanism   95

through Senegal and other parts of West Africa, such as Sierra Leone, Gambia, and Nigeria, by secretly circulating the *Negro World* in these colonies. Kamara was therefore a modern maroon who furtively eluded the French colonials while helping the UNIA to establish itself in Senegal. G.O. Olusanya explains:

> [T]he branch of the UNIA which was established at Rufisque in Senegal, as a result of the initiative of Sierra Leoneans such as Francis Webster, Farmer Dougherty, H.W. Wilson and John Kamara, became so active in disseminating the ideas of the parent body that the French colonial authorities became very worried, so much so that the members of the organization were kept under constant surveillance and the branch was in the end suppressed.
>
> (1994, 128)

However, while Garveyites in colonial Senegal tended to be Sierra Leoneans and Gambians, a few of them were born in the territory. Thus, according to Dramé, in 1922, a group of Senegalese men, including Diop Massylla, Ba Amadou, Louis Angrand, Joseph Gueye, Baye Diene, M'Baye William, Maurice Gueye, Moïse Diop, Fara Diop, and Alpha Guillabert, founded the *Comité pour l'action Sénégalaise* [Senegalese Action Committee] in Gorée (1988, 51). As Dramé also points out, Thiam has described the Committee as a group which donated 1400 French francs to Garvey's African Redemption Fund in 1922 (1988, 51). Ratified by ARTICLE XIV of the UNIA's Constitution, the African Redemption Fund was created in 1918 as a mechanism through which the organization encouraged "every member of the Negro race" to make a voluntary $5 contribution in order "to create a working capital for the organization and to advance the cause for the building up of Africa."[1] Based on the 1922 exchange rate (which was 0.82f to $1), the Senegalese Action Committee's contribution of 1400f amounted to $1707, which was a huge sum for Africans under colonial domination to collect.[2] Such a substantial contribution to UNIA's African redemption efforts shows the Senegalese Garveyites' dedication to an organization and a leader they perceived as meaningful in their destiny. One of these Senegalese Garveyites was Armand-Pierre Angrand, who created the *Comité pour l'action Sénégalaise*. Angrand was a descendant of a biracial (*métisse*) family from Saint-Louis, Senegal, and, ironically, Diagne's protégé. As a former World War I *tirailleur* who fought at Verdun and was wounded twice at war, Angrand later became involved in politics after his return home and served as a municipal councillor in 1923 before becoming mayor of Gorée from 1928 to 1932. He became Diagne's close friend and succeeded him as mayor of Dakar upon the deputy's death in 1934.[3]

Moreover, Angrand was the first leader of Le Comité d'études franco-africaines (CEFA) which, as Dieng suggests, aimed at "l'étude de toutes les questions concernant l'Afrique Noire, la création du Foyer franco-africain,

96   *Marcus Garvey's cosmopolitanism*

d'œuvres sociales, de groupements professionnels et de syndicats, l'organisation de la lutte contre les trusts coloniaux" [the study of all matters concerning black Africa and the creation of the Franco-African Foyer, social work, professional groups and trade unions, and the organization of the struggle against colonial trusts] (2011, 236). Angrand's leadership of an organization that explored major questions of black Africa and the struggle against colonial trusts indicates the influence of Garvey's radicalism in early twentieth-century Senegalese political culture. His devotion to Garveyism in a French colony in which anti-imperialism was severely punished was revolutionary. Yet this allegiance earned him the suspicion of colonials who perceived him as the Jamaican's supporter. The ninth volume of the UNIA Papers has an August 3, 1922, letter from Pierre Jean [Henri] Didelot [then Governor of Senegal] to the Governor-General of French West Africa, seeking "to obtain information" about "the native ANGRAND" of "38 rue Carnot in Dakar" to whom "6 packages containing tracts of anti-European propaganda," which "were to be distributed in our Colony," were addressed.[4] Another letter of Didelot to the Governor-General of FWA, dated post-August 1922, is more explicit about Angrand's support for the UNIA. Didelot writes:

> A search of his [Angrand's] home has led to the discovery of documents which prove that he is in correspondence with Marcus Garvey, as well as plans for the creation of a society called "the Senegalese Action Committee." The flyer distributed by this group is called "Appeal to all our racial brothers."[5]

Didelot's statements show the French colonials' perception of Angrand as a possible Garveyite who deserved monitoring and judicial action against him. Since he was the only member of the Angrand family who was accused of having ties with Garvey—though Johnson argues that the politician's brother, Joseph, also had Garveyite leanings (1997, 308)—Armand was subjected to the increasing scrutiny of a colonial police which perceived him as a nuisance to a French administrative establishment that desperately wanted to punish him despite his elite affiliations. This colonial disdain toward Angrand is apparent in Robert Hill's argument that, in December 1934, the "Former Diagne lieutenant Armand Angrand, who in 1922 was indicted by the French colonial authorities for his contacts with the UNIA, helps found the Parti Socialiste Sénégalais, which later becomes the Senegalese section of the French Socialist party" (Hill, 2006, clxi). Even if they did not incarcerate Angrand for his association with the UNIA, the French elite expressed deep contempt toward him and punished many of the organization's followers in Senegal. Hill explains:

> Following the accidental discovery of a registered-letter receipt with the address of the UNIA's headquarters in New York, colonial officials

Marcus Garvey's cosmopolitanism 97

launched wide-scale police searches and investigations that resulted in the detention of several UNIA supporters in Dakar and Rufisque and their eventual expulsion from Senegal. The French, however, were never able to apprehend the UNIA's elusive traveling commissioner, John Kamara, whose presence in Dakar and other parts of West Africa was confirmed by documents seized in the raids. Remaining UNIA activists in Senegal were thereafter kept under close police surveillance. French customs officials also reported discovering a bundle of *Negro World* issues addressed to Armand Angrand, a municipal councillor in Gorée, Senegal, whom the government believed to have been in correspondence with Garvey.

(1995, xlvii–xlviii)

Moreover, as Martin argues in *Marcus Garvey, Hero: A First Biography*, "The *Negro World* was banned throughout the French African colonies" (1983, 94). Such drastic measures show that the French took no chance with Garveyism when they fully noticed its growing influence in Senegal. Using Diagne's propaganda against Garvey, the French deployed another weapon against the Jamaican's clout in the colony. In *Blaise Diagne, Premier Député Africain*, Dieng says that after the Second Pan-African Congress, Diagne waged a vicious war against Garvey's "international Black Community" project because he was afraid of supporting a position that criticized the French colonial administration (1990, 133). Dieng also contends that Diagne attacked Garvey by describing his Pan-African theories as "dangerous utopias" that were beginning to have real influences on a few Senegalese intellectuals that colonial authorities had mostly accused as "Garveyist" and revoked (1990, 133). Therefore, as the only French deputy from West Africa, Diagne vowed to rid Africa of Garvey.

Incidentally, the French wanted Diagne to openly reject Garveyism in the way that president Charles Dunbar Burgess (C. D. B.) King, of Liberia, did for the American government. In an August 1921 article of *Les Annales Coloniales*, a reporter writes:

Il est donc certain, en tout cas, que la République de Liberia ne saurait devenir un foyer de propagande pour l'expulsion des blancs du continent africain . . . Mais nous croyons intéressant de signaler cette protestation énergique du président de la République de Liberia . . . Que va répondre Diagne (Blaise)?

[It is certain, in any case, that the Republic of Liberia cannot become a center of propaganda for the expulsion of whites from Africa . . . But it is interesting to note the energetic protest of the President of the Republic of Liberia . . . What is going to be the answer of Diagne (Blaise)?][6]

Therefore, the French expected Diagne to publicly challenge and discredit Garvey's growing influence in 1920s Africa, which they dreaded terribly.

98 Marcus Garvey's cosmopolitanism

Yet they were equally afraid of the growing influence of Garvey's nationalism in the United States and Liberia, as is visible in a passage from the September 14, 1921, issue of *Les Annales Coloniales*, entitled "Manifestation Américaine Pan-Noire," which reads:

> À New York, quinze-cents noirs ont défilé dans les rues du quartier Nord, précédés par une centaine d'automobiles environ, occupées par des femmes de couleur, manifestant à l'occasion de l'ouverture du congrès international des races noires du monde. Les manifestants portaient des drapeaux rouge vert et noir, couleurs internationales des nègres, et des bannières avec des inscriptions telles que: "L'Afrique pour les nègres!"

> [In New York, fifteen hundred blacks marched through the streets of the Northern quarter, preceded by about a hundred cars occupied by women of color, demonstrating on the occasion of the opening of the international congress of the black races of the world. Demonstrators wore red, green and black flags, international colors of negroes, and banners with inscriptions such as: "Africa for the blacks!"][7]

The statement suggests the real trepidation and shock that Garvey's "Africa for Africans" slogans created among French administrators who perceived it as a real threat to the profit, opulence, and unrestrained freedom they had received for centuries in Africa.

Moreover, Garvey's Pan-Africanist slogan was dreadful for colonials who associated the martial decorum and regalia of the UNIA's New York gatherings with Russian socialism. The following passage from the September 2, 1921, article of *La Dépêche Coloniale*, which describes the inaugural session of the congress's Paris meetings, reflects Diagne's association of Garveyism with communism:

> Dès ses premières paroles, il désavoua, en termes qui ne laissaient place à aucune ambigüité, les théories du noir Marcus Garvey. Il établit une comparaison entre la propagande faite par Garvey et le bolchévisme de Lénine; ce sont pour lui des tendances extrêmement dangereuses qui n'ont pour but que d'isoler des races et des peuples au seul profit d'ambitions personnelles. À ses yeux, le bolchévisme noir de Marcus Garvey ne pourra amener que ruine et dévastation, comme l'a malheureusement fait, en Russie, le bolchévisme jaune de Lénine.[8]

> [He began by disavowing, in clear and unambiguous terms, the ideas of the black American Marcus Garvey. He compared Garvey's propaganda with Lenin's Bolshevism; both are, he thinks, extremely dangerous tendencies, having as their only goal the isolation of races and peoples for the benefit of personal ambitions. In his view, the black

Marcus Garvey's cosmopolitanism 99

Bolshevism of Marcus Garvey can bring only ruin and devastation as, unfortunately, Lenin's yellow Bolshevism did in Russia].[9]

Diagne's reaction conveys his irrational and deceptive use of the claim of Bolshevist infiltration into France's colonies as an alibi for shielding the empire from Garveyism. Moreover, Diagne's association of Garveyism with Bolshevism aimed to discredit a movement that he did not understand. But, as Johnson explains, Diagne had other reasons for vilifying Garveyism as Bolshevism:

> [[A]fter the Russian Revolution [he] Diagne developed a fear of Bolshevism and preferred not to associate with Socialists. One reason for his attitude was the French lack of understanding of the Garvey movement—For several years the French believed Garvey was an agent of Moscow at work in the United States to help plan a negro revolution and to foment black American imperialism in the African colonies, which would possibly turn into a war of liberation.
>
> (1972, 174–175)

Incidentally, Du Bois expressed a similar aversion toward Garvey by associating him with Bolshevism and dangerous black radicalism, especially at the 1921 congress. Elliott M. Rudwick writes:

> DuBois found it necessary to make a public statement after it became known that Garvey had not been invited to the coming conclave [the 1921 Pan-African Congress], and the *Crisis* editor announced that the U.N.I.A. leader was ignored because his movement was "dangerous" and "impracticable."
>
> (1959, 425)

Du Bois and Diagne made a serious mistake by not inviting Garvey to the 1921 summit which was consistent with the UNIA's aim to connect Africa and the diaspora. By ostracizing Garvey and demeaning him, Du Bois and Diagne delegitimized the congress's claim of developing cosmopolitan inclusiveness and impartiality. Diagne and Du Bois might have realized their mistake since they later proposed a resolution to invite Garvey at the congress's next session. Yet Diagne did not seem enthusiastic about the proposition, as is apparent in the December 17, 1921, article in the *Negro World* in which Du Bois writes:

> I submitted a resolution which was rushed after having been refused by Mr. Diagne. In this resolution I requested that Marcus Garvey, having been charged without proof [of planning the removal of white Europeans from Africa and the establishment of three great African states] [;] be heard by the congress, which may ask him to do away with

100 *Marcus Garvey's cosmopolitanism*

whatever is considered dangerous in his policy. I intimated that it will be infamous on our part in the eyes of humanity to exclude a black man as Marcus Garvey from such a movement just because his ideas are different from ours.[10]

Even if Du Bois claims that he was willing to include Garvey in the 1921 congress, his previous complicity in Diagne's isolation of the Jamaican leader had already caused serious damages that maneuvering could not repair. This unavowed scheme led to Garvey's absence from the 1921 meeting, hampering the cosmopolitan claims of the convention's organizers and exposing their deep fear of the Jamaican's popularity. By justifying his disparagement of Garvey on anti-radicalism, Diagne, like Du Bois, revealed a vitriolic bias toward the Jamaican leader.

Fortunately, although he did not attend the 1919 and 1921 Pan-African congresses, Garvey was not less devoted to black liberation than its conveners were. Besides, the deliberations of both congresses resonated with his Pan-African aim to end Western global exploitation of blacks, let these people have the right to self-govern, develop education, and safely invest capital in their societies. It is therefore surprising that a reporter who commented on the 1919 congress, in the May 19, 1928, issue of the *Negro World*, did not point out these parallels between Garvey's disparagement of colonialism and the summit's resolutions. Instead, the reporter criticized the 1919 congress with the following statement: "Proceedings were moderate and reformist, steering clear of direct criticism of European colonial rule and in some cases pleading for better collaboration between African elites and colonial powers."[11] This declaration was made in 1928, a year after Garvey's imprisonment and removal from the United States had created deep aversion of UNIA followers toward Diagne. As a result of this injustice, many UNIA members disliked Diagne by perceiving him as a leader who had worked in tandem with Du Bois to prevent Garvey from being a spokesperson of the black world.

Diagne's dismissive attitude toward Garvey further appears in one of his speeches of the 1921 congress in which he depicts the Jamaican as a racial separatist. A summary of a part of Diagne's speech is as follows:

> Le président repousse les idées de M. Marcus Garvey, qui tendent à isoler la race noire. "C'est du temps et de la bonne volonté de ceux qui se chargeront de l'éducation des nègres que le congrès attend l'évolution de la race noire."[12]

> [The president rejects the ideas of Marcus Garvey which aim to isolate the black race. "It is through the time and good will of those who take care of the education of Negroes that the congress expects to see the evolution of the black race."]

Marcus Garvey's cosmopolitanism 101

Diagne's statement reflects his perception of blacks as people who cannot progress in civilization without the support of whites or members of other races. It is allegedly in defense of this cosmopolitan interracial cooperation that Diagne discredited Garvey as an enemy of the white race. From this perspective, Diagne, in agreement with Candace, repudiated Garvey's contention of "Africa for Africans!" and declared at the congress: "We do not hate the white race. What we seek is conciliation and collaboration. Our evolution and development depend upon relations with the white race. We would lose everything if we were isolated in Africa."[13]

By refusing to isolate Africans from Europeans, Diagne used the 1921 congress as an opportunity to reject Garvey's Pan-Africanism that French colonials regarded as racism and communism. It now appears that the colonial officers who accused Garvey of being an agent of Russian communism and socialism reached this conclusion after shoddy intelligence gathering. Johnson explains:

> Through a mistranslation, the French thought a Garvey subsidiary organization was the African Communists League instead of the African Communities League. A witch hunt for Garvey agents, believed to be Bolshevists, was carried on for the next two years in French West Africa.
>
> (1972, 175)

If France's colonial claim about Garvey was false, then its descendants owe apologies to a leader that their forefathers also vilified as a racist and an agent of German imperialism. Knowing that such charges were untrue, Garvey, who faced similar accusations in the United States, suffered personal trauma that probably contributed to his short life span.

However, Garvey did not delay in replying to Diagne's criticisms. He opposed Diagne's cosmopolitanism by demonstrating how France's relations with Senegal were based on exploitation rather than a desire to help Africans achieve freedom. In a speech delivered at Liberty Hall, New York City, on November 25, 1922, Garvey laments the heavy price that 2,100,000 black men from Africa, the United States, and the West Indies paid for France's freedom from Germany's invasion during World War I only to be excluded from the talks about world peace and prosperity that the victory against tyranny had inspired (*The Philosophy*, Vol II, 99). In the same address, Garvey asserts:

> When the white men faltered and fell back on their battle lines, at the Marne and at Verdun, when they ran away from the charge of the German hordes, the black hell fighters stood before the cannonade, stood before the charge, and again they shouted, "There will be a hot time in the old town to-night."
>
> (*The Philosophy*, Vol II, 99)

102 *Marcus Garvey's cosmopolitanism*

Unfortunately, many of these combats resulted in German soldiers' bloody slaughter of *tirailleurs*.

While acknowledging black soldiers' massive participation in France's liberation war from Germany, Garvey's statement denounces the hypocrisy of a Western world that betrayed the cosmopolitan solidarity that these combatants expressed in foreign trenches only to be forgotten after the upheaval. Garvey was dismayed by the lack of receipt for the heavy prices *tirailleurs* paid for a war which finally brought the freedom of whites only. Regarding the black soldiers' contributions to the war as unpaid African benevolence, Garvey develops the logical thesis that black cosmopolitanism should begin at home. He writes:

> If we [blacks] have been liberal minded enough to give our life's blood in France, in Mesopotamia and elsewhere, fighting for the white man, whom we have always assisted, surely we have not forgotten to fight for ourselves, and when the time comes that the world will again give Africa an opportunity for freedom, surely 400,000,000 black men will march out on the battle plains of Africa, under the colors of the red, the black and the green.
>
> (*The Philosophy*, Vol II, 100)

Indeed, black people's participation in World War I did not bring them freedom at home or abroad. For instance, at the end of the war, Africans who wanted to be recognized as cosmopolitans that had helped free the world from totalitarianism were asked to give up their weapons and return to the colonies without asking for independence. Likewise, African American and Caribbean soldiers were told to go back home without demanding civil rights. The Westerners' dismissal of blacks stemmed from a fear that these populations' realization of their equality to whites during World War I would lead them to demand freedom. Dreading this possibility, the French quickly disarmed returning *tirailleurs* for fear of rebellion in the colonies. As Garvey suggests, the presence of African veterans in France after the war revealed not the French's love for blacks, but their fear that the soldiers could use their newly gained knowledge of Europeans to start a revolution against them (*The Philosophy*, Vol II, 113–114). These statements show that Garvey was a stern enemy of colonialism.

Unfortunately, Garvey's rebuttal against Diagne often veered toward purism. For instance, he lampooned Diagne's representation of himself, at the 1921 congress, as a "French first" before he is "black."[14] This was a statement that the Senegalese deputy had made.[15] Yet Garvey viewed this declaration as Diagne's prioritizing of his ties to the French empire over his relations with blacks. Since Diagne had privileges that were denied to the majority of blacks in the colonies, Garvey would have won the arguments if he had simply condemned the deputy's undivided loyalty to the French empire as racial treason. The problem is that Garvey reverted to biological

Marcus Garvey's cosmopolitanism   103

essentialism by ridiculing Diagne with the unpersuasive theory that nationality cannot precede racial identity. In a speech that he gave at Liberty Hall, in New York, on September 7, 1921, Garvey said:

> Now, let us go back to the [n]atural existence of the individual. I had a black mother and a black father. Can you imagine that they could have conceived me as a British first before I was conceived as their offspring? (Laughter.) Just argue that out for yourselves. How impossible it is for a man to be first of a nationality before he was completely born. He was part of a man and a part of God's own image before he was brought to see the light of day, therefore he must first be of his race before he could be of his nation.[16]

Garvey's reaction to Diagne's devotion to France is counterproductive, because it essentializes the Senegalese leader's self-identifications as "French" before he is "black" as a preference of the "white" race over the "black" one. By representing race in such a divisive fashion, Garvey was biologically deterministic since he used science and religion to prove that racial self is an inborn character that precedes nationality, when other variants, including genetic changes, class, and culture can influence it. Furthermore, Garvey misunderstood Diagne's conceptualizing of his complex heritage since the deputy only meant to value his French identity first before treasuring his blackness. Ignoring the nuanced meaning of the Senegalese deputy's argument, Garvey interpreted it as Diagne's preference of France over his blackness. Diagne would have perceived Garvey's argument as being contrived since he equated a human's worth with intelligence, not skin color.

Another context in which Garvey lost the argument during his attacks on Diagne was miscegenation. Unlike Diagne, Garvey was racially prejudiced. In contrast to Diagne, who was married to a French white woman, Garvey was wedded to a black woman. Bringing this personal choice to the public realm, Garvey derided the deputy for engaging in interracial unions.[17] Garvey's dismissive attitude toward miscegenation suggests his intrinsic racial prejudices that often led him to envision the relations between blacks and whites in terms of biological polarities. Such prejudices hurt Garvey because they helped his critics label him as an essentialist and fanatic radical. This perspective has survived in black studies scholarship which usually identifies Garvey as an antithesis of Du Bois and Alain Locke, who are perceived as multiculturalists and cosmopolitan intellectuals who opposed racial separatism and embraced European cultures.[18] In this vein, Robert E. Washington alludes to critics' frequent portrayals of Garvey as an opposite of Claude McKay, who did "not celebrate racial pride or promote racial separatism" and who, unlike the UNIA's leader, strongly believed "that the great ideas of the West transcended racial concerns" (2001, 76).

Another criticism of Garvey against Diagne occurred in an October 2, 1921, speech that the Jamaican leader delivered in New York. In the address,

Garvey derided Diagne's political record and accused him for the tragic loss of *tirailleurs* in World War I. Garvey said:

> He [Diagne] went among the French colonial Negroes and I believe through his instrumentality over one million Negroes were recruited in Africa for France and sent over to France, and over 250,000 of them died in France and Flanders. They were used as shock troops, and they were killed by the hundreds of thousands. But they saved France.[19]

Garvey was right in his critique of Diagne's role in the deployment of thousands of *tirailleurs* who were killed in France and Flanders. Such a criticism helped Garvey show that Diagne was naive to believe that the French would reciprocate the cosmopolitanism that *tirailleurs* expressed toward them. The French returned these *tirailleurs*' sacrifices with racism and primitivizing, indicating Diagne's gullibility and instrumentality in a war that saved the métropole while killing tens of thousands of Africans.

Garvey's critical view of Diagne also stemmed from the different contexts out of which the two leaders had evolved. Diagne was raised by "*gens de couleur*" [biracial people] who instilled European cultures into him from a young age. Moreover, Diagne was the product of a hybrid and elite political culture that had social, economic, and political privileges denied to most blacks in colonial Senegal. This elite experience molded him into a fanatic

Figure 3.1 "Corps de tirailleurs sénégalais. Carte photo de source allemande, 1916" [Bodies of Senegalese tirailleurs. German source Photo Card, 1916].

Collections Eric Deroo.

Marcus Garvey's cosmopolitanism   105

believer in the superiority and universality of French civilization. In addition, as Dieng observes, "Diagne was an inheritor of the Enlightenment. He believed in the emancipating virtues of education. He believed that instruction was the major tool of liberation of Black people" (1990, 158). Unfortunately, Diagne was unable to radically organize this liberation due to his elite background and obsession with French civilization that somewhat alienated him from African masses and cultures. Noting Diagne's self-deprecating posture about Africa, Louise Delafosse writes:

> Mon père était toujours aussi opposé à l'assimilation dont Diagne faisait son cheval de bataille. On en arrivait à cette situation assez étonnante : c'était mon père, le Blanc, qui invitait les Noirs à revaloriser leurs coutumes propres, leurs traditions ancestrales, les plus belles pages de leur histoire; et c'était Diagne, le Noir, qui les incitait à s'intégrer dans la civilisation et le système européens.

> [The situation was startling. It was my father, the white man, who was encouraging Africans to reassert the value of their own customs, their ancestral traditions, the most beautiful pages of their history; and it was Diagne, the black man, who was inciting Africans to assimilate themselves into the civilization and system of Europeans].[20]

> (1976, 311)

Therefore, Diagne suffered from a cultural inferiority complex although such a psychological dysfunction did not lead him to dislike people because of their race.

By contrast, Garvey grew up poor and developed a combative attitude toward colonial whites who had subjected most Jamaican blacks of his generation to poverty. Born in 1887 in St. Ann's Bay, Jamaica, Garvey was the youngest of eleven children who confronted a difficult childhood marked by a decaying peasant economy, hurricanes, and undermined family bonds of affection (Stein, 1986, 24). Like most Jamaican children of his generation, Garvey received modern school education until the sixth grade only. In the British colonial school, he learned about racial separation, prejudice, religion and history, all things that helped shape his consciousness (Lewis, 1988, 20–21). At the age of sixteen, he became an apprentice printer in Kingston, Jamaica. Lawrence Levine writes: "It was in Kingston that Garvey became impressed with the power of the oratory" (1993, 109). During the printers' strike of 1907, Garvey was blacklisted for being the only foreman who supported the workers. His early confrontation with labor exploitation instilled in him an interest in political organization and struggle (Levine, 1993, 110). Garvey's unique radical life-trajectory later influenced his scathing criticisms against Diagne's undivided loyalty to France.

Garvey's critical views of Diagne mostly stemmed from political reasons, specifically, his perception of the deputy as an instrument of French colonial

106 *Marcus Garvey's cosmopolitanism*

propaganda. In his editorial letter to the *Negro World*, written on November 21, 1922, Garvey writes:

> Everybody knows that Diagne is but the puppet of France, like the Jack-in-the-box as France pulls the string he dances to the amusement of the gallery. This kind of propaganda stuff has been long exploded. Diagne must understand that neither France nor himself has a lease on Africa.[21]

Garvey was right in his portrayal of Diagne's role as France's marionette because he knew that the métropole was pleased with the deputy only when he provided them with *tirailleurs*, forced laborers, and propaganda. Whenever Diagne strayed from this mission, he was severely punished by France. Such was the case when the deputy co-organized the 1921 congress with Du Bois. Garvey explains:

> When Dr. Du Bois went to Paris to hold his Pan-African Congress, this great black French patriot [Diagne] was selected by Du Bois as President of the Congress, and immediately the French papers attacked this black man whom they had as it were honored in giving a battleship to take him to his native land to recruit black people to die for Frenchmen. They said: "We are surprised that you whom we love so much, for whom we did so much, should link up yourself with a proposition of 'Africa for the Africans.' Why you are ungrateful after all we have done for you; that is the thanks you are giving us."[22]

Garvey was, thus, aware of France's deceptive strategy of discrediting Diagne by likening him to black radicals or, in other cases, pitting him against other black leaders. Moreover, Garvey knew the dilemma Diagne faced by privileging his Frenchness over his race at a time when the métropole often classified him as a proponent of Pan-African liberation from colonialism. For instance, as Johnson argues, "when the agents of Marcus Garvey surfaced in West Africa, although there was not a shred of proof, [Martial Henri] Merlin's propaganda mill insinuated that Diagne was linked to Garvey" (1997, 309). Merlin was then the Governor-General of French West Africa. It was hypocritical for the French colonials to ask Diagne to attack Garvey in 1921 when they already perceived the parliamentarian as a potential radical. The French likened Diagne to Garvey because the former was asking for more naturalization and accommodation for *originaires* who fought for France during World War I. Another reason for the French's association of Diagne with Garvey was their fear of the Jamaican's ability to radicalize a deputy whom they perceived as having Pan-Africanist leanings.

The French's reservations against Diagne also originated from their disapproval of his ploy to speed assimilationism because they blamed him for continuing to unnecessarily supply the métropole with *tirailleurs* in the

Marcus Garvey's cosmopolitanism 107

1920s. In an article entitled "Pitié pour nos *tirailleurs*," Eugene Devaux proposed the repatriation of many of these *tirailleurs* from France to their homelands and their replacement with white troops. He writes: "Des troupes blanches doivent immédiatement relever les troupes noires que l'on renverra en Afrique où c'est leur place, et d'où, à mon avis, on n'aurait jamais dû les faire sortir" [White troops should immediately replace black troops that we will return to Africa, where they belong and, in my opinion, should never have been taken out] (Devaux, 1923, 1). Devaux's declarations corroborate Garvey's caricature of Diagne as a puppet of a hypocritical French empire. Here was Devaux writing in 1923 in an attempt to drive *tirailleurs* out of the "mother country" they helped liberate from Germany. Devaux's call for a resettlement of *tirailleurs* to West Africa was part of a French media and political campaign that he was running since October 1921 against Diagne's call for the betterment of the conditions of *originaires* of Senegal. Writing on October 28, 1921, in *Les Annales Coloniales*, Devaux opposed Diagne's proposal by rallying with Gabriel Angoulvant (then Commissaire de la République and former Interim Governor General of AOF during the war) against it. In agreement with Angoulvant, Devaux argued that the real victims of injustice were the Europeans who were "submergé par le flot des *originaires*" [overwhelmed by the flow of *originaires*] and "le danger du retour des anciens mobilisés dans leurs villages" [the danger of the return of the former mobilized to their villages] (1921, 1). While pretending to like *tirailleurs* who lived outside the four communes of Senegal, Devaux claimed that they suffered less than the Europeans who could be overtaken by the flow of naturalization which could grow from 25,000 in 1921 to 50,000 tomorrow, and possibly 100,000 afterwards—an increase, he maintained, that would delay the evolution of both *originaires* and *sujets* in the colony (1921, 1).

Focusing on *originaires*, Devaux also contended: "Chacun sait que ces hommes sont incapables de faire évoluer d'une façon sage ce pays où leur nombre leur assurera la direction suprême. Leur évolution n'est possible qu'en collaboration avec la race blanche" [Everyone knows that these men are incapable of developing this country in an intelligent way and assure supreme leadership accorded to their future number. Their evolution is possible only through collaboration with the white race] (1921, 1). Devaux was hypocritical because, like Angoulvant, he was unwilling to extend citizenship and full cosmopolitan rights and recognition to *tirailleurs*. By dismissing Diagne's proposal, Devaux confirmed Garvey's portrayal of the Senegalese as France's puppet. Like Devaux, Diagne's white colleagues frequently seemed to want to get rid of him. Such was the case when they accused Diagne of corruption in order to damage his political career. This character assassination is visible in an op-ed in *Les Annales Coloniales*, entitled "Diagne (Blaise) et Cie," written on June 3, 1921, in which one anonymous author accused Diagne and his immediate entourage of being corrupt leaders who were squandering away the colonies' funds.[23]

108 *Marcus Garvey's cosmopolitanism*

Knowing that he, too, was fighting for freedom from the colonizer's domain, Garvey somewhat understood Diagne's dilemma. In the 1920s, Garvey faced in the United States a plight similar to Diagne's when he took on the cause of social justice for African Americans. When Garvey demanded cosmopolitan equality for these blacks, racist plans to exterminate him were rapidly deployed. For instance, J. Edgar Hoover led an FBI campaign that accused Garvey of fraudulent activities in the UNIA, curtailing the Jamaican's activism in the United States. As Levine argues, in January 1922, Garvey and three of his associates were arrested and, in February, indicted "on twelve counts of fraudulent use of the mails to sell Black Star stocks" (1993, 134). Garvey was tried in June 1923 and imprisoned until December 1927 when he was deported as an undesirable alien. Therefore, like Diagne, Garvey was ultimately destroyed by a racist and imperial Western power that perceived him as a threat to the social and economic exploitation of blacks.

Moreover, in spite of their divergences, both Garvey and Diagne fought for black freedom within confines of racial segregation. Garvey sought Pan-African freedom within imperialist limits that white America established for blacks, while Diagne struggled for African sovereignty in colonialist restraints that France imposed on these populations. For example, when Diagne asked him for the permission to hold the First Pan-African Congress in Paris, Clemenceau agreed on colonialist conditions. Jean Suret-Canale explains: "Clemenceau, enchanté de cette occasion de faire pièce aux Américains, laissa faire et encouragea Diagne à y participer pour y chanter les louanges de la politique française. 'Ne le criez pas sur les toits dit-il à Diagne, mais allez-y'" [Clemenceau was pleased to have this opportunity to put the Americans in their place, and not only allowed it to take place but encouraged Diagne to take part and sing the praises of French policy. "Don't just proclaim it to the world in general," he said to Diagne, "but go to the congress itself"] (1957, 559–560). Defending French national policy in a summit that aimed to foster black transnational self-determination from the West was a delicate task. However Diagne emerged somewhat victorious from the meeting, because he partly reached out to the black world outside of Africa even if he served France's propaganda. Risking Clemenceau's reprobation, Diagne used the 1921 congress to develop his own Pan-Africanism. His subtle radicalism is apparent in his representation of the convention as a search for a private space where blacks could discuss their challenges in a liberal and democratic manner. A passage from a summary of Diagne's speech reads:

> En ouvrant la séance, M. Diagne tient à faire ressortir toute l'importance du congrès ... on pourra établir un programme suffisamment vaste pour que chacun y puisse adhérer et travailler utilement au bénéfice de la race noire ... De nouveau M. Diagne parle du projet de réclamer

Marcus Garvey's cosmopolitanism   109

l'Afrique pour que la race noire isolée du monde s'y organise et opère sa rénovation.

[In opening the session, Mr. Diagne emphasized the importance of the congress . . . . it will be possible to establish a broad enough program that everyone will be able to support it and work usefully together for the benefit of the black race . . . . Mr. Diagne spoke of the project of reclaiming Africa for the black race, which would be isolated from the world, so that the black race can organize there and effect its renewal].[24]

Even if he denied this affinity, Diagne's quest of Pan-African collaboration for the emancipation of the "black race" put him in Garvey's ideological camp. Yet Diagne refused to acknowledge this relationship due to many factors. One of these reasons was that Diagne was so entrenched in French cultural assimilation policy that he considered any ideology that was publicly critical toward the métropole as dangerous. Relatedly, Diagne's close ties to imperialism prevented him from recognizing Garvey's cosmopolitanism. Moreover, while Garvey wanted to gain freedom immediately, Diagne sought to achieve it incrementally. In this vein, Diagne was also a fractional Pan-Africanist even if he worked within the structures of French imperialism to weaken the métropole's dominance. Recognizing this Pan-Africanism that could have cemented the relations between Diagne and Garvey, Johnson observes:

Si Diagne et Garvey s'étaient rencontrés, il est probable que le malentendu aurait été éclairci. Diagne a donc aidé à lancer l'idée d'un mouvement pan-africain, parce qu'il s'intéressait à un mouvement pan-noir; mais Diagne voyait plus de progrès sous un Gouvernement français qu'ailleurs.

[If Diagne and Garvey had met, it is likely that the misunderstanding between them would have cleared up. Diagne helped launch the idea of a pan-African movement because he was interested in a pan-black movement; however, he saw more progress under a French Government than elsewhere.]

(1974, 47)

Johnson's comments show that the rift between Diagne and Garvey stemmed from a difficult context in which both France and the Senegalese misunderstood and feared the Jamaican. The remarks also show that Diagne was a complex black leader whose relationships with pan-Africanism were influenced by his complicated position in a colonial world in which lack of familiarity with Garvey made him lead France's vicious campaign against the Jamaican despite the ideologies they shared.

Ultimately, Diagne's Pan-Africanism and cosmopolitanism were thin in comparison with Garvey's since they did not inspire him to openly denounce

110 *Marcus Garvey's cosmopolitanism*

French colonialism or strongly embrace black struggle for autonomy and equality. Unlike Diagne, Garvey had the resolve and faith in the possibility of a free and independent Africa that was not obligated to mirror the West or surrender to its power. Being controlled by the French colonial administration, Diagne lacked the impetus of Garvey's Pan-Africanism and, thus, rejected the Jamaican's "Africa for the Africans" ideology as radicalism and Bolshevism. In doing so, Diagne surrendered to the colonial pressures that France put on him by expecting him to rid Senegal of Garvey. Resisting Diagne's propaganda, Garvey challenged the deputy's dubious role in the French empire in radical ways while indirectly influencing a few Senegalese to mobilize against colonialism. As is visible in the UNIA's presence in colonial Senegal, Garvey played an important role in the dominion's history by inspiring a few of its leaders to embrace the idea of Pan-African unity. As I will show in forthcoming chapters, Garvey's impact in Africa was more far-reaching, since the Jamaican also influenced other Francophone African leaders such as Touvalou and Lamine Senghor who also deployed radical resistances against Diagne's cosmopolitan and colonialist propagandas.

Bibliography

Adefuye, Adebowale. "Marcus Garvey and Nigeria." In *Garvey: His Work and Impact*, edited by Rupert Lewis and Patrick Bryan, 189–198. Trenton, NJ: Africa World Press, 1991.

"Africa for Africans! Is Not Negro Slogan." In *The Marcus Garvey and Universal Negro Improvement Association Papers*, Vol. 4, edited by Robert Hill, 32. Los Angeles: University of California Press, 1985.

Angrand, Jean-Luc. *Céleste ou le temps des Signares*. Sarcelles, France: Éditions Anne Pépin, 2006.

"Article in La Dépêche Coloniale et Maritime [Paris, 4 September 1921]. The Pan-Black Congress: Two Opposing Doctrines." *The Marcus Garvey and Universal Negro Improvement Association Papers*, Vol. 4, edited by Robert Hill, 176–182. Los Angeles: University of California Press, 1995.

"At the Pan-African Congress: 'Africa for the Africans... Bolshevik Talk!' Replies Mr. Diagne.'" *The Marcus Garvey and Universal Negro Improvement Association Papers*, Vol. 4, edited by Robert Hill, 158–159. Los Angeles: University of California Press, 1995.

"Au Congrès Pan-Noir ... 'L'Afrique aux Africains', a dit Marcus Garvey ... 'Langage de bolshevik !' réplique M. Diagne." *La Dépêche Coloniale et Maritime*, September 2, 1921: 1.

Cheah, Pheng. "The Cosmopolitical—Today." *Cosmopolitics: Thinking and Feeling beyond the Nation*, edited by Pheng Cheah and Bruce Robbins, 20–41. Minneapolis: University of Minnesota Press, 1998.

Colby, Frank Moore and Talcott Williams. *The New International Encyclopaedia*. New York: Dodd, Mead and Company, 1927.

"Constitution of the Universal Negro Improvement Association." In *Apropos of Africa: Sentiments of American Negro Leaders on Africa*, edited by Adelaide Cromwell Hill and Martin Kilson, 238–239. Garden City, NY: Anchor Books, 1971.

Marcus Garvey's cosmopolitanism 111

Contee, Clarence Garner. *W. E. B Du Bois and African Nationalism: 1914–1945.* Washington, DC: The American University, 1969.

Cornevin, Robert. *Hommes et destins (dictionnaire biographique d'Outre-mer),* Tome 9, *Afrique noire.* Paris: Académie des sciences d'Outre-Mer, 1989.

Delafosse, Louise. *Maurice Delafosse: Le Berrichon conquis par l'Afrique.* Paris: Société française d'histoire d'outre-mer, 1976.

Devaux, Eugene. "Pitié pour nos tirailleurs." *Annales Coloniales,* December 7, 1923: 1.

——. "Politique Noire." *Les Annales Coloniales,* October 28, 1921: 1.

"Diagne (Blaise) et Cie." *Les Annales Coloniales,* June 3, 1921: 1.

Dickerson, Debra J. *The End of Blackness.* New York: Pantheon Books, 2004.

Dieng, Amady Aly. *Blaise Diagne, premier député africain. Afrique Contemporaine,* Vol. 7, edited by Ibrahima Baba Kaké. Paris: Editions Chaka, 1990.

——. *L'Histoire des organisations d'étudiants africains en France (1900–1950).* Paris: L'Harmattan, 2011.

Dramé, Aly. L'impact du mouvement Garveyiste et la réaction de l'administration coloniale au Sénégal. B.A. thesis, Université Cheikh Anta Diop de Dakar, 1988.

Du Bois, W. E. B. "Pan-African Congress Adopted a Resolution to Invite Marcus Garvey to Next Session to Explain Aims and Objects of the U.N.I.A. Did You Know That?" *The Marcus Garvey and Universal Negro Improvement Association Papers,* Vol. 4, edited by Robert Hill, 276–281. Los Angeles: University of California Press, 1985.

Eschen, Penny M. Von. *Race Against Empire: Black Americans and Anticolonialism, 1937–1957.* Ithaca, NY: Cornell University Press, 1997.

Friedel, Tania. *Racial Discourse and Cosmopolitanism in Twentieth-Century African American Writing.* New York: Routledge, 2008.

Garvey, Marcus. "Defense of Ku Klux." In *The Marcus Garvey and Universal Negro Improvement Association Papers,* Vol. 4, edited by Robert Hill, 187–188. Los Angeles: University of California Press, 1995.

——. "Editorial Letter by Marcus Garvey in the Negro World [New York, November 21, 1922]." In *The Marcus Garvey and Universal Negro Improvement Association Papers,* Vol. 9, edited by Robert Hill, 694–696. Los Angeles: University of California Press, 1995.

——. "Liberty Hall, New York Crowded to Doors: Greet Marcus Garvey on Return from Boston." In *The Marcus Garvey and Universal Negro Improvement Association Papers,* Vol. 2, edited by Robert Hill, 241–59. Los Angeles: University of California Press, 1983.

——. *The Philosophy and Opinions of Marcus Garvey, or Africa for Africans,* Vol. 1 and 2, edited by Amy Jacques-Garvey and Tony Martin. Dover, MA: The Majority Press, 1986.

——. "The Principles of the Universal Negro Improvement Association." Speech Delivered at Liberty Hall, New York City, U.S. November 25, 1922. In *The Philosophy and Opinions of Marcus Garvey or Africa for the Africans,* Vol. 2, edited by Amy Jacques-Garvey and Tony Martin, 93–100. Dover, MA: The Majority Press, 1986.

——. "Speech by Marcus Garvey. [New York, October 2, 1921]." *The Marcus Garvey and Universal Negro Improvement Association Papers,* Vol. 4, edited by Robert Hill, 97–100. Los Angeles: University of California Press, 1985.

——. "Speech Delivered at Liberty Hall N. Y. C. During Second International Convention of Negroes August 1921." In *The Philosophy and Opinions of Marcus*

112 *Marcus Garvey's cosmopolitanism*

Garvey or Africa for the Africans, Vol. I, edited by Amy Jacques-Garvey and Tony Martin, 93–97. Dover, MA: The Majority Press, 1986.

Goyal, Yogita. *Romance, Diaspora, and Black Atlantic Literature*. Cambridge: Cambridge University Press, 2010.

Grant, Colin. *Negro with a Hat: The Rise and Fall of Marcus Garvey*. Oxford: Oxford University Press, 2008.

Hill, Robert "Chronology." In *The Marcus Garvey and Universal Negro Improvement Association Papers*, Vol. 10, edited by Robert Hill, cxxxvii–clxx. Los Angeles: University of California Press, 2006.

——. "Introduction." In *The Marcus Garvey and Universal Negro Improvement Association Papers*, Vol. 4, edited by Robert Hill, xlv–lii. Los Angeles: University of California Press, 1995.

——, ed. *The Marcus Garvey and Universal Negro Improvement Association Papers*, Vol. 4, 99. Note 1. Los Angeles: University of California Press, 1985.

Hill, Robert, ed. *The Marcus Garvey and Universal Negro Improvement Association Papers*, Vol. 7. Los Angeles: University of California Press, 1990, 183.

Hopquin, Benoît. *Ces noirs qui ont fait la France*. Paris: Calmann-Lévy, 2009.

Johnson, G. Wesley, Jr. "Discours de Monsieur Wesley Johnson." In *Blaise Diagne: Sa vie, son œuvre*, edited by Obèye Diop, 33-49. Dakar: Les Editions des Trois Fleuves, 1974.

——. "The Rivalry between Diagne and Merlin for Political Mastery of French West Africa." *AOF: réalités et héritages–Tome 1–2e partie*, edited by Charles Becker, Saliou Mbaye, and Ibrahima Thioub, 303–314. Dakar: Direction des archives du Sénégal, 1997.

——. "The Senegalese Urban Elite, 1900–1945." In *Africa & the West: Intellectual Responses to European Culture*, edited by Philip D. Curtin, 139–188. Madison: University of Wisconsin Press, 1972.

Jones, Hilary. *The Métis of Senegal: Urban Life and Politics in French West Africa*. Bloomington: Indiana University Press, 2013.

"Le Congrès Pan-Noir: Deux Théories en Présence." *La Dépêche Coloniale et Maritime*, September 6, 1921: 1.

"Le Congrès Pan-Noir." *Revue des Questions Coloniales et Maritimes* 486, no. 46 (July–September 1921): 122–123.

Levine, Lawrence. *The Unpredictable Past: Explorations in American Cultural History*. New York: Oxford University Press, 1993.

Lewis, Rupert. *Marcus Garvey: Anti-Colonial Champion*. Trenton, NJ: Africa World Press, 1988.

"Manifestation Américaine Pan-Noire" *Les Annales Coloniales*, September 14, 1921: 2.

Marable, Manning. *W. E. B. Du Bois: Black Radical Democrat*. Boulder, CO: Paradigm Publishers, 1986.

Martin, Tony. *Race First: The Ideological and Organizational Struggles of Marcus Garvey and the Universal Negro Improvement Association*. Westport: Greenwood Press, 1976.

——. *Marcus Garvey, Hero: A First Biography*. Dover, MA: The Majority Press, 1983.

Moore, Brenda. *To Serve My Country, To Serve My Race: The Story of the only African American WACS Stationed Overseas During World War II*. New York: New York University Press, 1996.

Marcus Garvey's cosmopolitanism 113

Moore, Jacqueline M. *Booker T. Washington, W.E.B. Du Bois, and the Struggle for Racial Uplift.* Wilmington, DE: Scholarly Resources Inc., 2003.

Nwankwo, Ifeoma Kiddoe. *Black Cosmopolitanism: Racial Consciousness and Transnational Identity in the Nineteenth-Century Americas.* Philadelphia: University of Pennsylvania Press, 2005.

Olusanya, G.O. "Garvey and Nigeria." In *Garvey: Africa, Europe, the Americas,* edited by Rupert Lewis and Maureen Warner-Lewis, 121–134. Trenton, NJ: Africa World Press, 1994.

"Pierre Jean Didelot to Governor-General of French West Africa." In *The Marcus Garvey and Universal Negro Improvement Association Papers,* Vol. 4, edited by Robert Hill, 557. Los Angeles: University of California Press, 1995.

"Qu'en pense Diagne (Blaise)." *Les Annales Coloniales,* August 12, 1921: 1.

"Report by Pierre Jean Henri Didelot to Governor-General of French West Africa." In *The Marcus Garvey and Universal Negro Improvement Association Papers,* Vol. 4, edited by Robert Hill, 581–584. Los Angeles: University of California Press, 1995.

Rudwick, Elliott M. "DuBois versus Garvey: Race Propagandists at War." *The Journal of Negro Education* 28, no. 4 (Autumn 1959): 421–429.

Skinner, Elliott P. "Ralph Bunch and the Decolonization of African Studies: The Paradox of Power, Morality, and Scholarship." In *Trustee for the Human Community: Ralph J. Bunche, the United Nations, and the Decolonization of Africa,* edited by Robert Hill and Edmond J. Keller, 42–68. Athens: Ohio University Press, 2010.

Stein, Judith. *The World of Marcus Garvey: Race and Class in Modern Society.* Baton Rouge. Louisiana State University Press, 1986.

Suret-Canale, Jean. *Afrique Noire: L'Ère Coloniale, 1900–1945.* Paris, Éditions Sociales, 1957.

The Emergency Tariff: And Its Effects on Cattle and Beef, Sheep and Mutton, Wool, Pork, and Miscellaneous Meats. Tariff Information Series, No. 29. Washington, DC: Government Printing Office, 1922.

Waldron, Jeremy. "What is Cosmopolitan?" In *The Cosmopolitanism Reader,* edited by Garrett Wallace Brown and David Held, 163–175. Cambridge, UK: Polity, 2010.

Walters, Ronald W. *Pan Africanism in the African Diaspora: An Analysis of Modern Afrocentric Political Movements.* 1993. Detroit: Wayne State University Press, 1997.

Washington, Robert E. *The Ideologies of African American Literature: From the Harlem Renaissance to the Black Nationalist Revolt.* Lanham, MD: Rowman & Littlefield Publishers, 2001.

4 Kojo Touvalou-Houénou's cosmopolitanism, anticolonialism, and relations with Marcus Garvey

Kojo Touvalou-Houénou and Marcus Garvey were similar in many respects although their cosmopolitanisms differed. Both leaders were strongly devoted to the liberation of Senegalese and other Africans from French colonialism. Moreover, both intellectuals desired the West's extension of cosmopolitanism to blacks worldwide. Yet, both Touvalou and Garvey sometimes lost faith in this dream and optimism when they reassessed their fascination with France's cosmopolitan tradition in light of the empire's racist treatment of Africans. Touvalou's rejection of French cosmopolitanism occurred in the 1920s, during the heyday of his Pan-Africanism, when he built strong ties with Garvey. During this period, Touvalou became increasingly radicalized and akin to the Jamaican who also condemned France for having denied integration to West Africans who had suffered to free it from the atrocities of World War I. Other connections between Touvalou and Garvey are apparent in the similar ways in which racist and colonialist forces finally curtailed their activisms and probably precipitated their premature deaths.

Yet, in spite of the convergences between them, Touvalou and Garvey diverged on the role that race played in their liberation ideologies. While Garvey's Pan-Africanist critique of Western cosmopolitanism was usually based on an essentialist view of race, Touvalou's was often founded on a hybrid and assimilationist conception of this idea. Consequently, Touvalou generally placed himself in a French cosmopolitan and assimilationist framework that partly alienated him from Garvey's Pan-Africanism. However, the differences between the two leaders were trumped by the Pan-African struggles that they shared. Also, both leaders saw each other as an opportunity to enhance their ideological ties and individual causes.

Touvalou was born on April 25, 1887, in Porto-Novo, Benin (formerly Dahomey) (Zinsou and Zouménou, 2004, 44). This is a state-city that fell under French domination by the end of the nineteenth century. Touvalou was the nephew of Béhanzin, the late nineteenth-century emperor of Dahomey, "who was deported to Martinique after his kingdom was conquered by France, and who later returned from exile to die in Algeria" ("Convention Report," 750). Touvalou was also a former *tirailleur* who had previously studied law in France and learned to speak French, German, and

Kojo Touvalou-Houénou's cosmopolitanism   115

English before serving in Europe during World War I.[1] After his education and World War I military service, he spent most of his life in Paris fighting for Africa's independence and unity between the continent and the diaspora.

Yet Touvalou's Pan-Africanism is little known. In order to resolve this problem, Patrick Manning and James S. Spiegler wrote a 1991 study entitled "Kojo Tovalou-Houenou: Pan-African Patriot at Home and Abroad" in which they declared:

> None of the studies published so far give[s] detailed analysis either of his thought or of his life ... His ideas were a profound reflection of political thinking among French-speaking Africans of his day, and an important source in the subsequent development of nationalist thought. But beyond this, we contend that these ideas stemmed in part from the complex experiences of two generations of coastal Dahomeans (i.e., the political econo[m]y of Dahomey). Not surprisingly, limits on his ideas and political activities also reflect peculiarities of colonial Dahomey.
>
> (1991, 1)

Certainly, Dahomey's social, political, and economic history has a major role in Touvalou's nationalism and activism, since it led him to criticize the French colonial administration in radical terms that Diagne and his colleagues severely punished. Yet Touvalou's radicalism can be fully understood only when it is assessed beyond Dahomey, that is, within the international context of the interwar years during which this leader became a contact point between Francophone and Anglophone Pan-Africanisms. This role is hinted in Langley's assertion that "his [Touvalou's] race consciousness was influenced by the pan-American movements which gained prominence between 1919 and 1925" (1969, 72). Touvalou's ties with the Pan-African movements are further evident in *The Practice of Diaspora*, where Edwards classifies him among the major black Francophone and Anglophone intellectuals who established mutual ties during the interwar period. Edwards writes:

> I have already argued that to a remarkable extent, the impetus for transnational communication and exchange among intellectuals of African descent in the interwar period arises from the Francophone side. Like René Maran opening a dialogue with Alain Locke, Kojo Tovalou Houénou pursuing ties with Marcus Garvey and W.E.B. Du Bois, or the Nardal sisters questioning Locke about translating *The New Negro*, Kouyaté was keen to engage black U.S. and Caribbean figures in correspondence.
>
> (2003, 292)

However, although he recognizes Touvalou's place among the Francophone blacks who bridged the divide with their Anglophone counterparts

116 *Kojo Touvalou-Houénou's cosmopolitanism*

during the 1920s, Edwards seems to ignore his ambiguity since he perceives his internationalism and fascination with Garvey as hasty and reckless. Discussing an address that Touvalou gave on August 31, 1924, at the UNIA Convention in Carnegie Hall, New York, Edwards states:

> At the closing session of the Convention, Touvalou Houénou spoke again, praising the UNIA's work for the "redemption of Africa" and adding that "the problem of the race in toto is not national, but international." . . . Touvalou Houénou's ardor for black internationalism was matched only by his ideological innocence.
>
> (2003, 103)

Touvalou's alliance with Garvey reflected not "an ideological innocence," but a mature and genuine political strategy for bringing freedom and equality to blacks worldwide. Incidentally, Touvalou's awareness about this oppression might have been partially influenced by the following racist experience that he had in Paris. According to Miller,

> Houénou was thrown out of a Montmartre cabaret by a group of white Americans who were shocked to see a black man seated alongside themselves. This expulsion turned into a cause célèbre in which French indignation against American racism furthered the myth of a nonracist and color-blind France. It was in the wake of this accident that the Frenchified dandy took up Garveyism and Pan-Africanism.
>
> (1998, 51)

Like Edwards, Miller views Touvalou's association with Garvey and Pan-Africanism as accidental when this coalition might have also derived from a stronger cause such as the Beninese leader's resolute aim to defeat racism and inequality on both sides of the Atlantic Ocean.

Touvalou's Pan-Africanism caught the attention of Garvey, who saw him as an opportunity to expand the UNIA's stature in Francophone Africa. Garvey's use of Touvalou to further his organization's influence is apparent in *Race First* where Martin asserts:

> Kojo suggested an alliance between the UNIA and his own Ligue Universelle pour la Défense de la Race Noire. This alliance would spearhead a worldwide federation of race organizations, in which the UNIA would provide the "heavy artillery." Kojo is also said to have led an abortive, UNIA-inspired revolt in Dahomey in 1925.
>
> (1976, 115)

Touvalou's search for relationships with the UNIA was concretized on August 31, 1924, when he delivered a speech at a convention of the organization in Carnegie Hall. In this speech, Touvalou agreed with Garvey's strong argument that the problem of blacks in the twentieth century was

Kojo Touvalou-Houénou's cosmopolitanism 117

global, and that blacks of the diaspora should help to resolve Africa's predicaments. Touvalou said:

> I brought you the greetings and salutations of Africa . . . I reiterate to you Africa's farewell. The U.N.I.A. has one supreme object, and that is Africa and its redemption. I do not know in detail the proceedings of the convention, but I know sufficient of its work in its various sessions to make all hearts vibrate in unison and solidarize or consolidate our efforts for this great objective—the redemption of Africa. The problem of the race in toto is not national, but international . . . we also want and must have our place, so that we can seek to have our own, and Africa, the cradle of the black race, will in [the] course of time have her own government and the world at large will realize that Africans are capable of their own government and will be welcomed in the concert of nations.
>
> (1986, 823)

In *The Practice of Diaspora*, Edwards interprets Touvalou's statements as "stunningly radical and hopelessly naïve" propositions (2003, 103). Representing Touvalou's transnationalism as monolithic, Edwards also states: "he [Tovalou Houénou] held the simplistic notion that all intellectuals of African descent are ultimately working toward the same end" (2003, 103). Edwards's representation of Touvalou's black internationalism as "simplistic" reinforces black Atlantic intellectuals' stereotyping of Africans' efforts to create their own version of modernity as a "naïve" romanticizing of black intellectualism and history. Edwards's argument resonates with Gilroy's dismissal of the idea of a shared black cultural and political destiny as essentialist (*The Black Atlantic*, 195). The charge of fundamentalism does not fit Touvalou who was not interested in mere celebration of blackness. Touvalou traveled from France to speak with Garvey, not because he shared any ideology of racial or cultural separatism with him, but because he partook in the Jamaican's idea that racial solidarity could help blacks of both Africa and the West to protect the continent from colonialism and segregation. Both leaders wanted to achieve these goals while remaining faithful to cosmopolitanism.

Touvalou's cosmopolitanism stems from his theorizing of human relationships as ties that transcend boundaries and his conception of the universe as a world in which metamorphoses in and between natural elements erase individualities. Touvalou bases his cosmopolitanism on a view of convergence as the process in which different entities naturally disrupt the polarities between them. Using religion as an example, he writes:

> Mon dessein dans cet ouvrage est de ramener les individualités irréductibles du système évolutif de l'univers à l'homogénéité, à l'identité primitive, à refluer le torrent des métamorphoses et des métempsychoses à Dieu, source infinie qui leur sert d'involution originelle et créatrice.

118   *Kojo Touvalou-Houénou's cosmopolitanism*

[My purpose in this book is to bring the irreducible individualities of the evolutionary system of the universe to homogeneity, the primitive identity, refluxing the torrent of metamorphosis and metempsychosis toward God, the infinite source that serves their original and creative involution.]

(Touvalou, 1921, 6)

This quotation reveals Touvalou's representation of God as the source of both the sameness and individualities that cosmopolitanism embodies. For him, cosmopolitanism evolved from this spiritual and original source that exemplifies perfection and symmetry. Describing the spiritual roots of his cosmopolitanism, Touvalou observes: "Dans l'ordre métaphysique qui seul préoccupe le penseur, l'égalité est absolue, tous les faits étaient pareillement sous ses yeux leur néant" [In the metaphysical order which only concerns the thinker, equality is absolute; all the facts before him were equally nothingness] (1921, 7). From this logic, equality is a natural part of life since it is not only integral to original sources but also to the universe's balanced evolution and functioning. By stressing the primacy of equality in human origins, Touvalou recognizes how particularities and commonalities can coexist. In his worldview, homogeneity is a form of cosmopolitanism referring to the similar desires, hopes, dreams, and situations that diverse societies share. Having been transformed by "the torrent of metamorphosis and metempsychosis," these communities are naturally drawn to the cosmopolitan core, or the "original and creative involution," from which different identities and spiritualities evolved and return. Therefore, Touvalou's cosmopolitanism stresses the deep yearnings for egalitarianism which lie in the hearts of all human beings.

However, Touvalou's cosmopolitanism was more than an abstract and metaphysical inquiry, since it was also a practical attempt to gain full admissibility for blacks in the French Republic. As an offspring of the Enlightenment, the French Revolution valued the cosmopolitan idea of assimilation which, although it was essentially racist, ethnocentric, and exclusive, sometimes gave colonized populations the opportunity to seek theoretical freedom within the empire. This abstract cosmopolitanism is perceptible in Francis Terry McNamara's description of the assimilationist zeal that the French Revolution ushered:

Eighteenth-century philosophers such as Montesquieu, Voltaire, Rousseau, and Diderot provided intellectual legitimacy to the concept of cultural assimilation. The French Revolution of 1789 had awakened a missionary zeal in the French. Many were driven to spread their culture, language, and political philosophy to the less fortunate non-Francophone. Their ultimate gift became language and culture. Human equality and the value of education as a corrective to environmental

Kojo Touvalou-Houénou's cosmopolitanism   119

differences were raised in republican France to the level of secular dogma by dedicated advocates of assimilation.

(1989, 35)

The idea of assimilation which emanated from the French Revolution botched the republicanism that inspired Touvalou. This assimilation was anticosmopolitan since it forced colonies to either adopt French civilization or be frozen in tradition. Alternatively, Touvalou proposed a balanced cosmopolitanism that accepts the benefits of French republicanism while rejecting the drawbacks of its assimilationism. For Touvalou, the only means to overcome the dangers of assimilation is to make it full and radical rather than partial and incremental. As Derrick (2008) indicates, in *Les Continents* issue of July 1924, Touvalou stated: "We ask to be citizens of some country or another. That is why, if France rejects us, we demand self-government (*autonomie*). If it accepts us, total, wholesale assimilation" (145). This quotation shows that Touvalou's cosmopolitanism is a radical and practical way of achieving black equality in the French empire. Yet this cosmopolitanism resists the ethnocentrism of French republicanism since it proposes fair and harmonious cohabitation between cultures and races as a means of resolving past historical inequalities. Conveying this cosmopolitanism, Touvalou said in his 1924 speech delivered at the Inter-Allied School of Higher Social Studies of the University of Paris:

We [African people] wish that you recognize our rights to citizenship—the elementary rights of man—and that living your life, suffering your sorrows, and rejoicing in your joys, we might be called to share your destiny, good or bad, but which we accept sincerely, loyally and faithfully.

(1924, 207)

This assertion indicates Touvalou's celebration of modern Africans' willingness to collaborate with the West and fully embrace its civilization with the hope of seeing this cosmopolitanism reciprocated through recognition of their human rights. In this sense, Touvalou's cosmopolitanism stemmed from the kind of recognition of humanism as a universal quality that later inspired Negritude. Langley explains:

[F]or in 1921 in Paris he [Tovalou] wrote a short book which can perhaps be described as a forerunner of the more literary theory of *négritude* of the 1930s ... Like his distinguished successor, Léopold Senghor, Tovalou argued, in a less artistic manner, that each people and culture was part of a whole and had its own distinctive contribution to that universal civilization.

(1969, 72)

120 *Kojo Touvalou-Houénou's cosmopolitanism*

However, Touvalou's cosmopolitanism is a valorization of European civilization that is not antithetical to radical black nationalist struggles for equal rights. Understanding Touvalou's theory of cosmopolitanism in this framework enables us to comprehend his concept of African modernity. First, one needs to define the notion of modernity in black Atlantic cultures. According to Gilroy, modernity is a concept which directs "attention toward the links between racial typologies and the heritage of the Enlightenment" and "makes that fateful compact fundamental to the task of grasping how knowledge and power produced the truths of 'race' and nation close to the summit of modern reflections on individuality, subjectivity, and ontology, time, truth, and beauty" (2004, 55–56). In French West African modernity, the fixation on racial axiology that dominates Gilroy's theorizing of black Atlantic cultures is usually absent. The modern Africans' priority is usually not to define blackness as better, worse, more, or less than whiteness, but simply to see themselves as complex and equal to anybody else. For instance, during the two world wars, Francophone West Africans did not totally reject French civilization; they reconfigured it through their modernity to achieve a sense of fullness and progress, just as any other members of human civilization has done. Touvalou personifies this black modernity in progress because his cosmopolitanism crosses human binaries by building new identities based on a mixing of European and African cultures. Discussing Claude McKay's views of Touvalou, Melvyn Stokes argues that "if Houénou cherishes his Dahomean roots, he was also at ease in the white western literary culture" (2009, 4). Quoting McKay again, Stokes asserts: "Plainly, McKay was positioning Houénou as a figure combining easily in his own character an African and a western identity. He seemed comfortable in both worlds" (2009, 4). These quotations show that Touvalou was a black cosmopolitan intellectual whose modern identity was fashioned from a blending of cultures. He unashamedly believed that it was important for the modern African to receive an education that will assure his or her "evolution" and "adaptation to European civilization" (Touvalou, 1924, 206).

Moreover, Touvalou's concept of modernity is premised on Africans' transformation of their societies from the inside-out. In this logic, adaptation to Western values is a natural choice to be accepted or rejected without outside impositions. Touvalou's modernity does not force French civilization into African cultures. Rather, it summons Africans to claim their right not only to decide which assimilation to other cultures might occur in their societies, but also the extent to which this accommodation will take place. Accordingly, Touvalou's cosmopolitanism is also a code word for free choice and swift independence from colonialism, not incremental integrationism into the métropole and its civilizations. He told France that there can be neither "half-measures" nor "compromise[s]" in the solutions to the corruption, violence, and inefficiency of its administration in the African colonies (Touvalou, 1924, 205). Providing a solution to this injustice,

Touvalou proposes "Absolute autonomy for the Colonies, with imperial relations to the Motherland on general questions; or otherwise total, complete assimilation without frontier—without distinction of race" (1924, 205). Here, Touvalou derides France's eagerness to alienate Africans rather than assimilate them into its métropole. In calling for either Africans' full "assimilation" into "the Motherland" or their complete "autonomy" from it, Touvalou exploited the paradoxes that prevented France from knowing what do to with members of its empire who were demanding the same rights that republicanism guarantees to all.

Thus, Touvalou's cosmopolitanism also stemmed from both his negotiations with France and his radical efforts to compel the métropole to extend freedom to blacks. At times, Touvalou praised the idea of universal freedom that was at the center of French republicanism. Focused on the Rights of Man, this republicanism is a radical philosophy that guarantees basic freedom to all members of society by proposing the end of customs which traditionally viewed monarchs as the extensions of a God whose divine representatives on Earth have the power to rule over men and nations. In republicanism, man, not kings and queens, govern nations in a constitutional democracy. Moreover, in republicanism, the power of the state and that of the people are intertwined. As Richard Kearney explains, "a single feature of the French *République* was the conviction that the Rights of Man and the Rights of the People were mutually inclusive" (2002, 24). As the originator of this philosophy, French republicanism rests on the idea of the Rights of Man and People that implies a theoretical reciprocity between the métropole and other freedom-seeking people.

Touvalou regarded French republicanism as a useful tool in black liberation struggles and global resistances against bourgeois hegemonies. In a 1928 article in *L'A.O.F.*, he urged France to preserve the republican and populist tradition of guaranteeing the freedom of all members of society, including working classes. Lamenting the despicable ways in which French colonials valued West Africa's groundnuts, palm oil, iron, skins, and mahogany rather than the "black people" who produced these resources, Touvalou writes:

> The continuation of such practices dishonours the name of Frenchmen and is treacherous because it results in the division of France, which should not be associated with the promotion of particular interests, the enjoyment of exorbitant privileges and of anti-republican (and therefore anti-French) prerogatives.
>
> (1979, 241)

These words convey Touvalou's fascination with cosmopolitanism's fearless defense of all people against exploitation. Embracing this cosmopolitanism as a Frenchman, Touvalou urges his compatriots to protect it by substituting colonialism in West Africa with a republican and

122 *Kojo Touvalou-Houénou's cosmopolitanism*

egalitarian system in which privileges are distributed to all without regard to family, creed, nobility, or other entities. Touvalou's faith in this republicanism is noticeable in his representation of "happiness" as a privilege "from which one indivisible France benefits" (1979, 239) and his argument that "the men of 1789 and 1848" wanted to protect all members of the great France from totalitarianism, since they did not decree "that only the members of the elite are allowed to live in the shadow of protective laws of freedom and human rights" (1979, 240). These statements suggest Touvalou's faith in a French cosmopolitanism that he associated with republican and revolutionary distributions of rights and liberties to all, not just to the elite. In this sense, Touvalou's cosmopolitanism was consistent with Garvey's aim to inscribe black liberation struggle into French republicanism. As Wilder points out, in this broad context, "here again, political practices in the republican public space mediated a Panafrican and internationalist vision on the one hand, and a commitment to the French national tradition and its political culture on the other" (2003, 248).

Assessing how the ideology was received on the other side of the Atlantic Ocean, Fabre states in *From Harlem to Paris*:

> Garveyism did not especially appeal to French anticolonialists because they attacked the colonial system through the principles of the rights of man and the workers' international, which made no allowance for racial specificity. French blacks began to question colonization because they considered themselves exploited like many other peoples, not just blacks.
> (1993, 147)

Touvalou was an exception to this group of French blacks, since he was attracted to Garveyism even if he despised its emphasis on racial particularity. Furthermore, Garvey was not totally different from Touvalou because he, too, admired a French cosmopolitanism that stressed the republican idea of the rights of man. Like Touvalou, Garvey strongly admired French cosmopolitanism though he attacked the métropole's colonial abuse of Africans. Garvey's fascination with cosmopolitanism also derived from his view and appreciation of the French Revolution as a catalyst of black global freedom struggles.

Garvey's fascination with French cosmopolitanism is recurrent in some of his writings and speeches of the 1920s in which he often invokes egalitarian ideals that France inherited from the 1789 Revolution. In the essay "A Solution for World Peace," Garvey expresses his enthrallment with this uprising's legacy when he states: "Yes, the Louis's [sic] laughed at the propaganda of the Liberals of France, but the French Monarchy is no more. Today Frenchmen take pride in the new democracy of France; so that others may laugh at us today because we are agitating the question of a free and independent Africa" (1922, 42). This quotation illuminates Garvey's view of the French Revolution as a crucial historical lesson that could inspire Pan-

Kojo Touvalou-Houénou's cosmopolitanism   123

African liberation struggles. In his August 1921 speech delivered at Liberty Hall, N.Y.C., Garvey alludes to the model of subversive resistance that the revolution represents for blacks. He states:

> As Pitt and Gladstone were able to work for the expansion of the British Empire, so you and I can work for the expansion of a great African Empire [sic] Voltaire and Maribeau were not Jesus Christs, they were but men like ourselves. They worked and overturned the French Monarchy. They worked for the Democracy which France now enjoys, and if they were able to do that, we are able to work for a democracy in Africa.[2]

This assertion shows Garvey's linking of the French Revolution with the UNIA's black liberation struggle. Even if he perceived France as a colonial oppressor, Garvey nonetheless viewed its democracy and freedom as ideas that could also benefit black revolutions for justice. Garvey was therefore akin to Touvalou since he, too, admired the French Revolution and theorized it as the catalyst of a global cry for human freedom in which black struggle was integral. In the above speech, Garvey also asserts: "Everywhere we hear the cry of liberty, of freedom, and a demand for democracy. In our corner of the world we are raising the cry for liberty, freedom and democracy."[3] Thus, like Touvalou, Garvey invokes the French Revolution and the long tradition of human struggles for liberty, freedom, and democracy to legitimize black resistances against oppression.

Yet, Garvey's fascination with France's cosmopolitan and republican traditions was sometimes idealistic since the colonial power was reluctant to grant blacks of its colonies the full benefits of this heritage. Like Touvalou, Garvey was initially so obsessed with France's cosmopolitan traditions that he naively trusted the métropole's natural propensity to integrate blacks to its republic. Enamored with France, Garvey often referred to this nation as a promoter of cosmopolitanism that Anglophone nations should emulate. In the editorial of the August 6, 1928, issue of the *Negro World*, Garvey writes:

> I must say that I am very much impressed with the genial hospitality of the French toward us as a race. My stay in France was in every way a pleasant one, made so by the attitude of the French toward the black man. If there has been any unpleasantness it came not from the French, but from the rude and vulgar white Americans we met on our way.[4]

This assertion displays Garvey's admiration of the cosmopolitan freedom that blacks could occasionally enjoy in France in the 1920s by being perceived as individuals with as much dignity and humanity as whites.

Another instance of Garvey's fascination with French cosmopolitanism is noticeable in a speech, delivered in West Kensington, London, on September

124 *Kojo Touvalou-Houénou's cosmopolitanism*

14, 1928, which expresses his preference of France's colonialism over those of other Europeans who alienated blacks. In the address, Garvey states:

> We admire the more liberal attitude of France in treating with us as a people, but we fully realize that the aim of the said treatment is skillfully calculated to make us more Frenchmen than self-respecting Negroes, inspired to self-reliance and political independence, such as we desire, in keeping with the principle of human liberty.[5]

Beside its reflection of Garvey's preference of French imperialism over those of other Europeans who did not treat blacks "as a people" whatsoever, this statement displays the Jamaican leader's theorizing of cosmopolitanism as a rejection of cultural assimilation and the affirmation of black people's ability to use the powers of the empires that have colonized them to achieve their own social, political, and economic development. Thus, Garvey invokes the idea of working within the Empire as a strategy for achieving black development.

In addition, Garvey was not unaware of the pitfalls of French cosmopolitanism since he knew that the majority of black Francophone subjects did not have rights. Although he liked France's hospitality, Garvey questioned its cosmopolitanism by depicting the nation's tolerance of blacks as a mere colonialist strategy. For instance, he knew that the French did not treat *tirailleurs* as equals and were often violent with them in the métropole. In the July 25, 1920, "Report of UNIA Meeting," Garvey states:

> "Give us liberty or give us death." After the French took a million and a half black men from Northern Africa and other parts of Africa and her colonial possessions, brought them into the war, used them as shock troops to stop the Germans at Verdun and at the battle of the Marne, their recompense is to lynch a Negro in a French city—a civilized French centre. It is a shame. It only goes to show that there is absolutely no trust to be placed in the white man's word—whether it is given by Clemenceau of France or Lloyd George of England or Orlando of Italy, we refuse now to trust the word of the white man any more.
>
> ("Hon. Marcus Garvey Speaks", 438)

The "lynch[ing] [of] a Negro in a French city" contradicts the cosmopolitanism that Garvey admired. France was a country where a black man could be hanged even if such a brutality was rarer in this nation than in the United States. Such racial violence suggests the paradox of a French cosmopolitanism in which openness toward blacks was ultimately a facade rather than a genuine expression of inclusion. Garvey was aware of this incongruity since he sometimes regarded France as a nation that was inherently prejudiced and exploitative toward blacks despite the small degree of assimilation it offered them. For instance, about a month after the 1921

Kojo Touvalou-Houénou's cosmopolitanism 125

congress, Garvey lampooned the ironic way in which French colonial officials, who had praised Diagne when he recruited soldiers for their war, now "ridiculed the idea that he should offer himself as a sympathizer of Africa for the Africans or to a Pan-African Congress."[6] Discussing this paradox, Garvey states:

> That reveals the hatred of France, the hypocrisy of France, the damnable lie of France that she loves Negroes and that she intends to help the development of Negroes. If they had loved Negroes so much—if their intention was so pure toward the Negro, they would have welcomed the Pan-African Congress and would have supported Diagne, the President of the Pan-African Congress. But they never meant it.[7]

Therefore, according to Garvey, European cosmopolitanism could be a veiled form of imperialism that aimed to pillage Africa. Garvey declares:

> Talk about love; there is no love but the love that you have for yourself, and all this farce, this hypocrisy [,] these [lies?] must be torn asunder. We are laboring under the hypocrisy of Great Britain, the hypocrisy of France, the hypocrisy of Italy, the hypocrisy of Belgium, of Portugal[,] of Spain, telling us about the larger humanity that causes them to go down to Africa to civilize and christianize. The rogues are going down to rob, to exploit, to plunder and to kill. They might fool a few French black deputies; they may fool fellows like Du Bois, but in the name of God they will never make fools of the Universal Negro Improvement Association.[8]

Garvey's pronouncements reflect the Pan-Africanist lenses through which he perceived imperialism as a global system in which European colonials made sure that blacks would be poor not just in Africa, through their international carving and sharing of the continent, but also in the diaspora. Garvey's Pan-Africanist lamentation of the conditions of blacks in the 1920s resonates with Touvalou's denunciation of the similar plight of French West Africans during the same period. In this sense, Touvalou was indeed one of Garvey's Pan-Africanist disciples that Moses describes in *The Golden Age of Black Nationalism* as the Africans "on the continent and in Europe" who "readily combined their Garveyism with a pro-Communist philosophy" (1978, 264).

Touvalou and Garvey were also in accord in their embrace of a Pan-Africanism that resisted the indignities of colonialism and racism against blacks of Africa and the diaspora. Moreover, they shared a strong Pan-Africanist belief in the right of all blacks to be free from oppression. In his 1924 speech delivered at the Inter-Allied School of Higher Social Studies, Touvalou said:

126 *Kojo Touvalou-Houénou's cosmopolitanism*

> We, Negroes of Africa, we raise our indignant protestation against the fate of our brothers in America. Shame to those Americans who feign to be civilized, but who have not yet condemned, by law, the outrage of lynching, and who continue to torture 15 millions of our brothers! Let the so-called civilized nations stop wholesale trade of Negroes by the purchase and sale of Colonies, after having condemned the slave trade in detail!
>
> (1924, 206)

This statement reflects Touvalou's Pan-Africanist conception of racism in the West and colonialism in other parts of the black world as subjugations that are integral to the same imperial exploitative system that began in slavery. In this sense, Touvalou aimed to liberate not just African Francophones, but also diasporan blacks. As Janet G. Vaillant argues, Touvalou "became a political activist on behalf of black people" (1990, 66). Touvalou's Pan-Africanist activism is also perceptible in his condemnation of the Western racial violence against blacks that prevailed in the 1920s. By denouncing in a same speech the atrocity of lynching and torture of blacks in the United States and the bondage of "Negroes" in the "Colonies," he provides a Pan-Africanist and transnational analysis of the plight of blacks that resonates with Garvey's. Like Touvalou, Garvey aimed to emancipate blacks from a global white racism that prevented them from gaining the cosmopolitan equality that freedom and nationhood required. Demanding black deliverance from this systemic domination, Garvey wrote in his 1923 essay, "Give the Blacks a Chance:"

> If the Negro is inferior why circumvent him; why suppress his talent and initiative; why rob him of his independent gifts; why fool him out of the rights of country; why imprison his intelligence and exploit his ignorance; why keep him down by the laws of inequality? Why not leave him alone to his own intelligence; why not give him a chance to grow and develop as he sees fit; why not free him from the incubus of a "forced upon" superiority; why not allow him, free and unhampered, to travel toward nationhood?
>
> (1986, 83)

Garvey's reference to the manner in which the West kept the "Negro" in "ignorance" and in positions of inferiority enforced by "laws of inequality" resonates with Touvalou's view of racism, lynching, and colonialism as systemic forms of European control of blacks. Both leaders regard shared legacies of oppression as historical forces that transcend the geographic boundaries separating modern blacks. Rather than simply mention Pan-African unity, Touvalou, like Garvey, wanted to concretize this solidarity in a blend of ideas that could uplift the conditions of blacks worldwide.

Kojo Touvalou-Houénou's cosmopolitanism 127

In this sense, Touvalou was inspired by Garvey's Pan-Africanism. As Langley points out, "Houenou was definitely a supporter of Marcus Garvey."[9]

Touvalou's Pan-Africanism is also visible in his August 31, 1924, speech at Carnegie Hall, in which he endorsed Garvey's immigration to Liberia project and his plans to extend the UNIA's influence across Africa. Touvalou told the UNIA members:

> You have chosen as your haven or port of landing that portion of Africa called Liberia. And, as its name indicates, it symbolizes and stands for liberty. And all other parts of Africa await you, and shall be thither guided, not by a little star of night, but thither shall your path be guided by the great sun which illuminates all Africa.
>
> (1986, 823)

Touvalou's words are the strongest validation Garvey received from an African intellectual. They contradict the notion that Garvey was an imperialist by recognizing the important role that the UNIA could play in Africa. Garvey strongly believed that Africans could take advantage of the black diaspora's intellectual, artistic, and scientific know-how to advance Africa. Referring to the delegations of UNIA members that Garvey had sent to Liberia in the 1920s, Touvalou asserts:

> What I have heard and seen I shall take back to my people, and next year, when I shall visit Liberia during my tours in Africa, I shall have the pleasure of saluting those of you who shall be in Liberia ... You are the elite of this race of ours; you will bring to the shores of Africa, our motherland, your Western civilization; you will bring to your brothers in Africa the arts and industries of the world in which you are living; you will bring all the education and morality and all that you have learned and all that you now possess you will bring over, and there shall be a fusion and community of ideas and spirit in our great motherland, Africa.
>
> (1986, 823–824)

Touvalou's praise of Garvey and the other members of the UNIA as "the elite of this race of ours" who bring "Western civilization," knowledge of the "arts and industries," "education and morality" to "Africa" reveals his fascination with the pragmatism of Garvey's Pan-Africanism. Such pragmatism is visible in the ways in which Garvey urged educated blacks worldwide to develop Africa with their knowledge. In this sense, as Goyal argues, "his [Garvey's] impact across the diaspora and on the continent was phenomenal albeit still little understood, especially in academic accounts of black history and intellectual life" (2010, 2). Goyal also observes, "And certainly, Garvey's historical impact on Africa and elsewhere may well be greater than that of his more illustrious rivals" (2010, 3).

128 Kojo Touvalou-Houénou's cosmopolitanism

Garvey's influence on Africa is further evident in Touvalou's fascination with the Jamaican's view of education as a pragmatic means to develop Africa. Speaking to UNIA followers in August, 1924, Touvalou said: "It was for the Negroes of the world . . . under whatever flag they might be, in whatever organization [,] to unite their forces and go marching back to their motherland and wrest it from the common enemy."[10] This passage shows Touvalou's strong allegiance to Garvey's "Back-To-Africa" ideology which gave blacks of the diaspora the sacred responsibility to go to Africa and protect it from Western imperialism. Such a direct and practical approach to Africa's problems, which relies on the global joining of blacks' efforts to resolve the continent's predicaments, shows that Touvalou was a Garveyite who employed pragmatic radicalism to organize African liberation from colonialism. Revealing Garvey's status as a spiritual and ideological force that crossed the Atlantic to inspire a continent he never visited, Martin writes in *The Pan-African Connection*:

> Houénou, in the 1920s became an avid supporter of the Jamaican Marcus Garvey, the scourge of the European colonialists in Africa. Houénou is even said to have led a Garvey inspired uprising against the French in Dahomey in 1923. The God of Africa, too, moves in mysterious ways, his wonders to perform.
>
> (1983, 16)

Therefore, Garvey played a major role in African anticolonialism of the 1920s since he was a strong circum-Atlantic ideological force that enabled Touvalou and his cohorts to imagine and actualize direct anti-imperial liberation struggle.

In retrospect, Garvey had the upper hand in his ideological conflicts with Touvalou since he knew that assimilation alone could not feed the millions of blacks who lived in French colonies. Moreover, Garvey knew that *francité* was meaningless because the French continued to represent Africans as cannibals and savages. Incidentally, Touvalou himself knew that black modernity and its struggle with Western colonialism could not escape the gaze of the French colonials who were unable to measure their humanity without opposing it to an inferior and exotic black "other." Associating this "othering" with Western primitivizing and exploitation of blacks would have allowed Touvalou to attenuate his obsessive adoration of French cosmopolitanism and republicanism and avoid the discord that such a mirage would bring in his relations with Garvey. Such a disjuncture was bound to occur because Touvalou, unlike Garvey, was a victim of a reckless faith in cultural assimilationism which, in the early twentieth century, made it difficult for black Francophone intellectuals to view racism as the major cause of their plight. By primarily inscribing their struggle in the ideals of French republicanism, such intellectuals as Touvalou, Diagne, and Candace prevented their racial outcry from being heard in an empire that claimed to

Kojo Touvalou-Houénou's cosmopolitanism   129

integrate blacks while ignoring the drastic consequences of colonialism on them. Martin Steins explains:

> Once the [first] war was over, the "assimilés" began by demanding the *immediate implementation of the promises* implicit in the colonial theory of political and cultural assimilation. They saw colonialism as a temporary phase leading to the elimination of the inequalities which had brought it about. However, by their insistence on basing their anti-colonialism on the principles of Republicanism, the élite deprived itself of a platform of its own.
>
> (1986, 357)

By writing race out of anticolonialism, French assimilationism and republicanism legitimized prejudice and exploitation in the post-World War I black Francophone world in both the métropole and abroad. This racism was exacerbated by the bias and abuse that white American soldiers brought to Europe during and after World War I. Touvalou was a direct victim of such bigotry. For instance, as Craig Lloyd points out, on August 3, 1923,

> Prince Kojo Tovalou of Dahomey, a decorated war veteran, possessor of a doctorate in jurisprudence from the Sorbonne, and a lawyer at the court of appeals in Paris, was literally thrown out of a Montmartre cabaret, breaking his glasses on the sidewalk of the rue Fontaine not far from Zelli's. Several months earlier, he had been chased out of the American-patronized Jockey-Bar in Montparnasse.
>
> (2006, 86)

Black and white French leaders, such as Candace and Raymond Poincaré respectively, were outraged by the incident. As Lloyd observes, Candace

> persuade[d] the French foreign ministry to order all French newspapers to publish on August 1, 1923, a stern note to foreign "guests" admonishing them to obey French law and custom with respect to people of color or else face sanctions from French authorities.
>
> (2006, 86)

In a similar vein, Vaillant states: "After all, when Tovalou had pressed charges against the unfortunate restaurant owner, had he not won damages in court and had not the prime minister, Raymond Poincaré himself, come to his support?" (1990, 66). Therefore, unlike those in the United States, blacks in 1920s France had some tangible, though minimal, legal means to protect themselves against racial injustice.

Yet the French colonials' support of Touvalou was hypocritical since it made anti-black discrimination appear as a foreign export rather than a homegrown phenomenon. After all, the owners of the public venues where

130   *Kojo Touvalou-Houénou's cosmopolitanism*

Touvalou was violated were white French whose complicity in the violence reflected entrenched racism against blacks in the métropole after post-World War I. Stovall explains:

> Many have exaggerated the color blindness of the French, and it is quite possible that some restaurant and hotel owners used their white American customers to mask their own prejudices. Yet discrimination against African Americans in Paris did occur most often in areas of the city frequented by their white countrymen.
>
> (1996, 73)

As is apparent in the savage treatment of Touvalou in the métropole, Francophone Africans were not shielded from the kind of racism that African Americans also faced in post-World War I France and the United States. Therefore, racial prejudice was not always a foreign export in France since it was also home-made.

Another parallel between Touvalou and Garvey is noticeable in the tragic ends of their lives as the results of racist and colonialist accusations. Garvey was a victim of an American racist system which was afraid of his growing power. Through Hoover's leadership, the FBI infiltrated spies in the UNIA's structures and activities, gathered false evidence against the organization, and charged its leader with allegedly illegal activities, leading to Garvey's incarceration and removal from the United States. In 1922, Garvey and three of his followers were convicted of mail fraud (Levine, 134). Traumatized by such humiliating experiences, Garvey, who had become seriously ill, passed away on June 10, 1940, at his West Kensington residence in London, thirteen years after his deportation. In "Memoirs of a Captain of the Black Star Line," Captain Hugh Mulzac says that Garvey died "a broken and embittered man" (1974, 137).

In similar ways, Touvalou was a victim of racist manipulations which curtailed his activism and certainly led to his premature death (in 1936). One of Touvalou's first ordeals occurred in France during the infamous trial that opposed Diagne and Maran, a black Guyanese novelist who was born in Martinique. In the October 15, 1924, issue of *Les Continents*, Maran wrote a scathing article entitled "Le Bon Apôtre" [The Good Apostle], in which he accused Diagne of having financially profited from the recruitment of World War I *tirailleurs*. Specifically, "Maran claimed that Blaise Diagne had received a commission for each of the fifty thousand Senegalese soldiers he had helped recruit to the French cause in 1918."[11] Diagne was angered by such serious accusations which, for him, put France's integrity at risk. Complicating the situation, Devaux and Delafosse were already infuriated when Maran received the Prix Goncourt in 1922 despite the fact that his 1921 book, *Batouala*, made strong criticisms against France.[12] Yet Diagne was more aggravated by the charges in *Les Continents* than his colonial colleagues were. As Conklin observes, "Diagne was incensed by an unsigned

Kojo Touvalou-Houénou's cosmopolitanism 131

article that had recently appeared in a new and struggling pan-noir journal critical of French colonial administration, *Les Continents*, of which Maran was vice-president" (2003, 302). In response to the allegations, Diagne took *Les Continents* and its white French editor, Jean Fangeat, to court. According to two articles in *Les Annales coloniales* covering the affair, Diagne won the case and was awarded 2,000 francs out of the total of 10,000 francs of *"dommages et intérêts"* [compensatory damages] that he had demanded. Mr. Fangeat received a 6-month prison Sentence and Diagne promised to donate the legal compensation to the assistance of the Committee of the Office of Colonial Troops in Paris.[13] However, Diagne's legal victory later backfired on him as it established his popular portrayal as a traitor to his race and a non-radical black leader.

Touvalou was implicated in the controversy between Diagne and Maran because he and the Guyanese had co-founded *Les Continent*. After Diagne sued for libel, Touvalou's effort to create a radical journal that would denounce France's colonial wrongdoings in Africa was halted. In an attempt to escape Diagne's scrutiny, Touvalou returned to Africa where he hoped to expand his activism. Yet, according to Steins, the trip "proved fruitless; once back in Africa, Tovalou took part in political activities only occasionally".[14] Yet Touvalou was not completely inactive in Africa since he was involved in Senegalese politics. What is true, however, was that Touvalou's life went on a downhill spiral after Diagne's legal case against his journal. After *Les Continents*'s circulation stopped, Touvalou was forcefully ejected from a French bar, a year later, and faced, afterwards, a series of arrests, imprisonments, and implications in scandals. For instance, according to his biography in the Garvey Papers,

> In 1926, while visiting Lomé, Togo, he [Tovalou] was arrested and returned to prison in Cotonou, initially on charges of failure to pay a debt in Paris. He remained imprisoned until at least September 1926. In December 1927 the appeals court in Dakar convicted him of libel against Germain [Ann Henry] Crespin [a Senegalese lawyer] and sentenced him to six months in prison. Upon release, he participated in Galandou Diouf's May 1928 electoral campaign against Blaise Diagne. Tovalou-Houénou then returned to Paris. Reconciling with Garvey in 1928 and 1929, he was described as a UNIA representative in Paris. In November 1928 he spoke at a meeting where Garvey, recently released from prison in Georgia, was the principal speaker.[15]

These revelations suggest the consistent way in which Garvey remained a strong influence for Touvalou who turned to him for inspiration and solace at times of trouble in Senegal that Diagne probably maneuvered against the Dahomean. Germain A. H. Crespin, with whom Touvalou had a legal dispute, was a Senegalese métis lawyer and the son of Jean Jacques Crespin. The latter was the brother of Diagne's adoptive father, Adolphe Crespin.

132 *Kojo Touvalou-Houénou's cosmopolitanism*

As the Marcus Garvey Papers suggest, Touvalou broke out from Germain, his family's lawyer, after the latter sided with his younger brother, Georges Quenum, over a "succession dispute for leadership of the Tovalou Quenum lineage, which included extensive lands, commercial holdings, and over a thousand members" in Dahomey.[16] Siding with the Lieutenant Governor Gaston-Léon-Joseph Fourn of Dahomey, Germain Crespin had a stake in the heritage dispute and might have contributed to Touvalou's isolation from the case. The story did not end here, because Touvalou was increasingly involved in local politics in Senegal between 1927 and 1936 by also siding with the lawyer, Lamine Gueye, who supported Senegal's rising political star, Galandou Diouf, in the struggle to remove Diagne from office in the 1928 electoral campaign of the colony.[17] Touvalou's alliance with a Senegalese leadership which opposed Diagne's colonialism and the deputy's partnership with corrupt Bordeaux traders and banks made him more susceptible to the veiled abuse of the representative. Diagne seized the opportunity to further isolate Touvalou from a distance when a dispute opposed the Dahomean to Crespin in 1934. As notes from the Marcus Garvey Papers indicate:

> In December 1932 Tovalou-Houénou returned to Dahomey, accompanied by his wife. In Cotonou he sued Crespin for fraud, apparently in connection with the sale of a building there. During the hearing in March 1934, a fight broke out; Tovalou was charged with contempt of court and with writing a bad check for twenty-five thousand francs. While appealing these charges, Touvalou-Houénou joined fellow Dahomeans—peasants and some officials in Allada—to complain against chief Djibode Aplogan. His appeals led him to Dakar, where he lost his case and was imprisoned for eighteen months at Cap Manuel. There, on 2 July 1936, he died of typhoid fever. Following his death, his wife [an African American woman from Chicago] tried repeatedly to remove the block placed on her dowry of one hundred thousand francs, which had been deposited in the colonial treasury against her husband's debts.[18]

According to Dieng, Touvalou was also charged for voluntary assault, injury, and disorderly conduct for having allegedly slapped Germain Crespin during the fight (2013, 64). These accusations reveal the despicable ways in which Diagne wielded a strong power against his opponents in Senegal, a dominance that was only equaled by the manipulations which had enabled Hoover to topple Garvey in the United States. Touvalou suffered from a similar propaganda spearheaded by Diagne since he was regarded in West Africa as a communist, just as Garvey was also perceived in the United States in the late 1920s when he took a radical stance against colonial capitalist interests in Africa. Touvalou faced a comparable demise as his Garveyite rhetoric earned him the close supervision of French colonial authorities. In *Russia and Black Africa Before World War II*, Edward T. Wilson states:

Houénou's extravagant praise of Garvey himself ("Zionist of the black race . . . the leader who can incite the masses"), as well as his often stated desire to work in conjunction with every existing association in the interests of Negro solidarity and the renaissance of Africa, gave observers still further cause to identify him with Garveyism. Thus the French government, which followed intently Houénou's activities, was prompted to regard his organization as "a Garveyite operation in France."

(1974, 114)

Therefore, France viewed both Touvalou and Garvey as communist agitators who could destabilize the métropole's imperial interests and lead the oppressed masses of the black world to rebel against Europeans. Moreover, although they lived in separate lands, both Touvalou and Garvey suffered from European colonials' attempts to stifle anti-imperialism in Africa. France helped engineer the elimination of Garvey and Touvalou from anticolonial activism despite the fascination that both leaders had for the métropole's cosmopolitan and republican ideas of universal justice and equality.

Both Garvey and Touvalou were mesmerized by certain parts of French cosmopolitanism that they identified with democratic principles of liberty, equality, and fraternity embodied in the spirit of the French Revolution. Both leaders expressed their fascination with France, hoping that the benefits of its cosmopolitan and republican ideals would be shared with blacks of Senegal and other parts of the world. However, both leaders later rejected French cosmopolitanism when they found out that colonialism and racism were inconsistent with romanticized liberty and justice, and that such ideologies had to be deconstructed in order to repair the damage of imperialism and restore the voice of the colonized masses.

Yet there were a few discrepancies between Touvalou and Garvey. For instance, because of its strict faith in French cosmopolitanism, Touvalou's Pan-Africanism sometimes lacked Garvey's radicalism and pragmatism. Moreover, unlike Garvey, Touvalou was aware of the continent's cultural and political heterogeneity and genuinely believed in the feasibility and applicability of French cosmopolitan and universalistic ideals in West Africa. Consequently, the two leaders had a few ideological differences even if they both opposed French colonialism in comparable ways and faced similar tragedies that probably contributed to their short life spans.

Bibliography

Blanchard, Pascal, Eric Deroo, and Gilles Manceron. *Le Paris Noir*. Paris: Hazan, 2001.

Centenaire de la Conférence de Berlin (1884–1885): actes du colloque international, Brazzaville, avril 1985, 435–436. Paris: Présence africaine, 1987.

134   *Kojo Touvalou-Houénou's cosmopolitanism*

Conklin, Alice L. "Who Speaks for Africa? The René Maran-Blaise Diagne Trial in 1920s Paris." In *The Color of Liberty: Histories of Race in France*, edited by Sue Peabody and Tyler Stovall, 302–337. Durham, NC: Duke University Press, 2003.

"Convention Report [New York, August 18, 1924]." *The Marcus Garvey and Universal Negro Improvement Association Papers*, Vol. 5, edited by Robert Hill, 747–752. Los Angeles: University of California Press, 1986.

Derrick, Jonathan. *Africa's 'Agitators': Militant Anti-Colonialism in Africa and the West, 1918–1939.* New York: Columbia University Press, 2008.

Devaux, Eugène. "L'épilogue logique de Batouala." *Les Annales Coloniales*, February 16, 1922: 1.

Dieng, Amady Aly. *Lamine Guèye: Une des grandes figures politiques africaines (1891–1968).* Paris: Editions L'Harmattan, 2013.

Edwards, Brent Hayes. *The Practice of Diaspora: Literature, Translation, and the Rise of Black Internationalism.* Cambridge, MA: Harvard University Press, 2003.

Fabre, Michel. *From Harlem to Paris: Black American Writers in France, 1840–1980.* Urbana: University of Illinois Press, 1993.

Garvey, Marcus. "A Solution for World Peace—1922." In *The Philosophy and Opinions of Marcus Garvey or Africa for the Africans*, Vol. 1, edited by Amy-Jacques Garvey and Tony Martin, 40–42. Dover, MA: The Majority Press, 1986.

——. "Editorial by Marcus Garvey in the Negro World [Berlin, Germany, 6 Aug. 1928]." In *The Marcus Garvey and Universal Negro Improvement Association Papers*, Vol. 7, edited by Robert Hill, 212–215. Los Angeles: University of California Press, 1990.

——. "Enclosure [West Kensington, London W, 14 September 1928]." In *The Marcus Garvey and Universal Negro Improvement Association Papers*, Vol. 7, edited by Robert Hill, 249–276. Los Angeles: University of California Press, 1990.

——. "Give the Blacks a Chance." In *The Philosophy and Opinions of Marcus Garvey, or Africa for Africans*, Vol. 2, edited by Amy Jacques Garvey and Tony Martin, 83. Dover, MA: The Majority Press, 1986.

——. "Hon. Marcus Garvey Speaks [New York, July 25, 1920]." In *The Marcus Garvey and Universal Negro Improvement Association Papers*, Vol. 2, edited by Robert Hill, 437–440. Los Angeles: University of California Press, 1983.

——. "Speech by Marcus Garvey [New York, October 2, 1921]." In *The Marcus Garvey and Universal Negro Improvement Association Papers*, Vol. 4, edited by Robert Hill, 97–100. Los Angeles: University of California Press, 1985.

——. "Speech Delivered at Liberty Hall N. Y. C. During Second International Convention of Negroes August 1921." In *The Philosophy and Opinions of Marcus Garvey or Africa for the Africans*, Vol. 1, edited by Amy Jacques Garvey and Tony Martin, 93–97. Dover, MA: The Majority Press, 1986.

Gilroy, Paul. *The Black Atlantic: Modernity and Double Consciousness.* Cambridge, MA: Harvard University Press, 1993.

——. *Between Camps: Nations, Cultures and the Allure of Race.* Routledge: London, 2004.

Goyal, Yogita. *Romance, Diaspora, and Black Atlantic Literature.* Cambridge: Cambridge University Press, 2010.

Herdeck, Donald E. Introduction to *Batouala: A True Black Novel*, by René Maran. 1–6. Washington, DC: Black Orpheus Press, 1972.

Kojo Touvalou-Houénou's cosmopolitanism   135

Hill, Robert, ed. *The Marcus Garvey and Universal Negro Improvement Association Papers*, Vol. 10. Los Angeles: University of California Press, 2006.

Kearney, Richard. *Postnationalist Ireland: Politics, Culture, Philosophy*. London: Routledge, 2002.

Langley, Jabez Ayodele. "Marcus Garvey and African Nationalism." In *Marcus Garvey and the Vision of Africa*, edited by John Henrik Clarke and Amy Jacques Garvey, 402–413. New York: Vintage Books, 1974.

——. "Pan-Africanism in Paris, 1924–36." *The Journal of Modern African Studies* 7, no. 1 (April 1969): 69–94.

Levine, Lawrence. *The Unpredictable Past: Explorations in American Cultural History*. New York: Oxford University Press, 1993.

Lloyd, Craig. *Eugene Bullard, Black Expatriate in Jazz-Age Paris: Black Expatriate in Jazz-Age Paris*. Athens, GA: University of Georgia Press, 2006.

Lunn, Joe. *Memoirs of the Maelstrom: A Senegalese Oral History of the First World War*. Portsmouth, NH: Heinemann, 1999.

"M. Diagne fait condamner ses diffamateurs." *Les Annales Coloniales*, November 27, 1924: 2.

"M. Diagne fera justice des potins de René Maran." *Les Annales Coloniales*, June 16, 1924: 1.

Manning, Patrick and James S. Spiegler. "Kojo Tovalou-Houénou: Pan-African Patriot at Home and Abroad." Paper presented at the African Studies Faculty Seminar, Stanford University, April 4, 1991.

Martin, Tony. *Race First: The Ideological and Organizational Struggles of Marcus Garvey and the Universal Negro Improvement Association*. Dover, MA: The Majority Press, 1986.

——. *The Pan-African Connection: From Slavery to Garvey and Beyond*. Dover, MA: The Majority Press, 1983.

McNamara, Francis Terry. *France in Black Africa*. Washington, DC: National Defense University, 1989.

Miller, Christopher L. *Nationalists and Nomads: Essays on Francophone African Literature and Culture*. Chicago: University of Chicago Press, 1998.

Moses, Wilson Jeremiah. *The Golden Age of Black Nationalism*. Hamden, CT: Archon Books, 1978.

Mulzac, Captain Hugh. "Memoirs of a Captain of the Black Star Line." In *Marcus Garvey and the Vision of Africa*, edited by John Henrik Clarke and Amy Jacques Garvey, 127–138. New York: Vintage Books, 1974.

Steins, Martin. "Black Migrants in Paris." In *European-Language Writing in Sub-Saharan Africa*, Vol. 1, edited by Albert S. Gérard, 354–378. Budapest: Akad. Kiadó, 1986.

Stokes, Melvyn. "Kojo Touvalou Houénou: An Assessment." *Transatlantica* no. 1 (2009): 1–9.

Stovall, Tyler. *Paris Noir: African Americans in the City of Light*. New York: Houghton Mifflin, 1996.

Tovalou-Houénou, Prince Kojo. "L'A.O.F. Extract." In *Ideologies of Liberation in Black Africa*, edited by Jabez Ayodele Langley, 239–241. London: Rex Collings, 1979.

——. *L'involution des métamorphoses et des métempsychoses de l'univers. Tome 1er. L'involution phonétique ou méditations sur les métamorphoses et les métempsychoses du langage*. Paris. L'auteur, 1921.

136 *Kojo Touvalou-Houénou's cosmopolitanism*

——. "Prince of Dahomey Speaks." In *The Marcus Garvey and Universal Negro Improvement Association Papers*, Vol. 5, edited by Robert Hill, 823–824. Los Angeles: University of California Press, 1986.

——. "The Problem of Negroes in French Colonial Africa." *Opportunity* (July 1924): 203–207.

Vaillant, Janet G. *Black, French, and African: A Life of Leopold Sédar Senghor.* Cambridge, MA: Harvard University Press, 1990.

Wilder, Gary. "Panafricanism and the Republican Political Sphere." In *The Color of Liberty: Histories of Race in France*, edited by Sue Peabody and Tyler Stovall, 237–258. Durham, NC: Duke University Press, 2003.

Wilson, Edward T. *Russia and Black Africa Before World War II*. New York: Holmes and Meier, 1974.

Zinsou, Émile Derlin and Luc Zouménou, eds. *Kojo Tovalou Houénou Précurseur, 1887–1936: Pannégrisme et Modernité*. Paris: Maisonneuve & Larose, 2004.

5 Lamine Senghor's cosmopolitanism, anticolonialism, and similarities with Marcus Garvey

Even if he had no personal relationships with Garvey, Lamine Senghor was ideologically similar to him since his criticisms against Diagne's exploitation of African masses during World War I for the sake of France resonates with those that the Jamaican made toward the deputy. Both leaders centered their liberation discourse on denunciations of the deceptive strategies that Diagne deployed to lead Africans to fight and sweat for a French empire that attached little value to their lives and conditions. Also, both Garvey and Senghor deplored France's refusal to extend to *tirailleurs* the cosmopolitanism that these Africans had defended by shedding blood for the métropole's liberty and freedom during World War I. Consequently, both intellectuals viewed Diagne as an elitist and corrupt leader who betrayed black people.

Another connection between Garvey and Senghor is that they both emphasized the importance of nationhood and cosmopolitanism in their fight for the freedom of blacks of Africa and the diaspora. Senghor based his Pan-Africanism and cosmopolitanism on the same idea of the universal right of mankind to achieve freedom that inspired Garvey. Yet, although he partook in this republican idea that fascinated Garvey, Senghor was partially different from the Jamaican since he believed in a crossracial cosmopolitanism which thrived to defend the freedom of both blacks and whites. Focusing on Senghor's memoir, *La violation d'un pays*, which was first published in 1927 and reprinted by Harmattan in 2012, this chapter will explore the Senegalese activist's denunciation of Diagne's and France's imperialism and mistreatment of *tirailleurs*. Moreover, the chapter will compare the Pan-Africanisms and cosmopolitanisms that both Senghor and Garvey deployed to resist the imperialism of Diagne and France.

A major gap in black studies is the neglect of the relationships between Garvey and the African Francophone activists who emerged in France in the 1920s after Touvalou's downfall. One of these leaders was the former *tirailleur* Lamine Senghor whose organization, the Comité de Défense de la Race Nègre (CDRN), was a precursor of another major association of black activists in 1920s France called la Ligue de Défense de la Race Nègre (LDRN). Garvey was a strong admirer of both organizations and, in 1928,

138 *Lamine Senghor's cosmopolitanism*

after Senghor's passing, reached out to the LDRN's new leaders, especially to its chairman, the Malian Tiémoko Garan Kouyaté. Discussing Garvey's attempts to establish ties with the LDRN, Edwards asserts:

> The UNIA leader was definitely in touch with Kouyaté by the beginning of 1928, when the French Colonial Ministry intercepted a letter in which Garvey wrote that he regretted that he could not send a financial contribution to the LDRN, but that he hoped to work together in the future "for the good of the blacks [*nègres*] of French Africa."
>
> (2003, 293)

Garvey finally encountered the African intelligentsia in 1928 when he and his wife Amy Jacques Garvey traveled to France and were well received by the Comité de Défense de la Race Nègre.[1] According to Edwards, it was during his visit to France that Garvey became a member of the LDRN (2003, 293–294).

Garvey's membership of the LDRN is also apparent in *Race First* where Martin writes:

> During his trip to France in 1928, Garvey claimed to have "cemented a working plan with the French Negro" and to have established a "sub-European headquarters" in France. He also joined the Comité de Défense de la Race Nègre, a Paris-based Pan-African organization associated with the French Communist Party and the Comintern.
>
> (1976, 115–116)

Even if Garvey's first direct contacts with the black French intelligentsia of Paris occurred in 1924 (through his contacts with Touvalou and, later, in 1928, via his membership of the LDRN), they were given the strongest expression by the ideological connections that he had with Senghor. Although he had no personal ties with Senghor, Garvey inspired the Senegalese's concept of self-reliance which later prompted the LDRN's future leaders to establish links with the UNIA. Yet Senghor's ideological relationships with Garvey remain generally ignored, probably because the Jamaican's ties with the LDRN evolved after the Senegalese leader's passing.

Beside Edwards's *The Practice of Diaspora*, a few studies have also tried to give Senghor the scholarly importance that he deserves. One of these texts is Holger Weiss's *Framing a Radical African Atlantic* (2014) which also re-inscribes Senghor in black Atlantic studies. Weiss describes Senghor's intervention at the 1927 Brussels Conference as "a passionate and mordant denunciation of French Imperialism" signified by "the photograph of him standing behind the podium with his determined look and hand clenched in a fist [which] was to be reproduced several times and symbolized the determination of the awakening political awareness of the exploited masses in Africa" (2014, 84). The quotations reflect the radical and anti-colonial posture that Senghor embodied in his activism.

Lamine Senghor's cosmopolitanism 139

Another seminal publication on Senghor is Derrick's *Africa's 'Agitators'* which suggests the important role the Senegalese played in the formation of black activism in France in the 1920s. Derrick writes:

> Lamine Senghor attended as representative of a new radical movement formed by Africans and West Indians in France, the Comité de Défense de la Race Nègre (CDRN) ... He declared, following the Communist line, that victims of imperialism in the West and in the colonies must stand together.
>
> (2008, 175)

In addition, like Steins's 1986 essay "Black Migrants in Paris," Derrick's book shows how Senghor replaced Touvalou as the leading voice of black anticolonialism in France in the mid-1920s after the rancid Diagne-Maran trial that finished *Les Continents*.[2]

Yet one of the most recent studies of Senghor's anticolonialism is the introduction of *La Violation du Pays* in which the editor, David Murphy, describes it as a radical departure from the paternalism and assimilationism that shaped France's relationships with *tirailleurs*. Murphy writes:

> La vision de l'Africain s'était transformée pendant la guerre: le bon *tirailleur*, ce "grand enfant", remplaça le "sauvage" dans l'imaginaire français. Mais Lamine Senghor révèle un nouveau visage au public français, celui du tirailleur radicalisé par ses expériences qui se lance dans un combat contre les injustices du système colonial, tout le contraire du tirailleur fidèle à la France présentée dans *Force-Bonté*.
>
> [The vision of the African was transformed during the war: the image of the good *tirailleur*, this "big kid," replaced the "savage" in the French imagination. But Lamine Senghor reveals a new face to the French public, namely, that of a *tirailleur* radicalized by his experiences who embarks on a fight against the injustices of the colonial system, which is the opposite of the true sharpshooter in France presented in *Force-Bonté*.]
>
> (2012, vii–viii)

Murphy's statement is crucial because it represents Senghor as a former *tirailleur* who became radicalized by his harsh conditions in colonial Senegal and the métropole. As this chapter argues, Senghor attributed these conditions to the fascist and assimilationist policies that Diagne and France developed against *tirailleurs*.

Senghor was born in either Kaolack or Joal, Senegal, in 1889, and moved to Dakar about a year before World War I to work as a "boy" [servant] and, later, as an employee of the Bordeaux trading house, Maurel et Prom, before enlisting in 1915 to fight at Verdun and the Somme.[3] He distinguished

140 *Lamine Senghor's cosmopolitanism*

himself in the war as an exemplary *tirailleur* who was ready to die for France. As Murphy indicates, between September and October 1917, Senghor was part of the 4th company of the 68th battalion of *tirailleurs* which was attacked with German mustard gas, an offensive which might have gravely impaired his lungs and killed him ten years later (2012, xx). After the war, Senghor received some recognition for his valor. Derrick writes: "He [Senghor] won the Croix de Guerre and was wounded and gassed. [He] was [d]emobilised back in Senegal in 1919 with the rank of sergeant and a 30 per cent invalid ex-serviceman's pension" (2008, 139). While Senghor was pleased with his Croix de Guerre, he was unhappy with the small French pensions which could not compensate for the suffering and loss of lives that *tirailleurs* incurred from the war. Such an injustice and the poverty and discrimination to which the combatants were subjected after the war transformed Senghor from a passive veteran to a bold, radical, and revolutionary activist. Yet, Senghor needed proper documents in order to be able to struggle for equality in France and Senegal. The plight of *tirailleurs* was his ticket to the métropole. Thus, according to Miller, in response to "the inequity of treatment between veterans who were French citizens and those who were not," Senghor "falsified his birth records, claiming to have been born in Dakar, not Joal; this earned him the status of French citizen" (C. Miller, 1998, 24). Yet, due to racism, Senghor was treated as an *indigène* in Senegal even if he once had an *originaire* status before he became a French citizen after the war.

However, Senghor's French citizenship was beneficial to him, since it facilitated his return to France and relative integration in a political and intellectual segment of the métropole after the war. Thus, as Derrick points out, Senghor "returned to France in 1921 and got a job with the PTT in the Paris 19th Arrondissement, and at some point became interested in left-wing politics" (2008, 139). Senghor's involvement in liberal politics and his anticolonialism and criticisms against Diagne triggered the French administration's backlash against him. Moreover, as Murphy argues, the French rescinded Senghor's citizenship probably because they found out that he was not born in one of the four communes of Senegal (2012, xix, xxi). Another possible reason for the French's nullification of Senghor's citizenship was to deter him from being involved in revolutionary activities. However, French colonials knew that an *indigène*'s falsification of papers for the improvement of his legal status was a common practice among wealthy Senegalese who had close ties to the administration. Referring to *indigènes* of the four communes, Johnson writes:

> The *sujets* rarely knew French and few had attended school in the countryside; an occasional literate and ambitious *sujet* might arrange to become an *originaire* if he could persuade influential *originaire* friends to testify in court that he was in fact a member of the chosen few.
>
> (1972, 146)

Though Senghor's successful attempt to become a citizen was a bold and risky endeavor, it was an effort that the French could have thwarted in Senegal if they had known that a Croix de Guerre would not have deterred the veteran from being an anticolonialist.

In March 1926, Senghor founded in Paris an organization called the Comité de Défense de la Race Nègre (CDRN).[4] This was an association which initially allied itself with the communist bloc called Union Intercoloniale. The latter was a branch of the political faction called *Parti Communiste Français* (PCF), which aimed to create a crossracial and transnational resistance against all forms of domination, including colonialism and capitalist exploitation. Senghor's involvement with the PCF occurred through his association with anticolonial and left-wing Asian and Caribbean activists who lived in France and were fighting for Third World liberation. Discussing this important phase of Senghor's history, Derrick highlights the Senegalese's collaboration with communist activists such as the three main Algerians—Hadj Ali, Menouard and Ben Lakhal—the white French socialist leader Henri Lozeray, the revolutionary Nguyen the Truyen, two other Vietnamese, and the West Indian Stéphane Rosso, among others, in order to establish a Colonial Commission that aimed to study the métropole's relations with its overseas territories (2008, 141). Another one of Senghor's collaborators was Max Clainville-Bloncourt, a Guadeloupan lawyer and socialist who was very aware of the colonial issues confronting blacks of Dahomey, the United States, and the Caribbean and might have inspired Senghor's Pan-African awareness. This influence is apparent in the book *In the Cause of Freedom: Black Internationalism from Harlem to London, 1917–1939*, in which Minkah Makalani highlights the manner in which both Senghor and the West Indian revolutionary denounced the United States as an imperialist nation that attempted to resuscitate slavery through the acquisition of Caribbean colonies in the early twentieth century when "black people were revolting against their limited freedoms and civil inequality" (2011, 141).

Although he worked on international issues, Senghor maintained a strong commitment to the plight of *tirailleurs* and other blacks. His devotion to *tirailleurs* sparked his interest in the transnational conditions of blacks. Thus, in 1927, a year after his creation of the Comité de Défense de la Race Nègre, Senghor co-founded an organization similar to Touvalou's LUDRN, called la Ligue de Défense de la Race Nègre (LDRN), with Kouyaté and the Martiniquan Camille Sainte-Rose, who were both intellectuals and activists based in France.[5] Kouyaté and Sainte-Rose found comfort in Senghor's new organization because they espoused its chief goal to provide a strong and collective defense of blacks against colonialism. Steins summarizes this Pan-African objective as follows:

> The C.D.R.N. for the first time united West Indians and Africans, the proletariat and the "assimilés," writers and politicians, in a single,

142   *Lamine Senghor's cosmopolitanism*

exclusively racial, organization whose aim was to speak for the blacks as one race ... The key idea was that racial solidarity should be the basis for all future action with a view to improving the position of colonized blacks. In order to achieve this, they must begin by organizing themselves in France.

(1986, 361)

The CDRN's emphasis on racial solidarity as the basis of unity and defense of blacks against colonialism resonated with Garvey's liberation ideology which perceived such a type of communalism as a solution to the dilemma of Africans at home and abroad. In this sense, Senghor's CDRN was similar to both Touvalou's LUDRN and Garvey's UNIA because all three groups regarded blacks of Africa and the diaspora as victims of a similar history of oppression in spite of their different locations. In this vein, Senghor wrote an essay, entitled "Ce Qu'est Notre Comité de Défense de la Race Nègre" [What our Committee for the Defense of the Black Race is], which was originally published in *La Voix des Nègres* on January 1, 1927. Senghor's article was partly a response to a French reporter, Pierre Bret, who, in the November 1, 1926, issue of the French journal *L'Écho de Paris*, summarized a general assembly of the CDRN that was just held at the Sorbonne. In his article, Bret says: "Ainsi, les noirs veulent se grouper, constituer une force et jouer un rôle. Ils pensent justement qu'ils sont Français et veulent servir la France" [Thus, the blacks want to come together, become a force, and play a role. They just know they are French and want to serve France] (2012, 95). Bret's quotation and entire article gave the impression that blacks of the colonies living in France in the early twentieth century were contented with their position in the métropole and were willingly coming together to serve the empire.

In response to Bret's claims, Senghor wrote "Ce Qu'est Notre Comité de Defense de la Race Nègre," which was first published in the January 1927 issue of *La Voix des Nègres*. In this essay, Senghor declares: "[R]ien n'est aussi faux que cette affirmation! Les nègres ne sont d'aucune nationalité *européenne* et ne veulent servir les intérêts d'aucun impérialisme contre ceux d'un autre impérialisme" [[N]othing is more false than this statement! The Negroes belong to no *European* nationality and do not want to serve the interests of any imperialism against those of another] ("Ce Qu'est Notre Comité de Défense de la Race Nègre," 47). Senghor's representation of the "Negroes" as people who did not count themselves in a European nationality or imperial venture refutes Bret's romanticization of France as a cosmopolitan nation that accepted its loyal colonial blacks. By rejecting Bret's cosmopolitanism, Senghor aimed to liberate the colonized Africans through a complete erasure of the French colonial state and its capitalist and imperialistic ventures. He equated the end of colonialism with the beginning of human freedom.

Lamine Senghor's cosmopolitanism   143

Many French intellectuals developed a similar thesis during the second part of the twentieth century. For instance, as Susan Gilson Miller argues, Jean Paul Sartre and Albert Memmi "saw in the end of colonialism the promise that a more rational moment was at hand, in which, as Memmi says, people would be 'whole and free'" (1991, 169). Senghor's representation of "Negroes" as people who "belong to no European nationality" and did not want to pander to imperialists made him appear as an extremist in the eyes of other black activists of his generation who did not want to alienate white members of the French Communist Party that supported the CDRN's struggle. Even if he desired crossracial alliances, Senghor refused any flattening of human experiences that dismissed the suffering and demands of blacks. Consequently, his radicalism prompted a few black members of the CDRN who feared it to leave the group. Thus, as Wilder points out,

> By 1927, ideological conflicts led to a split with the group between a reformist faction, led by Maurice Satineau (from Guadeloupe), and a communist faction, led by Senghor (from Senegal) and another African, Tiemoko Garan Kouyaté (from the French Sudan). The latter two seceded to create the more explicitly revolutionary League for the Defense of the Black Race (LDRN) whose newspaper *La Race Nègre* was also partly funded by the French Communist Party.
>
> (2003, 240)

Senghor's radicalism is further apparent in his additional criticism against Bret's article. Replying to Bret's portrayal of France's blacks as distinct from those of the United States, Senghor says:

> Au sein du Comité de Défense de la Race Nègre, il n'y a pas de distinction entre les nègres soumis au joug de l'impérialisme français et les nègres soumis au joug d'un autre impérialisme européen ou américain. Nous sommes tous des frères de la même race unis; nous subissons le même sort (sous différentes formes, bien entendu) esclavagiste par l'impérialisme international.

> [Within the Committee for the Defense of the Black Race, there is no distinction between the negroes under the yoke of French imperialism and the negroes under the yoke of another European or American imperialism. We are all united as brothers of the same race; we suffer from the same enslaving fate (in various forms, of course) through international imperialism.]
>
> ("Ce Qu'est Notre Comité", 47)

Thus, for Senghor, Bret's article was misleading because it did not address France's hypocritical mistreatment of blacks whose sole rewards for having

144 *Lamine Senghor's cosmopolitanism*

served the métropole for centuries was the kind of racism and imperialism that had also hampered the lives of blacks of the Americas.

Senghor's radicalism resonates with Garvey's conception of Pan-Africanism as a shared history of repression and a view of race as a motor force in the major historical tragedies that have shaped modern black societies. Race is so central in black history that Garvey begins the first chapter of his *Philosophy* with the idea that "the history of a movement, the history of a nation, the history of a race is the guide-post of that movement's destiny, that nation's destiny, that race's destiny."[6] Garvey's conception of history resonates with Senghor's which also recognizes blacks' limited power to achieve nationhood due to their racial identity.

Furthermore, like Garvey, Senghor knew that France's exploitation of Africans undercut its cosmopolitan discourse. Both leaders knew that France prioritized imperial prominence over its claim to improve the colonized blacks' welfare. Realizing France's hidden desires to remain a strong empire to be feared, Garvey criticized the country as anticosmopolitan. In a speech he delivered at Liberty Hall, on January 6, 1924, Garvey said: "France is at large in Europe menacing not only the peace of the Caribbean, but France to-day is a menace to civilization and to humanity."[7] Garvey's view of France as an anticosmopolitan nation resonates with Senghor's perception of the country as an empire that increasingly exploited blacks transnationally. Referring to the Republic of Haiti, that both France and the United States had occupied in 1924, Senghor states:

> Nous demandons la pleine et entière indépendance politique et économique pour les républiques de Haïti, Cuba, Saint-Domingue et les peuples de Porto-Rico et des îles de la Vierge. Nous demandons le retrait immédiat des troupes impérialistes envoyées dans ces pays. Nous désirons également obtenir pour les colonies caribéennes l'indépendance. La Confédération des Indes occidentales doit se réaliser et l'union de tous ces peuples doit s'accomplir.

> [We demand the full political and economic independence of the republics of Haiti, Cuba, Santo Domingo and the people of Puerto Rico and the Virgin Islands. We demand the immediate withdrawal of the imperialist troops that are in these countries. We also want the independence of Caribbean colonies. The Confederation of the West Indies must be achieved and the union of all these people must be fulfilled.]

> ("La question Nègre", 67)

Senghor's demand that Haiti, Cuba, Santo Domingo, Puerto Rico, and the Virgin Islands be freed from imperialism was consistent with Garvey's call for the Caribbean's independence from Western domination. Both leaders saw the Caribbean as a region that must be liberated from foreign

Lamine Senghor's cosmopolitanism 145

and colonial exploitation and allowed to develop economically. More than half a century before Edouard Glissant declared that Haiti is the focal point of the Caribbean, Garvey described this nation as a keystone of both the West Indies and the entire black world.[8] Garvey's opposition against French colonialism emanates from this shared history of black resistance that is anchored in Haiti where black cosmopolitanism was born. The desire to unite blacks and create peace between members of other races and them, that one notices in Pan-African liberation struggles, stemmed from this similar dream that Toussaint Louverture, the founder of the first independent republic of free slaves, pursued in his dealings with France and Napoléon.[9]

As discussed earlier, Garvey described Diagne, in a speech that he gave in New York, on October 2, 1921, as a leader who recruited thousands of Africans and led them to be slaughtered on the killing fields of Europe during World War I.[10] Garvey's representation of Diagne as a black deputy who brought his people to the killing fields in order to please the French resonates with Senghor's portrayal of the deputy as a traitor who helped to murder his brothers for the métropole's glory. In a 1924 article entitled "Un Procés Nègre," probably written by him, Senghor describes Diagne as "le commis recruteur, l'agent de liaison entre le vendeur d'esclaves (les chefs indigènes de l'AOF) et l'acheteur (la France impérialiste): marché de chair à canon pour la guerre de la civilisation" [the committed recruiter, the liaison between the buyer of slaves (*indigène* leaders of the AOF) and the seller of slaves (imperialist France): a market cannon fodder for the war of civilization] ("Un Procés Nègre," 33). Senghor expanded his disparagement of Diagne in his book *La violation d'un pays* where he satirizes the parliamentarian as the fictional character of "Dégou Diagne" who "Aidé de 'l'homme pale', enterra son frère qu'il avait assassiné, pour cacher les traces de leur crime" [collaborated with the "white man" to bury his brother that he killed and, thus, hide their crime] (*La Violation d'un pays*, 14). Senghor's indictment of Diagne came from the early post-World War I era in which Senegalese leaders sided either with the empire or its disenfranchised inhabitants. Having given his full allegiance to the métropole, Diagne automatically earned the disreputable mantle of betrayer of his people. In this vein, Dorothy S. Blair interprets the short story, *Prisonier du regard* (1975), as "an indictment of Blaise Diagne, portrayed not as one of Senegal's great political leaders but as the man who betrayed his countrymen's trust and was indirectly responsible for the deaths and untold suffering in the salt mines" (1984, 123). Diagne's indictment resulted from the rupture that occurred between Senegalese elite and the masses that they were supposed to represent. Diagne was an easy target of this schism because he had been a strong advocate of France's implementation of cultural assimilationism in Senegal since the early twentieth century, unlike the majority of the nation's subsequent political leaders, such as Lamine Senghor, Galandou Diouf, Léopold Sédar Senghor, Cheikh Anta Diop, and many others, who attacked such a policy as an aggression to the nation's humanity and sovereignty.

146 *Lamine Senghor's cosmopolitanism*

The denunciation of Diagne as a traitor was also part of a transnational intellectual tradition in which blacks of the diaspora were, like their counterparts in France and Africa, able to assess the effects of the deputy's partnership with the métropole on the continent. More than a decade before Senghor condemned Diagne's role in World War I, Garvey denounced the profit that the deputy made from the recruitment of *tirailleurs*. In his 1923 essay, entitled "Traitors," Garvey condemns blacks who profited from selling the less fortunate members of their race. He states:

> In the fight to reach the top the oppressed have always been encumbered by the traitors of their own race, made up of those of little faith and those who are generally susceptible to bribery for the selling out of the rights of their own people.
>
> (29)

Garvey's attack on "black" traitors resonates with the remonstrance that both he and Senghor made against Diagne by perceiving him as a leader who sacrificed *tirailleurs* on behalf of France.

Moreover, both Senghor and Garvey were accurate in their assessments of Diagne's horrid roles in the massacre of World War I *tirailleurs*. Many of these *tirailleurs* either died at the front or returned permanently maimed. Vaillant writes:

> Diagne pressed ahead with the conscription of African troops. Many of them, formed into units that carried on the name of Faidherbe's *tirailleurs Sénégalais*, fought and died on the fields of Flanders. Some educated Africans, especially the families of those conscripted with promises of citizenship that later were not honored, never forgave Diagne for what they believed to be his gross subservience to French interests.
>
> (1990, 47)

While the number of citizenships that Diagne obtained from the French in the aftermath of World War I is unknown, it is certain that it was not high. According to Philippe Dewitte, after the armistice, "la citoyenneté est accordée au compte-gouttes" [citizenship is granted by the dropper] (1985, 52). This situation was compounding to Senegalese *originaires* that Diagne had deployed to the war with the promise of a citizenship which was more valuable than the nominal and abstract French nationality that distinguished them from the *sujets*. *Originaires* were also disillusioned because the France they discovered after World War I was extremely racist and bent on giving them a semblance of privilege over the *sujets* as a means of preventing a collective unity between the assimilated elites and the rural class of traders and peasants.

To these problems, one must add the plight of blacks from other African colonies whose material conditions, dwellings, and infrastructures were worse than those of the rural inhabitants of Senegal. Few of these West Africans could obtain citizenship after the war. Those who had citizenship generally came from the elite that supported Diagne and the French administration. Echenberg refers to the example of Jean Adjovi, the son of a wealthy Dahomean trader who received citizenship in 1920 after he helped Diagne recruit Beninese soldiers for France, but was unable to help other Beninese gain this status (1991, 45–46). To such disparities, one should add the medical challenges of the wounded African veterans. In *Native Sons*, Mann observes:

> Many men were killed or injured in combat, but frostbite, tuberculosis, and other illnesses also took a heavy toll on the West African contingent ... By [World] [W]ar [I]'s end, approximately 30,000–31,000 of those who had served on the Western Front, in Africa, and in Turkey were dead, and many others had been sent home permanently disabled.
>
> (2006, 17)

Such dire effects of World War I on *tirailleurs* contradict the French cosmopolitanism that Diagne espoused with his fanatic belief in the métropole's love of blacks and willingness to reciprocate the sacrifices of these populations with fair treatment. Diagne's faith in this cosmopolitanism is displayed in the following words that he confided to Delavignette, a former French World War I soldier and official in West Africa: "Notre civilisation sera faite de la vôtre ou la vôtre tremblera" [Our civilization will be made of yours or yours will tremble].[11] This quotation indicates Diagne's romanticization of France and Senegal as entities bound by the same umbilical cord of cosmopolitan reciprocity and mutuality. A similar idealization of France appears in the February 16, 1924, issue of *La Dépêche Coloniale et Maritime* in which an anonymous article, entitled "Au syndicat de défense des intérêts sénégalais" [To the union for the defense of Senegalese interests], describes a meeting in Bordeaux, France, where Diagne proposed to build modern houses for the inhabitants of the four communes for many reasons including to "réaliser le maximum de securité à la fois pour les indigènes et pour les colons qui vivent à côté d'eux" [achieve maximum safety for both the natives and the settlers who live next to them] ("Au syndicat de défense des intérêts sénégalais," 1). This article suggests Diagne's plan to accommodate *originaires,* for whom he wanted to build modernized houses, and his alienation of *indigènes*, for whom he reserved chore rather than dwellings and comfort. Speaking to his Bordeaux merchant partners, Diagne represented *indigènes* as people who deserved more "semences" [seed] so that "l'intensification de la culture de l'arachide fut poussée dès cette année par tous les moyens possibles" [The intensification of cultivation of groundnuts be, from this year on, maximized by all possible

148 *Lamine Senghor's cosmopolitanism*

means] ("Au syndicat de défense," 1). Thus, Diagne was a fascist since he perceived *indigènes*, just as he did *tirailleurs*, as the empire's available laborers and servants.

Diagne's perception of *indigènes* as people whose sole purpose was to generate labor and seed for the French empire suggests his complete disregard of these populations in the cosmopolitanism that he loved so much. Diagne's sole interest in the material value of *indigènes* suggests his denial of these people's civil and human rights. Recognizing these rights would have led him to demand equal compensation for the negative outcomes of the war on *tirailleurs* and other *indigènes*. Unfortunately, by 1924, Diagne had partially abandoned his promise to seek France's accommodation for Senegalese soldiers (a combat that he had vowed to wage during the war) because he was, by then, entangled in conflicts of interests that tied him to business leaders of Bordeaux. Witnessing this tragedy, Lamine Gueye (another future Senegalese opponent of the black deputy), attacked Diagne by reverberating Garvey's and Senghor's claims that the deputy's loyalty rested more on the interests of capitalist French colonials than on those of Africans. According to Dieng, in a speech recorded by the French colonial police, Gueye described Diagne as follows: "C'est un déraciné—le coffre-fort bordelais—si vous ne l'éliminez pas, les mises à pied et les renvois vont pleuvoir en masse. À bas le vendu. Il a en main le commerce, les banques et le gouvernement" [He is uprooted—the safe of Bordeaux—if you do not get rid of him, there will be a long rain of layoffs and bounced checks. Down with the sellout! He has the trades, commerce, banks, and government in his hands].[12] Garvey perceived Diagne in comparable ways since he saw him as one of "the idols of France."[13] Garvey's observation signifies his view of Diagne as a fetish that France displayed in its national assembly in order to create the false image of a cosmopolitan and racially inclusive empire. For Garvey, the deputy was merely a subordinate politician whose role was to facilitate colonization.

Furthermore, Garvey's depiction of Diagne as one of "the idols of France" resonates with Senghor's appellation of the deputy as Dégou Diagne. This is a literary character who betrays West Africans by leading them to labor and fight to death for France in exchange for pittance or nothing. Diagne's betrayal of Africans reveals his role as a collaborator against his people—a behavior that prompted Senghor to fictively call the deputy "Dégou Diagne" or what Miller describes as "*jaaykatu dee* (vendeur dont la marchandise est la mort)" [seller of corpses] (C. Miller, 1998, 217). Such designations appropriately characterize Diagne as a fascist who exhibited the paradoxes of a French cosmopolitanism which perceived Africans mainly as laborers and fetish to use at time of war and discard afterwards as parasites. Ironically, Diagne's white collaborators perceived him in a similar fashion. Even if he continued to recruit *tirailleurs* for France after World War I, Diagne was depicted by French colonial journals as a charm that had become useless to the métropole in the 1920s. For instance, in some issues

Lamine Senghor's cosmopolitanism   149

of *Les Annales Coloniales* written during that period, a few white colonials and news reporters painted Diagne as a leader who had lost his value and purpose by falling into dandyism and narcissism while *tirailleurs* that he brought to France were being displayed as tools of entertainment.[14]

Unlike Diagne, Senghor had a steady empathy for the subjugated blacks of Senegal and France since he experienced discrimination against *tirailleurs* as well as forced labor in West Africa. His familiarity with the conditions of ordinary Senegalese is visible in a speech delivered at Le Congrès anti-impérialiste de Bruxelles [The Brussels Conference of the League Against Imperialism], held between February 10 and 15, 1927. In this speech, Senghor denounces the practice of forced labor in which African women and children in the colonies worked for ten hours per day at a salary of 1.50 francs while men served for the same duration at 2 francs per day.[15] Senghor's condemnation of the plight of these Africans resonates with the 1926 article entitled "Le Réveil des Nègres" in which he states:

> Après avoir forcé les nègres à travailler pour la gloire—ou pour la peau—de payer tous les impôts, y compris celui du sang, de faire deux et trois ans de service militaire, cependant que les fils des plus grands patriotes de leur patrie ne font que dix-huit mois, les envoyer se faire tuer sur les champs de "manifestation des civilisés" . . . pour la défense et la sauvegarde des droits de la liberté universelle, des peuples à disposer d'eux-mêmes; aujourd'hui on leur refuse (aux nègres), le bénéfice de ces droits et de cette liberté, pour lesquels des centaines de milliers des leurs pourrissent à des milliers de kilomètres en dehors de leurs pays d'origine, sous prétexte que ces droits et cette liberté sont faits pour les civilisés et non les autres.

> [After forcing the blacks to work for glory—or for their race—to pay all taxes, including the blood debt, to give two to three years of military service, while the sons of the greatest patriots of their homeland serve for only eighteen months, and be killed in the fields of "manifestation of the civilized" . . . for the defense and the safeguarding of people's right to universal freedom and sovereignty, today, they (negroes) are denied the enjoyment of these same rights and the liberty for which hundreds of thousands of them perished thousands of kilometers away from their country of origin, on the pretext that these rights and this independence are made for the civilized only and not the others].

> (41)

Later, Senghor condemns the discriminatory ways in which French law treated the injured *tirailleurs* after World War I. He writes:

> Un blessé de guerre 100 %, art. 10 et 12 (c'est-à-dire qu'il ne peut pas bouger et qu'on doit le porter partout où il va), si c'est un Français blanc,

150 *Lamine Senghor's cosmopolitanism*

on lui donne 15.390 francs; si c'est un nègre, on ne lui donnera que 1.800 fr.

[In accordance with Articles 10 and 12, a 100% war-disabled man (that is, a man who is no longer able to move and has to be carried everywhere) gets 15,390 francs if he is a white Frenchman; if he is a Negro he receives only 1,800 francs.][16]

This passage reflects the systemic racial discrimination that debunked the French's claims of regarding *tirailleurs* as equal members of their empire. By giving more disability benefits to white French veterans than the black Senegalese ones, the métropole belied the cosmopolitanism that it had celebrated since its official demise of slavery in 1848. Resuscitating this cosmopolitanism in a 1918 issue of *La Dépêche Coloniale et Maritime*, Delafosse says:

La France est un pays dans lequel la générosité vis-à-vis d'autrui est souvent plus forte que le souci des intérêts privés et publics. Elle est aussi un pays de bon sens, qui comprend que l'avenir d'une colonie est conditionné par la prospérité de ses habitants autochtones aussi bien, et parfois plus, que par celle des habitants immigrés.

[France is a nation in which generosity toward the other is usually stronger than the worry of private and public interests. She is also a country with common sense, which understands that the future of a colony is as determined by the prosperity of its autochthonous populations as it is, and sometimes more so, by that of its immigrant populations.]

(1918, 1)

Delafosse's declaration represents France as a cosmopolitan nation with sincere ethical willingness to assimilate and accommodate its colonized inhabitants. His cosmopolitan discourse was disproved by the inequalities between the maimed white and black soldiers. This inequity resulted from a new form of bondage that France had created in Africa during and after World War I. Depicting this new bondage, Senghor writes:

Les femmes et les enfants travaillent la même durée que les hommes et, avec cela, on vient nous dire que l'esclavage est aboli, que les nègres sont libres, qu'il y a l'égalité de tous les hommes, etc. Je considère ceux qui nous disent cela non comme des imbéciles, mais comme des hommes qui se fichent un peu de notre tête.

[Women, children, and men work for the same duration and, with this, we are told that slavery is abolished, that the Negroes are free, that there is equality of all men, etc. I consider those who speak like this not as fools, but as men who are joking.][17]

Locating French slavery in the global Western capitalist and colonialist relationship to the rest of the world, Senghor asserts later in "Ce Qu'est Notre Comité de Défense de la Race Nègre:"

> "*L'esclavagisme est aboli,*" crie-t-on à travers l'univers. Voyons cela! Les colonialistes internationaux se sont emparés de nos territoires et de nous-mêmes; puis, ils se les ont partagés. Pendant plusieurs siècles, ils se sont livrés à la traite des nègres, en nous vendant ou nous achetant comme de la marchandise. Aujourd'hui, ils prétendent avoir aboli l'esclavage cependant qu'ils s'octroient—démocratiquement—les droits de vendre et d'acheter un peuple tout entier sans demander l'avis de ce dernier. . . . Quelle hypocrisie! Quel mensonge! La vérité est *que la vente au détail est interdite, tandis que la vente en gros est permise.*"

> [Many people across the world are saying, "*slavery is abolished.*" If only this was true! International colonialists have taken our territories and us; then, they have shared what they have confiscated among themselves. For centuries, they engaged in the slave trade by selling or buying us as commodity. Today, they claim to have abolished slavery; however they grant—democratically—rights to sell and buy a whole people without asking for the latter's opinion . . . What hypocrisy! What a lie! The truth is that *retail is prohibited, while wholesale is allowed.*]

(47)

Senghor's declarations were criticisms against French colonials who regarded themselves as cosmopolitans despite the serfdom and segregation they brought to Africans. Such a cosmopolitan discourse was also contradicted by the abusive manner in which France and Diagne treated Senghor and other World War I veterans. Senghor was a personal victim of this violation when the terrible conditions that Diagne and his colonial administration reserved to returned and discharged soldiers forced him to exile himself from his homeland to France. This abuse of the released combatants is noticeable in Georges Bartelemy's following remarks at the French Chamber on December 21, 1922:

> [D]es *tirailleurs* et travailleurs démobilisés, débarqués à Dakar, Conakry, Bassam . . . ont été mis dans l'obligation de rejoindre à pied leurs villages d'origine, à 500, 1000 et parfois jusqu'à 1500 kilomètres: certains d'entre eux, blessés ou mutilés, attendent encore, après quatre ans, la liquidation de leur pension; pendant la guerre, ces *tirailleurs* avaient envoyé à leur famille des mandats qui, dans nombre de cas, ne sont jamais arrivés à leurs destinataires.

152 *Lamine Senghor's cosmopolitanism*

> [[*T*]*irailleurs* and demobilized workers, who landed in Dakar, Conakry, Bassam ... were obliged to return by foot to their villages located anywhere between 500, 1000, and sometimes 1500 km away; some of them, wounded or maimed, are still waiting after four years, for the receipt of their pension. During the war, *tirailleurs* sent to their families money orders that, in many cases, never reached their recipients].[18]

The predicament of World War I veteran *tirailleurs* is also perceptible in Mann's following testimonial:

> [S]ome men were discharged and sent home in spite of serious injuries or disabilities resulting from their service ... As civilians, many would decide that it was preferable to do without the pensions and often ill-fitting prosthetic devices that were offered to them.
>
> (2006, 100)

Such a wretched plight of returned *tirailleurs* in colonial Africa might have influenced Senghor's self-exile to France. Dewitte explains:

> Ce n'est pas un révolutionnaire qui retourne en France en août 1921, mais les espoirs déçus de l'après-guerre, les premiers contacts avec la France et les conditions d'existence réservées aux Nègres, peut-être aussi la 'trahison' de Blaise Diagne, sont à l' origine de son rapide ralliement au mouvement communiste.
>
> [This is not a revolutionary who returned to France in August 1921; but dashed post-war hopes, the first contacts with France and the life conditions reserved for Negroes, and perhaps the "betrayal" by Diagne, are at the origin of his [Senghor's] rapid alliance with the communist movement.]
>
> (1985, 127)

Dewitte's quotation echoes an argument that Miller has also made, which is that Senghor was a "model tirailleur" who became radicalized only after 1919 when he noticed the stark disparities between the treatments of French and black African World War I veterans.[19]

Another contributing factor in Senghor's radicalization was Diagne's efforts to restrain subversive anti-imperial movements in West Africa. In his battles against Garveyism and its supporters in Africa, Diagne tried to curtail both Touvalou's and Senghor's political activisms in Senegal. Diagne also wanted to shield Senegalese masses from the radical anti-French sentiments that Touvalou, Senghor, and Garvey were spreading in Africa. A September 1927 article of *La Race Nègre*, entitled "La générosité française sous la IIIᵉ République," laments how the French nation that previously defended the principles of 1789 would not allow its black people to hold a congress in Dakar, Bamako, Grand-Bassam, Porto-Novo, or Libreville or

Lamine Senghor's cosmopolitanism 153

receive newspapers from their black brothers of the United States, Brazil, and Argentina ("La générosité française sous la IIIe République," 75). Diagne was responsible for such a draconian media censorship which aimed to keep radicals like Senghor out of Africa.

Moreover, as they previously did to the UNIA's *Negro World*, the French banned Senghor's *La Race Nègre* in an attempt to prevent any black revolutionary movement in Africa. The French's fear of counter-insurgency in Africa is further apparent in a letter dated October 9, 1927, in which Captain Mademba, a black officer who served in Kati, Mali, wrote to a white Colonel Commander to report his seizure of a copy of "La Race Nègre" from a soldier. Captain Mademba intended to show the issue to his superior "et éviter dans nos camps la diffusion des idées subversives de quelques énergumènes, qui ne sont rien chez nous, mais qui deviennent des personnages, parce qu'il leur est permis en France d'insulter l'autorité et de prêcher la révolte" [And avoid the spread in our camps of subversive ideas of a few fanatics who are nothing to us, but who become known because they are allowed, in France, to insult the authority and preach revolt].[20] The Captain's fear of insurgency among *tirailleurs* of Mali reflects the French colonial administration's perception of subversive attitudes of *indigènes* or *originaires* as Bolshevik influence. *La Depêche Coloniale et Maritime* was not a stranger to this colonial fright of communist radicalism in the colonies since it had numerous alarmist articles warning against the rising threats of Bolshevik turbulence among *indigènes* who may succumb to Trotsky's and Lenin's propaganda.[21] Captain Mademba's perception of a few of his soldiers as potential radicals suggests his reinforcement of the French colonials' stereotyping of Bolshevism as an ideological activity that could jeopardize the empire's control of its black masses. Captain Mademba was so loyal to France that he perceived both *La Race Nègre* and *The Negro World* as dangerous alien indoctrinations that ought to be blocked from the colonial army. He writes:

> Par ailleurs, je sais, de militaires rentrés de l'extérieur, que des émissaires de la rédaction de la "Race Nègre" faisaient de la propagande auprès de nos gradés et tirailleurs de la Métropole ... Tous ces renseignements ont besoin d'être contrôlés. Dans tous les cas, des mesures sont à prendre contre les ennemis des blancs et de l'Armée Noire.

> [Moreover, I heard from military men who have returned from abroad, that emissaries of the journal "Race Nègre" [Negro Race] engage in propaganda among our officers and *tirailleurs* of the *Métropole* ... All this information needs to be controlled. In all cases, action must be taken against the enemies of the white race and the Black Army.][22]

Captain Mademba's declaration exhibits the French administration's use of black colonial army officers as means to stanch Senghor's radical influence in Africa.

154   *Lamine Senghor's cosmopolitanism*

Moreover, the French administration's fear of Bolshevism in Africa was traceable to Diagne's attempt to settle a score with Senghor over the Maran legal affair. In this trial, Senghor played an important role that upset Diagne by testifying against him and depicting him as a middleman of the French imperialists who tricked *tirailleurs* into fighting in World War I without fair compensation. An anonymous article, from the November-December 1924 issue of *Les Continents*, describes Senghor's testimony as follows:

> [I]l [Senghor] avait entendu les plaintes de ses camarades de tranchée. On ne payait pas aux autres militaires noirs les mêmes primes qu'aux électeurs sénégalais de M. Diagne. On leur avait promis beaucoup. On ne tint guère. Aussi, M. Diagne, "qui était assez payé pour n'avoir pas besoin de vingt sous par recrue" n'était plus aimé chez ses compatriotes."

> [H]e[Senghor] had heard the complaints of his fellow trenchmen. We did not pay the other black soldiers the same war veteran allowances that Diagne's Senegalese voters received. A lot was promised to the black soldiers. But such promises were not fulfilled. Also, Mr. Diagne, "who was paid enough for not demanding twenty cents per recruit" was not liked among his compatriots.][23]

Moreover, Senghor depicted the trial as a meeting between a slave trader and French imperialists.[24]

Responding to his explicit disparagement of Diagne, French colonials tried to weaken Senghor's capacity to organize a counter-colonialist revolution in West Africa by preventing the former *tirailleur* from returning to his homeland. In a posthumous tribute to Senghor, written in the May 1928 issue of *La Race Nègre*, and entitled "La Ligue est en deuil," Kouyaté writes:

> Depuis 1923, Senghor avait sollicité son rapatriement au Ministère des Colonies. Ce dernier le lui refusa. On craignait que le communiste Senghor ne fît une propagande dangereuse parmi ses compatriotes ... Nos compatriotes savent que, sous la paille des mots Civilisation, Justice, Liberté d'aujourd'hui, il y a des réalités abominées. Ils sentent qu'au nom de la France on nous impose un régime voisin de l'esclavage.

> [Since 1923, Senghor had been requesting from the Ministry of Colonies his repatriation. The latter was refused to him. It was feared that the Communist Senghor might develop a dangerous propaganda among his compatriots ... Our countrymen know that behind current words such as Civilization, Justice, Freedom, there are abominable realities. They feel that in the name of France, a system akin to slavery is imposed on us.]

(147)

Lamine Senghor's cosmopolitanism   155

Diagne probably was the driving force behind the denial of Senghor's repatriation request, since the Ministry of the Colonies was an office where he had strong clout. By preventing Senghor from going home, French colonials did Diagne a favor by attempting to suppress the activist's ideologies and organization in Senegal.

The French's refusal to repatriate Senghor was an atrocious decision that contradicted their celebration of cosmopolitanism. Such cruelty is evident in the vindictive mode in which the Minister of the Colonies rebuffed Senghor's request even if he admitted that such relocation would appease the patient's tuberculosis. In a very cordial and deferential letter to the Governor General of French West Africa (Jules Gaston Henri Cardé), Senghor desperately pleaded the official to grant his transfer *"qui seul me rendra à l'était[sic] normal de ma santé"* [*which* is the only thing that can make my health normal again] ("Texte de la lettre," 80). But the Governor ignored Senghor's appeal, demonstrating France's refusal to repay the cosmopolitanism that the Senegalese showed by voluntarily serving the métropole at his own fatal cost. Senghor later died from the effects of his war injuries in a French hospital.

Yet Senghor was not the only wounded World War I Senegalese *tirailleur* to suffer in France. Bakary Diallo had a plight similar to Senghor's despite his unmatched military record and praises of French cosmopolitanism. In 1926, Diallo wrote *Force Bonté*, a novel about his participation in the war and his views about the métropole. Diallo, who was gravely injured by an attack that impaired his mouth and tongue, leaving him hospitalized in France for years, recounts the goodness he received in the métropole. He was so enamored with France and its assimilationism that he refused to denounce this nation's colonial injustice against blacks. Reminiscing the words of Amidou Frama, a Senegalese *tirailleur* who talked to him in hospital 66 in Fréjus, France, and later died in battle in 1918, Diallo states:

> Beaucoup parmi nous croient que nous ne sommes considérés que comme des chiens de chasse, à lancer où besoin est . . . Eh bien, c'est une mauvaise croyance. La France est trop humanitaire pour avoir des sentiments contraires aux aspirations humaines. Pour bien comprendre ces inspirations-là, il est indispensable de comprendre le français.

> [Many of us believe that we are considered only as hunting dogs to release where need be . . . Well, this is a wrong belief. France is too humanitarian to have feelings contrary to human aspirations. In order to better understand these inspirations, it is essential to understand French.]

> (1973, 177)

Frama's romanticization of France as an empire that loved Africans is consistent with the popular glorification of the métropole as a compassionate and caring feminine angel who provided solace to the *tirailleurs*. As is apparent in the following illustrations, both this propaganda and imagery were pervasive in French media during and after World War I.

Like Frama's, Diallo's view of France fits into the logic of cultural assimilationism which perceived acquisition of French language, culture, and ideologies as essential for enabling the colonized to be civilized and benefit from the empire's cosmopolitanism and humanism. Since he is heavily indoctrinated by this discourse, Diallo romanticizes France by praising the people who greeted a battalion of *tirailleurs* on the streets of Cette (Hérault) at their arrivals, offered the combatants delicacies, invited them to their homes, treated his wounds when he was injured at war, and were willing to help him in other ways, as proofs of the "*bonté*" [goodness] of which France is blessed (1973, 117–118). Eulogizing France, Diallo writes:

> O vous, Français de France, vous que Dieu a faits nos maîtres depuis déjà de longues années, vous qui n'avez point hésité à nous confier, comme à vos propres fils, la défense de la France, vous qui nous avez vus au travail avec vous sur les terres africaines où nous sommes nés et avons grandi, vous qui, au milieu des erreurs, trouvez la justice, la vérité, la bonté, vous nation que Dieu a faite la foi de l'humanité de par sa grâce et par la grâce de vos idées, de votre raison et de vos bienfaits,

Figure 5.1 "Carte postale, fin 1914. Vendangeuse offrant du raisin à un blessé Sénégalais" [Postcard, end of 1914. Vintager offering grape to a wounded Senegalese].

Source: Collections Eric Deroo.

Figure 5.2 "Respectueux hommages" [Respectful homage]. Musere Goré, 1914.
Source: Collections Eric Deroo.

158 *Lamine Senghor's cosmopolitanism*

vous allez avoir la preuve totale de l'attachement que nous avons pour vous, la preuve de notre fidélité et d'un dévouement que votre justice ne saura méconnaître après les faits des jours qui vont venir.

[O ye French of France, that God has made our masters for many years already; you who have not hesitated to entrust to us, as to your own sons, the defense of France; you who have seen us at work with you on African land where we were born and grew up; you who, amidst errors, find justice, truth, and goodness; you, the nation that God has made the faith of humanity by his grace and the benevolence of your ideas, your reason, and your good deeds; you will have the full proof of the commitment that we have for you, the proof of our loyalty and dedication that your righteousness will not ignore after the events of days to come].

(1973, 117–118)

Diallo's homage displays his undivided cosmopolitan loyalty to France and his capacity to reciprocate the métropole's abusive historical legacy in Senegal with forgiveness and recognition of the European's humanity and "goodness." His perception of France as the epitome of "goodness" resonates with the idea of "*bonté*" that he celebrates in his narrative as the métropole's distinctive virtue. However, in spite of its cosmopolitan intent, Diallo's romanticization of France is troubling since it confirms the métropole's stereotypical representation of *tirailleurs* as noble savage warriors that the civilizing mission humanized. This paradoxical French cosmopolitanism is evident in the primitivizing imagery of African colonial soldiers that was popularized in the "*tirailleur Y'a bon*" commercial. According to Blanchard, Deroo, and Manceron, from 1913 through the World War I period, "La presse montre ces militaires dans les rues de Paris tandis que des milliers de cartes postales, affiches et illustrés reproduisent leur image, diffusant le mythe du 'tirailleur Y'a bon'" [The media show these soldiers in the streets of Paris while thousands of postcards, posters and caricatures capture their images, reflecting the myth of the "tirailleur Y'a bon"] (2001, 46). Popularized in the image of the *tirailleur* who says in Pidgin French "Y'a bon" [this is delicious] while eating from a cereal can, this caricature exemplifies Diallo's naïve praise of the métropole as the emblem of *bonté*.

Also, Diallo's tribute to France is a bit naïve since it depicts the métropole as the emblem of righteousness, thereby minimizing its exploitative relations with colonial Senegal. While he refers to the "errors" the nation has committed, Diallo does not charge France with wrongdoing in Senegal and keeps representing the métropole as a country that is naturally gifted with "*bonté*." By constantly praising France's cosmopolitanism, Diallo remains very abstemious toward the métropole. Consequently, he becomes the kind of docile colonial subject that Dewitte describes in the book,

Figure 5.3 "Banania y'a bon" / [Affiche non identifié] [Unknown image source], Bibliothèque nationale de France [National Library of France]

Source: gallica.bnf.fr

160 *Lamine Senghor's cosmopolitanism*

Les Mouvements Nègres en France, as "un dévot francophile" [a devout Francophile] (1985, 51). Diallo's Francophile devotion is apparent in one of the instances in which he celebrates the métropole's sense of "justice, truth, and goodness" as virtues that deserve the Senegalese's "full proof" of loyalty (1973, 117–118). In so doing, Diallo exemplifies a cosmopolitanism that takes pride in its unconditional allegiance to France despite the evidence of this nation's discriminatory attitudes toward *tirailleurs* who were stationed in the métropole during the World War I period.

Diallo himself was victim of this discrimination even if he does not fully admit it. There is a passage in which he hints at the prevalence of racism against the colonial black troops in France. Regretting the short duration that did not allow the French to like the black soldiers very much, Diallo writes:

> Mais nous n'avons pas eu jusqu'ici les moyens d'être aimés de près, pour longtemps, car si nous nous posions sur une autre nature quelconque, on n'avait pour nous que des sentiments de curiosité, notre couleur noire rendant sceptiques ceux qui ne cherchent que la lumière extérieure sans plus.

> [But we have not had, thus far, the opportunities to be loved closely, for long, because when we behaved in an unexpected manner, we only aroused feelings of curiosity about our blackness among skeptics who were interested in external light only.]
>
> (1973, 182–183)

Diallo's assertion evokes sadness and ambiguity in its admission of the French's racialized and superficial representations of *tirailleurs* and their recurrent failures to see them beyond exoticism and stereotypes. His acknowledgement of such limitations reveals ambivalence in his vision of the métropole. As Dominic Thomas points out, Diallo's autobiography "vacillates between praise for the colonial mission and a seeming disillusionment with it" (2007, 49).

Another example of racism against *tirailleurs* in France in Diallo's narrative is the legal challenge he faced after he was granted citizenship, following his reception of a Croix de Guerre and a decree of March 1920. When he went to get his salary as a French citizen, Diallo was told "qu'au point de vue civil j'étais français, mais qu'au point de vue militaire je ne l'étais pas" [that I was French from a civil point of view, not from a military aspect] (1973, 180–181). Diallo's inability to be compensated like a citizen, when he had fulfilled the same duties that whites, who had such privileges, had accomplished, suggests the discrepancy in a racist and colonialist cosmopolitanism that maintained economic and social disparities between veteran white French and black African soldiers. Senghor would have agreed with Diallo's admittance of French racism against former *tirailleurs*, since he, too, suffered from the same injustice. For instance, even if, as Murphy argues, he was accorded 30 percent of indemnity and, later, 100 percent, when his illness worsened (2012, xxi, vii), Senghor underwent the blatant discrimination of a French administration that considered *tirailleurs* as inferior to whites. In a January 1927 article of *La Voix des Nègres*, entitled "Pourquoi Sommes-Nous Inferiorisés?," that Murphy credits to Senghor,[25] the activist writes:

> Pourquoi un tirailleur Sénégalais, mutilé de la "Grande Guerre", domicilié en France, reçoit-il une pension 6 à 8 fois moins forte que celle payée à un Français de la métropole de la même mutilation et du même pourcentage d'invalidité? . . . Le sang d'un nègre ne vaut-il pas celui d'un blanc [?]

> [Why is it that a Senegalese infantryman, who was mutilated in the "Great War" and is domiciled in France, receives a pension 6 to 8 times less than that paid to a French of the métropole who experienced a similar mutilation and percentage of disability? . . . Isn't the blood of a negro equal to that of a white man [?]

(53)

Senghor's lamentations about France's discrimination against wounded *tirailleurs* contradict Diallo's romanticization of the métropole's relations with these soldiers.

In addition, like Senghor, Diallo was also badly injured in the war and remained poor and invalidated in France for many years. As he confesses numerous times in his narrative, after his war injuries, Diallo had difficulty masticating food due to a severed tongue. Yet Diallo was not paid for his injuries like a Frenchman. Even if he is not bitter about this injustice, Diallo nonetheless laments the prejudice that led him to consider returning to Senegal. This decision put him in a difficult condition as he desperately waited in France for his travel papers to be processed at a time when he was so poor and almost homeless (1973, 206). Fortunately, a French woman, Mme Hasselmans, offered Diallo a room where he could stay (1973, 206). In spite of his ordeals, Diallo naively believed that "Restent les garanties matérielles" [the material guarantees remain] (1973, 206). Until his death, Diallo continued to idealize the métropole as benevolent to Africans. Moreover, as the critic Buata B. Malela argues, even if "[i]l [Diallo] est discriminé dans le traitement des soldes . . . l'ancien tirailleur garde confiance en la 'bonté française' et n'en tire aucune conclusion contre la Métropole" [[h]e [Diallo] is discriminated against in the handling of salaries . . . the former tirailleur remains confident in the "French goodness" and does not use the prejudice against the métropole] (2008, 85–86).

Figure 5.4 "Prisonniers sénégalais blessés. Carte photo de source allemande, janvier 1918." [Senegalese wounded prisoners. German photo card source, January 1918].

Source: Collections Eric Deroo.

Lamine Senghor's cosmopolitanism 163

Moreover, Diallo's relentless celebration of *"bonté"* overlooks the systemic alienation and marginalization to which blacks in France, including former *tirailleurs*, were subjected after World War I when colonials treated them as less cultured, civilized, and acceptable than biracial black elite in the métropole. Steins explains:

> This small mulatto élite was separate in every way from those tens of thousands of blacks who, since 1914, had been arriving in France in the uniform of the *"Tirailleurs Sénégalais."* Once peace had been signed, many of them stayed on or came back. Fresh from their native bush in the depths of a continent colonized for less than a generation, these men were in no way assimilated. There were nonetheless among them a few autodidacts thrilled by their extraordinary adventure. They were not "citizens," but "subjects" who in France escaped the legal status of "the native." They were not integrated into the social life of the country; they lived on the fringes of society as social outcasts. Employed in the ports and in bars, they had access only to lowly occupations which, in turn, condemned them to becoming a bohemian proletariat. They were "les Nègres."
>
> (1986, 354–355)

Moreover, Diallo's romanticization of France as a nation that loved Africans was contradicted not just by the seclusion of blacks in the métropole, but also by the marginalization of *tirailleurs* in the colonies. For example, unlike Diallo, Baba Diarra, a Malian World War I veteran, expressed deep contempt for the métropole. In a letter published in the June 1927 issue of *La Race Nègre*, Diarra recounts the racism and abuse that he endured from the French both before and after World War I. Diarra explains how he was ill-treated in Bamako where he returned after his 1912 mission in Morocco. Diarra decries how he was beaten by the "sagent ropéen" [European sergeant] with the "manigolo" [chicotte] without the intervention of the white officers who also saw *indigène* soldiers as "sauvasi" [savages] (2012, 104). Diarra's account registers his sheer and justified rancor against the inequities of a French empire that traded cosmopolitanism with violence and segregation. Like Senghor, Diarra was repulsed by the French's classification of their white soldiers as superior to the African military who were mostly considered as non-citizens both before and after World War I. Furthermore, as is visible in Diarra's reference to his daily beatings, denigration, mal-nourishment, and treatment as "plus que esclave" [more than a slave] despite his distinction as a good soldier, the French used violence, racism, denial of humanity and equality to subject *tirailleurs* to a fascist colonialist apparatus. In this imperialistic machinery, the métropole's attitudes toward *tirailleurs* are dictated by the draconian and racist ideologies that Sartre describes in *The Colonizers and the Colonized*. According to Sartre, such views are

164 *Lamine Senghor's cosmopolitanism*

sustained by relations of production that define two sorts of individuals—one for whom privilege and humanity are one, who becomes a human being through exercising his rights; and the other, for whom a denial of rights sanctions misery, chronic hunger, ignorance, or, in general, "subhumanity."

(xxv)

Lamine Senghor was a radical black intellectual who had a major role in the history of Senegalese anticolonialism in France during the mid-1920s. With a determined and uncompromising tone, Senghor denounced the bigotry of a colonial France that had no real intentions to treat Africans in cosmopolitan ways. Moreover, he vehemently condemned the systemic ways in which the métropole kept *tirailleurs* in a slave-like status while using them as sacrifices in the trenches. Diagne contributed to the colonial inequities by enabling the métropole to recruit thousands of *tirailleurs* at a cheap cost without guarantee of citizenship and freedom for these wretched combatants of the empire. By defying Diagne at a time when he was just a former *tirailleur*, who later died from wounds that he sustained in World War I, Senghor demonstrated an exemplary courage and nationalism that deserves to be studied. He fought against the injustices of the empire from a métropole where the main policies holding back *tiralleurs* emanated. Such discriminations were corroborated in the trauma discussed earlier that other *tirailleurs* such as Diallo and Diarra also suffered from a World War I French military and colonial administration in which Diagne often served as a dictatorial and vengeful political leader who did not hesitate to punish Africans who appeared as enemies of France. Another important aspect of Senghor's history is the strong impact of Garvey's liberation ideologies on his activism. Like Garvey, Senghor resisted against not only French colonialism and cosmopolitanism but also against Diagne's role as a collaborator of a French empire that tightly controlled and punished subversive activities in West African colonies. Opposing Diagne's autocracy, Senghor, like Garvey, replaced it with a cosmopolitanism founded on justice and true appreciation for the subjugated and downtrodden blacks of colonial Senegal and the world at large.

Bibliography

"Au syndicat de défense des intérêts sénégalais." *La Dépêche Coloniale et Maritime,* February 16, 1924: 1.

Blair, Dorothy S. *Senegalese Literature: A Cultural History.* Boston: Twayne Publishers, 1984.

Blanchard, Pascal, Eric Deroo, and Gilles Manceron. *Le Paris Noir.* Paris: Hazan, 2001.

Boittin, Jennifer. "The Militant Black Men of Marseille and Paris, 1927–1937." In *Black France/France Noire: The History and Politics of Blackness,* edited by Trica

Lamine Senghor's cosmopolitanism 165

Danielle Keaton, T. Denean Sharpley-Whiting, and Tyler E. Stovall, 221–246. Durham, NC: Duke University Press, 2012.

Bret, Pierre. "Un Congrès de Nègres rue de la Sorbonne." In *Lamine Senghor: La Violation d'un Pays et autres écrits anticolonialistes*, edited by David Murphy, 93–95. Paris: L'Harmattan, 2012.

Cros, Charles. *La Parole est à M. Blaise Diagne, premier homme d'Etat africain*. Dakar: Edition Maison du Livre, 1972.

Delafosse, Maurice. "A Propos des indigènes Européanisés: La Théorie et les faits: Une conception originale de nos amis belges." *La Dépêche Coloniale et Maritime*, September 12, 1918: 1.

Delavignette, Robert. "Une Grande Figure Coloniale: Blaise Diagne." *La Dépêche Coloniale et Maritime*, May 15, 1934: 1.

Derrick, Jonathan. *Africa's 'Agitators': Militant Anti-Colonialism in Africa and the West, 1918–1939*. New York: Columbia University Press, 2008.

Dewitte, Philippe. *Les Mouvements Nègres en France*. Paris: L'Harmattan, 1985.

Diallo, Bakary. *Force-Bonté*. 1926. Nendeln/Liechtenstein, Germany: Kraus Reprint, 1973.

Diarra, Baba. "Réponse d'un ancien tirailleur sénégalais à M. Paul Boncour." In *Lamine Senghor: La Violation d'un Pays et autres écrits anticolonialistes*, edited by David Murphy, 104–105. Paris: L'Harmattan, 2012.

Dieng, Amady Aly. *Lamine Guèye: Une des grandes figures politiques africaines (1891–1968)*. Paris: L'Harmattan, 2013.

Echenberg, Myron. *Colonial Conscripts: The Tirailleurs Senegalais in French West Africa, 1857–1960*. Portsmouth, NH: Heinemann, 1991.

Edwards, Brent Hayes. *The Practice of Diaspora: Literature, Translation, and the Rise of Black Internationalism*. Cambridge, MA: Harvard University Press, 2003.

"Extrait d'un article-résumé des témoignages lors du procès Diagne-Les-Continents." In *Lamine Senghor: La Violation d'un Pays et autres écrits anticolonialistes*, edited by David Murphy, 110. Paris: L'Harmattan, 2012.

Garvey, Marcus. "Speech by Marcus Garvey. [Liberty Hall, New York, January 6, 1924]." In *The Marcus Garvey and Universal Negro Improvement Association Papers*, Vol. 5, edited by Robert Hill, 513–520. Los Angeles: University of California Press, 1986.

———. "Speech by Marcus Garvey. [New York, October 2, 1921]." In *The Marcus Garvey and Universal Negro Improvement Association Papers*, Vol. 4, edited by Robert Hill, 97–100. Los Angeles: University of California Press, 1985.

———. *The Philosophy and Opinions of Marcus Garvey, or Africa for Africans*, Vol. 1 and 2, edited by Amy Jacques Garvey and Tony Martin. Dover, MA: The Majority Press, 1986.

———. "Traitors." In *The Philosophy and Opinions of Marcus Garvey or Africa for the Africans*, Vol. 1, edited by Amy Jacques Garvey and Tony Martin, 29–30. Dover, MA: The Majority Press, 1986.

Glissant, Edouard. "Haïti, point focal de la Caraïbe." *Cultures Sud* no. 168 (2008): 28–31.

Hill, Robert, ed. *The Marcus Garvey and Universal Negro Improvement Association Papers*, Vol. 10. Los Angeles: University of California Press, 2006.

James, C. L. R. *The Black Jacobins: Toussaint L'Ouverture and the San Domingo Revolution*. 1943. New York: Vintage Books, 1963.

166 *Lamine Senghor's cosmopolitanism*

Johnson, G. Wesley, Jr. "The Senegalese Urban Elite, 1900–1945." In *Africa & the West: Intellectual Responses to European Culture*, edited by Philip D. Curtin, 139–188. Madison: University of Wisconsin Press, 1972.

Kaké, Ibrahima B. "The Impact of Afro-Americans on French-Speaking Black Africans, 1919–45." In *Global dimensions of the African Diaspora*, edited by Joseph E. Harris, 249–261. Washington, DC: Howard University Press, 1993.

Kolle, Samuel Same. *Naissance et paradoxes du discours anthropologique africain*. Paris: L'Harmattan, 2007.

"La générosité française sous la IIIe République." In *Lamine Senghor: La Violation d'un Pays et autres écrits anticolonialistes*, edited by David Murphy, 74–75. Paris: L'Harmattan, 2012.

"La Ligue est en deuil: son très dévoué président SENGHOR LAMINE est mort." In *Lamine Senghor: La Violation d'un Pays et autres écrits anticolonialistes*, edited by David Murphy, 145–149. Paris: L'Harmattan, 2012.

"La Propagande Bolchevik." *La Dépêche Coloniale et Maritime*, February 13, 1920: 1.

"Le Complot Bolchevik." *La Dépêche Coloniale et Maritime*, June 8, 1920: 2.

Mademba [Le Capitaine]. "Lettre relative à la distribution de 'La Race Nègre' en Afrique Occidentale Française." In *Lamine Senghor: La Violation d'un Pays et autres écrits anticolonialistes*, edited by David Murphy, 97–98. Paris: L'Harmattan, 2012.

Makalani, Minkah. *In the Cause of Freedom: Black Internationalism from Harlem to London, 1917–1939*. Chapel Hill: University of North Carolina Press, 2011.

Malela, Buata B. *Les écrivains afro-antillais à Paris (1920–1960)—Stratégies et postures identitaires*. Paris: Karthala, 2008

Mann, Gregory. *Native Sons: West African Veterans and France in the Twentieth Century*. Durham: Duke University Press, 2006.

Martin, Tony. *Race First: The Ideological and Organizational Struggles of Marcus Garvey and the Universal Negro Improvement Association*. Westport: Greenwood Press, 1976.

Miller, Christopher L. *Nationalists and Nomads: Essays on Francophone African Literature and Culture*. Chicago: University of Chicago Press, 1998.

Miller, Susan Gilson. "Afterword." In *The Colonizer and the Colonized*, by Albert Memmi. 155–169. Boston, MA: Beacon Press, 1991.

Monof. "A La Gloire des Tirailleurs Sénégalais." *Les Annales Coloniales*, July 11, 1921: 1.

Murphy, David. "Introduction." In *Lamine Senghor: La Violation d'un Pays et autres écrits anticolonialistes*, edited by David Murphy, vii–ixx. Paris: L'Harmattan, 2012.

Ros, Martin and Karin H. Ford. *Night of Fire: The Black Napoleon and the Battle for Haiti*. New York: Sarpedon, 1994.

Sartre, Jean-Paul. Introduction to *The Colonizer and the Colonized*, by Albert Memmi. 1965. xxi–xxix. Boston, MA: Beacon Press, 1991.

Senghor, Lamine. "Ce Qu'est Notre Comité de Défense de la Race Nègre." In *Lamine Senghor: La Violation d'un Pays et autres écrits anticolonialistes*, edited by David Murphy, 46–49. Paris: L'Harmattan, 2012.

——. "Pourquoi Sommes-Nous InférJiorisés?" In *Lamine Senghor: La Violation d'un Pays et autres écrits anticolonialistes*, 53–54. Paris: L'Harmattan, 2012.

Lamine Senghor's cosmopolitanism 167

——. "Discours de Senghor [au Congrès de Bruxelles]." In *Lamine Senghor: La Violation d'un Pays et autres écrits anticolonialistes*, edited by David Murphy, 57–63. Paris: L'Harmattan, 2012.

——. "La question Nègre devant le Congrès de Bruxelles. Résolution commune sur la question Nègre: Les décisions du congrès." In *Lamine Senghor: La Violation d'un Pays et autres écrits anticolonialistes*, edited by David Murphy, 63–68. Paris: L'Harmattan, 2012.

——. "La Violation d'un Pays." *In La Violation d'un Pays et autres écrits anticolonialistes*, edited by David Murphy, 1–30. Paris: L'Harmattan, 2012.

——. "Le Réveil des Nègres." In *Lamine Senghor: La Violation d'un Pays et autres écrits anticolonialistes*, edited by David Murphy, 41–43. Paris: L'Harmattan, 2012.

——. "Texte de la lettre de Lamine Senghor au Gouverneur Général de l'A.O.F. envoyé le 9 mars 1925." In *Lamine Senghor: La Violation d'un Pays et autres écrits anticolonialistes*, edited by David Murphy, 80. Paris: L'Harmattan, 2012.

——. "Un Procés Nègre." In *Lamine Senghor: La Violation d'un Pays et autres écrits anticolonialistes*, edited by David Murphy, 33–34. Paris: L'Harmattan, 2012.

Steins, Martin. "Black Migrants in Paris." In *European-Language Writing in Sub-Saharan Africa*, Vol. 1, edited by Albert S. Gérard, 354–378. Budapest: Akad. Kiadó, 1986.

Taylor, Ula Yvette. *The Veiled Garvey: The Life and Times of Amy Jacques Garvey*. Chapel Hill: University of North Carolina Press, 2002.

Thomas, Dominic. *Black France: Colonialism, Immigration, and Transnationalism*. Bloomington: Indiana University Press, 2007.

Vaillant, Janet G. *Black, French, and African: A Life of Leopold Sédar Senghor*. Cambridge, MA: Harvard University Press, 1990.

Weiss, Holger. *Framing a Radical African Atlantic: African American Agency, West African Intellectuals and the International Trade Union Committee of Negro Workers*. Leiden, NL: Brill, 2014.

Wilder, Gary. "Panafricanism and the Republican Political Sphere." In *The Color of Liberty: Histories of Race in France*, edited by Sue Peabody and Tyler Stovall, 237–258. Durham, NC: Duke University Press, 2003.

6 George Padmore's cosmopolitanism and views on French colonialism

George Padmore is uniquely important in the history of Pan-Africanism, anticolonialism, and cosmopolitanism of the interwar years because he was a Trinidadian intellectual who drew on his knowledge of Trotskyism in order to effectively assess France's inegalitarian relationships with Senegal. With determination and a genuine care for the plight of Senegalese, Padmore denounced how France endangered the lives of thousands of *tirailleurs* and black African farmers that it used to control colonies, maximize peanut productions, and impose forced labor. Such policies belied the discourse of cosmopolitan reciprocity and advantage that French administrators claimed to give to colonized blacks who were loyal to the métropole. Focusing on Padmore's 1931 book, *The Life and Struggles of Negro Toilers*, this chapter explores the extent to which the titanic Caribbean intellectual understood the geopolitical contexts out of which France used Senegalese *tirailleurs* and peasants as means of saving its declining empire between the post-World War I period and the beginning of World War II. This text shows Padmore's accurate depictions of France's colonialist and fascist views and policies toward blacks of Senegal during the interwar years. As Padmore's narrative suggests, these ideologies contradicted France's claims of extending cosmopolitanism to Africans. As the book also shows, France's power during the interwar period emanated from a highly structured colonial system that compelled West Africans to toil for the prosperity of an empire which gave little significance to their lives. Corroborating Leon Trotsky's negative assessment of French colonialism in the interwar years, Padmore draws on the example of Senegal where the métropole subjected *tirailleurs* to fascist conditions while using them occasionally to quell internal resistances against its languishing empire. As Padmore and his communist idol, Trotsky, reveal, fascism also signifies the racist and violent manners in which France and other Western capitalist nations confined colonized blacks and other working-class populations to subhuman conditions during the interwar years.

Between the end of World War I and the beginning of World War II, major historical developments fueled the tensions between France and other Western empires. One of these events was the development, in the middle

George Padmore's cosmopolitanism 169

of the 1930s, of a new and rigid divide between the wealthy and the poor of the world. Padmore calls this dichotomy "the regrouping of the great Powers into two armed camps: 'Haves' and 'Have-Nots' as a prelude to the second World War" (1972, 45). To this development, one must add the rise of Russian communism in 1917, which was an ideological approach to world problems through the equal distribution of wealth, as opposed to the capitalist and global conquest of territories. Russia set itself apart from the central policies of imperial powers such as France, Britain, and the United States, which were based on the systemic, direct, or indirect dominance of other countries. Consequently, Russia became the ideological champion of the wretched and browbeaten masses of the world who were toiling under the yoke of both reckless capitalism and colonial racism. In this vein, Padmore describes how world politics in the post-World War I era had

> been affected by the emergence of the proletariat and colonial liberation movements as independent political forces in the struggle against Capitalism and Imperialism and the existence of the U.S.S.R. which has removed one-sixth of the earth's surface from the imperialist system.
>
> (1972, 45–46)

According to Padmore, these developments "constitute the most significant features which distinguish the present from the past. For, here we have two irreconcilable social systems—Capitalism and Socialism—as well as two hostile classes—the bourgeoisie and the proletariat—openly struggling for world domination" (1972, 46). Padmore's assertions illustrate his indebtedness to communist ideology, specifically to Vladimir Lenin's interpretation of the West's approach to labor and money as a policy based on a ruthless race toward a "monopoly" of production which would ultimately kill capitalism by transforming global workers into discontented and downtrodden masses. Lenin views this stage as that of "socialization" of labor and the point when imperialism becomes "the highest stage of capitalism." Lenin states:

> Skilled labour is monopolised, the best engineers are engaged; the means of transport are captured ... Capitalism in its imperialist stage leads directly to the most comprehensive socialisation of production; it, so to speak, drags the capitalists, against their will and consciousness, into some sort of a new social order, a transitional one from complete free competition to complete socialisation.
>
> (1999, 41)

Thus, from Lenin's viewpoint, a positive outcome of capitalism's crisis is its production of a rising and socially-conscious and global workforce which is increasingly discontented with its conditions.

170 *George Padmore's cosmopolitanism*

Yet Padmore's critique of French colonialism also stemmed from his fascination with Trotsky's communism. Both Padmore and Trotsky developed, in the 1930s, an attraction to Russia's compassionate attitudes toward the poor and oppressed classes and races of the world. Like Trotsky, Padmore had such an admiration for communist Russia that he viewed it as the sole bastion of cosmopolitanism and humanism on Earth. He writes:

> While the capitalist world is on the decline, the Soviet Union is developing and successfully building a Socialist Society. The workers, and peasants of the Soviet Union, after the victorious overthrow of the capitalist system in their country in 1917, have since become the fortress of the revolutionary workers throughout the world. The Soviet Union is the only country that knows no oppression, knows no exploitation, has no imperialist aims and supports the revolutionary liberation movements of the workers and toiling peasants of all countries as well as the emancipatory struggles of the Negro toiling masses for self-determination.
>
> *(The Life,* 111)

Padmore's perception of Russia as the proletariat's defender against the international capitalist bourgeoisie was consistent with Trotsky's view of Western powers, such as France, Britain, and the United States, as nations that differed from the Soviet Union due to their foundation on a fictive democracy which is built upon working-class oppression. In this sense, Trotsky also saw Belgium, Germany, Italy, and other Western nations as fascist empires that blinded their people with pseudo-cosmopolitan rhetoric while hampering the rights and freedom of global workers and minorities. These nations were fascist since their attitudes toward Africans were primarily based on the capitalist logic of dominance and abuse of working classes. As Kai Hafez points out, not only did these nations have "few scruples about using violence in their colonial territories," but "Their actions were governed by an economic logic, and this meant showing no consideration for human life in the colonized territories. At best, the colonized countries were left with vague hopes of eventually being civilized by their colonial masters" (2010, 172).

By contrast, Russia did not colonize African territories or bribe its populations with fascism masked as "civilizing mission" or "cosmopolitanism." Instead, Russia related to colonial Africa as a part of the world's toiling societies to free from bourgeois capitalism and colonialism. In this context, Trotsky, like Padmore, singled out Russia as the pioneer of a true cosmopolitanism made possible by the rise of the world's first free working class. In his book, *Whither France?*, Trotsky argues that "it was only in Russia that the proletariat took full power into its hands, expropriated its exploiters, and knew how to create and maintain a Workers' State" (1936, 7). This quotation shows Trotsky's exceptionalist view of Russia as the only

George Padmore's cosmopolitanism   171

nation where unhampered cosmopolitanism existed in a post-World War I context in which democracy was in the hand of the masses rather than those of the bourgeoisie.

Trotsky's political ideology was akin to Padmore's which also thrived for a cosmopolitan world in which the international poor, peasants, colonized nations, and other alienated societies, would no longer be subjugated by the ruthless and fascist policies of many Western countries. Representing the exploited nations in ways similar to how Padmore envisioned the rise of the global poor against capitalism, Trotsky describes, in *Whither France?*, how, after World War I, the "parliaments, elections, democratic liberties" and other "remnants" that existed in France, Belgium, Holland, Switzerland, and Scandinavian countries were challenged by the fact that "in all these countries the class struggle is sharpening, just as it did previously in Italy and Germany" (1936, 7–8). Condemning Gaston Doumergue, who was France's twelfth president of the Third Republic, as a leader who "can permit no liberty for the civil servants or in general for employees of the state" (1936, 9), Trotsky berates the nation's status as a "'democratically' elected majority" which, however, depended "directly and immediately upon the bureaucratic apparatus, the police and the army" (1936, 9).

By describing France as a nation which relied on military and police forces rather than on its core democratic values, Trotsky revealed its transformation into a fascist country that traded its previous aspirations for republicanism and egalitarianism with new yearnings for social inequalities that solely benefited the bourgeois and their state. Speaking about the New France, Trotsky represents Doumergue, who led it between 1924 and 1931, as a puppet of a parliament that relied on empty rhetoric. Attacking this assembly, Trotsky argues that in France "Parliament exists, but it no longer has the powers it once had," adding "The appearance on the arena of armed Fascist bands has enabled finance capital to raise itself above Parliament. In this consists now the essence of the French Constitution. All else is illusion, phraseology or conscious dupery" (1936, 9). Trotsky's declarations display a critique of the French parliament as a sagging and anticosmopolitan institution since its rhetoric of social justice and fairness did not improve the lives of the working classes of the métropole and the colonies. Trotsky's disparagement of the French parliament's cosmopolitan discourse is further blatant near the end of *Whither France?* where he declares:

> The bourgeoisie operates with abstractions ("nations," "fatherland," "democracy") in order to cover up thereby the exploiting character of its rule. *Le Temps*, one of the most venal newspapers on the terrestrial globe, gives daily lectures to the popular masses of France on patriotism and altruism. Meanwhile, it is a secret to nobody that the altruism of *Le Temps* itself is on the market at fixed international rates.
>
> (Trotsky, 1936, 119)

172 *George Padmore's cosmopolitanism*

Trotsky's representation of the concepts of "nations," "fatherland," and "democracy" as abstractions that France used to dissimulate its exploitative policies suggests his criticism of this nation's betrayal of its cosmopolitanism through systemic inequalities between white citizens and colored colonial populations. The latter groups constituted the largest "popular masses" of the empire.

Paradoxically, France saw itself as the propagator of fairness across the world at a time when it ignored the misery that it spread to its colonies. Opposing this cosmopolitan discourse, Trotsky derides the French imperial autocracy that Doumergue promoted during his administration. He states: "This historic function of Fascism is to smash the working class, destroy its organizations, and stifle political liberties when the capitalists find themselves unable to govern and dominate with the help of democratic machinery" (Trotsky, 1936, 8). Trotsky encapsulates into his critique of Doumergue the anticosmopolitan contradiction of a French empire that used such fascist tactics as discrimination, military abuse, and other violent forces to sustain a vapid national bourgeoisie.

Padmore's view of colonialism resonates with Trotsky's because it also identifies fascism as a European imperial hegemony over working classes. In the February 1938 issue of *Controversy*, Padmore defines fascism as a force which "is bound to deprive the workers of their most elementary civil rights, such as freedom of the press, speech and assembly."[1] In this logic, fascism, colonialism, and capitalism are analogous since they refer to imperial powers' resolves to sustain inequalities for the sole benefits of industrial and bourgeois interests. It was from this vantage point that Padmore identifies imperialism and fascism as inseparable forms of exploitation. Makalani explains:

> Padmore closed the rhetorical distance European powers tried to create between empire and fascism. Padmore argued that "Hitler is a fascist dictator like Mussolini" . . . Italian aggression [on Ethiopia] was an instance of colonialism acceptable to European powers . . . Fascism was not simply the product of an abhorrent mind that deserved a unique response . . . Fascism could not be fought on the side of imperialism.
>
> (2011, 204)

Padmore's criticisms against fascism resonate with Trotsky's because they unmask European colonial powers such as France, England, Belgium, Germany and Italy that compensated their declines during the interwar years by developing autocratic policies toward their colonial laborers.

Quantifying *tirailleurs* stationed in West Africa in 1931, Padmore writes:

> At present there are 40,000 native soldiers. Of this number, 20,000 are stationed in West Africa, the remainder in France and various colonies. In addition, France maintains a local police force of about 15,000 men

George Padmore's cosmopolitanism 173

in her West African colonies. The West African troops are divided into 20 regiments of 2,000 men each.

(*The Life*, 116)

The statement suggests the highly policed and militarized structure of French imperialism in West Africa in 1931 when the métropole used *tirailleurs* as a means of keeping order in its overseas territories and impressing the British and Germans. In this sense, *tirailleurs* were symbolic and practical tools of instilling terror in enemies of France both in and outside the empire. Discussing such functions, Echenberg depicts the métropole as a nation that was different from Britain, Belgium, and Germany because "only France instituted universal male conscription in peace as well as in war from 1912 until 1960" (1991, 4) and had the "determination to use" its coercive police and military force (the *tirailleurs* Sénégalais) to employ "extensively as an expeditionary force in every corner of the French empire, whether for purposes of conquest, occupation, or later, counterinsurgency" (1991, 5). France did not treat these soldiers well in spite of its extreme reliance on them. Lunn describes atrocities to which French military

Figure 6.1 "Tirailleurs du 12e RTS sortant du métro porte de Clignancourt pour rejoindre leur casernement lors du défilé du 14 juillet 1939. Paris. Photographie." [Tirailleurs of the 12th RTS leaving Clignancourt's metro entrance to return to their barracks during the July 14, 1939, parade. Paris. Photography].

Collections Eric Deroo.

174 *George Padmore's cosmopolitanism*

officers subjected the combatants during their training in the colony and their naval deployments to Europe. As Lunn argues, French officers often called *tirailleurs* "slaves" or "niggers" in military camps (1999, 96) and habitually insulted and slapped them for allegedly "failing to execute orders" (1999, 107). Moreover, French officers tormented the combatants during the voyages to Europe by confining them "to the sweltering holds" of steamers, occasionally chaining them "to their places" (Lunn, 1999, 102) and expressing "wanton disregard of their welfare" (1999, 103).

Such fascist and anticosmopolitan French actions toward *tirailleurs* are consistent with those that Padmore derides in *The Life and Struggles of Negro Toilers*. Padmore condemns the fascist ways in which the métropole misused *tirailleurs* with the promise of a freedom that Africans did not see in the 1910s and 20s. Denouncing this colonial brutality and hypocrisy, Padmore writes:

> During the period of the [First] World War, over 200,000 African natives served in the French Army. The majority of these men were recruited under the direction of *Blaise Diagne*, a Senegalese Negro politician who was commissioned by Poincaré as the special representative of French imperialism in Africa during the war. Since then Diagne has been closely identified with the war plans of his imperialist masters, who in order to draw him still closer to them recently made him Assistant Minister for the Colonies in the Laval Government. This has been done to create the impression among the Negro petty-bourgeoisie and intellectuals that the French imperialists are liberal, while their true aim is to use Diagne's prestige to carry on war preparations in the African colonies.
>
> (*The Life*, 112)

Padmore's quotation reiterates the same criticism that Trotsky made against French fascism by viewing it as a rampant threat against proletarian workers. Describing Doumergue's administration, Trotsky asserts: "The Fascists find their human material mainly in the petty bourgeoisie. The latter has been entirely ruined by big capital . . . Its dissatisfaction, indignation and despair are diverted by the Fascists away from big capital and against the workers" (1936, 8). This statement is consistent with Padmore's assessment of France's relationships with Senegal as associations based on the métropole's selfish profits rather than on altruistic desires to enhance the lives of Africans. Padmore's disparagement of both the French's recruitment of "natives" and their promotion of a "Negro petty-bourgeoisie" suggests his conception of colonialism as fascism that impaired Africans. The real victims of colonialism were the recruits and the peasants that colonials abused through the collaboration of a class that Padmore calls "the Negro petty-bourgeoisie and intellectuals." Padmore's derision of this "Negro petty-bourgeoisie" is a subtle criticism against Diagne, because it revisits

George Padmore's cosmopolitanism   175

Lamine Senghor's depiction of the deputy as a traitor who sold *tirailleurs'* lives to France for personal profit. From this perspective, Diagne was an extortionist and a blackmailer who tricked Africans to fight in World War I as the "cannon fodder" of a French empire in which blacks were regarded as unworthy of freedom and equality. Christian Koller refers to a passage of a speech, delivered to the French Senate on February 20, 1918, in which Clemenceau said:

> We are going to offer civilisation to the Blacks. They will have to pay for that ... I would prefer that ten Blacks are killed rather than one Frenchman—although I immensely respect those brave Blacks—, for I think that enough Frenchmen are killed anyway and that we should sacrifice as few as possible!
>
> (2013, 120)

Here was the true face of a French cosmopolitanism which was just a ploy to get many "brave Blacks" to die in place of "one Frenchman" even if "the Negro petty-bourgeoisie and intellectuals," among whom Diagne was a part, had been indoctrinated to depict the métropole as republican and compassionate toward *tirailleurs*. Revisiting its insincere cosmopolitan rhetoric, France continued to depend on colonial troops, especially during the mid-1930s when it increased their numbers in the overseas headquarters where they used to be stationed just in case the métropole needed them.

Another example of Padmore's contempt toward Diagne is noticeable in *Pan-Africanism or Communism* (1956) where he subtly alludes to the parliamentarian's ambiguous role in World War I. In the book, Padmore states:

> Diagne was not without his critics, some of whom were sincere and others motivated by jealousy. He was called by some a traitor for having brought the Africans to fight for France and a tool of the rich white colonial interests. Others, however, praised him as having done more than any other to strengthen the position of coloured peoples in the French Empire.
>
> (1956, 121)

Although he seems to be supportive of Diagne's recruitment efforts and considers him as a key defender of "coloured peoples" in the French Empire, Padmore does not seem to be enthusiastic about the deputy. Padmore seems to be dejected by Diagne since his allusion to the critics who perceived the politician as a "traitor" rekindles the old blame that has tarnished the parliamentarian's legacy. Moreover, although he sees Diagne as a key defender of "coloured peoples," Padmore laments the deputy's ironic role as a possible betrayer of "coloured peoples in the French Empire." Padmore writes:

176 *George Padmore's cosmopolitanism*

Ironically enough, the Negroes, who are the most despised of the exploited races, seem to be always the ones destined to come to the aid of France in her hour of need. For twenty-five years before, when the Germans stood on the Marne, another black savior came out of Africa. He [sic] was Monsieur Blaise Diagne, the Negro deputy of Senegal, who, in response to the appeal of Prime Minister Clemenceau, recruited thousands of black troops from West and Equatorial Africa to help stem to [sic] German advance on Paris during the most critical period of the First World War.

(1956, 197)

Therefore, even if he might have recruited Africans to show their devotion to France, Diagne was a collaborator of this colonialism that was fundamentally anticosmopolitan due to its subjection of the combatants to inferior positions. By being a part of a French colonial administration that orchestrated this oppression behind the facade of cosmopolitanism, Diagne collaborated with a fascist system that marred the hopes of *tirailleurs*.

Yet, Padmore's most striking depictions of colonialism that contradict French cosmopolitan appear in *The Life and Struggles of Negro Toilers*. This book shows Padmore's deep anxieties about the sinister imperial project that France was preparing during the interwar years in order to dominate Europe through the use of Africans who were increasingly militarized to serve the empire's fascist ambitions. The French claimed to bring civilization to Africans when they were mainly interested in fleecing their poor peasants and using their men at war. It was this fascist cosmopolitanism that inspired Pierre de Taittinger, a French colonial leader, when he urged the métropole to draw on its colonial soldiers to defend its empire against Russia and Germany. Soucy writes:

In 1926 he [Taittinger] noted that colonial troops and foodstuffs ("tea, sugar, coffee, and rum") had greatly contributed to France's victory over Germany in 1918: "Only our colonies . . . permitted us to win." Mixing sentimentality with self-interest, he claimed that the empire "should be as dear to us as the cradle of our childhood or the tomb where our parents rest."

(1986, 85)

Such a colonialist discourse of a major French fascist leader such as Taittinger resonates with the imperialistic and pseudo-cosmopolitan rhetoric that Padmore denounces in *The Life and Struggles of Negro Toilers*.

In his revolutionary book, Padmore vituperates the tremendous efforts the French made in World War I by gathering *tirailleurs* to prepare for eventual conflicts with any Western nation. In its propaganda against Germany, Britain, Russia, and other rivals, France displayed the military and economic potentials of its West African colonies. African railroads had a pivotal role

George Padmore's cosmopolitanism 177

in France's imperial propaganda and global policy, as is noticeable in Padmore's following assertion:

> Finance-capital is rapidly pouring into the development of railroad construction in French Equatorial and West Africa. The railroad development in these countries is being pushed forward with phenomenal rapidity ... With the completion of such a railroad the report submitted to the Minister for the Colonies points out that half a million black soldiers could be transported quickly to the Mediterranean for service in Europe in the event of war or a proletarian revolution in France.
>
> (*The Life*, 32–33)

This statement shows the great extent to which France's imperial and geopolitical power after World War I relied on its African colonies. Yet France's use of such colonies in its propaganda and global policy was motivated by self-development rather than cosmopolitan improvement of Africans' conditions. Sarraut expresses this contrived French cosmopolitan ideology in *Grandeur et Servitude Coloniale* where he writes:

> Il [le français] s'approche des autres races pour les aider, leur plaire et s'en faire aimer ... Il a besoin de donner et de se donner, de porter partout les lumières qu'il croit capables d'éclairer les chemins où trébuchent douloureusement les races moins fortunées que la sienne.

> [He [the Frenchman] approaches the other races to help them, please them and win their love ... He needs to give and give, to carry everywhere the lights he believes capable of illuminating the paths where the races which are less fortunate than his own painfully stumble.]
>
> (79)

Sarraut's cosmopolitan discourse was contradicted by the appalling ways in which the French ill-treated West Africans. This oppression fits into the brutal abuse of colonialism that Murphy describes as "this brief reminder of the violence that accompanied the French conquest of Africa [and] provides a necessary counter-balance to France's colonial discourse of its 'civilizing mission'" (2008, 184). The violence that accompanied French colonialism is further evident in *The Life and Struggles of Negro Toilers* where Padmore reflects the challenges that *tirailleurs* faced in the 1930s when they were still not free from imperial domination. Revealing the soldiers' poor economic status, Padmore writes:

> The native soldiers receive about one dollar a month and serve a period of three years. They receive three months' instruction, after which they are sent in detachments of 600 to France, accompanied by one doctor.

178 *George Padmore's cosmopolitanism*

After three months' instruction in France they are then assigned to companies and sent to *Morocco, Algeria, Syria* or *Indo-China*.

(*The Life*, 116)

Therefore, *tirailleurs* were socially and financially discriminated against white French soldiers who were not only better paid, but suffered less than them since they were citizens. Moreover, as Thomas DeGeorges points out, France's colonial soldiers did not receive compensation for the "dangerous duty" they fulfilled in the métropole's wars and "instead, they suffered from racial discrimination in salaries and promotion" (2010, 523). In addition, as subjects, *tirailleurs* were kept in the colonial army for indeterminate years without equal retribution and were treated as inferior to both whites and *originaires*. Thus, another form of inequity was the schism that the French created between *tirailleur* and *originaire* soldiers by treating them unequally during the interwar years. Focusing on this period, Adria Lawrence asserts:

> *Originaires* who joined the army received a premium of 500–800 francs, but *tirailleurs* received only 50 francs; pay for a corporal was 6.5 francs per day for an *originaire*, but only 1.15 for a tirailleur. *Originaires* also received better housing, family benefits, and retirement benefits . . . Note that the colonial authorities never proposed addressing the inequalities between Senegalese citizens and subjects by elevating African subjects to the status of citizens; rather, they supported reducing the status of the *originaires* to that of colonial subject.
>
> (2013, 112)

Such inequalities between "subjects" [*sujets*] and *originaires* resulted from the deceptive cosmopolitanism that France encouraged by creating a form of "divide-and-conquer" strategy that separated the two classes of Senegalese. Such a discriminatory and misleading tactic is apparent in Padmore's assessment of the disparities that France fostered between its colonial populations in the early twentieth century by granting citizenship to a few of the black soldiers while confining them to the status of *sujets*. Padmore explains:

> In 1923 the term of military service for "citizens" in France was reduced to 18 months, but the term for "subjects" remained the same. The black "citizens" spend their 18 months in Senegal, but the "subjects" are sent to France, where the likelihood of death is much greater, due to climatic conditions. Natives physically unfit for regular military service are obliged to serve in labour battalions.
>
> (*The Life*, 115)

Padmore's declaration reveals the classism and elitism that France created in colonial Senegal by categorizing blacks along social lines. By giving

George Padmore's cosmopolitanism   179

special privileges to a group of Senegalese while depriving them to others, France initiated a rigid class division between a minority and a majority in the colony.

Yet, France did not hesitate to further exploit *tirailleurs* by using them as butchers of imperial power. This fascist employment of colonial troops was probably the reason which prompted a few *tirailleurs* to sometimes defy French military campaigns in West Africa. For instance, according to Manning, "The Dahomeans who had shown such enthusiasm for the conquest of [German] Togoland [at the start of World War I] lost interest rapidly when they were asked to serve for two years in the Kamerun campaign" (1998, 66). The "Kamerun campaign" was a military mission in which the French used West African *tirailleurs* to dismantle German ownership in the colony. This use of *tirailleurs* for conquest of German armies that were mainly composed of African soldiers shows the extent to which imperialism thrived on black-on-black militarism and violence when the real oppressors were the European occupiers. The battles between French and German troops featured Africans mainly, not their European officers. Consequently, the actual victims of imperial atrocity were usually the colonized fighters, not the small number of European soldiers who trained and pitted them against one another. Such a mercenary use of *tirailleurs* resonates with the fascist colonial policies and strategies that Padmore describes as "the sinister aims" of the French "imperialists" between 1918 and 1923 (*The Life*, 114–115).

France's fascist domination of *tirailleurs* is also perceptible in the section of *The Life and Struggles of Negro Toilers* in which Padmore further condemns the nation's status of a classical Western imperial force. He writes:

> In the early part of the 19th century France began the militarization of her black colonial natives by the sending of certain tribes on punitive expeditions to subjugate other recalcitrant tribes. This process of militarization has been developed to such a degree that France may be taken as a classical example of the present day military policy of the imperialist nations in Africa.
>
> (*The Life*, 113)

This passage shows the fascist role of enforcers of colonial violence that France assigned to *tirailleurs* by compelling them to punish other Africans who resisted imperialism. In this sense, *tirailleurs* contributed to colonialism in Africa, since they supported it through either violence or complicity. These combatants' appalling role of collaborators of France's imperial brutality is hinted at in the book *The Colonizer and the Colonized*, where Memmi writes:

> The representatives of the authorities, cadres, policemen, etc., recruited from among the colonized, form a category of the colonized which

180   *George Padmore's cosmopolitanism*

attempts to escape from its political and social condition. But in so doing, by choosing to place themselves in the colonizer's service to protect his interests exclusively, they end up by adopting his ideology, even with regard to their own values and their own lives.

(1991, 16)

The quotation suggests the extent to which *tirailleurs*, especially those who were *originaires*, consciously or unconsciously supported the fascist power of French imperialism. By enlisting in the colonial armies, even when the enrollment was done through force, *tirailleurs* became part of a fascist imperial machine which policed and killed other Africans. Both *tirailleurs* and the guards and squadrons called the *Spahis* (the original unit of Senegal's Gardes Rouges [Red Guards]) fulfilled this role of mercenaries and enforcers of fascist colonial authority through violence. Being often recruited from enslaved and other disenfranchised groups, many of these soldiers were sometimes eager to blindly follow the orders of fascist French officers that they viewed as saviors. Indoctrinated by the myth of the civilizing mission, these army men became France's most zealous and patriotic servants who did not hesitate to fight for it whether this meant quelling rebellions in Morocco, Algeria, or other parts of the empire or forcing other black Africans to join the corps of *tirailleurs*.[2]

Paradoxically, *tirailleurs* were usually victims of the fascism they supported since they experienced the same subjugation and alienation that confronted other *indigènes* in the colonies. This equal suffering was already apparent in the *originaire* soldiers' legal status which was somewhat comparable to those of the browbeaten *indigènes*. First, as Raffael Scheck points out, "most *Tirailleurs Sénégalais* did not have French citizenship" (2006, 157). Second, *tirailleurs* were victims of an ideological manipulation that led them to serve as strikebreakers, killers, and other enforcers of France's military and moral authority in Africa and abroad when their social and economic conditions in the colonies remained deplorable. Situating *tirailleurs*' ambiguous role and status in the colonial machine, Echenberg argues that

> Rather than being a caricature of colonialism, African soldiers were, perhaps more than other groups, a mirror of colonialism and a reflection of its most basic contradictions. The hierarchical and paternalistic institution to which they belonged was a metaphor for colonialism itself.
>
> (1991, 3–4)

Yet there were *indigènes* who defied French colonialism. Moreover, although many West Africans eagerly enlisted into the French colonial army, others did not do so without resistance. For instance, as Padmore contends,

George Padmore's cosmopolitanism 181

since the war, growing resistance of the Negroes to conscription and the whole militarist policy of the imperialists in the colonies in general, together with the inhuman French economic methods of exploitation, found its sharpest expression in the uprising of the natives in French Equatorial Africa in November, 1928, which lasted for several months.

(*The Life*, 116–117)

Padmore refers to a similar West African opposition to French militarization efforts when he says: "Furthermore, conscription in French West Africa has given rise to mass revolts and migrations of the natives to the surrounding territories, such as the Gold Coast, Nigeria, Gambia, Sierra Leone and Liberia" (*The Life*, 116). Padmore was therefore very familiar with the pervasiveness of resistances against French recruitment efforts in West Africa. He was a pioneer scholar since his assessments of the demeaning French colonial attitudes toward West Africans are corroborated by similar historical scholarships that also indicate *indigènes*' opposition to French recruitment efforts. For instance, in *Colonial West Africa*, Crowder observes:

French demands for African recruits for their army fighting against the Germans in the European War of 1914–1918, led to large scale revolts throughout French West Africa. Indeed such had been the violence of the reactions of French West Africans against the compulsory drafting of their able-bodied youth that France lost effective control over large areas of her vast federation, and in 1917 the new Governor-General, Joost van Vollenhoven, reported that further recruitment was impossible in view of the revolts that had taken place in Haut-Sénégal-Niger (Modern Mali, Upper Volta) Dahomey, Ivory Coast, Guinea and the Military Territory of Niger.

(1978, 179)

Likewise, in his essay "The First World War and its Consequences" (1985), Crowder discusses many West African *sujets*' protests against the French colonizers' recruitment system (the *indigénat*) and "the exactions of chiefs without traditional authority" during the World War I era (1985, 300). Describing the *sujets*' resistance methods, which included " 'protest migrations' to the neighbouring British territories," Crowder states:

To avoid recruitment teams, inhabitants of whole villages fled to the bush. Young men mutilated themselves rather than serve in the colonial army. The protest migrations were of such magnitude that it was estimated that French West Africa lost some 62,000 subjects as a result of them.

(1985, 301)

182   *George Padmore's cosmopolitanism*

However, the least reported form of the *indigènes*' anticolonial resistance is the series of social protests that Senegalese and other West Africans developed against French colonials during the interwar period. Many of these protests were caused by the daily abuse to which West African workers were subjected in colonial businesses such as railroads, ports, roads, and prisons in which they had no control. Describing similar protests, Frederick Cooper writes:

> The flourishing of unions in 1937 and 1938 went the further among civil servants, and they were decidedly centered on Dakar: 30 of the 42 unions enumerated were based there, most of the others in Senegal and Ivory Coast; 41 of the 55 recorded strikes occurred in Dakar or Senegal in 1936–38. In the Ivory Coast, labor protest—given the recruitment system—most often took the form of mass desertions.
>
> (1996, 98)

Such anticolonial resistances defied the fascist policies that the French were implementing in their West African colonies. One of these policies was the enlistment of blacks into the colonial army through draconian methods of persuasion. A young able-bodied West African *indigène*, especially from villages, had little chance to avoid conscription without suffering the fascist retributions of French colonials. These punitive methods included the village chief's ostracization of the recalcitrant Senegalese and the colonial administration's punishment of the *indigène* or his family with any possible alibi such as failure to pay for taxes or provide adequate forced labor. Such a fascism is visible in the dilemma that Richard Fogarty calls the French officers' "aggressive recruitment in the colonies," their "conviction that a black would march only if he was beaten," their tendency to see only the "faults" of *indigènes*, and their refusal to "recognize in them no quality" (106).

Furthermore, if an *indigène* openly resisted conscription or was involved in mass protests, he also put both his life and his family's existence in danger. Crowder explains: "These revolts were, whatever their cause, put down ruthlessly by the colonial authorities. 'Rebels' were impressed into the army, flogged or even hanged, chiefs exiled or imprisoned, and villages razed to the ground to serve as a warning" ("The First World War," 300). Such means of forcing West Africans to join the regiments of *tirailleurs* and fight for France were fascist, since they were based on coercion, intimidation, violence, and devaluation of the lives of individuals deemed dispensable. In fascism, the subjected group has only the duty of following draconian orders and is given no opportunity to express free will because the system is essentially antidemocratic and anticosmopolitan. Such traits of fascism coincide with those that Djibril Tamsir Niane and Suret-Canale depict in their classic textbook, *Histoire de l'Afrique Occidentale* (1961). Defining fascism, the two scholars write:

George Padmore's cosmopolitanism 183

C'est un mouvement politique au service de l'impérialisme, ayant pour objet de le consolider: devant les progrès de l'opposition populaire, l'impérialisme sent la nécessité de supprimer les libertés démocratiques. Le fascisme a pour objectif l'établissement d'une dictature brutale de l'impérialisme, brisant ses adversaires par la terreur, répandant les théories mensongères et abjectes du "racisme."

[It is a political movement in the service of the imperialism that it is designed to consolidate: as popular opposition increases, imperialism feels the need to remove democratic freedoms. Meanwhile, fascism seeks to establish a brutal dictatorship of imperialism by breaking its opponents with terror and spreading the misleading and abject theories of "racism."]

(Niane & Suret-Canale, 1961, 172)

This fascism resonates with the systemic repression and discrimination that French colonialism maintained in Senegal during the two great wars in an attempt to oblige blacks of the colonies to fight for the métropole.

Moreover, *tirailleurs* continued to experience multiple atrocities that contradicted French cosmopolitan rhetoric of civilizing them and improving their lives. One of these atrocities was the dilapidated health conditions in which *tirailleurs* lived between the two world wars. Focusing on *tirailleurs* who were assigned in France after World War I, Padmore states: "The mortality rate is very high among black troops, due to pulmonary affections, syphilis, malaria and other maladies. Nearly 82.32 per cent of Senegalese stationed in Europe contracted tuberculosis" (*The Life*, 116). Revealing the grim effects of tuberculosis and French winter on the soldiers, Padmore also asserts:

Thousands of able-bodied men die annually from consumption and other diseases contracted while serving in the army in France. The natives are not only unaccustomed to the European climate, especially its rigorous winters, but they are housed in unsanitary barracks and provided with the cheapest quality food.

(*The Life*, 35)

This excerpt shows the heavy toll that participation in World War I had on *tirailleurs* who had been deployed to Europe.

Moreover, instead of regarding maimed *tirailleurs* as equals for the lives they lost and the bravery they showed during World War I, many French colonials treated the wounded soldiers in fascist ways as natives who were racially inferior to whites. Such a blend of racism and fascism is apparent in the manner in which many French colonial officers were eager to put Africans in their place. In *Native Sons*, Mann describes how, after World War I, the French military administration regarded wounded African soldiers

184 *George Padmore's cosmopolitanism*

who stayed in the métropole as suffering from "warped mentality," "arrogance," "pretensions," and the expectation "to be treated like Europeans" (2006, 166). In an attempt to put *tirailleurs* in their natural place, the French administration created hospitals in Menton, Fréjus-Saint-Raphael, and Gourneau, all in France, where the soldiers were attended only by men and left "to die alone" (Mann, 2006, 166). Mann's observations reveal the mixture of racism and fascism that characterized French colonial officers' attitudes toward *tirailleurs*. By perceiving the sharpshooters as mentally deficient people who were unequal to Europeans, the French displayed fascism that they often masked with the biologically and ethnographically racist claim to keep and protect Africans in their proper environment.

The seclusion of World War I *tirailleurs* in France also derived from a colonial fascism that expressed itself in a virulent xenophobia and scientific racism toward ethnic minorities. Discussing similar prejudices toward Arabs and Berbers of Algeria during the interwar period, Samuel Kalman discerns an insidious fascist colonial rhetoric that perceived such populations as "malodorous, diseased" (2013, 9), "barbaric and inferior" (2013, 181). The isolation of *tirailleurs* in France during the interwar years resulted from comparable fascist and xenophobic sentiments that fractured the cosmopolitan romanticization of these soldiers as the empire's heroes. In this vein, Samuel Mbajum refers to the insidious manner in which fascism against *tirailleurs* in the métropole supplanted the ephemeral perception of these combatants as "brave Senegalese" who shed their blood for France during World War I, when conservative political voices, which were angered by the economic declines resulting from the 1929 financial crash, expressed virulent "Négrophobie" [Negrophobia] (2010, 69–70). The concealment of *tirailleurs* in France after World War I was empowered by the same kind of fascism that fueled French "Negrophobia" toward blacks in 1929.

Another French mistreatment of West Africans during the interwar era is visible in the fascist manner in which these populations were subjected to forced labor. This oppression is discernible in *The Life and Struggles of Negro Toilers* where Padmore reveals draconian colonialist policies of compulsory labor in French African colonies. Describing the conditions of the peasants and other *indigènes* in such territories, Padmore writes:

> The standard of life of the natives in these colonies is very low, due largely to the miserable wages paid to them on their plantations. Those who still "own" lands are also hardly better off. What [sic] with the primitive methods of cultivation, to which are added frequently [sic] droughts, and the invasion of insect pests and taxation, these toilers are unable to provide enough nourishment for themselves. This widespread condition of malnutrition produces great apathy, and leads to diseases and epidemics.
>
> (*The Life*, 31–32)

George Padmore's cosmopolitanism 185

Next, Padmore states:

> Their French masters nevertheless declare these black slaves the laziest beings in creation and have no hesitancy in "rationalising" their labour power by means of the whip. It is no uncommon sight to see thousands of natives toiling under the most devitalising tropical weather, hot sun or heavy rains, and standing over them armed guards with whips made of animal hide.
>
> *(The Life, 31–32)*

This portrayal of black workers toiling under the hot sun shows that French imperialism transferred to the colonies the fascism that was already pervasive in the métropole. Such fascism is apparent in the French colonials' perception of the Senegalese as mere producers of raw materials. But, as is evident in the French's view of *tirailleurs* as "black slaves" and "the laziest beings in creation," in spite of the vital labor force these workers contributed to the imperial economy, the Europeans' denigration of the colonized blacks reflected both racism and fascism. Padmore despised both oppressive systems because he saw how they alienated and exploited Senegalese people before trivializing them as being idle, lazy, and inferior.

Additionally, Padmore's diagnosis of France's exploitative relations with its African colonies reveals the symptoms of an empire that was in decline and was desperately holding to its dominions. France's imperial downfall partially derived from the 1929 stock-market crash that had drastic effects on world economies. According to Mbajum, this collapse impaired France's economy at a time when "Negrophobia" was on the rise in 1929.[3] But the causes of France's imperial decline were also homegrown since they partially resulted from both the empire's overreliance on the colonies' agricultural products for global trades and its inability to adjust commerce according to fluctuating market trends. Discussing the effects of the French empire's financial recession in 1930s in Senegal and other parts of Africa, Rodney writes: "In every part of colonial Africa, the depression years followed the same pattern . . . Then, prices of Senegalese groundnuts were cut by more than half . . . African peasants and workers bore the pressure, even if it meant forced labor." (1982, 158). Unfortunately, the direct victims of France's economic downturn in the early 1930s were African peasants who cultivated export crops, labored in fields, and paid taxes without seeing the benefits of these impositions. As *indigènes*, the peasant class of Senegal suffered greatly from the torturous conditions that France implemented to make up for financial losses that were accumulated from a depreciated economy. The Senegalese worked hard to increase production and make up for such losses while their bodies and souls succumbed to the labor's pressure. This toil that Rodney calls "pressure" attests to the prevalence of forced labor in Senegal during the 1930s.

186 *George Padmore's cosmopolitanism*

France's imperial decline is also perceptible in the October 7, 1934, issue of *La Dépêche Coloniale et Maritime* in which Jean Leune summarizes the following views of Doumergue, who was then prime minister and former president of the republic (1934, 1924–1931). According to Leune, Doumergue said, "In most of our overseas territories, the French and native populations deeply suffer from economic malaise, stemming from diverse causes, which severely affect them all" but also stated, "[F]or an equally serious crisis, there is more suffering in the colony than in the métropole" (1934, 1). Doumergue's assessments of the economic situation in the métropole and the colonies in 1934 reveal the symptoms of a French empire that was losing its might during the interwar period, because of the occupiers' long development of a reductive and exploitative economy that relied on the production of a monoculture rather than diverse crops in Senegal. Since the mid-nineteenth century, France had promoted an exclusive cultivation of groundnut that transformed the colony's peasants into a chattel-class that toiled for the métropole's industrial revolution rather than their own progress. Tracing the roots of such exploitation, Bernard Moitt states:

> In the second half of the nineteenth century, the Senegalese economy underwent a dramatic transformation. Peanuts replaced slaves and gum and became the single most important export crop in French West Africa. Peanuts remained an auxiliary crop which the household—the basic unit of production—cultivated to supplement its diet until well into the 1850s. From a paltry 1 metric ton in 1840, production rose to 5,000 metric tons in 1850.
>
> (1989, 27)

In a similar way, peanut cultivation in Senegal soared between the middle of the nineteenth century and the 1930s, when the produce increasingly became a monoculture that France promoted in the colony instead of developing diverse crops, manufactures, technologies, and industries. Alluding to this monopoly of peanuts in colonial Senegal, Moitt states: "Between 1880 and 1898, for example, exports rose from just over 34,000 metric tons to 95,000 metric tons, which means that production almost tripled" (1989, 27). France's overreliance on peanut cultivation in Senegal continued up through the interwar period and the middle of the twentieth century. Christophe Bonneuil explains:

> After British India, the French empire's peanut colony, Senegal, was the world's second largest exporter of peanuts in the inter-war period. Peanut exportation accounted for more than 85 per cent of the total exports from this territory, and French rulers directed their efforts at one goal: raising the peanut colony's exportation figures. Administrative

George Padmore's cosmopolitanism   187

structures, the creation of railways and roads, and economic policy were entirely driven by this aim.

(1999, 274)

Because of its over-reliance on peanut production, France's economy started to wane both at home and abroad due to inflation and competition with Britain, Russia, Germany, and the United States on world markets. Early signs of the inflation emerged near the end of World War I when the métropole's increasing dependence on fat created a groundnut crisis in Senegal. In order to palliate this crisis, Pierre Deloncle, a French economist, encouraged in French West Africa the production of grease from sources other than peanuts.[4] "Faisant allusion à la crise de l'arachide du Sénégal, il préconise l'utilisation des matières grasses comme carburants" [[R]eferring to the groundnut crisis in Senegal, he [Deloncle] advocates the use of fat as fuel].[5] Such measures could not tackle the "groundnut crisis," since the latter derived from France's long exploitation of African peasants. By confining Senegal's agriculture to groundnut, France further stifled and delayed the colony's industrial and technological development and made it a territory whose sole mission was to provide the métropole with the necessary grease for the métropole's factories and inhabitants. The métropole's dependency on Senegal's peanut and fat production is evident in Moitt's following statement:

The expansion in production was due to increased demands for fats and oils from Europe, the extension of the transportation network within Senegal (most notably the Dakar-Saint-Louis and the Thiès-Kayes railways), and more important, a massive inflow of servile labour from the Soudan before 1900, as well as a redirection of labour within the Peanut Basin after the end of slavery in 1905.

(1997, 577)

As West Africa's groundnut basin, Senegal strongly contributed to the realization of France's imperial project by providing the free workforce that sustained the métropole while keeping the colony's inhabitants in abject poverty and depravity. The Senegalese laborers who built roads, cleaned buildings, took menial jobs, and did other maintenance work included *indigène* prisoners who were also subjected to the kind of fascist forced labor that Padmore decries in *The Life and Struggles of Negro Toilers*. A similar servitude existed in colonial Senegal where the French built, between 1920 and 1940, a penal system which punished subversive *indigènes* accused of defiance of authority, indiscipline, or other fictive crimes by subjecting them to forced labor. As Ibra Sene has shown, this forced labor extended through the hinterland and was maintained by overseas administrators for the realization of France's colonial project which necessitated the building of

188 George Padmore's cosmopolitanism

roads.[6] According to Sene, "Prior to 1927, these prisoners were employed by private individuals and companies, but also by some high-placed officials of the administration for their own housework, and this against all the rules then in force."[7] Sene's revelations suggest the purely capitalist structure of French imperialism in Senegal and the fascist ways in which the penitentiary allowed the administrators to use colonial prisoners as private and personal labor that served as slaves. In this sense, the prison system in colonial Senegal was a fascist and capitalist venture in which penal law, compulsory work, and administrative culture transformed an already disenfranchised class of Senegalese peasants and other menial laborers into a wretched proletariat to exploit at ease in a slave-like fashion. Such a system was built on fascism, rather than cosmopolitanism, since it was part of an imperial doctrine that used penal sanction as a means to control a class of ostracized black laborers. It is from this structural form of dominance that the French transformed the convicted Senegalese into slaves of the empire by making them integral to the forced labor system. Sene writes: "Thus, in the particular field of construction and maintenance of roads, prison labor strengthened and even eventually substituted wage labor and forced labor effectively" (2004, 166). Therefore, *indigènes* in Senegal had limited rights since they performed plantation and public work just as condemned and forced laborers also did. Such imperial abuses had drastic effects on the peasants of Senegal by transforming them into wretched laborers whose temporary opposition to the colonial administrators was threatened by harsh measure such as imprisonment, physical violence, and death.

As Padmore's writings suggest, French colonialism was a fascist system in which Senegalese people suffered from forced labor, physical abuses, and other oppressions. Another effect of imperial domination was France's over-reliance on peanut production which brought more wretchedness, desolation, and depersonalization to a peasant class that was already transformed into a constricted proletariat. These subjugations resulted from a well-organized fascist and imperial system of control and domination of Africans who were judged as expendable and undesirable in their own lands despite their enrichment of the French empire. The blend of colonialism and fascism that legitimized this cruelty reveals the métropole's status as a nation whose imperialist policies toward Africans contradicted the cosmopolitan rhetoric of its colonial administrators. By denouncing the anticosmopolitan relationships between France and Senegalese peasants during the 1930s, Padmore accurately assessed the social and economic inequalities between the métropole and its West African colony between the interwar years. Such relations were based on fascist, racist, and elitist exploitations that French colonials masked under the pretext of a cosmopolitan discourse in which they rationalized imperialism as a means to bring human dignity to West Africans when their actual desire was to dominate these populations. As Padmore has shown, France was then beginning to lose its imperial might due to its reliance on a monoculture

George Padmore's cosmopolitanism   189

that jeopardized its standing among Western nations while further impoverishing Senegal.

Bibliography

Bonneuil, Christophe. "Penetrating the Natives: Peanut Breeding, Peasants and the Colonial State in Senegal (1900–1950)." *Science, Technology, and Society: A Journal Devoted to the Developing World* 4, no. 2 (1999): 273–302.

Cooper, Frederick. *Decolonization and African Society: The Labor Question in French and British Africa.* Cambridge, MA: Cambridge University Press, 1996.

Crowder, Michael. *Colonial West Africa.* London: Frank Cass, 1978.

——. "The First World War and its Consequences." In *General History of Africa*, Vol. VII: *Africa under Colonial Domination, 1880–1935*, edited by A. Adu Boahen, 282–311. Berkeley, CA: Heinemann and Unesco, 1985.

DeGeorges, Thomas. "Still Behind Enemy Lines? Algerian and Tunisian Veterans after the World Wars." In *The World in World Wars: Experiences, Perceptions and Perspectives from Africa and Asia*, edited by Heike Liebau, 519–546. Leiden, The Netherlands: Brill, 2010.

Deloncle, Pierre. "Au cercle intellectuel de la méditerranée. Une belle Conférence de Pierre Deloncle sur l'A.O.F." *La Dépêche Coloniale et Maritime*, November 16–18, 1934: 1–2.

Echenberg, Myron. *Colonial Conscripts: The Tirailleurs Senegalais in French West Africa, 1857–1960.* Portsmouth, NH: Heinemann, 1991.

Fogarty, Richard Standish. *Race and War in France: Colonial Subjects in the French Army, 1914–1918.* Baltimore, MD: Johns Hopkins University Press, 2008.

Hafez, Kai. *Radicalism and Political Reform in the Islamic and Western Worlds.* New York: Cambridge University Press, 2010.

Hartfield, James. *An Unpatriotic History of the Second World War.* Washington, DC: Zero Books, 2012.

Kalman, Samuel. *French Colonial Fascism: The Extreme Right in Algeria, 1919–1939.* New York: Palgrave, 2013.

Kelley, Robin D. G. *Freedom Dreams: The Black Radical Imagination.* Boston, MA: Beacon Press, 2002.

Koller, Christian. "The Recruitment of Colonial Troops in Africa and Asia and their Deployment in Europe During the First World War." In *Captivity, Forced Labour and Forced Migration in Europe during the First World War*, edited by Matthew Stibbe, 111–133. New York: Routledge, 2013.

Lawrence, Adria. *Imperial Rule and the Politics of Nationalism: Anti-Colonial Protest in the French Empire.* New York: Cambridge University Press, 2013.

Lenin, V. I. *Imperialism: The Highest State of Capitalism.* Sydney, Australia: Resistance Books, 1999.

Leune, Jean. "Après L'Appel du Président Doumergue: Front commun et Empire colonial." *La Dépêche Coloniale et Maritime*, October 5–7, 1934: 1–2.

Lunn, Joe. *Memoirs of the Maelstrom: A Senegalese Oral History of the First World War.* Portsmouth, NH: Heinemann, 1999.

Makalani, Minkah. *In the Cause of Freedom: Black Internationalism from Harlem to London, 1917–1939.* Chapel Hill: University of North Carolina Press, 2011.

Mann, Gregory. *Native Sons: West African Veterans and France in the Twentieth Century.* Durham, NC: Duke University Press, 2006.

190 George Padmore's cosmopolitanism

Manning, Patrick. *Francophone Sub-Saharan Africa, 1880–1995.* Cambridge, UK: Cambridge University Press, 1998.

Mbajum, Samuel. "Empire français et statut du colonisé: une ambiguïté permanente." In *Décolonisation de l'Afrique ex-française: Enjeux pour l'Afrique et la France d'aujourd'hui,* edited by Alexandre Gerbi, 55–80. Paris: L'Harmattan, 2010.

Memmi, Albert. *The Colonizer and the Colonized.* Boston, MA: Beacon Press, 1991.

Moitt, Bernard. "Peanut Production, Market Integration, and Peasant Strategies in Kajoor and Bawol before World War II." In *AOF: réalités et héritages: sociétés ouest-africaines et ordre colonial, 1895–1960, Tome 1,* edited by Charles Becker, Saliou Mbaye, and Ibrahima Thioub, 577–592. Dakar: Direction des Archives du Sénégal, 1997.

——. "Slavery and Emancipation in Senegal's Peanut Basin: The Nineteenth and Twentieth Centuries." *The International Journal of African Historical Studies* 22, no. 1 (1989): 27–50.

Murphy, David. "Sub-Saharan Africa." In *A Historical Companion to Postcolonial Literatures: Continental Europe and its Empires,* edited by Prem Poddar, Rajeev S. Patke, Lars Jensen, and John Beverley, 184–188. Edinburgh, UK: Edinburgh University Press, 2008.

Niane, Djibril Tamsir, and Jean Suret-Canale. *Histoire de l'Afrique Occidentale.* Paris: Présence Africaine, 1961.

Padmore, George. *Africa and World Peace.* 1937. London: Frank Cass, 1972.

——. "Fascism in the Colonies." *Controversy* 2, no. 17 (February 1938). Accessed June 21, 2014. http://www.marxists.org/archive/padmore/1938/fascism-colonies.htm.

——. *Pan-Africanism or Communism. The Coming Struggle for Africa.* New York: Roy Publishers, 1956.

——. *The Life and Struggles of Negro Toilers.* 1931. Hollywood: Sun Dance Press, 1971.

Rodney, Walter. *How Europe Underdeveloped Africa.* Washington, DC: Howard University Press, 1982.

Sarraut, Albert. *Grandeur et Servitude Coloniales.* Paris: Editions du Sagittaire, 1931.

Scheck, Raffael. *Hitler's African Victims: the German Army Massacres of Black French Soldiers in 1940.* Cambridge, UK: Cambridge University Press, 2006.

Sene, Ibra. "Colonisation française et main-d'œuvre carcérale au Sénégal: de l'emploi des détenus des camps pénaux sur les chantiers des travaux routiers (1927–1940)." *French Colonial History* 5, no. 1 (2004): 153–171.

Soucy, Robert. *French Fascism: The First Wave, 1924–1933.* New Haven, CT: Yale University Press, 1986.

Trotsky, Leon. *Whither France?* Translated by John G. Wright and Harold R. Isaacs. New York: Pioneer Publishers, 1936.

7 Léopold Sédar Senghor's cosmopolitanism and responses to French colonialism

Léopold Sédar Senghor's poems about World War II participate in black cosmopolitanism and anticolonialism, since they memorialize *tirailleurs* who defended France and Europe against Nazism. His war poems reveal a dualism in the blend of cosmopolitanism and anticolonialism that permeates his depiction of the disastrous effects of German invasion of France during the first years of the conflict. Although he empathizes with the suffering that the war brought to French people, Senghor is anguished by the connections that such a chaos had with colonial atrocities in Senegal. Counterbalancing his cosmopolitan sympathy for the French victims of Nazi invasion, Senghor denounces the comparable racism and dispossession that the métropole perpetrated against *tirailleurs* and other Africans during World War II. He purposefully disparages the injustices that France, under the Government of Maréchal Henri Philippe Pétain, perpetrated against *tirailleurs* and other Africans. Consequently, Senghor's poems reveal black cosmopolitanism through his humanistic concerns toward the plight of both African and French soldiers that he witnessed during the war. By sympathizing with the predicament of both blacks and whites, Senghor blended cosmopolitanism, anticolonialism, and transnationalism into a black Atlantic intellectual tradition from which he has often been excluded.

Senghor's poetic work has received strong scholarly attention that spans over decades. Yet, most of this scholarship focuses on the identitarian and cultural significance of the poet's writings, neglecting their political and ideological importance. Consequently, the extant scholarship on Senghor's oeuvre ignores his war poems and their relevance in the study of anti-colonialism and cosmopolitanism. One way to resolve this oversight is to interpret Senghor's poems in transnational contexts that center the role of France and its empire in the colonial predicaments of Senegalese people during the World War II era.

Aware of the need to go beyond traditional interpretations of Negritude, many contemporary critics have examined the writings of its founders in novel ways that acknowledge the philosophy's dichotomous characteristics. Such oppositional traits include the blend of complicity with and independence from the colonial order and the mix of particularistic and

192 *Léopold Sédar Senghor's cosmopolitanism*

universalistic patterns in Negritude. In *The French Imperial Nation-State*, Wilder asserts: "We need to be able to account for Negritude's contradictory character in relation to positions circulating in the interwar black public sphere and in relation to the contradictory logic of imperial politics" (2005, 202). In his next book, *Freedom Time: Negritude, Decolonization, and the Future of the World*, Wilder expands his complex assessment of Negritude when he observes:

> Scholarship is finally moving beyond focusing on Negritude as a (progressive or conservative) form of identitarian cultural nationalism or Africana philosophy that either helped or hindered struggles for national independence. Recent work reconsiders Senghor and Césaire as political thinkers in relation to broader fields of philosophy, critical theory, and aesthetics, and takes seriously their attempts to refigure universalism, humanism, and cosmopolitanism.
>
> (2015, 276)

This chapter aims to provide a similar study of Senghor's poetry beyond binaries while exploring the intellectual's embodiment of cosmopolitanism that France denied to *tirailleurs* and other blacks of its colonies during World War II. This history, which should compel us to study the effects of cosmopolitanism on Senghor's views on colonialism and his relations with France, cannot be ignored. To this effect, Cheikh Thiam writes in his book *Return to the Kingdom of Childhood: Re-envisioning the Legacy and Philosophical Relevance of Negritude*:

> Reading Senghor's philosophy of Negritude beyond the anti-colonial paradigm does not suggest, however, that the state and conditions of black men and women living in France between the two World Wars did not participate in the development of Negritude. Of course, these conditions were fundamental to the rise of a black racial consciousness in 1930s France. But, Negritude cannot be limited to a reaction to the West.
>
> (2014, 7)

Thiam's quotation cautions us against the danger of letting the study of Negritude "beyond the anti-colonial paradigm" force us to discard the social, political, and economic conditions of blacks in both France and the colonies during the 1930s and 40s. One way to avoid the catastrophic impulse is to give issues of empire and cosmopolitanism the same importance that is accorded to cultural and identitarian questions in the study of Negritude. Discussing these questions, Irele observes in "Negritude or Black Cultural Nationalism:"

> It is hardly an exaggeration to say that the advent of the European in Africa turned out to be for the African a shattering experience in more

than a metaphorical sense. Although the early phase of contact was marked by an ambiguously calm relationship, the European presence in Africa developed gradually into a situation of conflict, first through the slave trade, and later on with the establishment of colonial rule. African history since the coming of the white man presents examples of violent reactions to this situation—and resistance movements like those of Chaka in Zululand, and Samory in what is now Guinea, form an essential part of the stock of symbols that have nourished the nationalistic strain of *négritude*.

(1965, 322)

The deep scars of European imperial policies in Africa must be exposed despite the contemporary critics' call for studying Negritude beyond or within anti-colonial paradigms. This colonial history was so traumatic and debilitating that it left indelible imprints on the individual and collective identities that Senghor and Césaire uncovered as the painful source of black people's contributions to world civilizations. Describing the similar histories of oppressions that have made blacks feel as "one people" with a shared sense of tradition, Stuart Hall says that

Such a conception of cultural identity played a critical role in all the post-colonial struggles which have so profoundly reshaped our world. It lay at the centre of the vision of the poets of "Negritude," like Aimée Cesaire and Leopold Senghor, and of the Pan-African political project, earlier in the century.

(1990, 223)

Yet one should not interpret Negritude's celebration of collective identity as a denial of plural selves. As Thiam argues in *Return to the Kingdom of Childhood*, Senghor, "the theoretician of Negritude [,] lays the groundwork for a non-essentialist essentialism and sets the condition for the conception of Negro cultures as entities, which, since prehistory, develop, change, and mix with other cultures, while they remain fundamentally African" (2014, 7). In this sense, Negritude embraces both individual and collective identities.

Negritude is a literary and political movement founded in Paris by expatriate black students such as Senghor, Césaire, and Léon Gontran Damas. The movement grew out of the encounters and exchanges of these African and Caribbean intellectuals in the 1930s, especially at the Lycée Louis le Grand and the Sorbonne, where they developed a strong consciousness about the misrepresentations of black civilization in European textbooks. In response to these situations, the intellectuals looked up to Africa for inspiration in order to help blacks regain their humanity that Western civilization had belittled or ignored. Thus, as Irele points out, "Senghor's Negritude starts out as, and essentially remains, a defense of

194 *Léopold Sédar Senghor's cosmopolitanism*

African cultural expression" and what the poet calls "the sum total of African cultural values" (2011, 59). Yet, Negritude was not restricted to cultural issues, since its founders also aimed to achieve black freedom and economic development through a valuation of the cosmopolitanism that connects the suffering of both Africans and Europeans. According to Kanishka Chowdhury, the goal of Negritude was not only to assert the power and beauty of black culture through art and literature, but also to demand the political independence of Africans (1997, 36). Drawing from similar arguments, this chapter will analyze a selected number of Senghor's poems about World War II as anticolonial and anti-fascist texts in spite of their cultural import without minimizing their reflections of the intellectual's views on cosmopolitanism.

Another issue in the scholarship on Senghor is the neglect of his war poems. One exception is Jessie Carney Smith, who argues that it was in a German prison camp that "he [Senghor] produced some of his most poignant poems" (2002, 339). Yet the extent of this poignancy remains unknown since there are no extensive studies of the impact of World War II on Senghor's poetry. Although he has examined Senghor's poetry in relation to "the Negro origins of ancient Egyptian civilization" (Irele, 2011, 132) and Cheikh Anta Diop's refutation of "the argument that the Black race has produced no great world civilization" (ibid., 133), Irele's *The Negritude Moment: Explorations in Francophone African and Caribbean Literature and Thought* (2011) ignores the effects of World War II on Senghor's poetry. In a similar way, authoritative biographies of Senghor, such as Janeth S. Spleth's *Léopold Sédar Senghor* (1985) and Janet G. Vaillant's *Black, French, and African: A Life of Léopold Sédar Senghor* (1990), have overlooked the impact of World War II on Senghor's work even if they have examined the poet's cultural celebrations of blackness and have occasionally referred to Senghor's representations of *tirailleurs*.

On the other hand, many scholars have studied the relations between France and colonial Africa although such critics often explore these connections mainly as revealing the métropole's desire to culturally assimilate the colonies, forgetting to analyze this "civilizing mission" as a compulsory imperialistic policy and process that corrupted race relations in Africa. For instance, in *Senegal: A Study of French Assimilation Policy*, Crowder depicts Senegal as a colony where the métropole attempted to assimilate Africans by telling them that their ancestors were "the Gauls," and by detribalizing African soldiers in calling them *tirailleurs Sénégalais* and "black Frenchmen" (1962, 95, 99). Crowder's interpretation of the relations between blacks and whites in colonial Senegal overlooks these Africans' resistance against the French elite whom they saw as exploiters rather than cosmopolitan saviors. Crowder himself says that the term *"petit blanc[s]"* was used in colonial Senegal to refer to the local black élite that shared a "covert resentment" toward the "senior Frenchmen" who remained in the country after colonization (1962, 95). In order to understand the political and economic

Léopold Sédar Senghor's cosmopolitanism   195

basis of this resentment, one needs to interpret it in the historical context of the racist treatment of *tirailleurs* in the métropole during World War II and after their return to Senegal from combat only to be disappointed by French colonials who refused to treat them as equals. Like Senghor, these *tirailleurs* participated in the war in an attempt to be recognized as men of dignity and honor who deserved to be either integrated as full citizens into the French Empire or be given national independence without supervision.

First and foremost, one needs to define Senghor's cosmopolitanism which derived from his attempt to bring blacks toward other societies and cultures in a spirit of mutual dependence. His cosmopolitanism is in line with Appiah's conception of this idea as the belief that "we have obligations to others" and the notion that "we take seriously the value not just of human life but of particular human lives, which means taking an interest in the practices and beliefs that lend them significance" (2006, xv). Senghor was a pioneer of this cosmopolitanism since his Negritude sought to bridge the gaps between African and European societies and form a universal civilization to which people from all cultures could contribute without erasing differences amongst them. In a speech that he delivered at the 1956 Congress of Black Writers that was held in Paris, Senghor called the encounter between world cultures as the *"rendez-vous du donner et du recevoir"* [the meeting where one gives and takes].[1] His Negritude reveals a desire to reach out to this world outside of his immediate and local universe. As Sylvia Washington Bâ argues, "Senghor sees as a permanent characteristic of the black man a certain emotive sensitivity, an affective rapport with the forces and forms of the universe, a direct and immediate contact with 'the other'" (1973, 74). This yearning for intimacies with the world is a key tenet of Senghor's cosmopolitanism. Yet, as is apparent in his last remarks at the 1956 congress, Senghor knows that Europe can weaken the black person's desire to achieve cosmopolitanism. In the address, Senghor Laments Europe's requirement that Africans give up "culture" and "race" before they can be allowed to contribute to *"la civilisation de l'universel"* [the civilization of the universal].[2] Alternatively, Senghor believes that the creation of this new civilization "requires a certain unity among blacks even if this world culture is going to have everyone's contribution."[3]

Senghor's cosmopolitanism is also apparent in the way in which he perceives *Présence Africaine* as a major tool in the development of close relationships between Africans and the world. As Salah D. Hassan argues, Senghor defines *Présence Africaine* as "simultaneously a partner and a facilitator in the dialogue" between Africa and Europe (1999, 196). Hassan continues:

> Dialogue is here charged with a utopic potentiality, in which cultural exchange becomes the telos of the journal: *Présence Africaine* established the dialogue with the West; *Présence Africaine* has no other ambition but a dialogue; *Présence Africaine* represents the will of the "black man"

196 *Léopold Sédar Senghor's cosmopolitanism*

to dialogue. As formulated by Senghor and Rabemananjara in the late 60s, the dialogue takes place across cultures and races, between the colonizer and colonized, between the "black man" and various "others."
(1999, 196)

This cosmopolitan conception of *Présence Africaine* appropriates French republican discourse on the equality between races and cultures in order to place the human rights of Africans at its center, transforming the métropole into a site that integrates rather than rejects *tirailleurs*. Using the new framework, Senghor resisted French colonialism from within the métropole where he was able to expose its contradictions with republicanism. As Wilder argues, taking advantage of how "humanist reformers" adopted him during the late 1930s "as an exemplary native collaborator," Senghor opposed "his reformist counterparts," since he "illuminated the contradictions of republican colonialism and developed an explicit critique of the French racism that colonial humanists disavowed" (2005, 233).

However, Senghor's confrontation of French colonialism did not occur in the 1930s only, since it also resurfaced during the 1956 Congress of Black Writers in Paris where he legitimized Negritude as black people's passport to a free and cosmopolitan world. He said:

To be really ourselves, we had to embody Negro African culture in twentieth-century realities. To enable our negritude to be, instead of a museum piece, the efficient instrument of liberation, it was necessary to cleanse it of its dross and include it in the united movement of the contemporary world.[4]

Senghor's assertion validates Negritude as an intellectual and cosmopolitan weapon of resistance against colonialism and a movement toward continuous independence.

Senghor's cosmopolitanism is mostly apparent in many of his selected poems in which he uses it to attenuate the tragic consequences of World War II on the French. One of these poems is "Snow in Paris" (1945), in which Senghor counters Paris's bleak reality during World War II by conjuring the fall of soft and furry snow over the city as a way of soothing the wounds of its inhabitants whose houses and lives were shattered by the fascist violence of Hitler's army. The snow imagery is noticeable in the end of the poem where Senghor writes: "Lord, I have accepted your white cold, burning hotter than / salt" ("Snow in Paris," 12). With a forgiving and cosmopolitan voice that echoes the strong influence of his Catholic faith, Senghor implores God to pour the heavenly substance over a city that sin has paralyzed. He writes:

Lord, you have visited Paris on this day of your birth
Because it has become mean and evil,

Léopold Sédar Senghor's cosmopolitanism   197

You have purified it with incorruptible cold, with white
death.
This morning, right up to the factory smokestacks
Singing in unison, draped in white flags—
"Peace to Men of Good Will!"
Lord, you have offered the snow of your Peace to a torn
world,
To divided Europe and ravaged Spain
And the Catholic and Jewish Rebels have fired their fourteen
hundred
Cannons upon the mountain of your Peace.

("Snow in Paris", 12)

Senghor's representation of Paris as a sinful city that the Lord has "purified" with "incorruptible cold" and "with white death" is a redemptive biblical invocation that represents ice and blizzard as Christ's means for sanctifying a town that evil has corrupted with fascism, violence, and malice. The redemptive quality of Senghor's imagery of Paris is also noticeable in his portrayal of snowfall on the city as the sign of a divine message of "Peace to Men of Good Will" ("Snow in Paris," 12). These words reveal Senghor's use of cosmopolitanism as a means to offset the rancor he had against Hitler's Nazi army which attacked France and later besieged a "torn world," a "divided Europe," and a "ravaged Spain" ("Snow in Paris," 12). These predicaments resulted from Hitler's fascist collaboration with the authoritarian regimes of Italy's Mussolini and Spain's Franco in an attempt to bring Western Europe to its knees. As Doris Weatherford points out, Hitler "had conquered or neutralized all of western Europe" by the end of June 1940 (59).

According to Martin Gilbert, the attacks on France began on June 2, 1940, and were swiftly carried out by General Rommel

on June 3 [as] the German Air Force bombed Paris. In all, 254 people were killed, 195 of them civilians, the rest soldiers. Among the civilian dead were many schoolchildren who had taken refuge in a truck which had received a direct hit.

(2004, 85)

These attacks, which were followed by other German assaults against Rouen and other parts of France, led to the massive displacements of people who were fleeing from death. Describing the impact of the June 3rd tragedy on Paris, Rosemary Sullivan writes:

Now caught like the northern refugees in the debris of war, Parisians began to understand that this might be the end. Warplanes droned over the rooftops; the houses shook, the plaster cracked, the plates and glasses

198   *Léopold Sédar Senghor's cosmopolitanism*

slid from the tables. Powdered glass piled in small crystal mounds on the sidewalks and the acrid smell of cordite from the bombs thickened the air. It felt like Paris was dying.

(2007, 131)

This painful history had a strong influence on Senghor's poetry which provides an antidote against it. Senghor uses cosmopolitanism against the havoc by praying for Christ to dampen and pacify a war-torn Paris on the day of his "birth" ("Snow in Paris," 12). Since December 25 is considered as the day of Christ's nativity, Senghor might have written "Snow in Paris" during the Christmas of 1940 when the city of light experienced an unusually-severe cold weather. In *Agriculture et alimentation en France durant la IIe Guerre mondiale*, Michel Cépède describes a severe winter exceeding the normal 1.5 to 5 Celsius degrees, accompanied with heavy snowfall, that confronted half of Western and Eastern France during the second half of December 1940 (1961, 279). Senghor transforms this atrocious climate into a soothing weather that spiritually redeems France from an evil and unjust attack. He finds strength in his cosmopolitan and Christian faith that helps France resist Germany's scorching weapons with "white cold" that is "burning hotter than salt" ("Snow in Paris," 12). Senghor thus empowers an abused France with the cosmopolitan Catholic faith that he shares with the nation, namely, his strong belief in the power of goodness and purity of heart and actions to defeat fascism. Identifying a similar belief in Senghor's poetry, Aimé Adopo Achi states: "Ainsi, la seconde guerre mondiale ne lui est pas indifférente. Il décrit ses atrocités avec des accents de l'homme du monde, affligé et profondément touché" [Thus, Senghor was not indifferent to the second World War. He describes its atrocities with emphasis on the modern man who is both afflicted and profoundly hit] (2009, 14). By feeling afflicted by the atrocity of World War II in the métropole, Senghor expresses the kind of cosmopolitanism that Wilder depicts as the poet's "insistence that Africa forgive imperial France in order to build a common future, call forth a different kind of political association, and enact a form of reconciliation among peoples of the world" (2015, 71). From this peace-making and messianic stance, Senghor uses the image of snowfall in Paris as a means of dulling the pain that the city's inhabitants experienced when German soldiers nearly decimated their town during the raids that preceded the armistice of June 22, 1940.

Yet Senghor is not completely forgiving toward France since he links the empire with a global capitalistic system that had terrorized blacks for many decades before World War II. Denouncing this global tyranny, Senghor writes:

Lord, I know I'll never release this reverse of hatred
For diplomats who show their long canine teeth
And tomorrow trade in black flesh.

Léopold Sédar Senghor's cosmopolitanism 199

My heart, Lord, has melted like snow on the roofs of Paris
In the sunshine of your gentleness.
It is kind even unto my enemies and unto my brothers
With hands white without snow
Because of these hands of dew, in the evening,
Upon my burning cheeks.

("Snow in Paris", 13)

The passage suggests Senghor's dilemma as he develops a "reverse of hatred" against a French nation that subjugated blacks. Senghor's quandary resulted from the hypocrisy of a French society that refused to recognize that the violence which fractured it in June 1940 was a long-term result of the colonial and capitalist repression that the métropole historically perpetrated against Africans. As is apparent in Senghor's representation of the officials in "Snow in Paris" as "diplomats who show their long canine teeth" and wait until "tomorrow [to] trade in black flesh," France behaved like Germany by perceiving Africans as mere laborers and producers of raw materials. With this logic, France had, since the middle of the seventeenth century, exploited Senegal and other parts of its West African colonies through enslavement, forced labor, cultural and linguistic assimilation, and imprisonment of populations. Such a long history of colonial fascism led to the death, impoverishment, and ostracization of Senegalese and other black populations on whose parched bodies and souls France gained the human and economic resources that made it a global economic power by the 1930s. For instance, having extracted and shipped the colony's wealth for centuries, France left Senegal with very little infrastructure. Suret-Canale relates a famous anecdote about a French Professor, Auguste Chevalier, who returned to Senegal's rural areas in 1947 only to find their populations in the same deplorable conditions in which he left them at the end of the nineteenth century. Suret-Canale writes: "les cases sont toujours aussi misérables, les paysans toujours en haillons, et il interroge: 'Mais que sont devenus les millions de francs-or réalisés par la vente des cacahuètes?'" [the huts are still deplorable. The peasants are still covered in rags, and he asks: "But what happened to the millions of gold-francs gained from the peanuts trade?"] (1957, 200). The money was not in the colony's rural areas because it was not meant to benefit Senegalese peasants and *tirailleurs* who toiled and moiled only for France. Had France regarded the Senegalese as cosmopolitan equals, it would not have perceived them as mere workforce for the métropole's grandeur. In their book *Genocide and Gross Human Rights Violations: In Comparative Perspective*, Kurt Jonassohn and Karin Solveig Björnson convey Chevalier's awareness of the French colonials' exploitative attitudes toward Senegalese when they write:

According to Chevalier, the French colonials, especially the concession holders, considered the natives as freely available for forced labor and

200 *Léopold Sédar Senghor's cosmopolitanism*

proceeded to seize all their property, including cattle, under the pretext that the produce of soil was included in the concession. The few plantations still kept by the village people were "requisitioned" by the Europeans, their servants, or the Senegalese. Chevalier also quoted the opinion of the heads of trading stations and of army officers: "There is nothing to be got from these blacks here: the best thing to do is to exterminate them and so make the other regions more docile."

(1998, 242)

Senghor had a strong compassion for the plight of the Senegalese peasants and other workers on whose bare backs and limbs France built colonial power without knowing that its fascist and imperial abuses would haunt it later. Even if he had sympathy for France, Senghor knew that the empire contradicted cosmopolitanism and republicanism by harboring racism that later burgeoned into fascist policies and ideologies during the World War II era. Such a blend of racism and fascism is manifest in the above statement in which a petty French army officer proposes the liquidation of Senegalese villagers as a means of teaching their neighbors to become "docile" to the colonial authority. In this sense, French colonialism was akin to the anti-Semitism and Nazism that threatened to wipe out human civilization during the second war. Addressing this neglected French colonial racism, Conklin writes in *A Mission to Civilize*:

To the extent that racism is defined as the perception that certain groups—including Jews and various immigrant groups, as well as non-Western peoples of color—were fundamentally different from and inferior to white Europeans, then French officialdom was guilty of thinking in racialized categories and implementing oppressive measures throughout the life of the Third Republic.

(1997, 9)

Later, Senghor compares the French racism and violence against colonized Africans with Nazi Germany's prejudice and abuse against Jewish and French people during World War II. In the poem "Prayer to the Masks" (1945), he alludes to the early stages of Hitler's oppression against Jews when he urges Europeans to "Fix your steady eyes on your oppressed children / Who give their lives like the poor man his last garment" (14), anticipating the extortions, humiliations, violence, and other cruel abuse that the Nazi perpetrated against Jews before beginning to force them out of Germany by 1936. Senghor describes this tragedy in the sixth section of his poem, "Ethiopia: At the Call of the Race of Sheba" (1936), where he writes: "Here are the Asturian miner and the Liverpool stevedore, / The Jew driven out of Germany, and Dupont and Dupuis / And all the guys from Saint-Denis" (44). These references to Jews from a poem written in 1936 establish Senghor's moral and religious legitimization of a global cosmopolitan war against Nazi Germany. Defending this cosmopolitan mission, the narrator of "Snow in Paris" says: "And the Catholic and Jewish Rebels have fired their fourteen hundred / Cannons upon the mountain of your peace" (12). Senghor's references to Jews validate and empower the human brotherhood that he perceives as a crossracial and cosmopolitan blockade against tyranny and genocide.

Yet, the chaos that Senghor saw in Paris resembles the historical tragedies that also occurred in Africa. Senghor remembers a similar subjugation that Africans faced during slavery and colonization. Looking at the image of the white snow falling on Paris reminds him of

> The white hands firing the rifles that crumbled our empires,
> The hands that once whipped slaves, and that whipped you,
> The snowy white hands that slapped you,
> The powdery white hands that slapped me,
> The firm hands that led me to loneliness and to hate,
> The white hands that cut down the forests
> Of straight, firm palmyra trees dominating Africa,
> In the heart of Africa, like the Sara men,
> Handsome as the first men born from your brown hands.
> They tore down the back forest to build a railroad,
> They cut down Africa's forests to save Civilization,
> Because they needed human raw materials.
>
> ("Snow in Paris", 13)

These lines allude to the long history of colonial oppression in Africa that Senghor traces from the times Europeans destroyed the "empires" that they found in the continent to periods when they transformed these kingdoms' inhabitants into slaves, servants, railroad workers, and other menial laborers. In addition, Senghor represents French colonization as a violence that dispossessed Africans with a civilizing mission rhetoric. As is apparent in its decimation of Africa's "forests" and "straight, firm palmyra trees" ("Snow in Paris," 13), the French civilizing mission was not based on cosmopolitanism, since it intended to use the "railroad" as a means of extirpating Senegal's human, natural, and material sustenance, in the same way slavery emptied Africa's basic means of survival. To this history, one adds the humiliations that Africans faced during colonization as Europeans imposed forced labor on them, requiring them to work in conditions akin to New World bondage. These atrocities occurred in colonial Senegal where compulsory labor was pervasive between the 1920s and the 1940s. Describing the French colonials' establishment of "penal camps" in "the cercles (provinces) of Louga, Thiès, Diourbel, and eventually in Bignona" in 1936, Sene writes:

> They were used until 1940 to supply much of the work force for road building and maintenance along the main transportation routes of the

202 *Léopold Sédar Senghor's cosmopolitanism*

colony. Lacking any deterrent or rehabilitative objective, the penal camps epitomized the political and economic functions of colonial imprisonment.

(2004, 153)

Doubling the atrocity of a forced labor system that worked in tandem with the carceral institution, the French colonials also established prisons that resembled slave ships and concentration camps; these were small and insanitary confines where they kept Senegalese who defied their authority or became victims of its caprices. Such horrible conditions in colonial Senegalese prisons are apparent in the essay, "La prison coloniale au Sénégal, 1790-1960: Carcéral de conquête et défiances locales" [Colonial prison in Senegal, 1790-1960: Carceral conquest and local defiance] (2007), in which Babacar Bâ states:

> [C]es prisons qui avaient des capacités de 30 à 40 places ont régulièrement accueilli 70 à 80 détenus. Dans une prison où les ouvertures d'aération étaient limitées à de petits trous, les détenus étouffaient du fait d'un cubage d'air très faible, situé entre 1,5 et 8 mètres cube, loin de la norme des 15 mètres cube codifiés. Entassés dans une prison insalubre où régnaient en maîtres les odeurs et la vermine, c'est une humanité dégradante que vivaient les détenus partagés entre la malnutrition, la faim, la maladie et la mortalité: dans la prison de Dakar, celle-ci a évolué entre 15,98% et 24% entre 1931 et 1940.

> [[T]hese prisons, which were made for 30 to 40 cells, usually held 70 to 80 inmates. In a prison where the only ventilation consisted of a few small holes, the inmates suffocated from a lack of air. The holes were between 1.5 and 8 cubic meters, and way below the required 15 cubic meters. Piled in a dirty penitentiary full of stench and filth, the prisoners were losing their humanity as they faced malnutrition, hunger, disease, and death: in the prison of Dakar, the death rate was between 15.98 percent and 24 percent between 1931 and 1940.]

(2007, 89)

The horrible conditions in which the French kept the Senegalese inmates show the viciousness of their colonial and fascist carceral institution. Such a system was fascist because it aimed to depersonalize Senegalese people and force them to be "docile" and fearful of a metropolitan power that reaped the fruits of their labor and disposed of their bodies when no substance could be drained from them. Yet the French colonizers overestimated their power since they were unable to defend themselves alone when German Nazis brought to their nation domination that was somewhat akin to the ones they had perpetrated against Africans. Senghor was aware of this tragic irony, which is the reason why he uses poetry as an inventory of this bloody history.

Léopold Sédar Senghor's cosmopolitanism   203

His intention was to remind a torn French and European society that their dilemma was not unrelated to Africa's brutal colonial history, since the West's capitalist greed and violence had disrupted the lives of working class people in both continents. Describing the role of a pernicious collaboration between global financiers and Christian missionaries in Africa as well as in the Pacific seas during colonization, Senghor writes in "Prayer for Peace" (1945):

> Ah, I know that more than one of Your messengers
> Hunted down my priests like wild game and slaughtered
> Sacred images. We might have had an understanding,
> For those images were our Jacob's ladder
> From earth to Your heaven,
> The clear oil lamp for us to await the dawn,
> The stars foreshadowing the sun.
> And I know that many of your missionaries have blessed
> Weapons of violence and traded in banker's gold
> But traitors and fools have always existed.
>
> (72)

This poem suggests Senghor's denunciation of a form of Christianity that was corrupted by its cooperation with imperial authorities to colonize Senegalese. His disparagement of this Christianity is noticeable in his lamentation of the cruel manner in which the "messengers" of the French colonists "Hunted down my priests like wild game and slaughtered/Sacred images" ("Prayer for Peace," 72). The passage suggests collaboration between French missionaries and colonizers who subdued the Senegalese and robbed their lands and resources. Senghor could not tolerate this contradiction between his Catholic faith and a brutal history of imperialism that tormented him. In this history, the Church played a primary and longstanding role of destroyer of nations and people. Spleth explains: "While retaining the foundations of his faith, he [Senghor] was unable to justify the actions of Christians in the light of Christian principles" (1985, 7). But he was able to explain these actions as consequences of an imperialism that became antithetical to France's popular view of itself as a cosmopolitan and republican métropole.

Another significant aspect of Senghor's poetry is his condemnation of how Europe perpetrated violence against its own people during World War II. Senghor laments in his 1939 poem, entitled "Luxembourg," the shedding of Europe's lifeblood in a war that was foreshadowed by the stifling of "children voices" and the collapse of romantic dreams. These metaphors prefigure the tragic fall of the country's leaves, as soldiers

> dig trenches under the bench where I learned about
> The sweet budding of lips.

204 *Léopold Sédar Senghor's cosmopolitanism*

This sign, ah! yes, of dangerous youth! ...
I watch the leaves fall into these false shelters, into graves
Into trenches where the blood of an entire generation flows
Europe is burying the nations' leaven
And the hope of new races.

("Luxembourg", 48)

This passage suggests the influence of cosmopolitanism in Senghor's poetry, as is visible in the narrator's solidarity with Europeans who lost their lives in the trenches of Luxemburg during a tragic war that wasted their people's blood and natural world. Senghor draws on surrealism to show the chaos he witnessed in a cataclysmic world in which the only solace is the imagined sigh of death taking away the life and blood of the people's children, which is a heartbreaking reality that the poet depicts as the image of a "Europe [which] is burying the nations' leaven" ("Luxembourg," 48). This ghastly metaphor of a continent burying its own people is surrealistic since it suggests the poet's use of an abysmal image of self-interment in order to convey the extent to which World War II brought Europe to the brink of self-destruction. Surrealism enables a poet to realize, recall, or forebode impending chaos. Hans Sedlmayr writes:

The leading theme of Surrealism is chaos absolute, the movement seizes upon it wherever it can be found—in the dark regions of the world of dreams, in hallucination, in the "deranged" and irrational character of ordinary life, in that department of reality in which things that have no intrinsic connection with one another have been brought together in a fortuitous, senseless and fragmentary manner.

(2007, 142)

Senghor's poetry reflects this surrealistic use of chaos imagery since it helps him to depict the world in a cataclysmic way that illustrates the danger of war. In so doing, Senghor's poetry conveys the power of long-held moral virtues of peace, harmony, and cosmopolitanism against the terror of battle, discord, and egocentricity. He places cosmopolitanism at the center of surrealism since he uses poetry as a means of urging Europe to treat all people equally and decently. In teaching this parable, Senghor transgresses a major rule of surrealism, which is the rejection of established and mono-lithic notions of truth and morality. Such denial of exclusive rationality is noticeable in the "First Surrealist Manifesto" (1924) in which André Breton decries the philosophical dearth of the 1920s as follows:

We are still living under the reign of logic, but the logical processes of our time apply only to the solution of problems of secondary interest. The absolute rationalism which remains in fashion allows for the consideration of only those facts narrowly relevant to our experience .

Léopold Sédar Senghor's cosmopolitanism 205

.. In the guise of civilization, under the pretext of progress, we have succeeded in dismissing from our minds anything that, rightly or wrongly, could be regarded as superstition or myth; and we have proscribed every way of seeking the truth which does not conform to convention.

(1965, 66)

Yet, Senghor was partially in agreement with Breton's Surrealism since he espoused its cosmopolitan critique of a Western civilization that alienated itself from the rest of the world by interpreting culture and identity in narrow-minded ways and refusing to see value in other people's customs and stories. As is apparent in his denunciation of the self-centeredness, greed, and racism that brought about World War II, Senghor, like Breton and other surrealists, had a clear diagnostic of the historical consequences of colonial immorality. Being a cosmopolitan poet, Senghor found truth in the massive historical record that shows that Westerners are bound to kill one another and other people for profit or other immoral justifications unless reason, culture, and dialogue prevent them from doing so.

Senghor's conception of historical truth comes from his representation of logic as a belief stemming from a victimized people's collective memory of their tragic experiences. Barend van Dyk Van Niekerk recognizes this historical materiality of Senghor's literary work when he urges critics to place it "in a historical perspective and then to adduce a few reasons why the world in general" should "know more about the life and work of this poet" who could "one day, constitute a moderating influence in an eventual clash between the white and black cultures" of Africa (1970, 1–2). However, Senghor's poetry warns against the racial tensions that could occur not just in Africa but also in other continents if the racism, fascism, and ethnocentrism that led Europe to the "burying of the nations' leaven" are not eliminated. This historical materiality contradicts Appiah's argument that a "conflict arises most often when two peoples have identified the same thing as good" (2006, 78). Refusing to flatten human experiences, Senghor's cosmopolitanism reminds us that conflicts also occur from the West's propensity to hate and destroy other people by perceiving them as inferior, evil, enslaveable, and dispensable.

Moreover, Senghor was unambiguous about evil since it was blatant in the dislocation of European men from their wives and children during World War II when the same colonial greed and global capitalism that had turned Africans into forced laborers had also transformed many Westerners into a servile working class. In this vein, Senghor laments the deprivation of the European soldiers in the poem "Camp 1940," which, as Edward A. Jones argues, "was inspired by his experiences in the concentration camp" (1971, 20). These experiences are apparent in the image of a French community that is decimated by war. Senghor depicts the locality as "a huge village of mud and branches, a village crucified by two pestilential ditches"

206 *Léopold Sédar Senghor's cosmopolitanism*

and a place where "hatred and hunger ferment there in the torpor of a deadly summer" ("Camp 1940," 56). This appalling imagery of a society that is covered with mud, twigs, and fatal disease registers Senghor's perception of World War II as an apocalypse that brought death to Europeans who now experienced the kind of burden that had confronted blacks since slavery. This apocalypse is similar to the one that Senghor depicts in his 1939 poem "To The Music of Koras and Balaphon," in which he writes:

> Like the call on Judgment Day, a trumpet sound on Europe's
> Snowy graveyards. I choose my toiling black people, my
> peasant people,
> And the entire race of peasants throughout the world.
> "And your brothers are angry with you, and have made you
> till the soil."
>
> (19)

The excerpt registers Senghor's capacity to transform Europeans' apocalypse as a tragic opportunity that allows him to call for an erasure of all oppressions. Senghor imagines a world in which the deprivations of World War II lead to a subliminal moment when both the captured white and black soldiers in German prison camps of France rupture the apocalypse of racism and other subjugations in favor of a humanism they can experience during their last breaths. In this world that he captures in "Camp 1940," Senghor depicts "a large village surrounded by the immobile spite of barbed wire" and "under the tyranny of four machine guns/Always ready to fire" ("Camp 1940," 56). Yet he offsets his anticipation of imminent apocalyptic violence with the ephemeral hope and humanity that glimmer from the faces of the captured soldiers. Senghor praises the fallen white and black combatants for their capacity to keep "the whiteness of their laughter" and "the freedom of their fiery souls" ("Camp 1940," 56)]. These images anticipate a crossracial cosmopolitanism that is further noticeable in Senghor's representation of both the white and black World War II soldiers of France as combatants who share the human capacity to use dream as a way of overcoming pain, defeat, and destruction. In a world in which "the noble warriors beg for cigarette butts, Fight with dogs over bones, and argue among themselves/Like imaginary cats and dogs" ("Camp 1940," 56), Senghor salutes the humanity that these soldiers of different races regain at night when they dream of the freedom of their loved ones and other people. Senghor writes:

> When evening falls, it is a sob of blood setting free the night.
> They watch over their big pink children, their big blond
> Children, their big white children, who toss and turn
> In their sleep, haunted by the fleas of care
> And the lice of captivity.
>
> ("Camp 1940", 56)

Léopold Sédar Senghor's cosmopolitanism 207

This passage is very surrealistic because it reveals Senghor's capacity to use his imagination as a tool for inventing an idyllic cosmopolitan world that is free from the misery and depravity of World War II. His portrayal of soldiers watching the "big white children, who toss and turn" is an uplifting image that overcomes the dreary sound of "a sob of blood" to which the poet refers earlier. Senghor's use of positive imagery to outweigh a negative invocation of chaos reveals surrealistic poetry's vital reliance on the power of dreams to overcome personal and collective crises. In this sense, Breton acknowledges the crucial importance of dreams in poetic imagination when he writes:

> Man, when he ceases to sleep, is above all at the mercy of his memory, and the memory normally delights in feebly retracing the circumstance of the dream for him, depriving it of all actual consequence and obliterating the only *determinant* from the point at which he thinks he abandoned this constant hope, this anxiety, a few hours earlier.
>
> (1965, 67)

Senghor firmly believed in the ephemeral and transient nature of dreams since his imagination flows freely between multiple states of consciousness, revealing the relative nature of truth.

Yet, Senghor's abstract and elusive poetic imagination does not diminish his pity for the plight of *tirailleurs*. The enduring strength of his solidarity with *tirailleurs* is palpable in the way in which he empowers these soldiers in the German prison camps to reclaim their humanity through dream. Remembering their homelands, the captured *tirailleurs* recall

> Fireside stories [that] lull them to sleep, and the low voices
> That join the silent paths
> And the sweet lullabies [which] are songs without drums
> And without clapping black hands
> —Except that tomorrow, at siesta time, there will be the
> mirage of epics,
> The cavalcade of sunlight on white savannas of endless sand.
>
> ("Camp 1940", 57)

These lines suggest the cosmopolitan devotion to world peace and France's freedom that led *tirailleurs* to trade the comfort of their traditional African villages and families with the painful existence they had at the Western war fronts and in German prisons. In spite of these predilections, *tirailleurs* remained willing to die for world freedom and reclaim the same humanity that men of other races possess. In fighting and dying for humanity, *tirailleurs* displayed a cosmopolitanism that Senghor frequently celebrates in his poetry. This cosmopolitanism expresses itself in the patriotism that both Senghor and other *tirailleurs*, who were captured by German soldiers in mid-May

208 *Léopold Sédar Senghor's cosmopolitanism*

1940, felt toward France at the risk of imminent death. Such a loyalty is apparent in the historical episode that Martin Meredith describes in *The Fate of Africa: A History of Fifty Years of Independence* as follows:

> When his unit was taken prisoner by the Germans, all the blacks in it were pulled out of the ranks and lined up against a wall. Senghor quickly understood that the Germans intended to execute them on the spot. Just as the firing squad was about to shoot, he recalled, "we called out, 'Vive la France, Vive l'Afrique Noire.'" At that very moment, the Germans put down their guns. A French officer had persuaded them that such slaughter would be a stain on German honour.
>
> (2011, 60)

This account reflects the unflinching devotion and bravery that *tirailleurs* showed for France even if this republic did not consider them as equal. By shouting "Vive la France, Vive l'Afrique Noire" [Long live France, Long live Black Africa], Senghor and other *tirailleur* prisoners equated the métropole's freedom with the continent's liberation, establishing an exemplary cosmopolitan reciprocity of worth and dignity between these entities.

Yet the *tirailleurs'* search for cosmopolitanism was not easy since the discrimination, anguish, and alienation that they faced in the French Republic compromised it. The soldiers were disappointed in a republic that betrayed them even if they dearly cherished it. Their dejection is noticeable in the poem entitled "The Enlisted Man's Despair," in which Senghor pays tribute to one of the *tirailleurs* whose war sacrifices are unrecognized by a French sergeant of his unit who says, "I don't understand a thing ... Senegalese—and a volunteer!" when he sees the combatant's body ("The Enlisted Man's Despair," 69). The French sergeant's reaction suggests his refusal to believe that a Senegalese could die for France and his denial of the African soldier's integrity, valor, and humanity. Contradicting the white sergeant's incredulous comment about the *tirailleur* in his unit, Senghor says on behalf of the fallen soldier:

> For two weeks he has been there, turning around,
> ruminating
> On the new Great Joke and on the newest affront to his
> sacrifice—
> His sweating brow—bought with counterfeit coins.
> He never asked for fifty cents—not even one cent
> Only his identity as a man, granted posthumously.
> He has been given a servant's clothes, which he took to be
> The martyr's simple garment
> O naïve, natively naïve, and the plumed helmet
> And boots for his domesticated free feet.
>
> ("The Enlisted Man's Despair", 49)

Léopold Sédar Senghor's cosmopolitanism 209

This passage reveals the condescension, dehumanization, and infantilization that *tirailleurs* experienced in French war camps where they were ridiculed and belittled as circus materials. As Senghor also points out in "Liminary Poem" (1940), *tirailleurs* also suffered "the scornful praise" of French government ministers and generals and were portrayed in the society and on "all the walls of France" as "empty-pocket poor men without honor," who were displaying their "banana grins" ("Liminary Poem" 39). Such prejudices misrepresented *tirailleurs* and ignored how the West African soldiers sometimes fought better than their white French counterparts did. Scheck writes: "When Tirailleurs found themselves under air attack or under bombardment by mortars, they were less likely to surrender than white French troops even in hopeless situations" (134). Through their brave role of liberators of France, *tirailleurs* destroyed the myth of the white man's superiority to the black man. Breaking this legend which stemmed from the white man's view of himself as God's representative on Earth since the beginning of colonization allowed Africans to later demand their national independence from Europeans once World War II was over.

Moreover, the dismissive surprise of the white sergeant in "The Enlisted Man's Despair" exhibits the bias of a French society that ignored the heartfelt sacrifices of *tirailleurs*. The deceased *tirailleur*, whose "identity as a man" has been "granted posthumously," is a cosmopolitan combatant who values the humanity and sacrifices of other men without regard to race. This genuine cosmopolitanism is apparent in the soldier's brave walk in trenches "where dead men rot like sterile seeds" and his desperate attempt to see if any of his comrades has survived ("The Enlisted Man's Despair," 49). Dizzied by such a touching sight, Senghor ends his poetic homage with the following line: "O weak, too weak child, such a loyal traitor to your genius" ("The Enlisted Man's Despair," 50). This line signifies the paradox of a French society that does not appreciate the cosmopolitan valor, honor, intelligence, and blood sacrifices of *tirailleurs* due to racism. Senghor was aware of this prejudice since, as Chike Jeffers argues, a major theme of his cosmopolitanism was

> the idea that cultural sharing is not just a matter of introducing others to the novelty of your gift but also a matter of addressing a problem or deficiency of theirs, which your gift is uniquely qualified to solve or compensate for.
>
> (2010, 211)

Senghor firmly believed in this cosmopolitanism that thousands of *tirailleurs* exemplified by choosing to face the deadly guns of Nazi executioners rather than surrender their patriotic devotion to France during World War II.

Senghor's use of cosmopolitanism as a tool for denouncing the injustices of colonialism is also visible in the poems in which he further laments how

Figure 7.1 "Corps de tirailleurs sénégalais dont la disposition et l'absence de blessures peuvent indiquer une exécution collective. Front nord-est, juin 1940. Photographie de source allemande" [Bodies of Senegalese tirailleurs whose position and lack of injuries may indicate a collective execution. Northeast Front, June 1940. German source photograph].

Collections Eric Deroo.

Léopold Sédar Senghor's cosmopolitanism 211

French society ignored the physical and psychological pain that he and other *tirailleurs* experienced when they were Nazi captives. This agony appears in the poem "Liberation," in which Senghor describes how the "torrents" of his "blood whistled along the banks" of his "cell" and how his "whole body ached" during "weary sleepless nights" ("Liberation," 16). In spite of this suffering, Senghor and other *tirailleurs* defended France to regain the humanity and pride that it denied to blacks. Despite the betrayal, *tirailleurs* remained loyal to the métropole, as is also visible in Senghor's other poem, "To the Music of Koras and Balaphon," which describes the arrival of thousands of black soldiers in France as a moment of a "great jubilant shout" ("To the Music of Koras and Balaphon," 23). Senghor also writes: "They are seven thousand new Negroes, seven thousand / soldiers, / Seven thousand humble and proud peasants, who carry / The riches of my race on their musical shoulders, / Strength, Nobility, Sincerity" ("To the Music of Koras and Balaphon," 23). Senghor and his African comrades saw World War II as an opportunity to wash up the affront that their ancestors endured from French imperialism. By perceiving *tirailleurs'* war efforts as struggles to restore African dignity and honor, Senghor theorizes cosmopolitanism as a resistance against the minimization and agony that colonial soldiers felt for centuries. In this sense, Senghor corroborates Jeffers's argument that "a viable cosmopolitanism must be thoroughly and vigorously anti-Eurocentric" (2010, 2). Senghor's anti-Eurocentric cosmopolitanism is further noticeable in his disparagement of the colonials who "carved 'Mercenary'" on the "honorable weapons" of his "Fathers" and worked with "merchants," "bankers," and "lords of gold" in order to "banish" him "from the Nation" ("Return of the Prodigal Son," 33). By denouncing such French capitalist and imperialist misdeeds in Senegal, Senghor justifies his participation in World War II on both moral and racial grounds. He states:

> If I have planted my loyalty back in the fields of defeat,
> It is because God has struck France with his leaden hand.
> May you be blessed, my Fathers, may you be blessed.
> You who have endured scorn and mockery, polite offenses,
> Discreet slurs and taboos and segregation.
> And you have torn from this too-loving heart
> The ties that bind it to the world's pulse.
> May you be blessed, you who refused to let hatred turn a
> man's heart
> To stone.
>
> ("Return of the Prodigal Son", 33)

The poem registers the unconditional cosmopolitanism in Senghor's attitudes toward France. This cosmopolitanism recognizes the shared destiny of the métropole and Senegal and "this belief in the possibility and necessity of racial harmony" which, according to Jeffers "is connected" to "his

212 *Léopold Sédar Senghor's cosmopolitanism*

[Senghor's] conception of different cultures—especially African and European cultures—as *complementary*" (2010, 204). On the one hand, Senghor perceives the war as an opportunity to extend to France the cosmopolitan love for humanity that his ancestors demonstrated in their refusal to "hate" the métropole despite the colonial abuses and denigrations it perpetrated against them. Yet Senghor also considers the war as a pivotal moment for avenging his Senegalese "Fathers" that the French humiliated, despised, and ridiculed during colonization. By collating these two missions and perspectives in the same poem, Senghor reconciles both his abjuration and acceptance of France in his cosmopolitanism. Yet, he knows that he can protect France's liberty only when the métropole begins to treat *tirailleurs* as equals. He is so dedicated to the plight of this proletariat that he regrets to "have eaten the / bread / That brings hunger to countless armies of workers / And those without work" ("Return of the Prodigal Son," 33), shortly before his solidarity with his African comrades rescues him from moral disappointment. By seeking and finding solace in the solidarity of his black *tirailleur* brothers, Senghor strengthens his cosmopolitanism with African culture without abandoning his support of global humanism. As Wilder points out, "Although the relative emphasis he placed on either cultural specificity or human solidarity varied . . . his [Senghor's] commitment to embodied humanism, situated universalism, and concrete cosmopolitanism persisted" (2015, 234).

Another important part of Senghor's cosmopolitanism is Pan-Africanism since it enables him to embrace black brotherhood and solidarity with *tirailleurs* without falling into cultural essentialism. In "Liminary Poem" (1940), Senghor writes: "You Senegalese Soldiers, my black brothers with warm / hands under ice and death / Who can praise you if not your brother-in-arms, your / brother in blood?" ("Liminary Poem," 39). These lines register a sense of nationalist and Pan-African consciousness that Senghor develops at the front, in unity with other *tirailleurs*, without losing his cosmopolitanism. Such a non-essentialist Pan-African consciousness is consistent with Thiam's argument that in "the Negritude thinker's concept of time, one can claim that roots, tradition, or places of origin reinvent themselves, evolve, but can neither be lost nor be kept authentic" (2014, 44–45). Senghor uses this consciousness as a means to overcome the physical distance that separated him from Senegal during his time in the war by bonding with other *tirailleurs*. Alliance with his "black brothers" shielded him from the métropole's illusory cosmopolitanism, allowing him to overcome the isolation, belittling, and restlessness that Africans experienced in a dismissive French society.

However, while seeking refuge in black brotherhood and culture in his war poems, Senghor does not revert to essentialism. He simply wants France to recognize the sacrifices of *tirailleurs*. Alluding to such sacrifices in the 1938 poem, "To the Senegalese Soldiers Who Died for France," Senghor says:

Léopold Sédar Senghor's cosmopolitanism 213

Listen to me, Senegalese soldiers, in the solitude of the black ground
And of death, in your deaf and blind solitude,
More than I in my dark skin in the depths of the Province,
Without even the warmth of your comrades lying close to you.

(47)

Senghor later describes these Senegalese soldiers as "black comrades" who
"DIED FOR THE REPUBLIC" ("To the Senegalese Soldiers Who Died for
France," 47). In stressing that *tirailleurs* "DIED FOR THE REPUBLIC,"
Senghor urges France to remember the blood debt that it owes to Africans
and open up space for the racial and cultural inclusivity that true cosmopoli-
tanism embodies. In so doing, Senghor seeks Africans' admissibility into the
house of French republicanism that they helped to save from Germany's
World War II aggressions. However, Senghor's search for admissibility does
not signify assimilationism or fundamentalism since it only wants to remind
France of the imperial history that ties it to Africa. As Wilder explains,
"Rather than submitting to colonial assimilation or preserving a reified
tradition, he [Senghor] hoped to explore African cultural singularity and
rethink African culture in relation to contemporary imperial conditions"
(2015, 60–61). The imperial history and conditions that bind Senegal to
France were tragically revisited one night in December 1944, when French
army officers gunned in Camp de Thiaroye, Dakar, many *tirailleurs* who
demanded the pay that was promised to them before their return to their
countries. Manning explains:

> Toward the end of the war, West African soldiers who had been
> prisoners of war in Europe demanded to receive the back pay and
> premiums they were due before demobilization at Thiaroye near Dakar
> in December 1944. They briefly held the commanding general hostage.
> French officials labeled their demonstration a mutiny, and fired on the
> demonstrators, killing 35 and wounding 35 more. This incident became
> the source of widespread bitterness among African soldiers who felt they
> had contributed significantly to the liberation of France, only to be
> rewarded with denial of their back pay.
>
> (1998, 137–138)

Recalling this brutal history, Senghor denounces the massacre of Thiaroye
in his poem "Prayer for Peace" (1945) by portraying France as the country
"Who offers a hero's welcome to some, and treats / The Senegalese like
mercenaries, the Empire's black watchdogs" (71). The massacre of *tirailleurs*
at Thiaroye was a blatant example of the fascism that prevailed in Senegal
during World War II when the French government considered any act of
rebellion in the colony as treason. As the war continued, Maréchal Pétain
and Governor Pièrre Boisson had strengthened the fascism by punishing
members of the colony who opposed their racial hatred and collaboration

214 *Léopold Sédar Senghor's cosmopolitanism*

with the Nazis. Pétain and Boisson created in Senegal's communes fascist legions that replicated the bigotry of the Vichy Regime in the métropole. In *French Colonialism Unmasked* (2006), Ruth Ginio reveals the racism and tyranny of this transatlantic French fascism in colonial Senegal when she states:

> Jews and Freemasons were rejected, and every new member had to carry a warrior card from 1870, World War I, or the battles of 1940; declare alliance to France and the principles of the National Revolution; and accept the disciplinary rules of the organization. Membership in the legion was hardly voluntary. Boisson clarified to his subordinates that those who would not join its ranks would be considered hostile to the National Revolution.
>
> (51–52)

It is ironic that *tirailleurs* of Thiaroye were subjected to this kind of fascism in late November-early December 1944, six months after Paris was liberated from Germany and France chose General Charles de Gaulle as its leader in place of Pétain. The assassination of *tirailleurs* shows France's betrayal of the cosmopolitan and republican principles of liberty, equality, and fraternity upon which its revolution was founded. The genocide also exemplifies the colonial paradox that Miller represents as "a certain pattern" in which "the ideals of the Revolution, by the very fact that they are taken to be immutable and immortal, are pressed into service as justifications for various policies of domination and exploitation" (1994, 107). This inconsistent colonial blueprint that Miller also describes as a "pattern of forced and dubious reconciliation between the ideals of the Revolution and France's nationalistic and imperialistic tendencies" (1994, 107) contradicts Crowder's argument that

> for many years, Senegal has had a romantic and sentimental place in the eyes of the French, and the *tirailleurs Sénégalais*, who in fact enjoyed the services of recruits from all over West Africa, are known by most Frenchmen for their services to France in both world wars.
>
> (1962, 99)

The deadly shooting of *tirailleurs* betrayed the métropole's cosmopolitan claims to have affection for Africans and ultimately marred an already-conflicted policy of assimilation which regarded Senegalese as subjects rather than as equal human beings and citizens.

Senghor's World War II poems have a dualistic meaning since they reveal both his cosmopolitanism and anticolonialism. On the one hand, Senghor uses these poems as a means for demonstrating the cosmopolitan embrace of France and its ideals of liberty that inspired *tirailleurs* to fight for the métropole's freedom from German domination. On the other hand, Senghor

Léopold Sédar Senghor's cosmopolitanism 215

uses the verses as tools for showing the disappointment about France that these soldiers felt as they experienced rejection in a European society that refused to perceive them as equals in spite of the huge sacrifices they made for its liberation from Nazi occupation. Torn between these two realities, Senghor's World War II poems reveal the unresolved dilemma of a major Senegalese writer who deeply experienced the angst of sharing unrestrained cosmopolitan love and compassion for a French society that kept Senegalese in a debased colonial status akin to slavery and was unwilling to perceive its *tirailleur* liberators as equals. Ultimately, Senghor's World War II poems serve to remind French society that its republican ideals will remain empty slogans unless it sincerely and consistently fights for cosmopolitan equality, compassion, and justice between the former métropole and colonized Africans.

Bibliography

Achi, Aimé Adopo. "Le lexique dans l'œuvre poétique de Senghor: Ancrage culturel et ouverture sur le monde." *Revue du LTML (le laboratoire de recherche théories et modèles linguistiques)* no. 2 (January 2009): 1–17. Accessed June 12, 2012. http://www.ltml.ci/files/articles/ADOPO%20Achi.pdf.

Appiah, Kwame A. *Cosmopolitanism: Ethics in a World of Strangers*. New York: Norton. 2006.

Bâ, Babacar. "La prison coloniale au Sénégal, 1790–1960: Carcéral de conquête et défiances locales." *French Colonial History* 8, no. 1 (May 22, 2007): 81–96.

Bâ, Sylvia Washington. *The Concept of Negritude in the Poetry of Léopold Sédar Senghor*. Princeton, NJ: Princeton University Press, 1973.

Breton, André. "First Surrealist Manifesto." In *Surrealism*, edited by Patrick Waldberg, 66–72. London: Thames & Hudson, 1965.

Cépède, Michel. *Agriculture et alimentation en France durant la IIe Guerre Mondiale*. Paris, M.-T. Génin, 1961.

Chowdhury, Kanishka. "Afrocentric Voices: Constructing Identities, Displacing Difference." *College Literature* 24, no. 2 (June 1997): 35–56.

Conklin, Alice L. *A Mission to Civilize: The Republican Idea of Empire in France and West Africa, 1895–1930*. Stanford, CA: Stanford University Press, 1997.

Crowder, Michael. *Senegal: A Study of French Assimilation Policy*. London: Methuen, 1962.

Gilbert, Martin. *The Second World War: A Complete History*. New York: Henry Holt and Company, 2004.

Ginio, Ruth. *French Colonialism Unmasked: The Vichy Years in French West Africa*. Lincoln: University of Nebraska Press, 2006.

Hall, Stuart. "Cultural Identity and Diaspora." In *Identity: Community, Culture, Difference*, edited by Jonathan Rutherford, 222–237. London: Lawrence and Wishart, 1990.

Hassan, Salah D. "Inaugural Issues: The Cultural Politics of Présence Africaine, 1947–1955." *Research in African Literatures* 30, no. 2 (1999): 194–221.

Irele, Abiola F. "Negritude or Black Cultural Nationalism." *The Journal of Modern African Studies* 3, no. 3 (October 1965): 321–348.

216 *Léopold Sédar Senghor's cosmopolitanism*

——. *The Negritude Moment: Explorations in Francophone African and Caribbean Literature and Thought.* Trenton: Africa World Press, 2011.

Jeffers, Chike. *The Black Gift: Cultural Nationalism and Cosmopolitanism in Africana Philosophy.* PhD diss., Northwestern University, 2010.

Jonassohn, Kurt and Karin Solveig Björnson. *Genocide and Gross Human Rights Violations: In Comparative Perspective.* New Brunswick, NJ: Transaction Publishers, 1998.

Jones, Edward A. *Voices of Négritude: The Expression of Black Experience in the Poetry of Senghor, Césaire and Damas.* Valley Forge, PA: Judson Press, 1971.

Kesteloot, Lillian. *Black Writers in French: A Literary History of Negritude.* Philadelphia, PA: Temple University Press, 1974.

Manning, Patrick. *Francophone Sub-Saharan Africa, 1880–1995.* Cambridge, UK: Cambridge University Press, 1998.

Meredith, Martin. *The Fate of Africa: A History of Fifty Years of Independence.* New York: Public Affairs, 2011.

Miller, Christopher L. "Unfinished Business: Colonialism in Sub-Saharan Africa and the Ideals of the French Revolution." In *The Global Ramifications of the French Revolution,* edited by Joseph Klaits and Michael H. Haltzel, 105–126. New York: Cambridge University Press, 1994.

Scheck, Raffael. *Hitler's African Victims: the German Army Massacres of Black French Soldiers in 1940.* Cambridge, UK: Cambridge University Press, 2006.

Sedlmayr, Hans. 1957. *Art in Crisis: The Lost Center.* New Brunswick, NJ: Transaction, 2007.

Sene, Ibra. "Colonisation française et main-d'œuvre carcérale au Sénégal: de l'emploi des détenus des camps pénaux sur les chantiers des travaux routiers (1927–1940)." *French Colonial History* 5 (2004): 153–171.

Senghor, Léopold Sédar. "Conférence de Léopold Sédar Senghor: L'esprit de la civilisation ou les lois de la culture négro-africaine." *Presence Africaine* no. 8/10 (June-November 1956): 51–64.

——. "Camp 1940." In *Leopold Sédar Senghor: The Collected Poetry,* edited and translated by Melvin Dixon, 56—57. Charlottesville: University Press of Virginia, 1991.

——. "Ethiopia: At the Call of the Race of Sheba." In *Leopold Sédar Senghor: The Collected Poetry,* edited and translated by Melvin Dixon, 41–45. Charlottesville: University Press of Virginia, 1991.

——. "Liberation." In *Leopold Sédar Senghor: The Collected Poetry,* edited and translated by Melvin Dixon, 16. Charlottesville: University Press of Virginia, 1991.

——. "Liminary Poem." In *Leopold Sédar Senghor: The Collected Poetry,* edited and translated by Melvin Dixon, 39–40. Charlottesville: University Press of Virginia, 1991.

——. "Luxembourg 1939." In *Leopold Sédar Senghor: The Collected Poetry,* edited and translated by Melvin Dixon, 48. Charlottesville: University Press of Virginia, 1991.

——. "Snow in Paris." In *Leopold Sédar Senghor: The Collected Poetry,* edited and translated by Melvin Dixon, 12–13. Charlottesville: University Press of Virginia, 1991.

——. "The Enlisted Man's Despair." In *Leopold Sédar Senghor: The Collected Poetry,* edited and translated by Melvin Dixon, 49–50. Charlottesville: University Press of Virginia, 1991.

Léopold Sédar Senghor's cosmopolitanism 217

——. "Prayer for Peace." In *Leopold Sédar Senghor: The Collected Poetry*, edited and translated by Melvin Dixon, 69–72. Charlottesville: University Press of Virginia, 1991.

——. "Prayer to the Masks." In *Leopold Sédar Senghor: The Collected Poetry*, edited and translated by Melvin Dixon, 13–14. Charlottesville: University Press of Virginia, 1991.

——. "Return of the Prodigal Son." In *Leopold Sédar Senghor: The Collected Poetry*, edited and translated by Melvin Dixon, 31–35. Charlottesville: University Press of Virginia, 1991.

——. "To The Music of Koras and Balaphon." In *Leopold Sédar Senghor: The Collected Poetry*, edited and translated by Melvin Dixon, 17–24. Charlottesville: University Press of Virginia, 1991.

——. "To the Senegalese Soldiers Who Died for France." In *Leopold Sédar Senghor: The Collected Poetry*, edited and translated by Melvin Dixon, 46–47. Charlottesville: University Press of Virginia, 1991.

Smith, Jessie Carney. "Senegal." *Black Firsts: 4,000 Ground-Breaking and Pioneering Events*, edited by Jessie Carney Smith, 339. Detroit, MI: Visible Ink Press, 2002.

Spleth, Janice S. *Léopold Sédar Senghor*. Boston, MA: Twayne, 1985.

Sullivan, Rosemary. *Villa Air-Bel: World War II, Escape, and a House in Marseille*. New York: Harper Perennial, 2007.

Suret-Canale, Jean. *Afrique Noire: L'Ère Coloniale, 1900–1945*. Paris: Éditions Sociales, 1957.

Thiam, Cheikh. *Return to the Kingdom of Childhood: Re-envisioning the Legacy and Philosophical Relevance of Negritude*. Columbus: The Ohio State University Press, 2014.

Vaillant, Janet G. *Black, French, and African: A Life of Leopold Sédar Senghor*. Cambridge, MA: Harvard University Press, 1990.

Van Niekerk, Barend van Dyk. *The African Image in the Work of Senghor*. Cape Town, South Africa: A. A. Balkema, 1970.

Weatherford, Doris. *American Women During World War II: An Encyclopedia*. Abingdon, UK, and New York: Routledge, 2010.

Wilder, Gary. *The French Imperial Nation-State: Negritude and Colonial Humanism Between the Two World Wars*. Chicago: University of Chicago Press, 2005.

——. *Freedom Time: Negritude, Decolonization, and the Future of the World*. Durham, NC: Duke University Press, 2015.

Conclusion: Roadblocks to black cosmopolitanism and France's integration of its minorities

My objective in this book was to study how cosmopolitanism, which is the desire to make the world a better place in which people acknowledge one another's humanity and rights to be free and prosperous, permeates key black political and transnational writings produced between the two world wars. In these writings, cosmopolitanism expresses itself in the ways in which black intellectuals such as Du Bois, Garvey, Touvalou, Lamine Senghor, Léopold Sédar Senghor and Padmore assessed France's republican ideals and the impact of the métropole's colonialist and fascist mistreatment of West Africans between 1914 and 1945. As the archival and published texts of these black intellectuals suggest, *tirailleurs* and other West Africans were true cosmopolitans who suffered for a French empire and modern world in which they simply wanted to be considered as equal human beings. By validating the experiences of the *tirailleurs*, the black thinkers participated in a transnational freedom struggle that transcended the geographic, local, and linguistic barriers that separated them. In addition, they embraced French cosmopolitanism while resisting its imperial, racist, and fascist claims. Such resistances stemmed from the métropole's segregations against *tirailleurs* and other *indigène* populations who endured forced labor, alienation, disenfranchisement, and other inhumane conditions in both colonial Senegal and the métropole. Knowing that French policies in colonial Senegal fostered exploitation and racism rather than cosmopolitan cooperation and peace, Du Bois, Garvey, Touvalou, the two Senghors, and Padmore launched anticolonial attacks against the métropole's imperial attitudes that Diagne helped to enforce in the colony and in his cosmopolitan discourses. These thinkers did not seek refuge in theories of racial universalism or purism because they embraced their own individual types of black cosmopolitanism without negating the importance of mutual interdependency between Africa and the West.

Moreover, my book aimed to explore the contributions of the selected black intellectuals to cosmopolitan and transnational literary and political sites of resistances in which they established direct or circuitous relationships with one another through their close interests in the métropole's colonial relationships with Senegal. These relationships, that Gilroy's *The Black*

Conclusion 219

Atlantic neglects by focusing on the "internality of [diasporan] blacks to the West" (5–7), reveal Francophone West Africans' contributions to twentieth-century black cosmopolitanism. Diagne, Touvalou, and the two Senghors were cosmopolitans, anticolonialists, and Pan-Africanists in their own ways, just as Anglophone diasporan blacks such as Du Bois, Garvey, and Padmore also were. Their radicalisms were rarely essentialist because they often evolved out of humanistic and pluralistic visions of national and global black struggles and identities.

Moreover, in their speeches, writings, and other testimonies, the seven black intellectuals reflect a blend of radicalisms and compromises in their distinctive assessments of France's relations to Senegal and *tirailleurs*, suggesting the plural and complicated sinews of black cosmopolitanism during the two world wars. Exploring the ragged trajectories of such forms of solidarity shows that black cosmopolitanism is made of disjointed, yet sometimes consistent, discourses, just like anticolonialism and Pan-Africanism also are. Indeed, black cosmopolitanism is hardly monolithic since it developed in different ways and contexts depending on the scholar under consideration. At times, the black intellectuals discussed in this book oscillated between cosmopolitanism and radicalism, suggesting that black solidarity was not a uniformous and linear tradition. Rather than being a stable and unvarying aspiration, black cosmopolitanism was complicated by the different terms in which black intellectuals responded to French colonialism, racism, and republican claims according to their specific historical situations, geographic origins, and cultural backgrounds. The plural and incoherent nature of black cosmopolitanism is mostly apparent in the figure of Diagne whose similarities and differences with Du Bois, Garvey, and the two Senghors were blatant. Diagne was a far contrast to the other intellectuals since he was an avid devotee of French cosmopolitanism who often denied the full extent to which racism and violence against *tirailleurs* prevented this philosophy from being extended to blacks in the colonies and the métropole. Thus, his cosmopolitanism had stark paradoxes that one can hardly find in the political thoughts of the other leaders. Diagne's uncompromising faith in French cosmopolitanism made him closer to many white colonials who claimed to perceive West Africans as equals and free when the latter were under severe imperial dominance.

In contrast to Diagne, Du Bois, Garvey, Touvalou, Padmore, and the two Senghors denounced France's betrayals and ill-treatment of Africans and proposed alternative forms of cosmopolitanism that could repair the damage of French colonialism in West Africa. Known as black cosmopolitanisms, the alternative Pan-African forms of resistance and dialogue are not linear and undisturbed because, in a few instances, moments of contacts and exchanges between black diasporan and West African Francophone intellectuals have been historically determined to have produced failures of intellectual and political collaborations or cross-Atlantic understanding. This was the case during the discords between Diagne and Du Bois at the

220 *Conclusion*

1921 Pan-African Congress. These divergences are, however, minimal, compared to the success that the two black intellectuals achieved in co-organizing both the 1919 and 1921 Pan-African congresses and defending *tirailleurs* and Africa from their unique vantage points.

Evidently, the irony is that Diagne remained an outsider among the other black cosmopolitans since he was the only defender of colonialism and an obstacle for his contemporaries such as Garvey, Du Bois, Touvalou, and Lamine Senghor. Du Bois almost lost faith in Diagne due to the ways in which the Senegalese treated African Americans at the 1921 congress as strangers. As for Touvalou and Lamine Senghor, their personal and professional lives were heavily affected by Diagne who collaborated with French colonials to sabotage their political activities in both Africa and the métropole. In a similar way, Diagne mounted vile campaigns against Garvey in Africa, impairing the UNIA's chance to thrive in Senegal. In spite of these machinations, however, Diagne was not able to prevent his rivals from planting the seed of anticolonial revolution in Africa. The radicalisms that the early black intellectuals sowed in the early twentieth century had parallels in the Pan-Africanism that Padmore and Léopold Senghor developed by denouncing French colonialism and cosmopolitanism in defiant ways.

A major contrast to Diagne was Garvey, whose impact on the liberation ideologies of Francophone African intellectuals such as Touvalou and Lamine Senghor was tremendous. Garvey was similar to these African intellectuals since he agreed that blacks and whites must work together toward the advancement of human civilization. But Garvey was somewhat different from the Francophone intellectuals on the civilization question since his cosmopolitanism was not as broad and free of racial polarities as those of his African peers were. Yet Garvey was akin to Touvalou and Lamine Senghor because he also believed in the right of blacks to develop their own societies while indulging in and profiting from the benefits of cosmopolitanism. In addition, like Garvey, the African leaders believed in the importance of nationhood and social, political, and economic freedom.

Moreover, like Garvey, Touvalou and Lamine Senghor vehemently criticized Diagne as an agent of French imperial hegemony. Diagne's unyielding faith in French assimilationism, cosmopolitanism, and republicanism earned him the lingering title of traitor of his own race. Although it was historically determined, such a representation of Diagne must not be overemphasized since it neglects the complexity of a pivotal intellectual and politician who should not be dismissed in the study of black cosmopolitanism. Despite his assimilationism, Diagne was, at times, a black radical and a black cosmopolitan. Despite his loyalties to France, he often had a determined cosmopolitan will to enable blacks of Africa and the diaspora to be free and further contribute to world civilization and progress.

Another problem that I aimed to tackle in this book is the limited attention that has been historically accorded to the *tirailleurs*. This neglect partly stems from the fact that the history of the two world wars is dominated by Western

Conclusion 221

master narratives that mainly feature American, British, and Russian soldiers fighting against fascism and Nazism, forgetting the heroism and cosmopolitanism of Africans who also took part in these struggles. As is apparent in the extant films, documentaries, and books about the two great wars, the accounts have tended to ignore the contributions of Africans who fought in the historical moments. Such narratives are incomplete since they disregard the enormous sacrifices that *tirailleurs* and other Africans made for world freedom. Recognizing the contributions of *tirailleurs* requires a new approach to the study of the two world wars. Focusing on World War I, Gerwarth and Manela urge scholars to start

> thinking about the Great War as a war of empires rather than of nation states . . . [so that we can see] . . . how the various contenders mobilized, deployed, and demobilized different imperial populations in differential ways and why this mattered both to the general history of the war and to the mobilized groups themselves.
>
> (2014, 3)

In a similar vein, Gerwarth and Manela implore scholars to

> [A]dopt a perspective that does justice more fully to the millions of imperial subjects called upon to defend their imperial governments' interest, to theaters of war that lay far beyond Europe including in Asia and Africa and, more generally, to the wartime roles and experiences of innumerable peoples from outside the European continent.
>
> (2014, 3)

African intellectuals have a huge role to play in this scholarship since the task of correcting the oversight of Africa in world war studies cannot be left to Western scholars alone. French scholars have made tremendous contributions to the study of the métropole's historical relations with the colonies. Yet their works are not without problems since they may unconsciously assert imperial viewpoints on a history of which memories and narrations are dominated by the offspring of the métropole rather than by the descendants of the former colonies. In her 2010 essay, "L'aphasie coloniale française: l'histoire mutilée," Anna Laura Stoler laments how, with the exception of Georges Balandier's 1951 study, "La situation coloniale: approche théorique," white and French scholars, unlike colored Francophone or Anglophone intellectuals, such as Aimé Césaire, Frantz Fanon, Stuart Hall, and Edward Said, have generally avoided "[de] remarquer la pérennité des structures impériales et la ténacité des relations qu'elles mettaient en forme" [[to] draw attention to the pervasiveness of imperial structures and the persistence of the relationships they produce] (2010, 65). Knowing that French social sciences have been "réticentes vis-à-vis d'une réinterprétation qui plaçait la métropole et la colonie dans le même cadre

222   *Conclusion*

analytique" [reluctant to consider a reinterpretation that placed the métropole and the colony in the same analytical framework] (2010, 65), Stoler criticizes the ways in which the two great wars are unequally remembered in the former imperial nation (2010, 66).

Stoler, thus, casts doubt on the legitimacy of the waves of memorials about the two great wars in France. Her assertions empower us to rightfully lament how such memorials may ignore the endurance of inhumane and anticosmopolitan treatment of Africans and other members of postcolonial France who are subjected to racism, underemployment, xenophobia, Islamophobia, violence, and other injustices that recall the ill-treatment that *tirailleurs* suffered in the republic. In light of these circumstances, one can interpret the relative neglect of the history of *tirailleurs* in French studies as the empire's propensity to devise a selective memory that obfuscates the injustices of colonialism. In this vein, Bancel and Blanchard write: "Jusqu'au début des années 1990, la marginalisation de l'histoire coloniale a répondu à la double exigence d'oublier un traumatisme historique heurtant la représentation de la nation et de prévenir tout ressac des affrontements coloniaux" [Until the early 1990s, the marginalization of colonial history has answered the twofold requirement to forget historical trauma hurting the representation of the nation and prevent any resuscitation of colonial clashes] (2010, 506). France's desire to forget its colonial history contradicts its republicanism and reveals its difficult path to cosmopolitanism. France's road to cosmopolitanism requires its validation of this brutal history and its confrontation of what Mbembe calls "la question raciale" [the racial question] (2010, 212). As Mbembe argues, the métropole's path to cosmopolitanism is difficult due to 1) "son incapacité à embrasser le monde" [its incapacity to embrace the world] and "[son] excision de l'histoire de notre présence au monde et de la présence du monde en notre sein" [[its] excision of the history of our presence in the world and the world's presence in our midst] (2010, 212).

As I have attempted to show in this book, France's difficult path to cosmopolitanism is also traceable to the two world wars when its inferiorization of *tirailleurs* and other Africans mobilized many black intellectuals against colonialism. A study of *tirailleurs'* experiences, which served as a blueprint of France's historical relations with the colonies, can provide the former métropole with the consciousness that would allow it to have true and proper cosmopolitan attitudes toward the history of these combatants and their current descendants. Unfortunately, the blueprint has only served to stereotype *tirailleurs* in French culture or police and discipline blacks and other ethnic minorities of the former métropole. The root of this racism lies in France's reluctance to live up to its cosmopolitan promises. While preaching modernity and free circulation of people as means for building tolerance, global citizenship, and international exchange, France is prone to imposing strict barriers to such movements when they involve people from Africa and other parts of the "Third World." Addressing these

Conclusion 223

problems requires the development of egalitarian, social, political, and economic policies toward minorities as well as other members of society, and the promotion of positive attitudes that embrace mutual respect, diversity, parity, and dialogue as enduring goals of every righteous and fair-minded person and nation.

Bibliography

Bancel, Nicolas and Pascal Blanchard. "Colonisation: commémorations et mémoriaux. Conflictualité sociale et politique d'un enjeu mémoriel." In *Ruptures postcoloniales: Les nouveaux visages de la société française,* edited by Nicolas Bancel, Florence Bernault, Pascal Blanchard, and Valérie Amiraux, 480–508. Paris: La Découverte, 2010.

Gerwarth, Robert and Erez Manela. "Introduction." In *Empires at War: 1911–1923 (Greater War),* edited by Robert Gerwarth and Erez Manela, 1–17. New York: Oxford University Press, 2014.

Gilroy, Paul. *The Black Atlantic: Modernity and Double Consciousness.* Cambridge, MA: Harvard University Press, 1993.

Hargreaves, Alec G., and Mark McKinney. "Introduction: The Post-Colonial Problematic in France." In *Postcolonial Cultures in France,* edited by Alec G. Hargreaves and Mark McKinney, 3–25. New York: Routledge, 1997.

Mbembe, J. Achille. "La République et l'impensé de la 'race.'" In *Ruptures postcoloniales: Les nouveaux visages de la société française,* edited by Nicolas Bancel, Florence Bernault, Pascal Blanchard, and Valérie Amiraux, 205–216. Paris: La Découverte, 2010.

Peabody, Sue and Tyler Stovall. "Race, France, Histories." In *The Color of Liberty: Histories of Race in France,* edited by Sue Peabody and Tyler Stovall, 1–7. Durham, NC: Duke University Press, 2003.

Stoler, Anna Laura, "L'aphasie coloniale française: l'histoire mutilée." In *Ruptures postcoloniales: Les nouveaux visages de la société française,* edited by Nicolas Bancel, Florence Bernault, Pascal Blanchard, and Valérie Amiraux, 62–78. Paris: La Découverte, 2010.

Stovall, Tyler. "From Red Belt to Black Belt." In *The Color of Liberty: Histories of Race in France,* edited by Sue Peabody and Tyler Stovall, 351–369. Durham, NC: Duke University Press, 2003.

Notes

Introduction

1 See Lucie Couturier, *Des inconnus chez moi* (Paris: Éditions de la Sirène, 1920); Général [Charles] Mangin, *Comment finit la Guerre* (Paris: Librairie Plon, 1920); Charles Mangin, *Regards sur la France d'Afrique avec quatre cartes* (Paris: Librairie Plon, 1924); Charles Mangin, *La Force Noire* (Paris: Librairie Hachette, 1910).

2 For archived information on these events, see the website of the French research collective called Achac: http://www.achac.com/.

3 See "Le projet d'écriture d'une histoire générale 'vient combler un vide' (Iba Der Thiam)." http://www.seneweb.com/news/Societe/le-projet-d-ecriture-d-une-histoire-generale-vient-combler-un-vide-iba-der-thiam_n_122098.html. Accessed March 27, 2014.

4 Similar works that examine Negritude beyond traditional frameworks are: V.Y. Mudimbe, ed., *The Surreptitious Speech: Présence Africaine and the Politics of Otherness 1947–1987* (Chicago: University of Chicago Press, 1992); Elisabeth Mudimbe-Boyi, "Harlem Renaissance and Africa: An Ambiguous Adventure," in *The Surreptitious Speech*, ed. V.Y. Mudimbe (Chicago: The University of Chicago Press, 1992), 174–184.

5 See Paul Lovejoy, "The African Diaspora: Revisionist Interpretations of Ethnicity, Culture and Religion under Slavery," *Studies in the World History of Slavery, Abolition and Emancipation* 2, no. 1 (1997). Accessed January 1, 2014. http://www.yorku.ca/nhp/publications/Lovejoy_Studies%20in%20the%20World%20History%20of%20Slavery.pdf.

6 See Colonel Debon, "Les Troupes coloniales: Importance du Recrutement Indigène colonial," *La Dépêche Coloniale et Maritime*, April 1, 1920: 1.

7 See Moulaye Aïdara, L'Histoire Oubliée des Tirailleurs Sénégalais de la Seconde Guerre Mondiale (Paris: Le Manuscrit, 2005), 18; Pap Ndiaye, La condition noire: Essai sur une minorité française (Paris: Calmann-Lévy, 2008), 154 ; Colonel Debon, "Les Troupes coloniales," 1.

8 Pascal Blanchard, Eric Deroo, and Gilles Manceron, *Le Paris Noir* (Paris: Hazan, 2001), 46.

Chapter 1

1 See G. Wesley Johnson, Jr., "The Ascendancy of Blaise Diagne and the Beginning of African Politics in Senegal," *Journal of the International African Institute* 36, no. 3 (July 1966): 237; Jean-François Maurel, *Blaise Diagne et son temps: catalogue de l'exposition d'Archive* (Dakar: Archives du Sénégal, 1972), 1.

Notes 225

2 "Blaise Diagne est mort hier à Cambo," *Les Annales Coloniales*, May 12, 1934, 1.
3 See Maurel, 1.
4 See also Maurel, 1.
5 See Blaise Diagne, "Lettre de Diagne au maître de la loge maçonnique de Saint-Denis-de-la-Réunion. 8 aout, 1900," in *Blaise Diagne: Sa vie, son œuvre,* ed. Obèye Diop (Dakar: Nouvelles Editions Africaines, 1974), 24.
6 See Diagne, "Lettre de Diagne au maître de la loge," 25.
7 See Diagne, "Lettre de Diagne au maître de la loge," 25.
8 See Maurel, 3.
9 See also Amady Aly Dieng, *Blaise Diagne, premier député africain.* Vol.7 of *Afrique Contemporaine,* ed. Ibrahima Baba Kaké (Paris: Editions Chaka, 1990), 60.
10 See "A la chambre: le Budget des colonies: Deuxième séance du 30 Janvier: M. Varenne," *Les Annales Coloniales*, January 31, 1930: 2.
11 "A la Chambre," 2.
12 Blaise Diagne, "Le Gouvernement de demain et les colonies," *La Dépêche Coloniale et Maritime*, June 10–11, 1924: 1.
13 See Alice Conklin, Sarah Fishman, and Robert Zaretsky, *France and its Empire Since 1870* (New York: Oxford University Press, 2011), 17.
14 See Charles Cros, "Son premier discours à la tribune, sa première bataille, sa première victoire," *La Parole est à M. Blaise Diagne, premier homme d'Etat africain* (Dakar: Edition Maison du Livre, 1972), 81.
15 See Diagne, "Mon cher directeur," *Les Annales Coloniales*, April 8, 1926: 1.
16 See Diagne, "Mon cher directeur," 1.
17 See Gaston Valran, "Education du sens social chez les indigènes: Encourageons le génie de l'association," *La Dépêche Coloniale et Maritime*, August 25, 1922: 1 ; Maurice Delafosse, "Colonisateurs et colonisés: Juxtaposition, assimilation, association," *La Dépêche Coloniale et Maritime*, June 21, 1924: 1.
18 See "Courrier de l'Afrique Occidentale: Gouvernement General," *Les Annales Coloniales*, October 12, 1921: 1.
19 See "A la Chambre," 2.
20 See "A la Chambre," 2.
21 See "A la Chambre," 2.
22 "A la commission de l'Algérie, des colonies, et des protectorats," *Les Annales Coloniales*, December 1, 1924: 1.
23 "A la Commission de l'Algerie," 1.
24 Eugène Devaux, "Cinéma et causerie sur l'A.O.F.," *Les Annales Coloniales*, June 10, 1934:1.
25 Devaux, "Cinéma et causerie," 1.
26 Quoted from Robert Soucy, *French Fascism: The First Wave, 1924–1933* (New Haven: Yale University Press, 1986), 85.
27 See "A la Chambre," 2.
28 See "Les obligations militaires des Sénégalais," *Les Annales Coloniales*, June 10, 1916: 2.
29 Cited in Anne Douaire, Traces et absence de la Grande Guerre aux Antilles. In Mémoires et antimémoires littéraires au XXe siècle: la Première Guerre mondiale: colloque de Cerisy-la-Salle, 2005, ed. Annamaria Laserra, Nicole Leclercq, and Marc Quaghebeur (Bruxelles: P.I.E. Peter Lang, 2008), "Traces et absence," 132.
30 See Douaire, 133.
31 Charles John Balesi, *From Adversaries to Comrades-in-arms: West Africans and the French Military, 1885–1918* (Waltham, MA: Crossroads Press, 1979), 83; Cros, "Son premier discours à la tribune, sa première bataille, sa première

226 Notes

victoire," *La Parole est à M. Blaise Diagne, premier homme d'Etat africain* (Dakar: Edition Maison du Livre, 1972), 90; Marc Michel, *L'appel à l'Afrique: Contributions et réactions à l'effort de guerre en A.O.F. (1914-1919)* (Paris: Cujas, 1982), 63, 80, 131.

32 See Cros, "Son premier discours," 90.

33 See Cros, "Son premier discours," 90.

34 See Marc Ruedel, "Renforts Coloniaux," *Les Annales Coloniales*, January 1, 1916: 1.

35 See Cros, "La Parole est à M. Blaise Diagne," 91.

36 See Cros, "Son premier discours," 97.

37 "See Cros, "Son premier discours," 97.

38 See "Discours de Monsieur Fred Zeller," in *Blaise Diagne: Sa vie, son œuvre*, 25.

39 See Cros, "La première intervention à la Chambre, son premier succès," *La Parole est à M. Blaise Diagne, premier homme d'Etat africain* (Dakar: Edition Maison du Livre, 1972), 76.

40 See Cros, "La Première Intervention," 77.

41 See Niall Ferguson, *Civilization: The West and the Rest* (New York: Penguin, 2011), 183–184; Tyler Stovall, "Black Modernism and the Making of the Twentieth Century: Paris, 1919," in *Afromodernisms Paris, Harlem, Haiti and the Avant-garde*, edited by Fionnghuala Sweeney (New York: Columbia University Press, 2013), 27.

Chapter 2

1 W. E. B. Du Bois, "Letter to [Miss] Bernice E. Brand," November 16, 1927. W. E. B. Du Bois Papers (MS 312), Special Collections and University Archives, University of Massachusetts Amherst Libraries.

2 Du Bois, "Editorial," *The Crisis* 14, no. 5 (September 1917): 217.

3 "Three Members of Parliament," *The Crisis* 8, no. 4 (August 1914): 170.

4 "The World War: Causes and Effects," *The Crisis* 9, no. 2 (December 1914): 70.

5 Du Bois, "Editorial," *The Crisis* 17, no. 5 (March 1919): 215.

6 "Foreign," *The Crisis* 13, no. 5 (March 1917): 245.

7 "Miscellaneous," *The Crisis* 13, no. 6 (April 1917): 303. A similar admiration of *The Crisis* for the Senegalese soldiers is apparent on these pages: "Black Soldiers," *The Crisis* 15, no. 1 (November 1917): 33–34; "The War," *The Crisis* 16, no. 1 (May 1918): 21; "The War," *The Crisis* 15, no. 4 (February 1918): 192.

8 See Chad Williams, *Torchbearers of Democracy: African American Soldiers in the World War I Era* (Chapel Hill: University of North Carolina Press, 2013), 24–26, 56–58; Arthur E. Barbeau and Florette Henri, *The Unknown Soldiers: African American Troops in World War I* (Philadelphia, PA: Temple University Press, 1974), 21–32, 175–190; Frank E. Roberts, *The American Foreign Legion: Black Soldiers of the 93rd in World War I* (Annapolis, MD: Naval Institute Press, 2004), 193–202; Susan R. Grayzel, "Women and Men," in *A Companion to World War I*, edited by John Horne (Malden, MA: Wiley-Blackwell, 2010), 268;

9 "Benefits Forgot," *The Crisis* 19, no. 2 (December 1919): 76.

10 "War," *The Crisis* 14, no. 1 (May 1917): 38.

11 See Du Bois, "An Essay Toward a History of the Black Man in the Great War," *The Crisis* 18, no. 2 (June 1919): 64; Du Bois, "The Black Man in the Revolution of 1914–1918," *The Crisis* 17, no. 5 (March 1919): 218–219.

12 Du Bois, "The Black Man in the Revolution of 1914–1918," 219.

Notes   227

13 For biographies of George H. Jackson, see Benjamin R. Justesen, "African-American Consuls Abroad, 1897–1909," *Foreign Service Journal* (September 2004): 74; Louis R. Harlan and Raymond W. Smock, eds. *The Booker T. Washington Papers: 1906–8* (Urbana: University of Illinois Press, 1972), note 8.277.

14 George H. Jackson, "Letter to Blaise Diagne," December 27, 1918, W. E. B. Du Bois Papers (MS 312), Special Collections and University Archives, University of Massachusetts Amherst Libraries.

15 Blaise Diagne, "Letter to W.E.B. Du Bois," January 5 1919, W. E. B. Du Bois Papers (MS 312), Special Collections and University Archives, University of Massachusetts Amherst Libraries.

16 "Clippings," *The Evening Independent*, May 2, 1955: 18; "The War," *The Crisis* 16, no. 3 (July 1918): 134.

17 W.E.B Du Bois, "Letter to Blaise Diagne," October 18, 1919, W. E. B. Du Bois Papers (MS 312), Special Collections and University Archives, University of Massachusetts Amherst Libraries.

18 See "Crisis (Firm)," Clipping from *The Crisis*, March 1919. W. E. B. Du Bois Papers (MS 312), Special Collections and University Archives, University of Massachusetts Amherst Libraries.

19 See Diagne, "Letter to Du Bois," *The Crisis* 17, no. 5 (March 1919): 221.

20 "Memorandum from W. E. B. Du Bois to M. Diagne and Others on a Pan-African Congress to be Held in Paris in February 1919," January 1, 1919, W. E. B. Du Bois Papers (MS 312), Special Collections and University Archives, University of Massachusetts Amherst Libraries.

21 W. E. B. Du Bois, "Letter to A. Vinck," July 15, 1921, W. E. B. Du Bois Papers (MS 312), Special Collections and University Archives, University of Massachusetts Amherst Libraries.

22 "The Denial of Passports," *The Crisis*, 17, no. 5 (March 1919): 237.

23 See *W. E. B. Du Bois: A Biography in Four Voices*, directed by Louis Massiah (1995; San Francisco: California Newsreel, 1995), Videocassette (VHS).

24 Du Bois, "Letter to Jean de La Roche," *The Correspondence of W. E. B. Du Bois. Vol 3.* Selections, ed. Herbert Aptheker (Amherst: University of Massachusetts Press, 1978),59.

25 Du Bois, "Opinion of W. E. B. Du Bois," *The Crisis* 18, no. 1 (May 1919): 9.

26 Du Bois, "Opinion of W. E. B. Du Bois," *The Crisis* 18, no. 1 (May 1919): 9.

27 Du Bois, "The Pan-African Congress," *The Crisis* 17, no. 6 (April 1919): 271.

28 See "Memorandum from W. E. B. Du Bois to M. Diagne and Others on a Pan-African Congress to be Held in Paris in February 1919."

29 See "Memorandum from W. E. B. Du Bois to M. Diagne and Others on a Pan-African Congress to be Held in Paris in February 1919."

30 See "Memorandum from W. E. B. Du Bois to M. Diagne and Others on a Pan-African Congress to be Held in Paris in February 1919."

31 "Enclosure: Resolutions Passed at the 1919 Pan-African Congress," *The Marcus Garvey and Universal Negro Improvement Association Papers*, Vol. 4, ed. Robert Hill (Los Angeles: University of California Press, 1995), 4–7.

32 See "Discours inaugural de M. Diagne au Congrès Pan-Africain des 19-20-21 février 1919," ca. February 1919, W. E. B. Du Bois Papers (MS 312), Special Collections and University Archives, University of Massachusetts Amherst Libraries, 1–2.

33 See "Discours inaugural de M. Diagne au Congrès Pan-Africain des 19-20-21 février 1919," 1.

34 W. E. B. Du Bois, "Letter to Blaise Diagne," ca. August 1921.

35 See Wolters, *Du Bois and His Rivals*, 124–125.

228 Notes

36 "110 Delegates," 68–69.
37 See "Pan-African Delegates," 68–69; Jenkan, *Rayford Logan*, 54–56.
38 Du Bois, "Letter to Diagne," ca. August 1921, W. E. B. Du Bois Papers (MS 312), Special Collections and University Archives, University of Massachusetts Amherst Libraries.
39 Du Bois, "Opinion of W. E. B. Du Bois," *The Crisis* 21, no. 3 (January 1921): 101.
40 See Blaise Diagne, "Letter to W. E. B. Du Bois," November 15, 1920, W. E. B. Du Bois Papers (MS 312), Special Collections and University Archives, University of Massachusetts Amherst Libraries.
41 See "From N. Y. Tribune," *The Marcus Garvey and Universal Negro Improvement Association Papers*, Vol. 4, ed. Robert Hill (Los Angeles: University of California Press, 1995), 186.
42 See also "Au Congrès Pan-Noir: Une Séance de clôture Mouvementée," 1.
43 See "Article in *La Dépêche Coloniale et Maritime* [Brussel 2, 1921]," 165–166; See Du Bois, "The Pan-African Movement," 17–22.
44 See "Au Congrès Pan-Noir: Une Séance de clôture Mouvementée," *La Dépêche Coloniale et Maritime*, September 4–5, 1921: 1.
45 Du Bois, "Worlds of Color," *The Crisis* 3, no. 3 (April 1925): 433.
46 See "Au Congrès Pan-Noir: Une Séance de clôture Mouvementée," 1.
47 See Du Bois, "A Second Journey to Pan-Africa," *W. E. B. Du Bois: A Reader*, ed. David Levering Lewis (New York: Henry Holt, 1995), 665.
48 See "Le Congrès Pan-Noir," *La Dépêche Coloniale et Maritime*, September 9, 1921: 1.

Chapter 3

1 See "Constitution of the Universal Negro Improvement Association," in *Apropos of Africa: Sentiments of American Negro Leaders on Africa*, ed. Adelaide Cromwell Hill and Martin Kilson (Garden City, NY: Anchor Books, 1971), 238–239.
2 For my sources of conversion rates see Frank Moore Colby and Talcott Williams, *The New International Encyclopaedia* (New York: Dodd, Mead and Company, 1927), 1271; *The Emergency Tariff: And Its Effects on Cattle and Beef, Sheep and Mutton, Wool, Pork, and Miscellaneous Meats*. Tariff Information Series. No. 29 (Washington, DC: Government Printing Office, 1922), 155.
3 Robert Cornevin, *Hommes et destins: (dictionnaire biographique d'Outre-mer)*. Tome 9, *Afrique noire* (Paris: Académie des sciences d'Outre-Mer, 1989), 9–11; Jean-Luc Angrand, *Céleste ou le temps des Signares* (Sarcelles, France: Éditions Anne Pépin, 2006), 277; Hilary Jones, *The Métis of Senegal: Urban Life and Politics in French West Africa* (Bloomington: Indiana University Press, 2013), 189–190.
4 "Pierre Jean Didelot to Governor-General of French West Africa," *The Marcus Garvey and Universal Negro Improvement Association Papers*, Vol. 9, ed. Robert Hill (Los Angeles: University of California Press, 1995), 557.
5 "Report by Pierre Jean Henri Didelot to Governor-General of French West Africa," *The Marcus Garvey and Universal Negro Improvement Association Papers*, Vol. 9, 581.
6 "Qu'en pense Diagne (Blaise)," *Les Annales Coloniales*, August 12, 1921: 1.
7 "Manifestation Américaine Pan-Noire," *Les Annales Coloniales*, September 14, 1921: 2.
8 "Au Congrès Pan-Noir ... 'L'Afrique aux Africains', a dit Marcus Garvey ... 'Langage de bolshevik !' réplique M. Diagne," *La Dépêche Coloniale et Maritime*, September 2, 1921: 1.

Notes   229

9 "At the Pan-African Congress: 'Africa for the Africans... Bolshevik Talk!' Replies Mr. Diagne,'" *The Marcus Garvey and Universal Negro Improvement Association Papers*, Vol. 9, 158.

10 W. E. B. Du Bois, "Pan-African Congress adopted a Resolution to Invite Marcus Garvey to Next Session to Explain Aims and Objects of the U.N.I.A. Did You Know That?" *The Marcus Garvey and Universal Negro Improvement Association Papers*, Vol. 4, ed. Robert Hill (Los Angeles: University of California Press, 1985), 278.

11 *The Marcus Garvey and Universal Negro Improvement Association Papers*, Vol 7, ed. Robert Hill (Los Angeles: University of California Press, 1990), 183.

12 "Le congrès pan-noir," *Revue des Questions Coloniales et Maritimes* 486, no. 46 (July–September, 1921): 122.

13 "Africa for Africans! Is Not Negro Slogan," in *The Marcus Garvey and Universal Negro Improvement Association Papers*, Vol. 4, 32.

14 "Africa for Africans! Is Not Negro Slogan," 32.

15 See also Benoît Hopquin, *Ces noirs qui ont fait la France* (Paris: Calmann-Lévy, 2009), 129; Manning Marable, *W. E. B. Du Bois: Black Radical Democrat* (Boulder, CO: Paradigm Publishers, 1986), 101.

16 Marcus Garvey, "Defense of Ku Klux," in *The Marcus Garvey and Universal Negro Improvement Association Papers*, Vol. 9, 188.

17 Marcus Garvey, "Editorial Letter by Marcus Garvey in the Negro World [New York, November 21, 1922], in *The Marcus Garvey and Universal Negro Improvement Association Papers*, Vol. 9, 694.

18 See for instance, Tania Friedel, Racial Discourse and Cosmopolitanism in Twentieth-Century African American Writing (New York: Routledge, 2008), 105; Robert E. Washington, The Ideologies of African American Literature: From the Harlem Renaissance to the Black Nationalist Revolt (Lanham, MD: Rowman & Littlefield Publishers, 2001), 75–76.

19 See Robert Hill, ed. The Marcus Garvey and Universal Negro Improvement Association Papers, Vol. 4, 99.

20 See Louise Delafosse, *Maurice Delafosse: Le Berrichon conquis par l'Afrique* (Paris: Société française d'histoire d'outre-mer, 1976), 311.

21 Garvey, "Editorial Letter by Marcus Garvey in the Negro World," 695.

22 "Speech by Marcus Garvey. [New York, October 2, 1921]," *The Marcus Garvey and Universal Negro Improvement Association Papers*, Vol. 4, 99.

23 "Diagne (Blaise) et Cie," *Les Annales Coloniales*, June 3, 1921: 1.

24 "Le Congrès Pan-Noir: Deux Théories en Présence," *La Dépêche Coloniale et Maritime*, September 6, 1921: 1; "Article in La Dépêche Coloniale et Maritime [Paris, September 4, 1921] The Pan-Black Congress: Two Opposing Doctrines," *The Marcus Garvey and Universal Negro Improvement Association Papers*, Vol. 9, 176.

Chapter 4

1 See Centenaire de la Conférence de Berlin (1884–1885): actes du colloque international, Brazzaville, avril 1985 (Paris: Présence africaine, 1987), 435; Joe Lunn, Memoirs of the Maelstrom: A Senegalese Oral History of the First World War (Portsmouth, NH: Heinemann, 1999), 204; Pascal Blanchard, Eric Deroo, and Gilles Manceron, Le Paris Noir (Paris: Hazan, 2001), 46.

2 Marcus Garvey, "Speech Delivered at Liberty Hall N.Y.C. During Second International Convention of Negroes August 1921," in *The Philosophy and Opinions of Marcus Garvey or Africa for the Africans*, Vol. 1, ed. Amy Jacques Garvey and Tony Martin (Dover, MA: The Majority Press, 1986), 95–96.

230 Notes

3 Marcus Garvey, "Speech Delivered at Liberty Hall N.Y.C. During Second International Convention of Negroes August 1921," 94.

4 "Editorial by Marcus Garvey in the Negro World [Berlin, Germany, 6 Aug. 1928]," in *The Marcus Garvey and Universal Negro Improvement Association Papers*, Vol. 7, ed. Robert Hill (Los Angeles: University of California Press, 1990), 212.

5 "Enclosure," *The Marcus Garvey and Universal Negro Improvement Association Papers*, Vol. 7, 268–269.

6 Marcus Garvey, "Speech by Marcus Garvey [New York, October 2, 1921]," *The Marcus Garvey and Universal Negro Improvement Association Papers*, Vol. 4, ed. Robert Hill (Los Angeles: University of California Press, 1985), 99.

7 Marcus Garvey, "Speech by Marcus Garvey [New York, October 2, 1921]," 100.

8 Marcus Garvey, "Speech by Marcus Garvey [New York, October 2, 1921]," 100.

9 Jabez Ayodele Langley, "Marcus Garvey and African Nationalism," in *Marcus Garvey and the Vision of Africa*, ed. John Henrik Clarke and Amy Jacques Garvey (New York: Vintage Books, 1974), 412.

10 "Convention Report [New York, August 18, 1924]," in *The Marcus Garvey and Universal Negro Improvement Association Papers*, Vol. 5, ed. Robert Hill (Los Angeles: University of California Press, 1986), 750.

11 Robert Hill, ed., *The Marcus Garvey and Universal Negro Improvement Association Papers*, Vol. 10 (Los Angeles: University of California Press, 2006), 172. Note 1.

12 For the reactions of these French colonials toward Batouala, see Donald E. Herdeck, "Introduction," in *Batouala: A True Black Novel*, by René Maran (Washington, DC: Black Orpheus Press, 1972), 2–3; Eugène Devaux, "L'épilogue logique de Batouala," *Les Annales Coloniales*, February 16, 1922: 1.

13 See "M. Diagne fait condamner ses diffamateurs," *Les Annales coloniales*, November 27, 1924: 2; "M. Diagne fera justice des potins de René Maran," *Les Annales Coloniales*, June 16, 1924: 1.

14 Martin Steins, "Black Migrants in Paris," *European-Language Writing in Sub-Saharan Africa*, Vol. 1 (Budapest: Akad. Kiadó 1986), 356.

15 See Robert Hill, The Marcus Garvey and Universal Negro Improvement Association Papers, Vol. 10, 164.

16 See Robert Hill, The Marcus Garvey and Universal Negro Improvement Association Papers, Vol. 10, 164.

17 For a discussion of Touvalou's relations with Lamine Gueye, see Amady Aly Dieng, *Lamine Guèye: Une des grandes figures politiques africaines (1891–1968)* (Paris: Editions L'Harmattan, 2013), 64.

18 See Robert Hill, The Marcus Garvey and Universal Negro Improvement Association Papers, Vol. 10, 164.

Chapter 5

1 To study this rupture of the LDRN, see Jennifer Boittin, "The Militant Black Men of Marseille and Paris, 1927–1937," in *Black France/France Noire: The History and Politics of Blackness*, ed. Trica Danielle Keaton, T. Denean Sharpley-Whiting, and Tyler E. Stovall (Durham, NC: Duke University Press, 2012), 224; Ula Yvette Taylor, *The Veiled Garvey: The Life and Times of Amy Jacques Garvey* (Chapel Hill: University of North Carolina Press, 2002), 96.

2 See Jonathan Derrick, *Africa's 'Agitators': Militant Anti-Colonialism in Africa and the West, 1918–1939* (New York: Columbia University Press, 2008), 145–46; Martin Steins, "Black Migrants in Paris," in *European-Language Writing in Sub-Saharan Africa*, Vol. 1, ed. Albert S. Gérard (Budapest: Akad. Kiadó, 1986), 362–363.

Notes 231

3 See Philippe Dewitte, *Les Mouvements Nègres en France* (Paris: L'Harmattan, 1985), 127; Christopher L. Miller, *Nationalists and Nomads: Essays on Francophone African Literature and Culture* (Chicago: University of Chicago Press, 1998), 2, 217; Brent Hayes Edwards, *The Practice of Diaspora: Literature, Translation, and the Rise of Black Internationalism* (Cambridge, MA: Harvard University Press, 2003), 28–29.

4 See Robert Hill, ed, *The Marcus Garvey and Universal Negro Improvement Association Papers*, Vol. 10 (Los Angeles: University of California Press, 2006), 174, Note 10; Steins, "Black Migrants in Paris," 361.

5 See Samuel Same Kolle, *Naissance et paradoxes du discours anthropologique africain* (Paris: L'Harmattan, 2007), 72; Ibrahima B. Kaké, "The Impact of Afro-Americans on French-Speaking Black Africans, 1919–45," in *Global dimensions of the African Diaspora*, ed. Joseph E. Harris (Washington, DC: Howard University Press, 1993), 258.

6 Marcus Garvey, *The Philosophy and Opinions of Marcus Garvey, or Africa for Africans*, Vol. 1, ed. Amy Jacques-Garvey and Tony Martin (Dover, MA: The Majority Press, 1986), 1.

7 Garvey, "Speech by Marcus Garvey [Liberty Hall, New York, January 6, 1924]," in *The Marcus Garvey and Universal Negro Improvement Association Papers*, Vol. 5, ed. Robert Hill (Los Angeles: University of California Press, 1986), 518.

8 See Edouard Glissant, "Haïti, point focal de la Caraïbe," *Cultures Sud* no. 168 (2008): 28–31.

9 For a study of Toussaint's relations with France, see Martin Ros and Karin H. Ford, *Night of Fire: The Black Napoleon and the Battle for Haiti* (New York: Sarpedon, 1994); C. L. R. James, *The Black Jacobins: Toussaint L'Ouverture and the San Domingo Revolution* (New York: Vintage Books, 1963).

10 See Garvey, "Speech by Marcus Garvey [New York, October 2, 1921]," in *The Marcus Garvey and Universal Negro Improvement Association Papers*, Vol. 4, ed. Robert Hill (Los Angeles: University of California Press, 1985), 99.

11 See Robert Delavignette, "Une Grande Figure Coloniale: Blaise Diagne," *La Dépêche Coloniale et Maritime*, May 14–15, 1934: 1.

12 See Amady Aly Dieng, Lamine Guèye: Une des grandes figures politiques africaines (1891–1968) (Paris: L'Harmattan, 2013), 64.

13 Garvey, "Speech by Marcus Garvey [New York, October 2, 1921]," 99.

14 See Monof, "A La Gloire des Tirailleurs Sénégalais," *Les Annales Coloniales*, July 11, 1921: 2.

15 See Lamine Senghor, "Discours de Senghor [au Congrès de Bruxelles]," in *Lamine Senghor: La Violation d'un Pays et autres écrits anticolonialistes*, ed. David Murphy (Paris: L'Harmattan, 2012), 60.

16 Senghor, "Discours de Senghor [au Congrès de Bruxelles]," 62.

17 Senghor, "Discours de Senghor [au Congrès de Bruxelles]," 60.

18 See Charles Cros, *La Parole est à M. Blaise Diagne, premier homme d'Etat africain* (Dakar: Edition Maison du Livre, 1972), 105.

19 See Miller, Nationalists and Nomads, 24; Dewitte, Les Mouvements Nègres en France, 51.

20 See Mademba [Le Capitaine], "Lettre relative à la distribution de 'La Race Nègre' en Afrique Occidentale Française," in *Lamine Senghor: La Violation d'un Pays et autres écrits anticolonialistes*, 97–98

21 See "La Propagande Bolchevik," *La Dépêche Coloniale et Maritime*, February 13, 1920: 1; "Le Complot Bolchevik," *La Dépêche Coloniale et Maritime*, June 8, 1920: 2.

22 See Mademba, "Lettre," 98.

232 *Notes*

23 See "Extrait d'un article-résumé des témoignages lors du procès Diagne-Les-Continents," in *Lamine Senghor: La Violation d'un Pays et autres écrits anticolonialistes*, 110.
24 See Senghor, "Un Procés Nègre," in Lamine Senghor: La Violation d'un Pays et autres écrits anticolonialistes, 33.
25 See David Murphy, "Introduction," in Lamine Senghor: La Violation d'un Pays et autres écrits anticolonialistes, xlv.

Chapter 6

1 George Padmore, "Fascism in the Colonies," *Controversy* 2, no. 17 (February 1938). Accessed June 21, 2014. http://www.marxists.org/archive/padmore/1938/fascism-colonies.htm.
2 See James Hartfield, *An Unpatriotic History of the Second World War* (Washington, DC: Zero Books, 2012), 101–102.
3 See Samuel Mbajum, "Empire français et statut du colonisé: une ambiguïté permanente," in *Décolonisation de l'Afrique ex-française: Enjeux pour l'Afrique et la France d'aujourd'hui*, ed. Alexandre Gerbi (Paris: L'Harmattan, 2010), 70.
4 See Pierre Deloncle, "Au cercle intellectuel de la méditerranée. Une belle Conférence de Pierre Deloncle sur l'A.O.F.," *La Dépêche Coloniale et Maritime*, November 16–18, 1934: 2.
5 See Deloncle, "Au cercle intellectuel de la méditerranée," 2.
6 For an original version of the quotation in French, see Ibra Sene, "Colonisation française et main-d'oeuvre carcérale au Sénégal: de l'emploi des détenus des camps pénaux sur les chantiers des travaux routiers (1927–1940)," *French Colonial History* 5 (2004): 154.
7 See Sene, "Colonisation française," 157–158.

Chapter 7

1 See Léopold Sédar Senghor, "Conférence de Léopold Sédar Senghor: L'esprit de la civilisation ou les lois de la culture négro-africaine," *Présence Africaine* no. viii-ix-x (June-November 1956): 51.
2 See "Conférence de Léopold Sédar Senghor," 377.
3 See "Conférence de Léopold Sédar Senghor," 377.
4 Senghor's statement is quoted in Lillian Kesteloot, *Black Writers in French: A Literary History of Negritude* (Philadelphia, PA: Temple University Press, 1974), 103.

Index

abolition of slavery in France 41
Achac 5, 224n2
Achi, A. A. 198
Adefuye, A. 88
Adi, H. 11
Africa: Diagne against Garveyism in 97; French colonials against Garveyism in 98; Garvey's influence in 88–9, 94, 127–8
"Africa for Africans" slogan: feared by colonials 98, 229n13; rejected by Diagne 98, 101
Africa's 'Agitators' (Derrick) 15–16, 119, 139–41, 230
Les Africains et la grande guerre (Michel) xi, 5–6
African Americans: angered by Diagne 79–80; at the 1919 Pan-African Congress 79
African American soldiers: compared to *tirailleurs* 67, 102; Du Bois fascinated by 67; France's respect for 68; as viewed by Garvey 101; in World War I 67–9
African modernity: defined 120; Touvalou as symbol of 120 *see also* modernity
African soldiers: as seen by France, 48 *see also tirailleurs*; World War I *tirailleurs*; World War II *tirailleurs*
Aïdara, M. 23
aims of this book 4, 10–15
Anglophone Africa: Garvey's influence in 88–9
Anglophone blacks 1–3, 8–19, 31, 60, 65–7, 72, 78–82, 115, 123, 219–21 *see also* Francophone blacks

Anglophone intellectuals *see* black intellectuals
Angrand, A.: colonials' disdain toward 96; Garvey's influence on 96; viewed by the French 96
Angrand, J. 228n3
Les Annales Coloniales 2, 15, 23, 32, 42–4, 46, 52, 97–8, 107, 131, 149, 225–31
"L' A.O.F. Extract" (Touvalou-Houénou) 121–2
Appiah, K. A. 5, 43, 195, 205
"Atlantic Aporias" (Piot) 9

Bâ, B. 202
Bâ, S. W. 195
Balesi, C. J. 225n31
"Banania y'a bon" [Banania is good] 159
Barbeau, A. E. 226n8
Bell, B. W. 72
Benin: Touvalou in 131–2
Björnson, K. S. 199
black anticolonialism 2–3, 11–12, 16, 20, 25, 32–3, 61, 73–4, 94, 128–9, 139–40, 164, 168, 191, 214, 219; of Garvey 126; Garvey's influence on 127–8; of Garvey and Lamine Senghor 137, 144; and Garvey's Pan-Africanism 125; Garvey's role in 88; of Garvey and Touvalou 133; of Lamine Senghor 137–8, 141, 164; of Léopold Senghor 191, 196, 209; of Négritude 196; of Padmore 168, 176; of Touvalou 120–1, 126
The Black Atlantic (Gilroy) xi, 9–10, 117, 218–19

234 *Index*

black Atlantic theory 9–11; and Africa 9; Americocentrism of 10; assessments of 9–10, 18, 61; black cultures in 9; strengths and weaknesses of 9–10, 18, 61
black cosmopolitanism 2–4, 9, 13, 31–2, 71–2, 145, 191, 218–20; as consistent and disjointed 219; defined 4, 11, 218; as failure and success 219–20; hybridity in 4; as non-linear and plural 219; roadblocks to 71; as solidarity 4; and Western concepts of civilization 3–5, 16, 29, 39–40, 44–7, 60, 90–3, 120–1, 127, 144–55, 176, 193–5, 201, 204–5, 220
Black Cosmopolitanism (Nwankwo) 4, 93
black diaspora 3–4, 8–20, 31–3, 60, 75, 78–81, 89, 92–4, 99, 115–17, 125–8, 137–8, 142, 146, 219–20, 224n5, 231n3, 231n5; defined 19
Black France (Thomas) 13, 160, 230n1
black intellectuals: and Africa 1, 218–20; cosmopolitanisms of 9, 218–20; diversity among 4; against French colonialism 1; and French cosmopolitan discourse 1, 218–20; and republican principles 8; solidarity between 2, 218–20
black internationalism 10, 15, 116–17, 141; archives and the study of 15; translation and the study of 15 *see also* black transnationalism
"Black Man in the Revolution of 1914–1918" (Du Bois) 67, 226n11
black Paris scholarship 10–11
black radicalism: 1, 3–4, 13–14, 17, 22, 31–7, 90, 93, 96, 99–100, 103–21, 128, 131–3, 138–44, 152–3, 164, 219–20; before Negritude 13–14; defined 33; of Diagne and Garvey 109; of Garvey and Lamine Senghor 144; of Garvey and Touvalou compared to Diagne's 128; of Lamine Senghor 138, 143, 152, 164; rejected by French assimilationism 129; of Touvalou 115; and Touvalou's cosmopolitanism 120
black soldiers 67, 102, 150, 154, 160, 177–8, 206, 211, 226n7; compared

to white soldiers 101; Garvey's praise of 101 *see also* white soldiers
black transnationalism 10–11, 14, 61; black women in 14; defined 21; Garvey's influence on 87–8; of Touvalou 115 *see also* black internationalism
Black Writers in French (Kesteloot) 12–13, 232n4
blacks: of Africa 3, 92, 147; of Africa and the diaspora 3, 11–15, 18, 31, 78, 89, 125–6, 137, 141–2, 146; of the African diaspora 9, 78, 128, 144, 219; of the Caribbean 105, 141, 144–5, 153; of colonial Senegal 6, 8, 15–17, 24, 37–9, 87, 104, 133, 138, 164, 178, 183–5, 194, 199–200; in France 163, 184, 192, 208, 211, 222; of the French empire 25, 59, 62–3, 67, 118, 121–2, 128–30, 138, 141–4, 147–9, 155, 168, 175, 192, 198–9, 219; of Jamaica 105; of La Réunion 38; of the United States 10, 15–17, 19, 59, 62–5, 66–73, 76, 87–8, 92–4, 98–9, 101, 108, 126, 129–30, 143, 153; worldwide 2, 4, 19–21, 25, 64, 68–77, 82, 90, 93, 100–3, 114–17, 123–7, 143–5, 191–3, 198, 206, 220
Blair, D. S. 145
Blanchard, P. 5–6, 23, 158, 222, 224n8, 229n1
Boahen, A. A. 32, 42
Bogues, A. 33
Boittin, J. 230n1
Bonnett, A. W. 19
Bonneuil, C. 186
Bret, P. 142–3
Breton, A. 204–7
Brown, G. W. 39

"Camp 1940" (Senghor) 205–7
Campbell, J. 11–12, 69
Candace, G. 72, 77–81, 101, 128–9; and Poincaré on Touvalou's racial incident 129
capitalism: Lenin on 169; Léopold Senghor and 211
Caribbean soldiers: Garvey on 101; compared to *tirailleurs* 102

Index 235

"Ce Qu'est Notre Comité de Défense de la Race Nègre" (Lamine Senghor) 142–3, 151
Cépède, M. 198
Césaire, A. 12–13, 20–2, 34, 192–3, 221
Cheah, P. 74, 90
Chowdhury, K. 194
Chrisman, L. 11; black Atlantic scholarship of 61; on Du Bois 61; on Gilroy's transatlanticism 18; transatlantic methodology of 18
Civil Code: of France 41–2
"*la civilisation de l'universel*:" defined 195
Clipping from *The Crisis* 70
Colby, F. M. 228n2
Colonel D. 22–3, 224n6–7
Colonial Conscripts (Echenberg) 7, 147, 173, 180
Colonial troops: France's treatment of 64–5
colonialism: compared to racism 126; defined 20; the 1919 Pan-African Congress on 76
colonies: as boundless reservoirs of soldiers 52; France and 42
colonization: Césaire on 20–1
Le Comité de Défense de la Race Nègre (CDRN) 137, 139–43; Garvey and 138
La Condition noire (Ndiaye) 23, 224n7
"Conférence de Léopold Sédar Senghor" (Léopold Senghor), 195–6, 232nn1–3
Conklin, A. L. 13, 16–17, 31, 130, 200
Contee, C. G. 80–1, 91
continental Africans: compared with blacks of the diaspora 31
Les Continents: Diagne's legal case against 131
Cooper, F. 182
Cornevin, R. 228n3
"Corps de tirailleurs sénégalais" [Bodies of Senegalese tirailleurs] *104*
"Corps de tirailleurs sénégalais" [Bodies of Senegalese tirailleurs] *210*
cosmopolitanism: between black and white soldiers 51; defined 39–40, 218; as mutuality and reciprocity 40;

of *Présence Africaine* 195; universal scope of 40; Wilder on 198;
Cosmopolitanism (Appiah) 5, 43, 195, 205
cosmopolitanism of Diagne: as association 43; common profit in the 43; as conjoined sacrifice 47; contradictions in the 31, 56; as equality 53; as equal blood sacrifice 54; France and colonies in the 45; French nationality in the 40; and French republicanism 54–5; as idealization of France 147; imperialism in the 46; rights of Senegalese in the 148; the métropole in the 46; as moral solidarity 54; as mutual dependence 40; as national devotion to empire 47; origins of the 39–41, 43; and paternalism 47–8; romanticizing in the 40; and slavery's abolition 41; against unequal dependence 42
cosmopolitanism of Du Bois: ambivalence toward France in the 61; compared to Diagne's 59, 61; race in the 74–5
cosmopolitanism of Garvey 90–1; autonomy in the 124; compared to Diagne's 87, 91 109–10; compared to Du Bois's 91–2; critics' neglect of the 90; and rights of blacks 93; as transnational resistance 91–2; and western republicanism 91
cosmopolitanism of Lamine Senghor 141–2; compared to Garvey's 137
cosmopolitanism of Léopold Sédar Senghor 27, 191–2, 207, 209; African culture and humanism in the 212; Christianity in the 196–9; dualism in the 191; surrealism in the 204; world peace in the 207–8
cosmopolitanism of Padmore 168; and Trotsky's antifascism 168, 171–2
cosmopolitanism of Touvalou-Houénou: convergence in the 117; equality in the 118; and Garvey's 114, 122–3, 133; God in the 118; homogeneity in the 118; humanism in the 119; Negritude and the 119
Couturier, L. 5, 224n1

236 *Index*

The Crisis 2, 11, 24, 61–72, 76–7, 80, 99, 226nn2–7, 226nn9–11, 227n16, 227nn19, 227n22, 227nn25–7; views on Diagne in 64
Cros, C. 23, 225n14, 225n31, 226nn32–7, 226nn39–40, 231n18
Crouch, S. 60–1
Crowder, M. 34, 181–2, 194, 214

"Débarquement aux Dardanelles" [Disembarking in Dardanelles] 26
Debré, J. 73
DeGeorges, T. 178
Delafosse, L. 105, 229n20
Delafosse, M. 105, 130, 150, 225n17, 229n20
Delavignette, R. 147, 231n11
Deloncle, P. 187, 232n4, 232n5
La Dépêche Coloniale et Maritime 2, 15, 23, 32, 40, 43, 98, 147, 150, 153, 186, 224n6, 225n12, 225n17, 228n8, 228nn43–4, 228n48, 229n24
Deroo, E. xi, 5–6, 23, 26, 48, 53, 66, 104, 156–8, 162, 173, 210, 224n8, 229n1
Derrick, J. 15–16, 119, 139–41, 230
Devaux, E. 107, 130, 225nn24–5, 230n12
Dewitte, P. 146, 152, 158, 231n3, 231n19
Di Méo, N. 63
Diagne, B.: as assimilationist 31, 34–5, 105, 220; biography of 34–9; and black anticolonialism 32–3; as black cosmopolitan 31, 34–6; and black nationalism 42; and black radicalism 32–3, 36–7; in Cayenne 37; compared to Garvey 102–05; cosmopolitan idealism of 38–9; criticized by Padmore 174–6; as fascist leader 148; and forced labor 32; and freemasonry 39; and French republicanism 31, 36–9, 220; Garvey's criticisms against 104–6, 146; as liberator and oppressor of *indigènes* 31–2, 148; and Pan-Africanism 33, 71; paradoxes of 24; as perceived by Du Bois 68–9,

72; as perceived by Lamine Senghor 145; against race and racism 36–9; as supporter of French colonialism 32–3, 220; as treated by white French colonials 107, 125, 149; UNIA followers and 100; used by France 146–9; viewed by critics 32, 34
Diakhaté, A. 22
Diallo, B. 155–8, 160–64; discriminated in France 160
Diarra, B. 38, 163–4
Diawara, M. 40
Dickerson, D. J. 92
Dieng, A. A. 34, 39, 95, 105, 132, 148, 225n9, 230n17, 231n12
Diouf, M. 21, 50
"Discours de Senghor [au Congrès de Bruxelles]" (Lamine Senghor) 140–51, 231nn15–17
Douaire, A. 225nn29–30
Doumergue, G.: criticized by Padmore and Trotsky 174
Dramé, A. 89, 94–5
Du Bois, W. E. B.: as advocate for African Americans abroad 69; on Africa 60; as anti-racist Race Man 74; collaboration between Diagne and 73–4; compared to Diagne 73–5, 82–3; and Europe 60–1; and Judeo-Christian cosmopolitanism 60; Negritude and 14; relationships between Diagne and 24, 59, 68–9, 77; scholarship on 59–60

Echenberg, M. 7, 147, 173, 180
Edwards, B. H. 10, 15–16, 60, 81, 115–17, 138, 231n3
Empires at War (Gerwarth and Manela) 7, 221
England 7, 19, 25, 61, 65, 76, 124–5, 169–73, 176, 187
"The Enlisted Man's Despair" (Léopold Senghor) 208–9
Eschen, P. M. V. 94
"An Essay Toward a History of the Black Man in the Great War" (Du Bois) 67, 226n11
"Ethiopia: At the Call of the Race of Sheba" (Léopold Senghor) 200

Index 237

Europe: as symbol of cosmopolitanism 62; as viewed by Du Bois 62
The Evening Independent 227n16

Fabre, M. 12, 35, 62, 122
fascism: attacked by Trotsky 168–72; in colonial Senegalese prisons 201–2; colonialism and 22; defined 22; denounced by Padmore 168; in France's attitudes toward *tirailleurs* 179–80; French colonialism as 188; against interwar *tirailleurs* 173–5, 183; in the poetry of L. S. Senghor 200–02; racism and 22; in Senegal 213–14; slavery and 22
Fauset, J. 14, 76, 80–2; Diagne viewed by 80–2; elitism of 81
Ferguson, N. 54–5, 226n41
Fogarty, R. S. 182
Force-Bonté (Diallo), 155–64
Forced Labor: in colonial Senegal 187–8
Ford, K. H. 231n9
Foster, E. 47
France 1–27, 33–56, 59–83, 87–91, 99–110, 114–25, 130–3, 137–64, 168–88, 192–4, 197–200, 203, 206–15, 218–22; decline of the empire of 187; Diallo's romanticized views of 155–8, 160; idealism of 41; liberalism of 41; perception of empire in 47; photographic romanticizing of 155–7; relations between colonies and 39; as romanticized by Du Bois 62, 64; as symbol of cosmopolitanism 8; as symbol of universal equality 63; as viewed by Diagne 39
Francophone Africa: Garvey's influence in 89–90
Francophone blacks, 1–3, 8–19, 31, 59–60, 67, 71–2, 79–82, 88–90, 110, 115–20, 124–30, 137, 219–21, 231n3 *see also* Anglophone blacks
Francophone intellectuals *see* black intellectuals
Francophone Sub-Saharan Africa (Manning) 179, 213
Freeman, C. 34

French citizenship: selectively given 147
French civilizing mission: contradicted by colonialism 17; and republicanism 16
French colonization: as a brutal system 44; as exploitation of West Africa 121; as a moral and national duty 46
French cosmopolitanism: as abstract 118; ambiguous nature of 8; black intellectuals' ambivalence toward 16; as colonial ideal and romanticization 39–42; contradicted by colonialism and fascism 2, 8, 176, 188, 218; contradicted by France's ill-treatment of *tirailleurs* 155, 177, 184; contradicted in West Africa 168; development of 1–2; Diagne's support of 1–2; Du Bois fascinated by 59, 63, 65; France-Afrique, EurAfrique, and Francité in 40; Garvey's criticisms against 124–5; Garvey's praise of 122–4; Lamine Senghor against 142; origins of 1, 39; paradoxes of 209; and republicanism 16; roadblocks to 222–3; romanticizing of blacks in 142; Touvalou's fascination with 121–4; universalistic 16; as veiled imperialism 125
French republicanism: Garvey's admiration of 122–3; paradoxes of 16; and *Présence Africaine* 196; as represented by Trotsky 171–2; and Touvalou's anticolonialism 121; Touvalou's fascination with 121–3
The French Revolution 55–6; and Diagne's cosmopolitanism 36–7; and Touvalou's cosmopolitanism 118–19
Friedel, T. 90, 229n18
From Harlem to Paris (Fabre) 12, 35, 62, 122

Garvey, M. as advocate of African American rights 94; biography of 87–8, 105; as champion of black cosmopolitanism 93–4; compared to Diagne 103, 108; compared to

238   *Index*

McKay 103; and colonial Senegal 24, 89, 94–7; Diagne against 24, 97–9, 101; Diagne criticized by 106; and French cosmopolitanism 24; and French republicanism 24; Hoover against 108; as perceived by French colonials 106; as portrayed at the 1920 Pan-African Congress 99–100; racial prejudices of 103; relations between Diagne and 101; scholarship on 87–90; Senegalese supporters of Garvey, 89, 94–5; Sierra Leonean supporters of, 94–5; *tirailleurs* as viewed by 101; Touvalou's fascination with 127; viewed as opportunist and fearmonger 88; and West Africa 24
Gerbi, A. 34, 234n4
Gerwarth, R. 7, 221
Gikandi, S. xi
Gilbert, M. 197
Gilroy, P. 9–10, 18, 61, 117, 120, 218
Ginio, R. 214
Glissant, E. 145, 231n8
The Golden Age of Black Nationalism (Moses) 11, 125
"Le Gouvernement de demain et les colonies" (Diagne) 39
Goyal, Y. 92, 127
Grant, C. 88
Grayzel, S. R. 226n8
Grosholz, E. R. 72
Gueye, D. 36–7, 49
Gueye, L. 41, 50, 132, 148, 230n17, 231n12

Hafez, K. 170
Hall, S. 193, 221
Harlan, L. R. 227n13
Hartfield, J. 232n2
Hassan, S. D. 195
Held, D. 39
Henri, F. 226n8
Herdeck, D. E. 230n12
Hill, R. 2, 11, 19, 96, 226n8, 227n31, 228n1, 228n4, 228n41, 229n10–11, 229n19, 230, 230n4, 230n6, 230n10–11, 230n15–16, 230n18, 231

Histoire du Sénégal (Diouf) 21, 50
L'Histoire Oubliée des Tirailleurs Sénégalais de la Seconde Guerre (Aïdara) 23
Hollinger, D. A. 71
Hopquin, B. 229n15

imperialism: defined 20
indigènes 5–6, 21–2, 31–2, 37–9, 42, 45, 49–50, 54, 140, 145–8, 153, 163, 180–5, 187–8, 218; defined 21; Diagne's support for 42, 50; forced labor of interwar 184–5; French citizenship denied to 146; as loyal to France 5–6; in Senegal 38; treated like slaves 185; in West Africa 38 *see also originaires*; *indigènes sujets*
interwar *tirailleurs*: as perceived by Padmore 173; as treated by French colonials 173–4; as used by French colonials 176–80
Irele, A. F. 13–14, 192–4; On Negritude 192–3

Jackson, G. H. 68, 227n13–4
Jacobs, N. J. 41
James, C. L. R. 231n9
Janken, K. R. 76
Jeffers, C. 209, 211
Jeffery, T. 18
Jézéquel, J. 73
Johnson, G. W. 35–8, 50, 96, 99, 101, 106, 109, 140, 224n1
Jonassohn, K. 199
Jones, E. A. 205
Jones, H. 32, 35, 228n3
Justesen, B. R. 227n13

Kaké, I. B. 225n9, 231n5
Kalman, S. 184
Kamian, B. 35, 53
Kearney, R. 121
Kelley, R. D. G. xi, 22
Kesteloot, L. 12–13, 232n4
Kolle, S. S. 231n5
Koller, C. 175

Langley, J. A. 11, 115, 119, 127, 230n9
Law of 1848: importance of the 41

Index 239

Law of October 19, 1915: and the Four Communes 49
Lawrence, A. 178
Lenin, V. I. 98–9, 153, 169
"Lettre de Diagne au maître de la loge" (Diagne) 36
Leune, J. 186
Levine, L. 105, 108, 130
Lewis, D. L. 59–60, 63, 65, 228n47
Lewis, R. 105
"Liberation" (Léopold Senghor) 211
The Life and Struggles of Negro Toilers (Padmore), 170, 173–9, 181–5
Ligue de Défense de la Race Nègre (LDRN), 137–8, 141–3, 230n1
"Liminary Poem" (Léopold Senghor), 209, 212
L'Involution des métamorphoses et des métempsychoses de l'univers (Touvalou-Houénou) 117–18, 123
Lloyd, C. 129
Loingsigh, A. N. 10
Lovejoy, P. 19, 224n5
Lunn, J. 7, 23, 173–4, 229n1
"Luxembourg 1939" (Léopold Senghor) 203–4

Makalani, M. 141, 172
Malela, B. B. 161
Manceron, G. 6, 23, 158, 224n8, 229n1
Manela, E. 7, 221
Mangin, C. 5, 52–4, 224n1; Diagne's views about 53–4; *tirailleurs* as perceived by 53
Mann, G. 7, 147, 152, 183–4
Manning, P. xi, 115, 179, 213
Marable, M. 23, 229n15
Maran, R. as perceived by Diagne, 130–1
Marcus Garvey, Hero (Martin) 97
The Marcus Garvey and Universal Negro Improvement Association Papers (Hill) 2, 24, 229n10–11, 229n13, 229n19, 229n22, 230n4–6, 230n10–11, 230n15–16, 230n18, 231n4, 231n7, 231n10
Martin, C. 5
Martin, G. 40

Martin, T. 12, 89, 97, 116, 128–9, 138, 229n2, 231n6
Maurel, J. 34, 224, 225n3–4, 225n8
Mbajum, S. 184–5, 232n3
Mbembe, A. 8, 222
McNamara, F. T. 118
Memmi, A. 143, 179
Memoirs of the Maelstrom 7, 23, 173–4, 229n1
Meredith, M. 208
methodology: used in this book 2, 11, 16–19
métropole: defined 34
Michel, M. 5–6
Miller, C. L. 13, 34, 116, 140, 148, 152, 214, 231n3, 231n19
Miller, M. L. 74
Miller, S. G. 143
A Mission to Civilize (Conklin) 16–17, 200
"Mitrailleurs sénégalais à l'exercice" [Senegalese gunners in exercise] 53
modernity 10, 14, 22, 117, 120, 128, 222 *see also* African modernity
Moitt, B. 186–7
"Mon cher directeur" (Diagne) 42–3
Monof. 231n14
Moore, J. M. 92
Moses, W. J. 11, 125
Mudimbe, V. Y. 12–13, 224n4
Mudimbe-Boyi, E. 224n4
Mulzac, H. 130
Murphy, D. 25, 40, 139–40, 161, 177, 231n15, 232n25

Nationalism of Garvey: not antithetical to cosmopolitanism 90
Nationalists and Nomads (Miller) 13, 34, 51, 116, 140, 148, 231n3, 231n19
Native Sons (Mann) 7
Ndiaye, P. 23, 224n7
Negritude: and black nationalism 13; and black radicalism 13; current scholarship on 191–2; importance of 193–4
Negritude Moment, The (Irele), 13–14, 193–4
Niane, D. T. 182–3
Nwankwo, I. K. 4, 93

240 *Index*

Oboe, A. 9, 10
Olusanya, G. O. 95
originaires 21, 38, 41–2, 49–50, 55, 66–7, 106–7, 140, 146–7, 153, 178, 180; compared to *indigènes* 140–1; Diagne's support for 49; racism against 146 *see also sujets*; *indigènes*
Otlet, P. 78

Padmore, G.: and black anticolonialism 25; and black cosmopolitanism 25; on fascism 25; on French classism and elitism 178; on French treatment of *tirailleurs* 177; and Trotsky 168
Pan-African Congress of 1919: black cosmopolitanism at the 72; Diagne's dilemma at the 73; disagreements between Diagne and Du Bois at the 76; history of the 71–6; platform of the 75; as viewed by Du Bois 72, 77
Pan-African Congress of 1921: African and Caribbean participants of the 76–7; Diagne's attitudes toward African Americans at the 77–9; Otlet's motion at the 78; tension between Diagne and Du Bois at the 78–80
The Pan-African Connection (Martin) 128
Pan-African History (Adi and Sherwood), 11
Pan-Africanism: as conceptualized in this book 19–20, 219; conventional definition of 19–20; of Diagne 82; of Diagne and Garvey 109–10; of Garvey 125–7, 137; of Garvey and Lamine Senghor 144–5; of Lamine Senghor 137; of Léopold Senghor 212–13; of Padmore 168; scholarship on 11–12; of Touvalou 115, 125–7
Paris: in poems of Léopold Senghor 197–9; as site of black transnationalism 11
Le Paris Noir (Blanchard, Deroo, and Manceron) 6
La Parole est à M. Blaise Diagne (Cros), 23, 225n14, 225n31, 226n32–7, 226n39–40, 231n18
The Philosophy and Opinions (Garvey) 2, 24, 229n2, 231n6

Piot, C. 9
Pogge, T. 54
Postcolonial Contraventions (Chrisman) 61
"Pourquoi Sommes-Nous Infériorisés?" (Lamine Senghor) 161
Pouvourville, A. 42
The Practice of Diaspora (Edwards) 10, 15–16, 60, 81, 115–17, 138, 231n3
"Prayer for Peace" (Léopold Senghor) 203, 213
"Prayer to the Masks" (Léopold Senghor) 200
Présence Africaine 195
"Prince of Dahomey Speaks" (Touvalou-Houénou) 116–17, 126–7
"Prisonniers sénégalais blessés" [Senegalese wounded prisoners] *162*
"The Problem of Negroes in French Colonial Africa" (Touvalou-Houénou) 120–1, 126–8
"Un Procés Nègre" (Lamine Senghor), 154–5, 232n24

"La Question Nègre devant le Congrès de Bruxelles" (Lamine Senghor) 144

Race First (Martin) 12, 89–90, 116, 138
racism: toward black soldiers in the United States 67; in Cayenne 37; in colonies 36; denounced by Lamine Senghor 143; toward disabled World War I *tirailleurs* 150, 161–2; in France 124; toward Garvey and the UNIA 108; toward *indigènes* 50, 150; toward interwar *tirailleurs* 183–4; in La Réunion 38; toward Touvalou in France 116, 129–31; toward World War I *tirailleurs* 49–50, 107, 161–2
Recharting the Black Atlantic (Oboe and Scacchi) 9, 10
"Réponse d'un ancien tirailleur sénégalais" (Diarra) 38, 163–4
"La République et l'impensé de la 'race'" (Mbembe) 8, 222
"Respectueux hommages" [Respectful homages] *157*

Index 241

"Rethinking Black Atlanticism" (Chrisman) 18
"Return of the Prodigal Son" (Léopold Senghor) 211–12
"Le Réveil des Nègres" (Lamine Senghor) 149
Roberts, F. E. 226n8
Rodney, W. 185
Ros, M. 231n9
Rudwick, E. M. 99
Ruedel, M. 42–3, 52, 226n34
Russia: as champion of the poor 169; and colonialism in Africa 170; Padmore's view of 170

Sarraut, A. 43–5, 177; collaboration in the cosmopolitanism of 44; colonized populations in the cosmopolitanism of 44; cosmopolitanism of Diagne and 43–5; in Dakar 44; and imperialism 44
Sartre, J. 143, 163
Scacchi, A. 9, 10
Scheck, R. 180, 209
Schmeisser, I. 20
"A Second Journey to Pan-Africa" (Du Bois) 80, 228n47
Sedlmayr, H. 204
Sene, I. xi, 187–8, 201
Senegal: France and colonial 194; as France's peanut colony 186–7; forced labor in colonial Senegal 201; influence of Garvey and the UNIA in 94–5; prison conditions in colonial 202; Touvalou's plight and imprisonment in 131–2
Senghor, L. biography of 139–40; and Blaise Diagne 25, 145, 152; on colonial treatment of Africans 151; compared with Touvalou 152; cosmopolitanism of 25; denied repatriation from France 154–5; Diagne and the French against 153; and French communists 15, 141; on French treatment of disabled *tirailleurs* 141, 149–50; and Garvey 16, 25, 137, 145, 152, 164; on labor exploitation of *tirailleurs* 149; scholarship on 137; and Third World liberation struggle 141; viewed as

promoter of Bolshevism in Africa 153–4
Senghor, L. S. capitalism in the poetry of 199; Christianity in the poetry of 196, 203; dualism in the poetry of 214; Europe in the poetry of 206; fascism in the poetry of 200–2, 213–14; German captivity in the poetry of 206; Nazi invasion of France in the poetry of 197–201; Nazi oppression of Jews in the poetry of 200–1; patriotism in the poetry of 208; scholarship on 191–4; surrealism in the poetry of 204–7; *tirailleurs* in the poetry of 27, 205–15; World War II in the poetry of 206–15
Sharpley-Whiting, T. D. 13–14, 230n1
Sherwood, M. 11
Sierra Leone: influence of the UNIA in 94–5
"Sketches from Abroad" (Du Bois) 61–3
Skinner, E. P. 88–9
Smith, J. C. 194
Smock, R. W. 227n13
"Snow in Paris" (Léopold Senghor) 196–9, 201
"Soldat africain originaire de l'une des Quatre communes et une amie" [African soldier from one of the four communes and a friend] 66
Soucy, R. 176, 225n26
Spencer, R. 69
Spiegler, J. S. 115
Spleth, J. S. 194, 203
Stein, J. 87, 105
Steins, M. 129–31, 139–41, 163, 230n2, 230n14, 231n4
Stephens, M.A. 21
Stewart, J. B. 72
Stokes, M. 120
Stovall, T. 55, 130, 226n41, 230n1
sujets 21, 49–50, 107, 140, 146, 178, 181 *see also originaires*; *indigènes*
Sullivan, R. 197
Sundquist, E. J. 59–60
Suret-Canale, J. 108, 182–3, 199

242 *Index*

Taylor, U. Y. 230n1
"Texte de la lettre" (Lamine Senghor) 155
Thiam, C.: on Negritude 192
Thiam, I. D. 6, 7, 95, 224n3
Thiaroye Massacre 213; and fascism 214; in Léopold Senghor's poetry 213–14
Thomas, D. 13, 160
Thomas, M. 34
tirailleurs: origins of 22–3; role of Africans in the scholarship on 7; scholarly neglect of *tirailleurs* 220–1; scholarship on 5–7; and world war memorials 222 *see also* World War I *tirailleurs*; World War II *tirailleurs*
"Tirailleurs du 12e RTS sortant du métro porte de Clignancourt" [Tirailleurs of the 12th RTS leaving Clignancourt's metro entrance] *173*
"To The Music of Koras and Balaphon" (Léopold Senghor) 206–11
"To the Senegalese Soldiers Who Died for France" (Léopold Senghor) 212–13
"Tournée de recrutement au Soudan" [Recruitment tour in Soudan] *48*
Touvalou-Houénou, Prince Kojo: activism of 13; biography of 114–15; Diagne against 13, 131–3; and French colonists 13, 131–2; and French cosmopolitanism 25, 118–22; and French republicanism 118–22; and Garvey 16, 13, 25, 114–17, 122–33; Pan-Africanism of 115; perceived as essentialist 117; scholarship on 115–17; and the UNIA 117, 127 *see also* cosmopolitanism of Touvalou
Trotsky, L. 153, 168–74; on French imperialism 172; and Padmore's anticolonialism 170
Tyson, L. 18

"Unfinished Business" (Miller) 214
The United States: compared to Europe 63; compared to France 64–5, 72; Du Bois's dejection about 71; lack of cosmopolitanism toward blacks in 71

The Universal Negro Improvement Association (UNIA), 20–5, 88–100, 103, 108–10, 116, 123–4, 127–31, 138, 142, 153, 220, 228n1; and Africa 127

Vaillant, J. G. 126, 129, 146, 194
Valran, G. 225n17
Van Niekerk, B. v. D. 205
Varenne, M. 45; Diagne's contention with 45–6
"Vendangeuse offrant du raisin à un blessé Sénégalais" [Vintager offering grape to a wounded Senegalese] *156*
"La Violation d'un Pays" (Lamine Senghor) 145 *see also* Senghor, L
La Violation d'un Pays et autres écrits anticolonialistes 231n15, 231n20, 232n23–25 *see also* Senghor, L.

Waldron, J. 93
Walters, R. W. 12, 19, 60, 89
Washington, R. E. 103, 229n18
Watson, G. L. 19
Watts, J. G. 20
Weatherford, D. 197
Weiss, H. 32, 138
West Africans 3, 6–9, 15, 24–5, 39, 59, 62, 67, 77–9, 87, 92, 104, 118, 121–2, 128–30, 133, 138, 141–4, 147–9, 155, 163–6, 168, 175, 178, 182–5, 192–4, 198–200, 208, 211, 219, 222; horrible conditions of 151; punished for resisting French recruitment 181–2
Western cosmopolitanism: as universalistic and absolutist 4–5
white soldiers 47, 51, 163, 178, 183, 191, 206–9, 219 *see also* black soldiers
Wilder, G. 16, 122, 143, 192, 196–8, 212–13; on Negritude 192
Williams, C. L. 226n8
Wilson, E. T. 132
"Who Speaks for Africa?" (Conklin) 31, 130–1
Wolters, R. 227n35
World War I *tirailleurs*: cosmopolitanism of 5, 104; Diagne's treatment of 48–51, 55; France's

treatment of 6, 51, 102, 160–4; and French citizenship 55; French disarmament of 102; French stereotypes about 5, 52, 139, 158–9; health conditions of 161–2, 183; as loyal to France 5; number of 23; perceived as inexhaustible forces 52; as represented in archived materials 5; sacrifices and plight of 53, 102–4, 151; scholarship on 5–7, 22–3; as a trope 8; white French soldiers' solidarity with 51; wounded 161–2

World War II *tirailleurs*: 195; in the poetry of Léopold Senghor 206–15

Wright, M. M. 8, 12

Young, R. J. C. 20

Zinsou, É. D. 114

Zouménou, L. 114

Taylor & Francis eBooks

Helping you to choose the right eBooks for your Library

Add Routledge titles to your library's digital collection today. Taylor and Francis ebooks contains over 50,000 titles in the Humanities, Social Sciences, Behavioural Sciences, Built Environment and Law.

Choose from a range of subject packages or create your own!

Benefits for you
- Free MARC records
- COUNTER-compliant usage statistics
- Flexible purchase and pricing options
- All titles DRM-free.

Benefits for your user
- Off-site, anytime access via Athens or referring URL
- Print or copy pages or chapters
- Full content search
- Bookmark, highlight and annotate text
- Access to thousands of pages of quality research at the click of a button.

REQUEST YOUR FREE INSTITUTIONAL TRIAL TODAY

Free Trials Available
We offer free trials to qualifying academic, corporate and government customers.

eCollections – Choose from over 30 subject eCollections, including:

Archaeology	Language Learning
Architecture	Law
Asian Studies	Literature
Business & Management	Media & Communication
Classical Studies	Middle East Studies
Construction	Music
Creative & Media Arts	Philosophy
Criminology & Criminal Justice	Planning
Economics	Politics
Education	Psychology & Mental Health
Energy	Religion
Engineering	Security
English Language & Linguistics	Social Work
Environment & Sustainability	Sociology
Geography	Sport
Health Studies	Theatre & Performance
History	Tourism, Hospitality & Events

For more information, pricing enquiries or to order a free trial, please contact your local sales team:
www.tandfebooks.com/page/sales

The home of Routledge books

www.tandfebooks.com